THE Holy Spirit AND Spiritual Gifts

IN THE NEW TESTAMENT CHURCH AND TODAY

REVISED EDITION

MAX TURNER

HENDRICKSON PUBLISHERS

To Duncan and Abbie

First published 1996 by Paternoster Press
This edition 1998

Hendrickson Publishers
P.O. Box 3473
Peabody, MA 01960

ISBN 1–56563–352–0

Hendrickson Publishers edition printed by arrangement with
Paternoster Press,
an imprint of Paternoster Publishing
P.O. Box 300, Carlisle, Cumbria CA3 0QS, U.K.
http://www.paternoster-publishing.com

Printed in the United States of America

Library of Congress Cataloging-in-Publication Data

Turner, Max, 1947–
The Holy Spirit and spiritual gifts: in the New Testament church
and today / Max Turner. — [Rev. ed.]
Some chapters have been presented as lectures and seminars in 1984
and 1985; some chapters have appeared as articles in various publications.
Includes bibliographical references and indexes.
ISBN 1–56563–352–0 (pbk.)
1. Gifts, Spiritual—Biblical teaching.   2. Bible.   N.T.—Criticism, interpretation,
etc.   3. Gifts, Spiritual—History of doctrines—Early church, ca. 30–600.
4. Gifts, Spiritual—History of doctrines—20th century.   I. Title.
BS 2545.G47T87   1998
234'.13'09—dc21   98-20222
CIP

Contents

Acknowledgements

This work owes a great deal to many, but special mention must be made of the following:

(1) The editors of *Evangelical Quarterly, New Testament Studies, Novum Testamentum,* and *Vox Evangelica* as well as Inter-Varsity Press and Paternoster Press, for permission to revise and incorporate material from articles earlier published with them.
(2) Antony Billington, who read the material and saved me from many errors.
(3) My students, at Aberdeen and London Bible College, who have been a constant source of stimulation.
(4) Elria Kwant of Paternoster Publishing, who has not only provided many corrections, but has also greatly enhanced the usefulness of the book by expanding the table of contents, by supplying the select bibliography, and by refining the index.
(5) My family, especially my wife Lucy, without whose constant and loving support the project would have withered. This book is dedicated, however, to our son Duncan and daughter Abbie. They have given us more pleasure than they can imagine, and have even had the grace not to complain when I withdrew 'yet again' to the study!

Preface

This book arises from an invitation from a British degree-awarding open-learning Faculty (the Open Theological College, Cheltenham) to write a half-module for its third-year BA course on the Holy Spirit and spiritual gifts. It was already essentially something I had embarked on teaching at London Bible College. The contents of this work, however, are not 'the half-module' itself. They merely provide an indication of many of the subjects to be covered, and constitute *one* of the basic resources for such a course. There are inevitably other more important works to react with, and other exciting questions to face. As it stands, this book is more of a Level 2 text, and so the kind of work that is readily accessible to busy pastors, church leaders, and other more general readers. Most of the chapters are a slightly revised version of lectures to BA students at LBC. Having said that, I should add that its often compressed style owes much to the fact that it was intended to be expanded in those lectures. I have left many portions in their 'compressed' form in order to limit the length of the book.

This work, as I have already indicated, has something of a 'history'. As a busy lecturer, I have inevitably compiled it partly out of publications which I have already made available in other forms. Chapters 2, 4 and 5 depend quite heavily on my article on 'Holy Spirit' in the *Dictionary of Jesus and the Gospels* (this article itself owed much to lectures delivered to Aberdeen students in 1987). Chapter 3 is a slightly shortened version of an essay in *The Book of Acts and Its Theology* (eds. I.H. Marshall and D. Peterson), which is volume 6 in the *Acts In Its First-Century Setting* series. More significantly, perhaps, Chapters 12–20 are a revised version of a long article first published as 'Spiritual Gifts Then and Now' in *Vox Evangelica* 15 (1985), 7–64. This article was an edited version of papers presented at three seminars of the Fellowship of European Evangelical Theologians in Altenkirchen, 1984. The mood there was predominantly (often sharply) 'cessationist', and this may explain the sustained, if usually implicit, critique of such a position in my 'response'. However, as a member of the Evangelical Alliance's Committee on Unity and Truth (ACUTE), I would wish to support any attempt to find unity between the Pentecostal/Charismatic and the more tradition-al forms of Evangelicalism. In that respect, Part 2 of this work is intended to be bridge-building, not polemical; many of its asser-tions should be heard as tentative questions rather than as dogmatic statements.

The purpose of this book is to explore the significance of the gift of the Spirit in the New Testament. It consists of two parts. Part 1 begins with a brief examination of OT and intertestamental views of the Spirit. In this initial chapter I argue that at the turn of the eras the Spirit was largely understood as the 'Spirit of prophecy' ena-bling revelation, wisdom and inspired speech. But while Schweizer, Menzies and others have concluded that the Spirit was thus merely an empowering for certain types of service, and not soteriologically necessary, I argue that even in Judaism these gifts of the 'Spirit of prophecy' could be anticipated not as empowering alone, but also as the very 'life' of the restored community, and the power of its holiness. Chapters 2–8 suggest that Luke, John and Paul have developed this understanding and see the one gift of the Spirit to believers as a Christianized version of the 'Spirit of prophecy'. Precisely *as* the 'Spirit of prophecy', the Spirit *simultaneously* provides the 'life' of the saved community and its empowering for service and mission. Chapters 9–11 then explore the significance of the NT witness as we move towards a contemporary and systematic *theology* of the gift of the Spirit. In Chapter 10 it is argued that the classical Pentecostal two-stage view of Spirit-reception needs to be replaced by a more broadly charismatic one-stage conversion-in-itiation paradigm. In Chapter 11 we examine the extent to which the New Testament witness prepares the ground for later trinitarian understanding of the Spirit. In speaking of 'the New Testament witness', however, one important qualification must be made: limitations of space have required me to restrict the enquiry to the three major witnesses to New Testament pneumatology (Luke-Acts, John and Paul).

Part 2 begins with an examination of three prototypical 'gifts of the Spirit' (prophecy, tongues and healing) and the nature and purpose of these and other spiritual gifts in the New Testament Church (Chs. 12–15). I then discuss the cessationist claim (stemming largely from Warfield) that these gifts were given primarily as divine attestation to Jesus and the apostles as bearers of divine revelation, to provide the revelation necessary for the writing of the New Testament books, and to guide the church until the canon was completed. The corollary drawn by Edgar, Farnell, Gaffin, Masters and others, is that the New Testament writers anticipated that, with the death of the apostles and their co-workers, such spiritual gifts would cease. This view is investigated in Chapter 16. Nearly all NT scholars would dismiss such a view as a curiosity, but the cessationist view at least raises, in an interesting form, the question of the real nature and purpose of such spiritual gifts (even if its 'answer' is entirely unacceptable to serious NT scholarship and to that of Early Church history). Subsequent chapters inquire into the nature and significance of the prophecy, healing and tongues speech claimed in the Pentecostal and Charismatic renewal movements and their relation to the NT gifts denoted by the same terminology. The book ends by asking to what extent the phenomena in question are unique to such movements, and whether there is any theological or empirical reason to suppose that some post-conversion crisis experience is actually *needed* in order to receive such gifts.

Two further points concerning the scope of this work perhaps invite further comment. First, I am conscious of the extent to which the discussion in the pages which follow is mainly (though by no means exclusively) with evangelical and other relatively 'conservative' writers (whether Pentecostal, Charismatic or from more traditional Evangelicalism). This is not out of any hesitation to listen to theology from other quarters, but perhaps reflects a greater interest in pneumatology in those circles than elsewhere. Had the course been on christology or ecclesiology there would undoubtedly have been a much wider range of dialogue partners.

Second, I am aware that it is not entirely usual for a New Testament course to cross the disciplinary borders and to ask questions about the appropriation of the New Testament witness today. I am aware of some of the vigorous debates on this issue, and side with those who believe New Testament scholarship and systematic theology should learn from each other. Those being trained at London Bible College will be expected in their ministries to be able to fuse the horizons of New Testament studies and contemporary theology. This being so, it seems not unreasonable that some New Testament courses should at least take a first step towards systematic theology. If anything, my regret is that limitations of space have prevented me from a much fuller discussion of the relevant issues.

Abbreviations

A1CS	*Acts in its First-Century Setting* (Carlisle: Paternoster, 1995)
ABD	*The Anchor Bible Dictionary*, ed. D.N. Freedman (6 vols.; New York: Doubleday, 1992)
ANRW	*Aufstieg und Niedergang der römischen Welt*, ed. H. Temporini and W. Haase (Berlin: de Gruyter, 1980)
ATR	*Anglican Theological Review*
BAGD	W. Bauer, *A Greek-English Lexicon of the New Testament and Other Early Christian Literature*, eds. W.F. Ardnt, F.W. Gingrich and F.W. Danker (Chicago: University of Chicago, 1979)
Beasley-Murray	G.R. Beasley-Murray, *John* (Waco: Word, 1987)
BBR	*Bulletin of Biblical Research*
BDF	F. Blass, A. Debrunner, and R.W. Funk, *A Greek Grammar of the New Testament* (Cambridge: CUP, 1961)
Bib	*Biblica*
BJRL	*Bulletin of the John Rylands Library*
Brown	R.E. Brown, *The Gospel According to Saint John* (2 vols.; London: Chapman, 1971)
BSac	*Bibliotheca Sacra*
BTB	*Biblical Theology Bulletin*
BZ	*Biblische Zeitschrift*
Carson	D.A. Carson, *The Gospel according to John* (Leicester: IVP, 1991)
CUP	Cambridge University Press
CBQ	*Catholic Biblical Quarterly*
DBSupp	*Dictionnaire de la Bible, Supplement*
DJG	*Dictionary of Jesus and the Gospels*, eds. J.B. Green and S. McKnight (London: IVP, 1993)
DPL	*Dictionary of Paul and his letters*, eds. G.F. Hawthorne and R.P. Martin (London: IVP, 1993)
DSD	*Dead Sea Discoveries*

DSS	Dead Sea Scrolls
EDNT	*Exegetical Dictionary of the New Testament*, eds. H. Balz and G. Schneider (3 vols.; Grand Rapids: Eerdmans, 1990–93)
ERT	*Evangelical Review of Theology*
EtB	*Etudes Bibliques*
ETL	*Ephemerides Theologicae Lovanienses*
EvQ	*Evangelical Quarterly*
EV	English Version (EVV = English Versions)
ExpT	*Expository Times*
Fitzmyer	J.A. Fitzmyer, *The Gospel According to Luke* (2 vols.; New York: Doubleday, 1981, 1985)
GNB	Good News Bible
HeyJ	*Heythrop Journal*
HTR	*Harvard Theological Review*
IBS	*Irish Biblical Studies*
Int	*Interpretation*
ITP	Intertestamental Period
ITQ	*Irish Theological Quarterly*
IVP	Inter-Varsity Press
JASA	*Journal of the American Scientific Association*
JANES	*Journal for Ancient Near Eastern Studies*
JBL	*Journal of Biblical Literature*
JET	*Journal of Empirical Theology*
JETS	*Journal of the Evangelical Theological Society*
JJS	*Journal of Jewish Studies*
JPT	*Journal of Pentecostal Theology*
JSNT	*Journal for the Study of the New Testament*
JSP	*Journal for the Study of the Pseudepigrapha*
JSS	*Journal of Semitic Studies*
JTS	*Journal of Theological Studies*
LXX	Septuagint (Greek Bible)
MMS	Marshall, Morgan and Scott
MT	Masoretic Text (Hebrew Bible)
NEB	New English Bible
Neot	*Neotestamentica*
NIDNTT	*New International Dictionary of New Testament Theology* eds. L. Coenen, E. Beyreuther, H. Bietenhard and C. Brown
NIV	New International Version
NJB	New Jerusalem Bible
NRSV	New Revised Standard Version
NRT	*La Nouvelle Revue Théologique*
NovT	*Novum Testamentum*

NT	New Testament
NTS	*New Testament Studies*
OT	Old Testament
OUP	Oxford University Press
OTP	*Old Testament Pseudepigrapha*, ed. J.H. Charlesworth (2 vols.; London: Doubleday, 1983, 1985)
PBI	Pontifical Biblical Institute (Rome)
RB	*Revue Biblique*
REB	Revised English Bible
RefR	*The Reformed Review*
Rel	*Religion*
RevRel	*Review for Religions*
RevSR	*Revue des Sciences Religieuses*
RSPT	*Revue des Sciences Philosophiques et Théologiques*
RSR	*Recherches de Science Religieuse*
RSV	Revised Standard Version
SAP	Sheffield Academic Press
Schnackenburg	R. Schnackenburg, *The Gospel According to St John* (3 vols.; London: Burns & Oates, 1968–82)
SE	*Studia Evangelica*
Sem	*Semitica*
SJT	*Scottish Journal of Theology*
SLJT	*Saint Luke's Journal of Theology*
SNTU	Studien zum Neuen Testament und seiner Umwelt
ST	*Studia Theologica*
TDNT	*Theological Dictionary of the New Testament*
Theol	*Theology*
TrinJ	*Trinity Journal*
TS	*Theological Studies*
TynB	*Tyndale Bulletin*
TWNT	*Theologisches Wörterbuch zum Neuen Testament*
TZ	*Theologische Zeitschrift*
UPA	University Press of America
VoxEv	*Vox Evangelica*
WTJ	*Westminster Theological Journal*
ZNW	*Zeitschrift für Neutestamentliche Wissenschaft*
ZTK	*Zeitschrift für Theologie und Kirche*

In the interests of economy of space, references to standard commentaries (after the initial reference) are given without a title or short title: e.g. Haenchen, 135 [= E. Haenchen, *Acts of the Apostles* (Oxford: Blackwell, 1971), 135].

PART I
THE DEVELOPMENT OF NEW TESTAMENT
PNEUMATOLOGY

Chapter One

The Background to New Testament Pneumatology: The Spirit in the Old Testament and in 'Intertestamental' Judaism

New Testament beliefs about the Spirit did not fall ready-made from heaven amidst the tongues and fire of Pentecost. The early disciples already had the fundamentals of a theology of the Spirit from their Jewish understanding of the Old Testament, and this understanding would have been extended by the 'revival' of the Spirit in the ministries of John the Baptist and Jesus. We shall examine what may have been learned from Jesus' ministry in the next chapter, but we must begin further back, as it were, with the *presuppositions* Jesus' hearers would probably have shared about the Spirit. It is largely only from these presuppositional foundational beliefs about the Spirit that Jesus and the disciples could have been expected to recognize certain activities of God amongst them as derived from the *Spirit*, rather than from some other means of God's presence (whether his 'power', his 'hand', his 'name', an angel, or whatever). Accordingly we must start by asking how *typical* Jews would think about the Spirit in the period leading up to Jesus' ministry.

While first-century Jews may have been expected to derive their understanding of the Spirit from the Old Testament, heard (e.g.) in the weekly synagogue readings, we need to be aware that they were as prone to hear 'selectively' as their twentieth-century Christian counterparts. The various groups within Judaism thus came to emphasize different aspects of the Spirit's work and to play down others. In what follows, however, we have space only to discuss the main elements of shared beliefs.

I. THE OLD TESTAMENT LEGACY TO JUDAISM ON THE 'SPIRIT OF GOD'

The Old Testament had spoken in diverse and fragmentary fashion of God's Spirit.[1] Its language was strongly metaphorical, and was often the language of vivid experience, but it offered comparatively little help to the reader attempting to forge a 'theology' of the Spirit.

Part of the problem was that the Hebrew word used – *rûach* – sometimes denotes a storm wind, sometimes 'breath', sometimes 'vitality' or 'life', and so it was not always easy to be sure whether or not a particular instance of *rûach* referred to God's Spirit. Anyone who has compared the different English versions of Genesis 1:2 will have become acutely aware of the problem: while NIV reads 'and the Spirit of God was hovering over the waters', NRSV (like one of the oldest translations of the OT, the Aramaic targum) renders, 'while a *wind* from God swept over the face of the waters'. It was thus unclear whether or not this passage expressed the view that God's Spirit was involved in creation. Similar ambiguities attach to the other references usually quoted to support the view that the Spirit was involved in creation.[2]

Another potential problem arose, with the Old Testament material, when the reader posed the question of how 'the Spirit of the Lord' was related to God. While some New Testament writers may have been coming to think of the Spirit as fully God, a personal being at one with the Father and the Son (see Ch. 11, below), such a view was to be discerned only with very great difficulty (if at all) in the Old Testament.

---

[1]For brief (but serviceable) overviews of the Spirit in the OT, see (e.g.) E. Schweizer, *The Holy Spirit* (London: SCM, 1981), ch. 2, or A. Heron, *The Holy Spirit* (London: MMS, 1983), ch. 1, or the standard dictionary articles. Better (fuller) are G.T. Montague, *The Holy Spirit: Growth of a Biblical Tradition* (New York: Paulist Press, 1976), chs. 1–8 and L. Neve, *The Spirit of God in the Old Testament* (Tokyo: Seibunsha, 1972), *passim.*

[2]For example, when Ps. 33:6 said 'By the word of the Lord the heavens were made, and all the host by the *rûach* of his mouth', did this refer to God's Holy Spirit, or to 'the breath of his mouth', referring (poetically) to the breath with which the creative command was uttered? Similarly Ps. 104:30, speaking of all God's creatures, said 'when you send forth your spirit they are created'. But was this a reference to the Holy Spirit in creation, or was God's *rûach* here simply the 'vitality' he gives living organisms or the 'breath of life' like that which he breathed into the first man, Adam, according to Gen. 2:7? (Cf. Ps. 104:29; Job 27:3; 33:4; 34:14–15).

In each of these occasions it is not clear that we have a reference to what might properly be called 'the Spirit of God' or the 'Holy Spirit' (a term found for sure only at two places in the OT: Ps. 51:11 and Isa. 63:10–14).

Indeed, if one were to ask Jewish readers of the Hebrew Bible, most would have been liable rather to explain the Spirit as God's *own* life and vitality in action, just as a person's 'spirit' is his or her own 'vitality' or 'life'. To speak of 'the Spirit of the Lord' performing some act was thus analogous to speaking of the 'arm of the Lord' or 'the hand of the Lord' performing the same action: it would be understood as a way of speaking of Yahweh himself in action; the extension of his own invisible presence. Thus, when Isaiah 63:10 said, 'But they rebelled and grieved his Holy Spirit; therefore he became their enemy; he himself fought against them', a Jew might naturally read this to mean that Israel in the wilderness grieved *Yahweh himself*, God whose inner Spirit was present and active with the Israelites through Moses and the seventy elders. Those with a particular interest in Jewish wisdom, however, may have been more inclined to identify the Spirit as God's own 'mind' or 'will' at work (cf. Isa. 30:1–2; 40:12–14; Wisdom of Solomon 7–9; Philo, *Creation* 135, 144; *Special Laws* 4.123; *The Worse Attacks the Better*, 80–81, 83–84; *On Noah's Work as Planter*, 18; *Allegorical Laws* 1.142).

What, in brief, would a reading of the Old Testament have indicated concerning the usual *actions* of the Spirit of God? The Spirit was primarily represented in two ways:

(1) *as the invisible activity of God in power*, and
(2) *as his presence in revelation and wisdom.*

In both, God's Spirit was typically related to God's *covenantal* activities *in and on behalf of Israel*, so the locus of the Spirit's work was restricted almost exclusively to the holy nation.

1. The Spirit of the Lord in Israel's Past

Within Israel, the Spirit was said to be 'on', 'with' or 'in' (the terms are interchangeable) Israel's *leaders*, enabling them to act with God's power or to reveal his will. Accordingly God's *rûach* was portrayed as a charismatic endowment on the judges, such as Othniel (Jdg. 3:10), Gideon (Jdg. 6:34) and Jephthah (Jdg. 11:29), flaring into action on behalf of God's covenant people in times of crisis. Indeed, even the at-first-sight bizarre eruptions of the Spirit of power through Samson (e.g. 14:6,19; 15:14–15) appear to have been understood as the divine protection of this champion of Israel,[3] and for the routing of her enemies (14:19 and 15:14).

---

[3]Cf. Judges 14:6 (Samson tears apart a threatening lion), 15:14–15.

Working at a more personal level (rather than as naked power), the Spirit of the Lord was perceived as an endowment on Moses (Num. 11:17,29) through which he liberated and led Israel at God's direction. Joshua was understood to have had a similar endowment (Num. 27:18 and elsewhere). The same endowment was shared with the seventy elders (11:25–29) and gave them wisdom (with Moses) to adjudicate disputes (cf. Neh. 9:20, a retrospective view). God's wisdom and enabling were also portrayed as given by God's Spirit to the craftsmen who made the cultic furniture (Exod. 28:3; 31:3; 35:31). Later in the biblical chronology God's Spirit acted in power on behalf of Israel, the unseen sceptre of his righteous rule, through her kings, such as Saul in 1 Samuel 10:1–11 and notably through David in 1 Samuel 16:13 and elsewhere (cf. Zech. 4:6).

In perhaps the majority of these various Old Testament incidents the Spirit of God acted as the channel of communication between God and a human person. This was 'the Spirit of prophecy' as Judaism came to understand it. The Spirit was perceived to have made God's will and wisdom known to the charismatic leader, to the king, and even to the cult carpenter, especially (though not exclusively) through the phenomenon of oracular speech termed 'prophecy', in which a message of the Lord was granted by the Spirit in a dream, vision or word. Thus God's revelation was directly or indirectly traced to the Spirit in early prophecy (as in Num. 11:25–29; 24:2; 1 Sam. 10:10; 19:20) and in classical prophecy. Micah 3:8 and Hosea 9:7 effectively equated 'prophet' with 'man of the Spirit'. A similar message was expressed in Ezekiel 11:5–25 and elsewhere (Isa. 48:16; 61:1–3; Zech. 7:12).

2. Israel's Future Expectation of the Spirit

In the Old Testament the ministry of the Spirit seems to have been limited, with few exceptions, to the leaders and prophets; theirs was the responsibility, through the Spirit, to bring Yahweh's direction to his people. By contrast, a future was anticipated in which *all* Israel would share in the Spirit of prophecy (Joel 2:28; cf. Num. 11:29); indeed, such immediate knowledge of God lay at the heart of the hoped-for new covenant. In the new covenant each would 'know the Lord' for himself or herself (Jer. 31:34). The future was thus expected to be an epoch characterized by the lavish outpouring of God's Spirit (as in Isa. 32:15; 44:3; Ezek. 39:29) and the revelation of his glory and power (Hab. 2:14). This was in part to be accomplished (according to some elements of the OT tradition) through a righteous prophetic liberator (Deut. 18:15; Isa. 61), and/or a king endowed with the Spirit of wisdom and power

(Isa.11:1–9). But the universalizing of the Spirit amongst God's people was anticipated as leading to the deep existential renewal of Israel – like a mass resurrection from dead bones in the wilderness (cf. Ezek. 37). It would amount to the re-creation of the very heart of humankind in obedience (Jer. 31:31–40; Ezek. 36:24–29; cf. Ps. 51:10–14 for an analogous individual expression of such hope).

It is to the more specific question of how these various activities of the Spirit came to be understood in Judaism that we may now turn in more detail.

II. THE SPIRIT AS THE 'SPIRIT OF PROPHECY' IN JUDAISM[4]

By far the most widespread understanding of the Spirit in Judaism was as something like what later came to be called the 'Spirit of prophecy'. While the term 'Spirit of prophecy' only became *regular* in the targums (the from first-century BC to mediaeval Aramaic interpretive renderings of the Hebrew Bible given in the synagogues),[5] it was used in the pre-Christian writing *Jubilees* (31:12[6]) and in Philo (*On Flight and Finding* 186[7] and *Life of Moses* 1.277[8]), and something like the *concept* denoted by

---

[4]On the Spirit in Judaism, serviceable brief surveys are given by Bieder and Sjöberg, Πνεῦμα, κτλ', *TDNT* VI: 367–75 and 375–89; J.D.G. Dunn, *Christology in the Making* (London: SCM, 1980), 132–6; M.E. Isaacs, *The Concept of Spirit* (London: Heythrop Monographs, 1976), chs. 2, 3, 5 and 6; Schweizer, *Spirit*, ch. 3; David Hill, *Greek Words with Hebrew Meanings* (Cambridge: CUP, 1967), 205–41, and Montague, *Spirit*, chs. 7–11. More extended, and more important, are J. Breck, *The Origins of Johannine Pneumatology* (Crestwood: St. Valdimir's Seminary Press, 1991); R.P. Menzies, *Empowered for Witness: The Spirit in Luke-Acts* (Sheffield: SAP, 1994), chs. 2–5; M. Turner, *Power From On High* (Sheffield: SAP, 1996), chs. 3–5.

[5]It is especially common in *Targum Jonathan* to the Former and Latter Prophets (which contains both tannaitic (pre-200 AD rabbinic tradition) and amoraic (AD 200–500) material); but also in *Targum Onqelos* on the Pentateuch (also relatively early) and *Targum Pseudo-Jonathan* (on the Pentateuch, but later than *Onqelos* (probably finally edited in the seventh century), and much more interpretive in its paraphrases).

[6]'And a spirit of prophecy came down upon [Isaac's] mouth' and he blessed Levi and Judah. For convenient text of *Jubilees* (written mid-second century BC), see *OTP* 2:35–43.

[7]'Telling . . . in another [passage] of the divine Spirit of prophecy bestowed on only seventy elders', Philo, a Greek-speaking Jew of Alexandria, wrote in the years AD 25–40+.

[8]'[Balaam] straightway became "possessed", and there came upon him the prophetic Spirit'.

the phrase 'Spirit of prophecy' (as used in the targums) is older.[9] For someone from outside the Jewish tradition the name 'Spirit of prophecy' is potentially misleading, for it might suggest Jews thought of the Spirit primarily as giving prophecies. In fact, by the term 'Spirit of prophecy' Jews meant something much wider, namely the Spirit acting as the organ of communication between God and a person, typically inspiring at least four different types of gifts.

1. The Gifts Prototypical to the Concept of the 'Spirit of prophecy'[10]

We shall inspect the relevant activities of the Spirit in the order of frequency with which they are described:

(1) *Most commonly, in Jewish writings, the 'Spirit of prophecy' affords charismatic revelation and guidance.*[11]

The examples of this kind of activity in the rabbis and targums are too numerous to mention, but many of them are also perhaps rather too late to count as strictly 'intertestamental'; one text, however, relating to Gamaliel (probably the grandson of the Gamaliel that taught Paul, and teaching mainly AD 80–90) may be given in full as a typical example:

> Rabban Gamaliel was going along from Akko to Kezib. He found a loaf of cheap bread on the road. He said to his slave, Tabi, 'Take the loaf.' He saw a Gentile. He said to him, 'Mabegai, take this loaf of bread.' R. Le'ii ran after him [to find out about him] . . . He said to him, 'What is your name?' He said to him, 'Mabegai.' He said to him, 'Now, did Rabban Gamaliel ever in your whole life meet you?' He said to him, 'No.' On the basis of this event we learn that Rabban Gamaliel divined by the Holy Spirit. (*Tosefta Pesaḥim* 2.15[12])

---

[9]For detailed consideration see Turner, *Power*, ch. 3.

[10]For a fuller account, *ibid.*

[11]See *ibid.*, §2(A), where we define this 'charismatic revelation' as: 'a certain type of event in the psyche of an individual; namely one which that individual (or some observer) conceives to be the communication of revelatory knowledge from God. For ITP Judaism the knowledge in question would prototypically be granted in a visionary experience, a dream, or in the hearing of words (or by some combination of these), and it would have as its content either foreknowledge of the future, or revelatory insight into some aspect of the present world or of the heavenly realm.'

[12]The Mishnah was the great rabbinic codification of Law first taught orally, but then committed to writing at the end of the second century. This inscription was a landmark dividing the period of the *tannaim* (rabbinical schools from AD 10 to 200) from the later *amoraim* (extending from the writing of the Mishnah to

Here, clearly, the 'Spirit of prophecy' has nothing to do with 'prophesying' as such. Gamaliel utters no oracle. Rather, his disciples deduce that, if he had never before met the man in question, it must have been the Holy Spirit who disclosed Mabegai's name to Gamaliel. In this instance, what is revealed is of course merely an incidental detail, not unlike what some Pentecostals or Charismatics might call a 'word of knowledge'. Such gifts of revelation are regularly attributed to the 'Spirit of prophecy', even when they are not actually themselves 'prophecies', nor lead to them, because charismatic revelation provides the usual *basis* for prophetic utterances. In the Old Testament and Judaism most 'prophecy' was not immediately or invasively inspired utterance, but the relating to a target audience of some revelation given earlier. As for the revelatory content afforded by the Spirit, this could naturally be of considerably greater import than in Gamaliel's case!

Rabbinical and targumic examples, as intimated, are plentiful. By the Spirit of prophecy it is revealed:

to *Abraham*, that a woman will one day save a whole city ((Abel) *Tanḥuma* (Buber) וירא §12)

to *Isaac*, that Esau's descendants will oppress Jacob's (*Midrash Psalms* 10.6)

to *Rebecca*, the content of Esau's thoughts (*Midrash Psalms* 105.4 (cf. *Targum Pseudo-Jonathan* Gen. 27:5, 42))

to *Jacob*, that Joseph is in danger of being 'devoured' by Potiphar's wife (*Genesis Rabbah* 84.19); that he (Jacob) will not be buried with Rachel (*Midrash Ha-Gadol Gen.* 513); that he should lay his hands on and bless Ephraim then Manasseh (*Num. Rab.* 14.5), and (during famine) that there is corn in Egypt (*Fragmentary Targum Gen.* 42:1)

to *Joseph*, that there will be two temples built in Benjamin (*Gen. Rab.* 93.12), and that Jacob is unwell (*Pesiqta Rabbati.* 3.4 cf. *Fragmentary Targum Gen.* 37:33, etc.)

to *Miriam*, that the saviour Moses is to be born ('Pseudo-Philo' = *Biblical Antiquities* 9.10//Babylonian Talmud, tractate *Soṭah* 11b)

to *Moses*, that the Egyptian taskmaster really deserves the fate Moses is about to inflict on him (*Exodus Rabbah* 1.28 and//s (!)); that the future Temple will be destroyed (*Tanḥuma* תבא §1), and that the Temple service will resume under Ezra (*Jalqut* שפטים §915, etc.)

to the *Israelites* in general, both where the Egyptians had hidden their treasures (*Mekilta Pisha* 13 (on Exodus 12:36)) and Pharaoh's strategy against them (*Mek. Shirata* 7 (on Exodus 15:9–10))

to *Rahab* the prostitute, that the searchers will return in three days (*Ruth Rab.* 2.1)

to *Solomon*, that Pharaoh's work-party for the Temple will all need burial shrouds within the year (*Num. Rab.* 19.3)

(footnote 12 continued)
that of the Talmuds). Tosefta, meaning 'supplement', was material 'additional to' the legal discussions in the Mishnah. Many tosefta passages were set alongside their corresponding Mishnah section in the Talmuds.

and, to proceed without further ado to the other temporal extreme, to *Rabbi Simeon ben Yohai*, that the peasant himself has buried the corpse he pretends to Simeon to have discovered (*j. Shebi* 9.1 and//s).

One of the most amusing illustrations is the story told of Rabbi Meir (third generation tannaim: so circa AD 150. The story first occurs in the Jerusalem Talmud (*Sotah* 1.4), though the fuller text given here is from *Num. Rab.* 9.20):

R. Zechariah, the son in law of R. Levi [c.300], related the following incident: R. Meir used to hold regular discourses in the Synagogue every Sabbath. A certain woman was present who made it a habit to listen to him. On one occasion he discoursed to a late hour. She went away and when about to enter her home she found the lights out. Her husband asked her: 'Where have you been?' She told him: 'I have been listening to the discourse.' Said he to her: 'This woman [= You] will not enter the house unless she goes and spits in the face of the preacher.' R. Meir saw it all by means of the Holy Spirit. He pretended therefore to be suffering from pain in the eyes, and announced: 'If there is any woman skilled in whispering charms for the eyes, let her come and whisper.' Her neighbours said to her: 'Behold your opportunity of going back home! Pretend you are a charmer and spit into his eyes.' When she came to him he said to her: 'Are you skilled in whispering charms for the eyes?' Being overawed by his presence she answered in the negative. He said to her: 'Nevertheless, spit into this one seven times and it will get better.' After she had spat he said to her: 'Go and tell your husband: "You bade me do it only once; see, I have spat seven times!" '

According to Sirach 48:24[13] it was 'by the Spirit of might' that Isaiah 'saw the last things', and so 'comforted those who mourned in Zion' (similarly Enoch, in 1 *Enoch* 91:1,[14] promises Methuselah and his children that when the Spirit is poured upon him, 'I [will] show you everything that will happen to you for ever.' Cf. 4 Ezra 14:22 for 'retrospective' prophetic revelation, on which see below[15]).

(2) *'The Spirit of prophecy' affords charismatic* wisdom.[16]

This is the second most common gift attributed to the 'Spirit of prophecy' (though rare in the rabbis). Archetypal biblical examples, regularly commented on by later Judaism, would be Bezalel filled with the Spirit for all wisdom in crafting the covenantal furnishings (Exod.

---

[13]Sirach – also called Ecclesiasticus – was written in Hebrew at the beginning of the second century BC, and translated into Greek by ben Sirach's grandson, c. 132 BC. The text can be found in any version of the Apocrypha.

[14]1 *Enoch* is a composite work of mainly second century BC origin, but redacted at the turn of the eras: for text see *OTP* 1:13–89.

[15]See also (e.g.) Philo, *On Dreams* 2.252; *Biblical Antiquities* (also referred to as *Pseudo-Philo* or as *LAB*) 9.10; 31.9.

[16]At *Power*, ch. 3 §2(B), we distinguish two terms: 'charismatic *communication* of wisdom' and 'charismatic *infusion* of wisdom'. By the former we denote a single

31:3); similarly the seventy (-two?) elders who were granted the Spirit to enable them to lead and adjudicate in Israel. For a typical example from outside the biblical witness we may refer to Philo's *Life of Moses* 2. 265. In the immediate co-text Philo discusses Moses' instructions with respect to the Sabbath. Impressed by the wisdom revealed in them, which he regards as God-given, he says:

> I need hardly say that conjectures of this kind [Moses' teaching on the Sabbath] are closely akin to prophecies. For the mind could not have made so straight an aim if there was not also the divine Spirit guiding it to the truth itself.

This revealing remark by Philo largely explains *why* 'wisdom' is attributed to the 'Spirit of prophecy': from Philo's perspective, charismatic wisdom is similar to charismatic revelation in so far as the unaided human mind could not achieve it; God must intervene by his Spirit and guide the mind in order to make such understanding possible. Similarly, in *4 Ezra* 14:22,[17] Ezra requests, 'send the Holy Spirit to me, and I will write everything that has happened in the world from the beginning.' This request is almost certainly to be understood largely as a request for charismatic *revelation*, but the close relation to charismatic wisdom is also demonstrated in the context in that, in answer to his prayer, Ezra is given a cup which fills him with the *wisdom* and *understanding* to articulate what he receives (vv. 25, 40–41).

A further significant example is provided by Sirach 39:6. In the midst of a section praising the wise man who devotes himself to a study of the Law the sage expresses his hope that:

> 'If the great Lord is willing he [that is, the man who devotes himself to the Law] will be *filled with* the *spirit of understanding*; he will pour forth words of wisdom and give thanks to the Lord in prayer.'

Here, clearly, charismatic wisdom means a lively enthusiasm and understanding of God's word that is characterized by doxological joy in God and enables the sage to become a charismatic teacher. It is quite

---

(footnote 16 continued)
charismatic event (perhaps immediately consciously perceived) communicating divine wisdom; i.e. an event in the psyche of an individual in which the cognition is perceived to be altered by God thereby enabling improved analysis of a particular situation or handling of a skill or problem. By 'charismatic *infusion* of wisdom', we wish to denote a series of such events – virtually a process extended over time – and not necessarily consciously perceived by the beneficiary, perhaps, rather deduced by observers.
[17] An apocalypse, written c. AD 100, in Palestine. For text see *OTP* 1: 525–39.

similar to what is prayed for by Paul in Ephesians 1:17–20; 3:16–21, and
what he commends to them 5:18b–20.[18]

(3) *'The Spirit of prophecy' sometimes affords* invasively inspired
prophetic speech.

By 'invasive' is meant that as the Spirit comes upon the person they are
caught up and inspired to speak. This is quite different from the usual
form of prophecy, which was not immediately inspired, but involved
the relating to a target audience of some revelation given (perhaps days
or weeks) beforehand. We may take as an example of this invasive type
of speech what Josephus[19] attributes to the non-Israelite prophet-and-
sorcerer Balaam. The context is the story in Numbers 23–24 where
Balak, the king of Moab, wished to force Balaam to utter a prophetic
curse on Israel, who were threatening his kingdom. Balaam received
prophetic words of blessing for Israel instead. When Balak fumes
against him, Balaam is made to reply (echoing Num. 22:38; 24:12–14):

> Balak . . . have you reflected on the whole matter, and do you think
> that it rests with us at all to be silent or to speak on such themes as
> these, when we are possessed by the Spirit of God; for that (Spirit)
> gives utterance to such language and words as it will, and of which
> we are unconscious. (Josephus, *Antiquities* 4.119)

On the whole, examples of 'invasive' prophetic speech are more common in hellenistic Judaism than in Palestinian (where it is rare), especially amongst those writers who owe a debt to Greek philosophical
ideas of mantic prophecy.[20] Such notions are reflected in the example
just given when it is suggested the prophet actually becomes *unconscious* of what is being said – which goes back to the Greek idea that the
human mind must be evicted or eclipsed as the divine mind takes over.
Other significant examples of invasive prophetic speech are provided
by (e.g.) targums to Numbers 11.26–27; *Jubilees* 25.14; 31.12; Philo, *Special Laws* 4. 49; *Life of Moses* 1. 175 and 277, and *Bib. Ant.* 28.6.

---

[18]For other examples see, e.g. targums to Exodus 31:3; *Frg. Tg. Num.* 11:26–27;
Tg. Onq. Deut. 34:9: *Jos. and As.* 4:9; Josephus, *Ant.* 10.239; *Jub.* 40:5; Philo, *Jos.*
117; *Giants* 24; Sir. 39:6; Sus. 45b (Theod); Wis. 7:7; 9:17–18; and cf. 1QH 12.11–
13; 13.18–19; 14.12–13.
[19]Josephus (AD 37-100+), an aristocratic priestly Pharisee, held a command in
Galilee during the Jewish War but surrendered into the hands of Vespasian,
whom he prophesied would become emperor, and whose protégé he became.
Later he accompanied Titus to Rome, where he wrote his (pro-Roman and
apologetic) *Jewish War* (c. 75–79) and later his twenty-volume *Antiquities of the
Jews* (c. 93–95).
[20]See Ch. 12 below.

(4) *'The Spirit of prophecy' sometimes (but rarely) affords* invasively inspired charismatic praise or worship.

This is the closest analogy in Judaism to the phenomenon of tongues on the day of Pentecost and when others first received the Spirit (e.g. Acts 10:46; 19:6). The most obvious Jewish examples, perhaps, are those associated with the Saul tradition in 1 Samuel 10 and 19. At 10:6, for example, Samuel tells Saul that as he approaches Gibeah he will meet a band of prophets. The Masoretic Text goes on: 'The Spirit of the Lord will come upon you in power and you will prophesy with them; and you will be changed into another man.' The targum changes this to read:

> 'And *the spirit of prophecy from before the Lord will reside* upon you, and you will *sing praise* with them, and you will be changed into another man.'

Similar changes are then repeated at 1 Samuel 10:10 and 19:20,23. An analogous understanding is represented in *1 Enoch* at two points. In *1 Enoch* 71:11 the messianic Enoch figure relates how he ascended into heaven, and saw the holiest angels, the heavenly rivers of fire, and then beheld God himself. He says: [on seeing God] 'I fell on my face . . . Then I cried with a great voice by the *spirit* of the power, blessing, glorifying, and extolling.' A similar understanding is found earlier at 61:7 and 11,12, but this time it is the whole heavenly congregation which blesses, extols and worships God with charismatic wisdom 'in the Spirit of life' (v.7) and a spirit of 'faith', 'wisdom', 'patience' and 'mercy' (11,12).

In the rabbis we find another tradition cropping up in several forms to the effect that all Israel were charismatically inspired to sing the song of triumph in Exodus 15 (the so-called 'song of Moses'). One of the earlier forms of the tradition, as preserved in *Mekilta Beshallaḥ* 7 (on Exodus 14:26–31),[21] describes the matter thus:

> Great indeed is faith before Him who spoke and the world came into being. . . . R. Nehemiah says: Whence can you prove that whosoever accepts even one single commandment with true faith is deserving of having the Holy Spirit rest upon him? We find this to have been the case with our fathers. For as a reward for the faith with which they believed, they were considered worthy of having the Holy Spirit rest upon them, so that they could utter the song, as it is said:

---

[21]*Mekilta* is primarily legally orientated commentary (midrash) on some important texts from Exodus. *Beshallah* covers from 13:17 to the end of chapter 14. While a core may go back to the tannaitic period, it has been substantially edited in the amoraic period (AD 200–400+).

'And they believed in the Lord . . .' Then sang Moses and the children of Israel (Exod. 14:31; 15:1; cf. *Exodus Rabbah* 23.2).[22]

Charismatic revelation, charismatic wisdom, invasive prophetic speech and invasive charismatic praise are the four gifts prototypically associated with the 'Spirit of prophecy'. As we shall see, there are others occasionally associated with the Spirit/Spirit of prophecy, though this will lead us into disputed territory. The foregoing description of the types of charismata regularly attributed to the Spirit in Judaism could easily give a misleading impression of bland uniformity in Jewish pneumatologies. Such is not intended. There was indeed considerable diversity,[23] but this was less at the level of which charismata the divine Spirit enabled than in the import of the respective charismata for the life of the individual and of the nation.

2. The Alleged Withdrawal of the 'Spirit of prophecy' and the Hoped-For Universal Return of the Spirit

It is often held that Judaism believed in the complete withdrawal of the Spirit following the last canonical prophets (cf. *Tosefta Sotah* 13.3–4), a cessation that would last until the eschaton. This almost certainly rests on misunderstanding (as we shall see in Ch. 12). It would be nearer the truth to say that many Jews thought experience of the Spirit of prophecy was relatively rare in their own day (except, perhaps, in the sense of pious wisdom), and comparatively lacking in quality and power. If one asked why this was so, an important answer was that it was because of the nation's sin (cf. *b. Sanh.* 65b). Correspondingly it was also hoped (especially on the basis of Joel 2:28–32 (= MT 3:1–5)) that the Spirit of prophecy would be poured out on *all* of the restored Israel at the end. Thus *Numbers Rabbah*[24] 15.25 states:

---

[22]From J.Z. Lauterbach, *Mekilta de Rabbi Ishmael* (Philadelphia: JPSA, 1933–35), 252–3. Cf. *Bib. Ant.* 32:14 (Deborah sings praises by the Holy Spirit). *Testament of Job*, chs. 48–50, describe Job's daughters putting on spiritual sashes which immediately cause them to burst forth into charismatic praises including angelic glossolalia. But these chapters are probably a Christian (perhaps Montanist) addition to the *Testament*.

[23]For a (rather overdrawn) description of the diversity, see e.g. Breck, *Origins*, chs. 4–6.

[24]*Numbers Rabbah* is one of a series of *homiletic* commentaries (midrashim) on the biblical books. The section on Numbers 15 onwards is derived from Tanhuma, the midrashic compilation attributed to the rabbi of that name

The Holy One, blessed be He, said: 'In this world only a few individuals have prophesied, but in the world to come all Israel will be made prophets', as it says: *And it shall come to pass afterward, that I will pour out my spirit upon all flesh, and your sons and your daughters will prophesy, your old men*, etc. (Joel 3:1). Such is the exposition given by R. Tanhuma, son of R. Abba.

This would bring Israel immediate knowledge of God and of his will, and thus promote ongoing obedience fulfilling the hope of Ezekiel 36:27 (*Deut. Rab.* 6.14; *Targum Ezek.* 36:25–26: cf. *b. Ber.* 31b–32a). In the meantime the Spirit had afforded the repository of wisdom and revelation in Scripture, and some pious Israelites were thought to have at least a measure of the Spirit of prophecy:[25] men and women of the Spirit such as Zechariah, Simeon and Anna depicted in Luke 1–2, would thus not be out of place in a first-century Palestinian context. Philo and ben Sirach would extend the Spirit of prophecy to a wider sector of the 'wise', while the Qumran community appear to have considered all their members to share some measure of the eschatological promise of the Spirit.

3. Disputed Questions: the 'Spirit of Prophecy' as the Source of Acts of Power and as the Inspiration of Ethical Renewal

In his famous article on Spirit for *TDNT*, E. Schweizer was to claim

Luke adopts the typically Jewish idea that the Spirit is the Spirit of prophecy . . . This prevents him from attributing to the Spirit either miracles of healing or strongly ethical effects like the common life of the primitive community (*TWNT* VI:407 (ET (mistranslated) *TDNT* VI:409).

There are two important claims here.

(1) According to this view the Spirit in Judaism acts *only at the cognitive* (or pre-cognitive) *level, not in the physical/ tangible realm*. It seemed self-evident to him that as the 'Spirit of prophecy' the Spirit will not heal the lame and cleanse lepers but rather gives

---

(footnote 24 continued)
(c. AD 350–375), but edited between the fifth and ninth centuries. Despite the late date of the redaction of *Num. Rab.* it contains early material.
[25]We have noted the cases of Gamaliel and Meier: cf. also R. Akiba (In *Lev. Rab.* 21.8) and Simeon ben Yohai (*j. Shebi* 9.1).

revelation or wisdom and inspires speech — which for Schweizer largely meant preaching.

(2) For Schweizer, the Spirit in Judaism is clearly an empowering for special tasks, not a soteriologically *necessary* gift (and, by implication, the same applies for Luke). On his understanding, a person does not need the gift of the Spirit of prophecy in order to be 'saved'. Rather, God gives this gift to people who are already part of the community of salvation, and it is given as a *donum superadditum* (an 'additional gift' or, one might say, as a 'second blessing'). Schweizer's position has been especially strengthened by the writings of Pentecostal scholar R.P. Menzies, whose doctoral dissertation was published recently under the title *The Development of Early Christian Pneumatology with Special Reference to Luke-Acts.*[26]

But strong arguments stand against the Schweizer/Menzies understanding of the Spirit of prophecy in Judaism. In the first place, however incongruous it may seem, *Judaism did attribute miracles of power to the 'Spirit of prophecy'.*[27] That is, Jews did not think of the 'Spirit of prophecy' as 'the Spirit of the inspiration of "prophetic" phenomena *alone*', but something more like 'the Spirit which is *typically* associated with "prophetic" phenomena, but also at other times revealed as the "Spirit of power"'. The LXX and the much freer biblical 'translations' of the targums retain the word 'Spirit' (even 'Spirit of prophecy' in the latter) in contexts where miraculous power is meant, e.g. to overcome enemies (*Tg. Jon.* Judges 3:10: cf. 6:34; 11:29; 13:25; 14:6, 19; 15:14), or to transport the prophet to another place (1 Kgs 18:12; 2 Kgs 2:16; Ezek 2:2; 3:12,14; 8:1, 11:1,24, etc), while in 2 Kings 2:9–15 the power by which Elisha divides the waters is specifically identified by the targum as the 'Spirit of prophecy' upon him. Outside the 'translations', we find the Spirit as the author of creation and resurrection first in *2 Baruch* (21:4; 23:5[28]) and *4 Ezra* (6:39–41), but then also on several occasions in the rabbis.[29] We may then also note that the

---

[26](Sheffield: SAP, 1991) This has subsequently been brought out in a more user-friendly form as *Empowered For Witness* in the new *Journal of Pentecostal Theology Studies* series (Sheffield: SAP, 1994).

[27]See M. Turner, 'The Spirit and the Power of Jesus' Miracles in the Lucan Conception', *NovT* 33 (1991), 124–52 (esp. 132–6). More fully, *Power*, ch. 4.

[28]'O hear me, you who created the earth, the one who fixed the firmament by the word and fastened the height of heaven by the Spirit . . .' (21:4); 'No creature will live again unless the number that has been appointed is completed. For my Spirit creates the living . . .' (23:5).

[29]See *Power*, ch. 4: cf. *m. Sot.* 9.15; *Gen. Rab.* 96.5 (but only in a late MS); *Exod. Rab.* 48.4; *Cant. Rab.* 1.1 §9 and *Pesiq. R.* 1.6. See also Ch. 8 below.

Spirit as the power of miraculous deeds is clear in the Palestinian *Biblical Antiquities* (27.9–10; 36.2), in the hellenistic writings of Josephus (*Antiquities* 8.408), and above all in the 'messianic' traditions based in or reflecting Isaiah 11:1–4, discussed below, which in different ways take up the idea of the Spirit as the source of the Messiah's 'might' against his enemies.

We should also challenge Schweizer's claim that as the 'Spirit of prophecy' the Spirit would not be anticipated to have any significant direct ethical influence. Examination reveals the opposite is closer to the truth. It would appear various sectors of Judaism expected the 'Spirit of prophecy' to give such important and/or transforming revelation, and such ethically *renewing* wisdom, that these activities would almost inevitably be regarded as *virtually essential* for fully authentic human existence before God,[30] and so also for that future state of it which writers mean by 'salvation'.[31]

This is plainly the case at Qumran, which considered itself a community enjoying the beginnings of eschatological salvation, attributed largely to the Spirit. The following medley of assertions, taken from the Qumran hymns alone, adequately illustrates the point:

> 'I praise Thee, O Lord, for Thou didst uphold me with Thy might and Thy Holy Spirit thou hast shed upon me that I might not stumble. And thou hast strengthened me in face of battles of wickedness (1QH 7.6–7)
> . . . Thou hast upheld me with certain truth; thou hast delighted me with Thy Holy Spirit and [hast opened my heart] till this day (1QH 9.32).
> . . . I, the Master, know Thee O my God, by the Spirit which Thou has given to me, and by Thy Holy Spirit I have hearkened to Thy marvellous counsel. In the mystery of Thy wisdom Thou hast opened knowledge to me and in Thy mercies [Thou hast unlocked for me] the fountain of Thy might (12.11–13).

---

[30]Thus *Targum Pseudo-Jonathan* can even amend Genesis 6:3 to generalize the point, making the Lord say, 'Did I not put my Holy Spirit in them that they might perform good deeds?' More in the wisdom tradition, Philo can explain the total consecration, obedience, and virtue of the first man in terms of the divine Spirit flowing in full measure in him (*Creation*, 144), and can characterize the prophetic Spirit on Moses and the seventy elders — and all other wise — as the Spirit which leads in every journey of righteousness (*Giants*, 55; cf. 28–29, 47, 53). These are not accidental references, but go to the heart of his pneumatology: experience of the divine spirit is participation in the rational and moral mind of God. *Cf.* also *Test. Simeon* 4.4; *Test. Benj.* 8.1–3; *Test. Levi* 2.3B7–8, 14 (manuscript E); *Joseph and Aseneth* 4.11.

[31]See M. Turner, 'The Spirit of Prophecy and the Ethical/Religious Life of the Christian Community', in M. Wilson (ed.), *Spirit and Renewal: Essays in Honour of J. Rodman Williams* (Sheffield: SAP, 1994), 166-90, or, more fully, *Power*, ch. 5.

. . . And I, Thy servant, I know by the Spirit which Thou hast given to me [that Thy words are truth], and that all Thy works are righteousness, and that Thou wilt not take back Thy word (1QH 13.18–19).

. . . And I know through the understanding which comes from Thee, that in thy goodwill towards [ashes, Thou hast shed] Thy Holy Spirit [upon me] and thus drawn me near to understanding thee (1QH 14.12b–13).

. . . And me, your servant, you have favoured with the Spirit of knowledge (1QH 14.25).

. . . Bowing down and [confessing all] my transgressions, I will seek [Thy] spirit [of knowledge]; cleaving to Thy spirit of [holiness], I will hold fast to the truth of Thy Covenant that [I may serve] Thee in truth and wholeness of heart, and that I may love [Thy Name] (1QH 16.6–7).

. . . And Thou sheddest (Thy) favour upon me through Thy compassionate spirit and Thy [glo]rious splendour (1QH 16.9).

. . . And I know that man is not righteous except through Thee and therefore I implore Thee by the spirit which thou hast given [me] to perfect Thy [favours] to Thy servant [for ever], purifying me by the Holy Spirit, and drawing me near to Thee by Thy grace according to the abundance of Thy mercies (1QH 16.11b–12).

. . . to wipe out in my midst, for a spirit of fle[sh] . . . is Thy servant . . . Thou didst sprinkle [Thy] Holy Spirit upon Thy servant . . . his heart (1QH 17.25–26).[32]

Here the 'Spirit of prophecy' — i.e. the Spirit which brings revelation, knowledge, and wisdom — delights with truth, the Law and knowledge of God (9.32; 12.11–13), and so draws towards Him (14.12b–13), but in the process purifying *by* such a vision and understanding (16.11b–12). The revelatory Spirit has thus itself become simultaneously the soteriological Spirit, the very basis of the transformed 'life' and sustained righteousness of the restored community. This new kind of existence is seen in terms of Ezekiel's new creation (1QH 17.25–26 (echoing Ezek. 36:26–27); similarly 4Q504.5 and 1QS 4.20–23), brought about by Spirit-given understanding (cf. 4Q434). As Breck summarizes the matter:

In the thought of the Dead Sea community . . . the titles 'Holy Spirit', 'Spirit of the Lord,' and 'Spirit of Truth' represent one and the same divine Spirit which reveals true knowledge of Torah and leads the faithful to perform works of righteousness in preparation for the coming Visitation.

---

[32]Menzies argues these are all late parts of the Qumran evidence and so just after the beginnings of the Christian movement. That is not clear. In any case, they come from the same *general* period and show how Jews at the time could conceive of the 'Spirit of prophecy' as soteriologically necessary.

. . . the function of the divine Spirit . . . can be generally characterized as both *revelatory* and *soteriological.*

The Spirit . . . exercises what can be termed an essential *hermeneutic function,* insofar as it inspires both correct interpretation of the divine will and the believer's ethical response to that will in the form of works of righteousness.[33] (Breck's emphases)

We have argued that essentially the same view is held in the later rabbinical traditions on Ezekiel 36,[34] and analogous ones elsewhere. We shall find further important evidence in Jewish conceptions of the Spirit on the Messiah.

4. The Spirit on the Messiah

A special case of 'the Spirit of prophecy' was to be that of *the Spirit on the Messiah.* A major strand of Judaism anticipated a Messiah mightily endowed with the Spirit as *both* the Spirit of prophecy (affording unique wisdom and knowledge of the Lord as the basis of his dynamic righteousness and 'fear of the Lord') *and* the Spirit of power (i.e. of the 'might' by which he asserts liberating rule against opposition). The model is first David, then more especially the 'Davidic' figure of Isaiah 11:1–4, endowed with the Spirit of wisdom, knowledge and might. The Targum renders Isaiah 11:1–2

> And a *king* shall come forth from the *sons* of Jesse, and *the Messiah* shall *be exalted* from *the sons of* his *sons.* [2] And upon him shall rest *the* spirit *of prophecy,* a spirit of wisdom and understanding, a spirit of counsel and might, a spirit of knowledge and the fear of the LORD.[35]
> (Italicized material is what the targumist has added to the Hebrew text.)

It is this combination, with strong echoes of the very language of

---

[33]The first two quotations are from *Origins,* 161, the third from *Origins,* 163.
[34]See Turner, *Power,* ch. 10, §2.7.
[35]For a defence of this reading, see C.A. Evans, 'From Anointed Prophet to Anointed King: Probing Aspects of Jesus' Self-Understanding', in *Jesus and His Contemporaries* (Leiden: Brill, 1995), 437–56, esp. 449–50. Others (including Chilton) read 'a spirit from before the Lord' in place of 'the spirit of prophecy', but this does not materially affect our argument, as the 'spirit from before the Lord' is identified *co-textually* as the Spirit giving wisdom, knowledge, etc. and so (as when the term is used elsewhere) as the 'spirit of prophecy'.

Isaiah 11:1–4, that provides the different 'messianic' portraits in *1 Enoch* 49:2–3; 62:1–2 (where the ethical dimension of the Spirit's endowment of the messianic figure is underscored by describing it as the 'Spirit of righteousness'); *Psalms of Solomon* 17:37; 18:7; 1QSb 5.25; 4Q215 iv.4; 4QpIsa^a 7–10 iii.15–29; 4QMess ar (= 4Q536) 3 i.4–11; *Targum Isaiah* 11:1–16, etc.[36] Other rather rarer strands of Jewish messianic hope also involve Spirit-endowed figures, whether the Elijah-like prophet based on Malachi 4:5 (Sir. 48.10); a Priestly Messiah (e.g. 1QS 9.10–11; T. *Levi* 18); a Prophet-like-Moses based on Deuteronomy 18:15–16 (e.g. 1QS 9.10–11); a Servant-Herald based on Isaiah 42:1–2; a liberating Servant-Warrior derived from Isaiah 61:1–2 (e.g. 11QMelchizedek; cf. 4Q521), or some combination of these. In each case the quality of the endowment of the Spirit might be nuanced slightly differently, but would combine wisdom, revelation, and some kinds of acts of power.[37]

III. CONCLUSION

The Spirit in intertestamental Jewish literature was above all the 'Spirit of prophecy'. The most typical gifts anticipated from the Spirit were accordingly various types of charismatic revelation, charismatic wisdom, and invasive charismatic speech. But this did not preclude the Spirit of prophecy from being associated with different kinds of acts of power (including healings and raising from the dead in 4Q521). Nor was the 'Spirit of prophecy' merely a *donum superadditum* of little ethical consequence. The Spirit's revelatory and wisdom-granting roles were understood (in many quarters) as transformative, and thus as potentially soteriological. In several of the messianic figures anticipated the one Spirit of prophecy was simultaneously to be the radically ethically-orientated Spirit of knowledge and fear of the Lord, and the Spirit of wisdom and might to rule.

---

[36]On the Qumran passages see, e.g., C.A. Evans, 'Jesus and the Messianic Texts from Qumran: A Preliminary Assessment of the Recently Published Materials', in *Jesus*, 83–154.
[37]See Turner, *Power*, ch. 4, §3, and ch. 5, §2.9 and §3.

Chapter Two

Jesus and the Spirit in the Synoptic Tradition

The nature of the gift of the Spirit received by Jesus in his Jordan experience[1] has been at the centre of three significant twentieth-century debates: (i) the extended controversy since Gunkel's day over the relation of Jesus' 'religion' to that of Paul (this has been stated as an antithesis: Jesus preached the Father and his kingdom; Paul, the Son); (ii) early mid-century discussions concerning whether the Spirit given to Jesus provides a paradigm for the sacrament of confirmation, and (iii) similar debates between classical Pentecostals and more traditional Protestantism on the question of whether Jesus' Jordan experience was a 'second' grace of empowering and the pattern for future Christian 'baptism in the Holy Spirit'.

In one of the most significant books to be written on New Testament pneumatology this century, James Dunn brought the debates together.[2] Fighting a war on three fronts, Dunn opposed the sacramentalist assertion that the regenerative gift of the Spirit is automatically given *in* the water rite, while against the Pentecostals and Confirmationists he argued the gift granted is no 'second blessing' given beyond conversion-initiation (even years later), but always *closely associated* with conversion-initiation — viz. as God's saving response to the human act of conversional repentance acted out in water baptism. This gift of the Spirit brings believers their knowledge of forgiveness and of eschatological new creation and sonship. To receive the Spirit is to receive nothing less than the downpayment and first fruits of the kingdom of God. *This*, argues Dunn, is what Jesus' Jordan experience was all about.[3] The Spirit descended upon him as the eschatological Spirit of new creation sonship and of the kingdom of God. That descent marked the turn of the eras. At least for Jesus, who alone entered the new

---

[1] Mk. 1:10,11 = Mt. 3:16,17 = Lk. 3:21,22.

[2] J.D.G. Dunn, *Baptism in the Holy Spirit: A Re-examination of the New Testament Teaching on the Gift of the Spirit in Relation to Pentecostalism Today* (London: SCM, 1970).

[3] For Dunn's account of the experience of Jesus at Jordan, *see Baptism*, ch. 3.

experience of the Spirit; the old covenant gave way to the new, the age
of Satan's rule was passing, the kingdom of God had come. But this
was an experience the disciples could enter only *at Pentecost*, after Jesus
had taken into himself the purging fire of the Spirit/kingdom in his
death at Calvary.[4] The 'religion' of Jesus and that of Paul are thus
transparently related: Jesus' experience of God through the Spirit is
archetypal of all later Christian experience of new covenant life and
sonship, and without this new creation gift of the Spirit there is no
experience of 'salvation'.[5]

As we shall see, Dunn's analysis of Paul has been largely convincing.
But he has been less successful with the Gospels, especially with Luke-
Acts. Building on Schweizer's analysis, Roger Stronstad,[6] Robert Menzies and others have argued, *per contra*, that in Luke the Spirit on Jesus
is the 'Spirit of prophecy'. According to Menzies, Luke intended his
readers to perceive Jesus' Jordan experience as providing a paradigm
for the post-Easter experience of the disciples' 'baptism in Holy Spirit'.
For all concerned, the gift of the 'Spirit of prophecy' is exclusively a
prophetic empowering for mission. It is *not* (as in Paul) the regenerative
and soteriologically necessary gift of the Spirit as the basis of sonship
and new covenant life, the power that redeems men and women from
the power of *sarx* ('the flesh' i.e. rebellious human nature). Rather, for
Luke, the Spirit is given only to those of faith, who are *already* part of
the community of salvation.[7] The Spirit has little, if anything, to do
with the ethical renewal of the individual or of the community, but
comes as the driving power to mission and witness, impelling the
gospel from Jordan to Jerusalem, and thence, in the period of the
church, to the ends of the earth.[8] As we have seen, for Schweizer and
Menzies, even the accompanying signs of healings and exorcisms are
excluded from this concept of the 'Spirit of prophecy' in Judaism and
from its counterpart in Luke-Acts.

---

[4]See Dunn, *Baptism*, ch. 4.
[5]This perspective was more explicitly developed in Dunn's later *Jesus and the Spirit* (London: SCM, 1975).
[6]*The Charismatic Theology of Saint Luke*, (Peabody: Hendrickson, 1984).
[7]See Menzies, *Development*, chs. 6–11; *Empowered*, chs. 6–11.
[8]Hans von Baer's pioneering monograph, *Der Heilige Geist in den Lukasschriften* (Stuttgart: Kohlhammer, 1926), was the first to demonstrate Luke's redactional interest in the Spirit as the driving force of salvation history, especially as empowering for witness — hough he did not set this 'Spirit of prophecy' in antithesis to the Spirit of sonship, of ethical renewal, and of power to perform liberating miracles, as Schweizer and Menzies were subsequently to do. For von Baer's important contribution see ch. 3 below.

Dunn and Menzies offer radically different and competing hypotheses about the nature of the gift of the Spirit to Jesus and to his disciples. In this chapter and the next we shall note considerable weaknesses in both positions, and work towards what we consider a more probable explanation of developments from Judaism to Luke-Acts and to Paul. In the present chapter we shall address the question of how the Synoptic Gospels understood the Spirit upon Jesus, but considerations of space require that we limit ourselves largely to Luke (who incorporates, adapts and considerably adds to the Marcan and Q material).[9]

I. THE SPIRIT IN THE GOSPEL INFANCY NARRATIVES (LUKE 1–2)[10]

1. The Spirit as the 'Spirit of Prophecy' in Expectant Israel

Luke (alone of the gospels) portrays a number of prophetic activities in association with Jesus' conception, birth and infancy. Elizabeth and Zechariah experience the Spirit of prophecy in invasive prophetic speech (the invasive quality denoted here by the Lucan favourite idiom 'filled with' the Holy Spirit) at 1:41–42 and 1:67, and as a result give oracles of recognition and assurance of salvation. Simeon too receives charismatic revelation (2:26, and perhaps Anna at 2:38), guidance (2:27) and prophetic utterance (2:29–35). This so closely tallies with the picture of the Spirit of prophecy in Judaism (see Ch. 1) that it has been suggested Luke here creates an idealized picture of the 'old covenant' epoch of Israel, to be succeeded by those of Jesus and the Church (so von Baer, Dunn), and also that the deliberate likeness of the activities of the Spirit to those portrayed in the Acts is intended by Luke to establish Christianity as the continuity and fulfilment of Judaism (so M.A. Chevallier[11]). Menzies, appealing to

---

[9]For a general portrait of Jesus and the Spirit seen through the evidence of the Gospels, but not attempting to elucidate the separate perspectives of the Evangelists, see G.F. Hawthorne, *The Presence and the Power*, (Waco: Word, 1991). For a more critical account of the 'historical Jesus' and the Spirit, see C.K. Barrett, *The Holy Spirit and the Gospel Tradition*, (London: SPCK, 1966[2]), and Dunn, *Jesus*, 11–92. For Jesus and the Spirit in Matthew, see (e.g.) Montague, *Spirit*, ch. 24. For the same in Mark, see M.R. Mansfield, *"Spirit and Gospel" in Mark*, (Peabody: Hendrickson, 1987); Montague, *Spirit*, ch. 20; J.E. Yates, *The Spirit and the Kingdom*, (London: SPCK, 1963).

[10]For detailed treatment and bibliography on the Spirit in the Lucan infancy narratives, see Turner, *Power*, ch. 6.

[11]See M.A. Chevallier, 'Luc et l'Esprit à la Mémoire du P. Augustin George (1915–77)', *RSR* 56 (1982), 1–16.

the allegedly widespread belief in the withdrawal of the Spirit from Israel
until the end, and the strongly christocentric focus of the Spirit's activities
in Luke 1–2 (it is exclusively those awaiting the messianic salvation of
Israel that experience the Spirit), suggests rather that Luke portrays here
the dawn of the eschatological *restoration* of the Spirit of prophecy to
Israel; not the period of 'old covenant' Israel as such. Each of these positions builds in a different way on the assumption that the above cases
depict extraordinary actions of the Spirit. But there is little exceptional
about the idea of the Spirit of prophecy being manifest through occasional holy people,[12] especially in connection with the temple, and/or
at the birth of significant liberator figures. Rather, such could be expected.
*It is what is said of the Spirit in relation to John and to Jesus in these chapters
that strikes the new and eschatological note.*

2. The Spirit on the Baptist

The eschatological quality of the Spirit restored to God's people is
evidenced in the unique features within the portrayal of John the Baptist as prophet. If he is the greatest (Lk. 7:26–28), that is because he
fulfils the role of the awaited 'Elijah' to initiate restoration in Israel
through repentance before the fuller eschatological visitation (Lk. 7:27;
Mal. 3:1 (cf. Mal. 4:5)).[13] This view has been carefully sculpted into the
Infancy Narratives, not only in stepwise parallelism between John, the
Prophet of the Most High (1:76), and Jesus, the Son of the Most High
(1:32) who comes to effect the promised salvation, but also in the
specific identification of John as the one who 'will go before him in the
Spirit and power of Elijah' to prepare the Lord's people (Luke 1:17
again strongly echoing the Malachi tradition).[14] In accordance with his
eschatological stature and role, the gift of the Spirit to John is unprece-
dented: he is 'filled with the Holy Spirit' even from his mother's womb
(1:15): hence even in *utero* he recognizes with joy the bearer of the

---

[12]Even the rabbis can occasionally speak of pious individuals experiencing the
Spirit of prophecy (see *t. Pesaḥ* 2:15; *Lev. Rab.* 21:8; *j. Šeb.* 9:1 and *j. Soṭa* 1:4
(and//s)).

[13]This is denied by Conzelmann, but see J.A. Fitzmyer, *Luke the Theologian* (London: Chapman, 1989), 86–116.

[14]In Judaism the collocation 'Spirit and power of Elijah' (probably pre-Lucan)
would normally suggest a miracle-working prophet, but in the Lucan redaction
it means rather that John preaches powerfully — according to Luke 7:21–23
miracles are what *distinguish* Jesus from John, and are offered to John's disciples
as evidence to their master that Jesus is indeed the 'Coming One'.

Messiah (1:41, 44), and from birth he grows and becomes strong in the Spirit (or possibly 'in spirit'), (1:80).

3. The Spirit and the Conception of the Messianic 'Son of God'

The new eschatological quality of the Spirit in Israel is manifest especially in connection with its role in the conception of the Messiah (1:32–35, cf. Mt. 1:18). The child born to Mary is to be hailed 'Son of the Most High' and given the eschatological throne of David (1:32–33), because he will be no child of ordinary wedlock (1:35). As Fitzmyer now admits, following the semi-miraculous conception of John the Baptist to his aged parents in 1:5–25, the ascending parallelism of the narrative requires that this means a *virgin* conception of Jesus, by the creative activity of the Holy Spirit.[15] The angelic oracle asserts that, through the action of the Spirit (perceived as the new creation 'power of the Most High': cf. 1:35b), the child which is born shall be 'holy, the Son of God'. With respect to this tradition we may note six relevant points:

(1) The passage clearly presents Jesus as the fulfilment of the same kind of *Davidic* messianic hopes that we encountered in the Jewish developments from Isaiah 11:1–4. The title 'Son of God' takes up the messianic use of Psalm 2:7 and 2 Samuel 7:11–14 (cf. 4QFlorilegium i.10–12), which specifically refers the latter to the awaited ruler from the house of David, and, most strikingly, an expected royal heir who is to be 'great' and hailed both 'Son of God' and 'Son of the Most High' is due to be given an 'everlasting kingdom' according to 4Q246 (1.1–2.9, esp. 1.7; 2.1,5), in a passage with important allusions to *Targum Isaiah* 11.[16] The heavenly 'annunciation of birth' to a 'virgin' (*parthenos*) from 'the house of David' (Lk. 1:27), given in a form which otherwise virtually paraphrases the wording of the Emmanuel prophecy in Isaiah 7:14, could only confirm the fundamentally Davidic/messianic import of the 'sonship' in 1:32–35.

(2) While the Spirit in Luke 1:35 may well be understood as the same 'Spirit of prophecy' by which Mary later utters the

---

[15]Fitzmyer, 338, against his former position which denied there was any real implication of virginal conception in 1:35 (cf. 'The Virginal Conception of Jesus in the New Testament', *TS* 34 (1973), 541–75).

[16]See C. A. Evans, *Jesus*, ch. 3, esp. 107–11.

Magnificat (1:47–55), here, as even Menzies concedes, the Spirit is primarily the *miraculous power of new creation*.[17]

(3) The specific form of 'new creation' concerned is further indicated as essentially bound up with Israel's restoration by the allusions to Old Testament passages in 1:35. The reference to the Spirit 'coming upon' Mary 'from on High' is to be identified as a clear allusion to (LXX) Isaiah 32:15 (the beginning of a passage (32:15–20) concerning Israel's 'New Exodus' restoration), and Luke's statement to the effect that the power of God will 'overshadow' (*episkiazein*) Mary has been recognized as most probably an allusion to (LXX) Exodus 40:35, and to the cloud of God's presence (cf. Lk. 9:34) which brought God's glory into Israel's camp and led her through the wilderness to the promised land. In sum, the Spirit's creative activity in relation to the messianic 'Son of God' assures he will embody and become the fountainhead of Israel's restoration.

(4) The Spirit here, at the opening of Luke's work, indubitably also has profound ethical orientation. *Because* of the Spirit's action, the one to be born 'shall be called "Holy" ' (1:35b). This, as we have noted, is in accord with hopes built from Isaiah 11:1–4, where the Messiah of the Spirit exhibits a radical righteousness grounded in the wisdom, knowledge, and fear of the Lord granted by the Spirit.

(5) As H.J. de Jonge has shown, the outcome of the conception by the Spirit is portrayed in Luke 2:41–51 in terms of the special *wisdom* and *knowledge* of God as *'Father'*, that would be anticipated of the Davidic Messiah in circles that developed the hopes of Isaiah 11.[18] Already Jesus shows a wisdom that startles the leaders of Israel; knows a duty to his Father which transcends that to his parents (2:49) and a unique divine 'sonship' (compare *ho patēr mou* ('my Father') here with the same expression at 10:22; 22:29 and 24:49), the depths of which Luke underscores by the redactional notice in 2:50 that Mary and Joseph did not understand the significance of what Jesus said.

---

[17] There is no need to dispute the authenticity of 1:35 on the grounds that Judaism could not associate the Spirit with works of power or of creation. We have seen this is simply incorrect. The Spirit is also associated with the power of new creation/resurrection at Ezek. 37:9–10, 14; 2 *Bar.* 23:5; *m. Soṭa* 9.15; *Pesiq. R.* 1.6, and *Cant. Rab.* 1.1 §9.

[18] H.J. de Jonge, 'Sonship, Wisdom, Infancy: Luke II. 41–51a', *NTS* 24 (1977–78), 317–54.

(6) The above considerations inexorably point in the opposite direction to Dunn's view. It is quite impossible in the light of the above to argue that Jesus only first began to experience what Dunn means by 'new covenant' existence and eschatological 'sonship' with his reception of the Spirit in or after his baptism. If the Baptist's own experience of the Spirit was itself an eschatological novum, Jesus' surpasses it. As Gerd Schneider put it: 'Jesus is not merely filled with the Spirit, like John, rather his very *being* is attributed to the Spirit.'[19]

II. THE BAPTIST'S PROMISE: MARK 1:8//MATTHEW 3:11 = LUKE 3:16[20]

John contrasts his own baptizing activity with that of one to come who 'will baptize you with Holy Spirit-and-fire' (so the older Q version: Mark omits 'and fire'). The 'you' in question is all Israel (not merely the righteous), and syntactically 'Holy Spirit and fire' is probably a hendiadys (i.e. a single 'baptism' consisting in Spirit and fire; not a baptism of Spirit for the righteous and one of fire for the wicked).

Speculation about whether the Baptist originally promised only judgement in the form of a baptism of *fire* alone (Bultmann), or of 'wind and fire' (so Best[21]), is as unverifiable as it is unnecessary. A number of scholars have quite correctly argued that the concept of some kind of an eschatological deluge of Spirit-and-fire is understandable enough within apocalyptic Judaism. There, for example, we find an eschatological stream, deluge or flood of fire (a burning counterpart to Noah's: cf. Dan. 7:10; 1QH 3.20–36; 1 *Enoch* 67:13; 4 *Ezra* 13:10–11), destructive of the wicked, but purging the righteous (cf. *T. Isaac* 5:21–5; *T. Abr.* 13), and the connection of the Spirit with cleansing, purging, even 'fiery' judgement was traditional: cf. especially Isaiah 4:4 and 1QS 4:21–22.[22]

There are problems with this, however, that are sometimes passed over too lightly. In the first place, the apocalypses do not quite speak

---

[19]*Lukas*, 53. Cf. G. Schneider, 'Jesu Geistgewirkte Empfängnis (Lk 1, 34f)', *Theologisch-Praktische Quartalschrift*, 119 (1971), 105–16.
[20]For detailed discussion of the tradition-history and sense of the Baptist's promise, see Turner, *Power*, ch. 7.
[21]E. Best, 'Spirit-Baptism', *NovT* 4 (1960), 236–43: Best takes his cue from the winnowing image which follows in Q, and from the observation that the Hebrew/Aramaic word *ruach* inevitably used by John could mean both 'wind' and 'spirit' — but does one 'baptize' with 'wind'?
[22]These points were ably made by J.D.G. Dunn, 'Spirit and Fire Baptism', *NovT* 14 (1972), 81–92.

of a flood of *Holy-Spirit-and-fire*, and, second, in Judaism a flood of divine *Spirit* could only be anticipated from God himself, not from the Messiah (though 4 *Ezra* 13:8–11 perhaps comes close in anticipating a stream of flame and fiery *breath* from the Messiah). Indeed this is the main objection to the authenticity of the Baptist's promise as it stands: it is alleged that a promise of any *human* agent pouring out *God's* Spirit is simply inconceivable (*T. Jud.* 24:2–3 is precisely suspect as *Christian* interpolation), for reasons that will be elucidated in Chapter 11.

But such considerations probably misunderstand John's promise. He does not speak of the Messiah 'deluging' Israel with the Spirit (nor of his 'bestowing' the Spirit). While the Greek verb *baptizein* ('to baptize') may sometimes be used metaphorically to mean 'deluge with' or 'over-whelm with', the Aramaic term almost certainly used by John himself will have been *tabal*, and was not used in a comparable sense: it meant simply 'to dip', 'to bath', or 'to wash (by immersing)'. The last of these, we have argued, provides the probable key to the Baptist's meaning: i.e. he contrasts his own water rite, which cleanses Israel through repentance and forgiveness, with the mightier baptism (i.e. cleansing (and purging) of Israel) that will be effected by the coming agent of God's reign. In this case we have no need to posit that John went beyond the traditional expectation of a messianic figure powerfully fulfilling Isaiah 11:1–4 (and 9:2–7 — as in *1 Enoch* 49:2–3; 62:1–2; *Pss. Sol.* 17:37; 18:7; 1QSb 5.24-25; 4Q215 iv.4; 4QpIsa[a] Fragments 7–10 Column iii. lines 15–29, etc.). The arrival of such a figure to rule, with his decisively authoritative Spirit-imbued command, burning righteousness, and dramatic acts of power, effecting both judgment and salvation, *would itself be sufficient to suggest the metaphor of his cleansing Israel with Spirit-and-fire* (cf. *Targ. Isa.* 4:4 where the 'Spirit of judgement' and 'Spirit of fire' become the Messiah's powerful com-mand of judgement and of extirpation respectively). Support for this view can be found in the immediate co-text of 3:17. From the Baptist's perspective, the task of the coming one is not to sift the wheat from the chaff in Israel, nor is the instrument in his hand a threshing fork (as is usually maintained). John understood himself largely already to have accomplished the sifting process through his preaching and baptismal ministry. From his point of view what remains is for the coming one to *'cleanse the threshing floor'* (17b), and deal with the already-separated wheat and chaff: so, appropriately, he comes with a *spade* (*ptuon*) in

---

[23]For the view that the coming one's instrument is the spade, and that he comes to cleanse/clear the threshing floor, see R.L. Webb, 'The Activity of John the Baptist's Expected Figure at the Threshing Floor (Matthew 3.12 = Luke 3.17)', *JSNT* 43 (1991), 103–11.

hand.[23] In short, both parts of 3:16–17 convey the same message: viz., the coming one will cleanse/restore Israel in the fiery power of the Spirit.

The imagery of washing/cleansing with Spirit and fire was clearly capable of being applied by the Evangelists (i) to the Spirit *in* Jesus' ministry, (ii) to the continuation of his ministry through the church in Jesus' Lordship over the Spirit, and (iii) to the final act of judgement and re-creation, without requiring it to be applied *exclusively* to any one. Yates is probably right to think Mark saw Jesus' baptismal reception of the Spirit, and powerful ministry, as fulfilment of the Baptist's promise,[24] but wrong to restrict it to that; because for Mark a climactic new phase in the revelation of Christ and of God's reign is initiated with the Easter events. Exegetes are right to suggest Luke saw the fulfilment of John's promise in Pentecost (Acts 1:5; 11:16 (and Matthew in the eschaton, cf. 'fire' in Matthew)), but wrong to restrict it to this if it means denying Luke thought Jesus' messianic ministry (empowered by the Spirit, directed to the transformative and restorative cleansing of Israel, and casting 'fire' on the earth (12:49)), already *began* to fulfil John's logion.

III. THE SPIRIT COMES IN THE WILDERNESS

The Gospels portray the Baptist as preparing the way of the Lord in the *wilderness* and explaining this location in terms of Isaiah 40:3 (Mk. 1:3 and//s). This was to evoke a recurring intertestamental pattern of ideas based in an Isaianic New Exodus theology. It amounted to a hope that God (through a Spirit-empowered Servant (61:1–2) who embodies 'Israel', and who bears both 'Davidic' and 'Mosaic' (cf. Isa. 42:1–7) characteristics) would destroy Israel's enemies (at the time partly identified as the spiritual forces behind idolatry and Israel's blindness) and shepherd her along 'the way' through a transformed wilderness to a restored Zion where he would rule. The announcement of this 'good news' to her was to be her 'comfort' and bring her the joy of her 'salvation'. The pattern is widely reflected in Judaism (cf. 1QS 8.12b–16a; 9.17–20; 4Q176; Sir. 48:24–25; *T. Moses* 10:1–8; *Pss. Sol.* 11, etc.), and is woven through the Spirit traditions in both Mark and Q, and expanded in Luke.[25]

---

[24] Yates, *Spirit*.

[25] For the claim that Mark has worked this theme into a dominating *ideology* in his Gospel — i.e. a construal of a symbolic world through which the community understands itself as 'true Israel' (over against Judaism) and rehearses its

1. Jesus 'Receives' the Spirit: Mark 1:10–11 = Matthew 3:16–17 = Luke 3:21–22[26]

Dunn rightly observes that, for the Evangelists, Jesus receives the Spirit only after he comes out of the water (and, for Luke, whilst he is praying); his baptism was thus not the first Christian 'sacrament'.[27] Strictly speaking the Synoptic Gospels do not even actually record an objective 'reception' of the Spirit by Jesus, but a *vision* which includes a descent of the Spirit. The clause 'the heaven(s) opened' in Matthew and Luke is a standard formula to denote the beginning of a visionary experience, cf. Acts 7:56; 10:11, etc. (Mark's different wording, 'the heavens *rent*', simply heightens the Isaianic New Exodus connections by using the language of Isa. 64:1.) Within the structure of such visions, what is seen and what is heard are mutually interpretive. Taken this way, the import of the vision is that *from that time the Spirit will be with Jesus as the power to exercise the messianic task*. The Davidic aspect of this task is indicated in the use of Psalm 2:7 in the voice which addresses Jesus, 'You are my . . . Son' (Mark 1:11b//s). But attention falls perhaps more particularly on Jesus' forthcoming role as the Servant-Herald, adumbrated in the allusion to Isaiah 42:1–2 in the second part of the address ('my beloved . . . in whom I am well pleased' (Mark 1:11c//s: cf. also Isa. 53:7 and 61:1–2)). This 'Servant-Herald' role is also perhaps highlighted by the dove motif. To see the Spirit descend as a *dove* most probably evokes the symbolism of the dove as a herald or as a trustworthy messenger (so *b. Git.* 45a; *b. Sanh.* 95a) and bearer of good tidings (cf. Gen. 8:11), and so further interprets the Spirit on Jesus as the power to proclaim the messianic 'good news'.

It would be possible to understand this visionary experience as nothing more than a disclosure to Jesus of the impending significance of the Spirit already upon him: i.e. the Spirit he received in the miraculous conception (Lk. 1:35) was about to empower the messianic task through him. The fact that Jesus 'sees' the Spirit come to him need not imply some 'real' second descent from heaven, any more than Peter's vision of a sheet containing unclean animals descending from heaven

---

(footnote 25 continued)
origins in Israel's founding (and refounding) moments — see R.E. Watts, 'The Influence of the Isaianic New Exodus on the Gospel of Mark', unpublished PhD dissertation, Cambridge, 1990. For the special importance of the theme in Luke, see M.L. Strauss, *The Davidic Messiah in Luke-Acts: The Promise and its Fulfillment in Lukan Christology* (Sheffield: SAP, 1995), 285–97, and Turner, Power, ch. 9, §4.
[26]See more fully, Turner, *Power*, ch. 8, §1.
[27]Dunn, *Baptism*, ch. 3.

(Acts 10:11) implies that real animals were lowered to the ground for him to kill and eat. We must let visions be visions. But that Jesus' Jordan experience coincided with the beginning of some dramatic new nexus of activities of the Spirit in and through him is apparent from each of the Gospels: both the Marcan and the Q tradition agree he was thereupon immediately impelled or 'led' by the Spirit into the wilderness contest with Satan which was a key to the ministry ahead (see below).

Dunn (following a long line of exegetical tradition from Büchsel and von Baer on) attempts to explain the 'gift' here primarily in terms of Jesus' *paradigmatic* experience of the Spirit in eschatological sonship, new age 'life', life of the kingdom of God, etc. and only secondarily as empowering. But anyone holding the sort of messianic hopes outlined above would immediately recognize this narrative as being primarily, if not exclusively, concerned with messianic empowering. And for Luke, especially, it is clear that Jesus had already experienced a sonship to God deeper than that to which believers might aspire (cf. 1:35; 2:41–52). For him, any further dimension of sonship added by Jesus' 'reception' of the Spirit at the Jordan is of a more distinctively messianic rather than generally paradigmatic nature.[28]

2. The Spirit and the Defeat of Satan in the Wilderness: Mark 1:12–13//Matthew 4:1–11 = Luke 4:1–13, 14[29]

The Spirit who comes upon Jesus in the wilderness now leads him deeper into the wilderness into the trial with Satan; but nothing is said of the Spirit's role in the encounter itself in Mark or Matthew. The redactional change in Luke (4:1a), however, ensures that the emphasis falls more on the one 'full of the Spirit' now being led (by God) *in the wilderness trial itself*, and that he is led *in a way that manifests the messianic empowering* (cf. 'in the Spirit'). The final 'temptations' echo Israel's in the wilderness but, while they 'rebelled and grieved his Holy Spirit' there (Isa. 63:10), the new representative of Israel remains faithful and overcomes the tempter. Luke does not specify whether this is because the Spirit affords Jesus new depths of charismatic wisdom and insight, which is the basis of the hoped-for Messiah's redoubtable righteousness (1 *Enoch* 49:2–3; *Pss. Sol.* 17:37; 18:7; 1QSb 5.25; *Tg. Isa.* 11:1–2, etc.), but such is probably to be inferred — for to what else could the redactional

---

[28]See M. Turner, 'Jesus and the Spirit in Lucan Perspective', *TynB* 32 (1981), 3–42.

[29]For fuller treatment and bibliography see Turner, *Power*, ch. 8, §§2–3.

statement that he was led 'in the Spirit', *during* this period of temptations, otherwise reasonably refer?[30]

The redactional notice in Luke 4:14 that Jesus then returned 'in the
power of the Spirit' to Galilee not only highlights the 'power' character
of the gift of the Spirit to Jesus but may also be intended to indicate that
the successful encounter with Satan lies at the root of Jesus' later success in 'healing all who were under the power of the devil' (Acts 10:38;
cf. Lk. 11:21,22). In this light the whole section (Lk. 4:1–14) then appears
to relate the beginning of Israel's New Exodus in God's messianic Son,
and 'the turning of the tide' through Jesus' victory over the captor as
the Servant Warrior of Isaiah 49:24,25, who will accomplish Israel's
liberation (see below).

IV. THE SPIRIT IN JESUS' MINISTRY

1. The Messiah-of-the-Spirit, Exorcisms and Blasphemy Against the
Spirit

Matthew 12:28 (= Q: 'If it is by the Spirit of God that I cast out demons,
then the kingdom of God has come upon you') explicitly attributes
Jesus' exorcisms to his empowering with the Spirit, and concludes they
manifest the inbreaking of God's reign. This is striking, as no available
Jewish sources directly connect exorcisms with the Spirit nor do they
explicitly interpret exorcisms as evidence of the arrival of the kingdom.
The same assumption — that Jesus exorcizes by the power of the Spirit
— is made in the Marcan tradition warning of blasphemy against the
Spirit (Mk. 3:28–30//Mt. 12:31–3). This, with the saying that immediately precedes it (the Parable of the Strong Man Bound: Mk. 3:27//Mt.
12:29), may provide a clue to the connections of thought.

The most obvious Old Testament background to the charge of 'blasphemy against the Spirit' is Isaiah 63:10, with its accusation that the
perverse and blind rebellion of the wilderness generation 'grieved his
Holy Spirit', and turned God into their enemy. Equally, the closest Old
Testament parallel to the parable of the Strong Man Bound is widely
recognized to be Isaiah 49:24–26, with its New Exodus theme of the
Yahweh Warrior taking back the captives from the warriors, and
plunder from the fierce — i.e. releasing Israel — so that all mankind
will know he is Israel's saviour. By the intertestamental period these
'enemies' from whom deliverance was awaited were especially the
powers of Belial, and the Messiah was the one who would act as God's

---

[30]For substantiation see Turner, *Power*, ch. 8, §2.

agent in effecting the New Exodus release: so e.g. *Testament of Dan* 5:10–13[31] and 11QMelchizedek. The New Exodus hopes thus offer a plausible background to explain why the Messiah (already traditionally regarded as empowered by the Spirit to deliver Israel from her enemies) should be connected with exorcisms, and these in turn with the advent of God's reign — and provide an inviting background too for labelling as 'blasphemy against the Holy Spirit' the rebellious refusal to recognize such acts of redemption as *God's* work.[32]

Luke 11:20 has changed the Q saying, represented in Matthew 12:28, to attribute exorcisms to 'the finger of God' rather than to the Spirit. It is often alleged Luke has made this change because he regarded the Spirit (as in Judaism) as 'the Spirit of prophecy', and, for that reason, could not accept the Spirit was also the power of miracle. But this is based on a false antithesis (see Ch. 1), and Luke's change is more readily explained in other terms: the shift in terminology from 'Spirit of God' to 'finger of God' (a clear reference to Exod. 8:19) is probably in the interest of Luke's prophet-like-Moses christology, but still probably *refers* to the Spirit (in the OT, the parallel term 'the hand of the Lord' was interpreted to refer to the Spirit at e.g. Ezek. 37:1, and cf. *Joseph and Aseneth* 8:9, where Joseph prays, 'Bless this virgin, and renew her by your Spirit, and form her anew by your hidden hand').

2. The Spirit and Miracles of Healing

To the extent that illness was regarded as both directly and indirectly Satanic (e.g. Acts 10:38; Lk. 13:10–15, etc.), we might expect healings to be regarded as part of the messianic deliverance. They would be regarded as the acts of the Messiah endowed with the Spirit (cf. Mt. 11:2) to liberate Israel from her enemies. The strong connection between healings and pronouncements of the inbreaking reign of God supports the view (notably Lk. 9:2 and 10:9,11//Mt. 10:7–8). In addition, the Q tradition (Mt. 11:5//Lk. 7:21,22) that Jesus responded to the Baptist's

---

[31]Cf. also *Testament of Zebulon* 9:8 and *Testament of Levi* 18:12.

[32]Luke has shifted the blasphemy against the Spirit saying to a different context (12:10–12). The 'blasphemy' concerned still probably means obdurate and rebellious unbelief that opposes God's redemptive initiative, now in persistent antagonism to the gospel preached in the power of the Spirit (so Fitzmyer) — a theme which dominates Acts. Of the alternative suggestion (Schweizer, George, Menzies, etc.), that 'blasphemy against the Spirit' denotes failure of the Christian to confess Jesus when prompted by the Spirit in situations of trial, there is simply no trace in Luke-Acts.

doubt by highlighting the blind seeing, the lame walking, lepers cleansed, deaf hearing and 'good news' being preached to the poor, evokes a medley of Isaianic New Exodus texts (29:18; 35:5–7; 42:18) including the most significant of them, Isaiah 61:1–2 (see below). This tradition thus appears to attribute the miracles to the Spirit on the anointed Isaianic messianic Prophet-liberator.

> Interestingly, a newly published fragment from Qumran, 4Q521, draws especially on Isaiah 61 and anticipates a similar collection of miracles with the appearance of the Messiah. Like the Q tradition, it includes the surprising reference to 'raisings from the dead' on which the Isaianic texts themselves had nothing to say. And while the text has gaps which make the interpretation uncertain, it seems likely that these miracles are performed by the Messiah through the Spirit (of Isaiah 61).[33]

Similarly, Matthew specifically and redactionally traces the healings to the Spirit on the Servant-Herald of Isaiah 42:1,2 (Mt. 12:15–21). The occasional Elisha or prophet-like-Moses allusions in the miracle tradition of Luke (7:11–17; 9:10b–17,28–36; 10:1–12; 13:32,3) should not be taken as providing a competing explanation, but as reflecting a merging of prophetic and more traditional messianic views (anticipated in 'New Exodus' contexts and elsewhere).

3. The Interpretation of the Spirit on Jesus in Terms of Isaiah 61:1,2

Using careful redactional bridges (4:1 and 4:14), Luke interprets the 'gift' of the Spirit to Jesus in 3:21,2 in terms of fulfilment of Isaiah 61:1,2 (4:18–21). The unusual text form of the citation, and other non-Lucan features, suggest he has received the substance of 4:16–30 from a source,[34] but Luke has given it programmatic significance.

The use of Isaiah 61:1,2 to explain the Spirit on Jesus has both christological and soteriological significance. Isaiah 61:1,2 was understood in contemporary Judaism to encapsulate the New Exodus hopes for a messianic jubilee and 'release' of 'the poor' (=Israel in need of salvation) from captivity to the powers of Belial (compare

---

[33]On the fragment, and its relation to Lk. 7:20,21 (Q), see e.g. J.J. Collins, 'The Works of the Messiah', *DSD* 1 (1994), 98–112; J.D. Tabor and M.O. Wise, '4Q521 "On Resurrection" and the Synoptic Gospel Tradition: A Preliminary Study', *JSP* 10 (1992), 149–62. For the argument that the miracles are worked by the Spirit on the Messiah, see Turner, *Power*, ch. 4, §3.

[34]See Turner, *Power*, ch. 9 §§1–3, for a review of the tradition-history of this passage.

11QMelch; 4Q521).[35] That the citation was understood this way is indicated by the intercalation of the thematic words 'to set the oppressed free' from Isaiah 58:6. Jesus claims to be the one empowered by the Spirit to effect the 'release' of Israel from the variety of forms of Satanic oppression. That this includes healings and exorcisms is clear from Luke 7:21 (Lucan redaction) with 7:22 (Q), and from Acts 10:38 (which echoes the language of Lk. 4:18–21: cf. also, e.g. Lk. 13:10–15). But that it also goes beyond these to include release from Israel's idolatrous 'blindness' and 'deafness' also to God (cf. 8:4–15: Acts 28:26,27) is evident from the way Isaiah 61:1,2 shapes the Beatitudes (Mt. 5:3–6; Lk. 6:20,21).

Christologically, the use of Isaiah 61:1,2 (and 42:1,2) with a New Exodus theme probably indicates a prophet-like-Moses motif, rather than the more traditional regal Messiah; but the two are complimentary, not antithetical, and whether the Messiah is Davidic or Mosaic makes only a slight difference to the pneumatology: both figures are expected to experience the Spirit in acts of power and deliverance, and both experience the Spirit in charismatic *wisdom*. A Mosaic motif enables an emphasis on the Spirit as the source of charismatic *revelation*, and on the outcome in foundational and authoritative *teaching*, more easily than the regal. In the final analysis, however, the Synoptics are surprisingly reticent to speak of Jesus receiving revelation (contrast the paucity of such reference in Luke (only 3:21,22; (10:18?) and 10:22) with the numerous occasions on which *disciples* receive revelations in Acts), and this is never specifically attributed to the Spirit. And while Jesus is presented as the giver of foundational *teaching*, the authority of the content is presented as his own ('I say to you . . .'), rather than attributed to the Spirit. The Spirit has become the power that works *through* Jesus' words and deeds to affect others.

V. CONCLUSION

The main emphasis in the Synoptic Gospels' portrait of Jesus and the Spirit, and especially of Luke's, supports the views of Schweizer, Stronstad, Menzies and others, who have seen Jesus' Jordan experience almost exclusively in terms of empowering for mission, rather than as bringing him 'new covenant life' or 'eschatological sonship' (as Dunn argued). Luke 10:21 alone speaks of a psychological effect of the Spirit on Jesus, and even here the description 'he exulted in the Holy Spirit

---

[35]Cf. R.B. Sloan, *The Favorable Year of the Lord: A Study of Jubilary Theology in the Gospel of Luke*, (Austin: Schola, 1977).

and said' serves more to designate the content of the speech event which follows as charismatic and revelatory than to highlight a benefit to Jesus' own religious life and perception. We should be unwise to build too many theological conclusions from these silences, but it will be apparent that the gospels were more interested in assuring their readers *that* Jesus was the expected Messiah of the Spirit and *that* he was so empowered for his mission than they were in explaining what Jesus' endowment at the Jordan contributed to his own life before God. In his later works Dunn has increasingly recognized that, for Luke, the Spirit on Jesus is primarily (if not exclusively) to be understood in terms of prophetic empowering,[36] and he has openly conceded that his earlier argument, to the effect that the Spirit brings Jesus archetypal Christian experience of eschatological sonship and new covenant life, does not take adequate account of Luke 1:35.[37]

With Schweizer and Menzies, we must agree that Luke presents the Spirit on Jesus primarily as some kind of *donum superadditum* of the 'Spirit of prophecy'. But we do not find Luke explicitly ascribing to Jesus any of the prototypical gifts of the 'Spirit of prophecy' except, on one occasion, invasive doxology (Lk. 10:22). The 'Spirit of prophecy' upon him is more specifically the unique messianic version of this endowment. This interest may explain why Luke shows no real reserve about connecting the Spirit on Jesus with works of power (*pace* Schweizer and Menzies; cf. 1:35; 4:18–25; 7:21,22; Acts 10:38). The traditions of the Messiah of the Spirit expected the one endowed to be empowered by the Spirit to liberate Israel, and within the context of Isaianic New Exodus hopes this 'liberation' was readily extended to miracles of healing and deliverance.[38] Equally (again *contra* Schweizer and Menzies) the traditions of the Messiah of the Spirit expected the one so endowed to exhibit a robust righteousness through the Spirit of wisdom, knowledge, and fear of the Lord upon him (he was to purge Israel by it), and Luke 4:1b echoes this. The same traditions also to some extent anticipate the Spirit as a charismatic power acting *through* the Messiah's instruction, giving it compelling authority and influence. This is the nearest Judaism comes to the Spirit as 'the power of

---

[36] Cf. Dunn, *Christology*, 138–43.

[37] J.D.G. Dunn, 'Baptism in the Spirit: A Response to Pentecostal Scholarship on Luke-Acts', *JPT* 3 (1993), 3–27, e.g. 17.

[38] Against the contention of Menzies and Schweizer, that Luke distances the Spirit from miracles of power, see M.M.B. Turner, 'The Spirit and the Power', 124–52. Menzies replies in 'Spirit and Power in Luke-Acts: A Response to Max Turner', *JSNT* 49 (1991), 11–20, to which see the surrejoinder in Turner, *Power*, chs. 4 and 9.

preaching', which was to emerge as a characteristic emphasis within Christian pneumatology.[39]

The clear emphasis on the Spirit as the *Messiah's* endowment should also warn us against too quickly assuming Luke presents Jesus as a pattern for all other Christians' experience of the Spirit. Both the timing of his reception of the Spirit and the nature of his endowment with the Spirit might be anticipated to have unique elements corresponding to his unique mission.[40]

---

[39]For this argument in detail see M.M.B. Turner, 'The Spirit of Prophecy and the Power of Authoritative Preaching in Luke-Acts: A Question of Origins', *NTS* 38 (1992), 66–88.
[40]Cf. Turner, 'Jesus and the Spirit', 3–42.

Chapter Three

The Gift of the Spirit in Acts: The 'Spirit of Prophecy' as the Power of Israel's Restoration and Witness[1]

I. INTRODUCTION

This introductory part of the chapter will first summarize the main points of Lucan pneumatology on which scholarship appears to be agreed,[2] then highlight the areas of dispute which we shall address in subsequent parts. Part II then argues that the Holy Spirit in Acts can be understood as a Christianized version of the (Jewish) 'Spirit of prophecy'. Part III indicates that Luke regards this gift as granted (normatively) in conversion-initiation, and Part IV attempts to explain why this is so by showing that for Luke the 'Spirit of prophecy' is necessary to what the evangelist understands as the 'salvation' of Israel.

1. Areas of Consensus on Lucan Pneumatology

Hans von Baer set the agenda for subsequent scholarship, both methodologically (as a forerunner of redaction criticism) and in his intent to discover the specifically Lucan view of the Spirit. On the following points later research has done little more than to offer minor corrections and variations to his pioneering work.

---

[1]This is a shortened version of 'The "Spirit of Prophecy" as the Power of Israel's Restoration and Witness' published in A1CS Volume 6. All issues addressed are dealt with in considerably greater detail in Turner, *Power*.
[2]Constraints of space forbid a formal review of the *Forschung*. For an account of the development of scholarship see Turner, *Power*, chs. 1–2. For other types of survey of the literature see e.g. F. Bovon, *Luke the Theologian: Thirty-three Years of Research (1950–1983)* (Allison Park: Pickwick, 1987), ch. 4; Menzies, *Empowered*, ch. 1; and O. Mainville, *L'Esprit dans l'Oeuvre de Luc* (Montreal: Fides, 1991), 19–47.

(1) The essential background for Luke's pneumatological material is Jewisn and deeply rooted in the Old Testament.

Von Baer maintained, especially against H. Leisegang, that Luke did not draw any significant traits of his conception of the Spirit from Greek mysticism, nor from Mantic prophetism.[3] The Spirit is not mere 'substance', but the presence, empowering and saving activity of the God of Israel himself, the self-revealing extension of his person and vitality into history. In maintaining an Old Testament background to Luke's pneumatology, however, von Baer was also affirming a contrast with the more developed and distinctively Christian Johannine and Pauline portraits of the Spirit. The Spirit in Luke-Acts has often since been considered 'Old Testament' in character both in the range of broadly charismatic activities attributed to the Spirit and in the language used to describe them,[4] although it would almost certainly be safer to characterize the language and ideas as 'early Jewish Christian', as it is usually recognized that Luke's material also reflects distinctive ITP understandings of the Spirit and significant Christian developments too.

(2) The Spirit is the uniting motif and the driving force within the Lucan salvation history, and provides the legitimation of the mission to which this leads.

One of von Baer's central arguments against the alleged Hellenism of Luke's pneumatology was that the diverse manifestations of the Spirit in Luke-Acts all combine to serve this distinctively Jewish motif. In Luke 1–2 the Spirit brings about the birth of the Messiah who is to redeem Israel (1:32–35), affords prophecies relating to the saving events about to unfold (1:42,43, 67–79; 2:25–32), and empowers the Elijianic

---

[3]H. Leisegang argued that Philo's conception of the prophetic Spirit provided a bridge between Greek concepts of πνεῦμα and those in the Church (cf. *Der Heilige Geist: Das Wesen und Werden der mystisch-intuitiven Erkenntnis in der Philosophie und Religion der Griechen*, (Berlin: Teubner, 1919)). His second monograph attempted to derive virtually all the pneumatological material in the Synoptic Gospels from Hellenism, cf. his title: *Pneuma Hagion: Der Ursprung des Geistesbegriffs der synoptischen Evangelien aus der griechischen Mystik*. For analysis and criticism of the latter, see (*inter alios*) von Baer, *Geist, passim*; C.K. Barrett, *Spirit*, especially 3–4; 10–14; 36–41.
[4]So especially G.W.H. Lampe, 'The Holy Spirit in the Writings of Saint Luke' in D.E. Nineham (ed.), *Studies in the Gospels: Essays in Memory of R.H. Lightfoot* (Oxford: Blackwell, 1955), 159–200; A. George, 'L'Esprit Saint dans l'Oeuvre de Luc', *RB* 85 (1978), 500–42 (esp. 513–15; 528–9); Chevallier, 'Luc', 1–16; Mainville, *L'Esprit*, esp. 323–32.

forerunner who prepares the way of the Lord (1:15,17). In Luke 3–4 the
Spirit then comes as Jesus' messianic empowering for the redemptive
mission, while Pentecost brings a parallel endowment for the church's
mission, over which the Spirit remains the initiator (cf. esp. Acts 2:4;
8:29; 10:19, 44; 11:12; 13:2,4, etc.), the driving power (Lk. 24:49; Acts 1:8;
4:31; 9:17,31), the guide in significant decisions (16:6,7; 19:21; 20:22,23),
and the legitimator of the whole endeavour, especially at its most delicate points (cf. 5:32; 8:17,18; 10:44,45,47; 11:15–18; 15:28).[5] For von Baer
these different activities of the Spirit divided salvation history into
three sharply distinguished epochs (each characterized by its own distinctive type(s) of activity of the Spirit[6]): — (1) the OT/time of promise
terminating with Jesus' baptism,[7] (2) the period of Jesus' ministry
during which he alone is empowered (cf. Luke 4:14, 4:18–21) by the
Spirit (John the Baptist having effectively been removed from its commencement by the notice in Luke 3:19–21, and the epoch concluding
with Jesus' ascension and the redactionally highlighted 'Spiritless' in-
terregnum of Acts 1:12–26[8]), and (3) the period of the church empowered for witness by the Pentecostal Spirit. As we shall see, the
significance of this periodization has proved more contentious.

*(3) For Luke the Spirit is largely the 'Spirit of prophecy'; in Acts especially
as an 'empowering for witness'.*

Von Baer saw that the Spirit was essentially the 'Spirit of prophecy' in
each of the 'epochs', though in different ways — mainly as oracular
speech in Luke 1–2; as the unique messianic endowment to proclaim
eschatological liberation and God's reign (and to effect these with
words of power) in the ministry of Jesus, and the power of inspired
witness to Jesus in the period of the church. In connection with the third
of these, von Baer drew attention to Luke 24:49 and Acts 1:8 (gateway
redactional texts into Acts) which above all characterize the Spirit as
the power to witness;[9] to Peter's Pentecost speech which programmatically describes the promise of the Spirit to all Christians as the gift of

---

[5]*Cf.* Shepherd, whose (broader) thesis is that the function of the Spirit in Luke's
writings 'is to signal narrative reliability' and so to provide the confirmation of
the gospel throughout Luke-Acts (W. Shepherd, *The Narrative Function of the
Holy Spirit as Character in Luke-Acts* (Atlanta: Scholars, 1994), 247 and *passim*).
[6]See esp. *Geist*, 111, but also the majority of Part 1 (43–112).
[7]Von Baer can, however, also speak of 1:35 as the beginning of the new epoch
in which 'der Geist Gottes als Wesen des Gottessohnes in dieser Welt erscheint'
(*Geist*, 48).
[8]*Geist*, 79–85.
[9]*Ibid.*, 84.

the 'Spirit of prophecy' promised by Joel (2:17,18, 33 and 38,39), and to the way the narrative of Acts repeatedly associates the Spirit with witness, if in different ways.

> (a) As a gift that is God's own witness to the gospel, especially towards Jews (2:33–36; cf. 5:32); (b) as God's witness to those who are his people, i.e. through the gift of the Spirit he attests to them as his own (esp. 15:8; cf. 5:32); (c) as the mediator of confident *assurance* of the gospel testimony to the believer;[10] (d) as the inspiration to *give* witness (esp. 4:31);[11] (e) as providing charismata which make the *content* of the witness more dramatic and effective (including e.g. signs and wonders alongside the preaching, but also charismatic wisdom enhancing the speech event and other forms of inspiration empowering them); (f) as part of the *content* of the witness (Acts 2!) and (g) as the Lord of the witnesses (guiding, encouraging, etc.).[12]

In continuity with von Baer, the major works on Lucan pneumatology have increasingly emphasized Luke's tendency to portray the Spirit as the 'Spirit of prophecy', even if they have drawn quite different conclusions from it.[13]

(4) Correspondingly, Luke shows relatively little interest in the Spirit as the power of the spiritual, ethical and religious renewal of the individual.

Gunkel had argued the Spirit in the primitive community reflected in Acts was naked supernatural power (especially of miraculous speech, such as prophecy and tongues), and discerned simply by cause and immediate effect, not in terms of the inspiration of less 'charismatic' activities furthering some divine plan and/or working towards some theological goal. As the charismatic 'Spirit of prophecy', the Spirit might thus be expected to have little or no bearing on ordinary Christian life.[14] Von Baer pointed out the weaknesses of such a portrait. The miraculous speech in question for Luke was mainly witness to Christ, and the Spirit was evidently the driving power of the church's mission, and of salvation-history more generally. It seemed to follow that the

---

[10]According to von Baer the Spirit in Acts 2 provides the robust assurance (going beyond mere 'faith') of Jesus' exaltation as Christ and Lord (*Geist*, 99).
[11]*Geist*, 102–3.
[12]Hence the Spirit cannot be reduced to Gunkel's 'naked supernatural power' (see von Baer, *Geist*, 103–4; 184–92).
[13]Most notable in developing von Baer's emphasis are the contributions by Lampe, 'Spirit'; Schweizer, 'πνεῦμα, κτλ.'; G. Haya-Prats, *L'Esprit Force de l'Église*, (Paris: Cerf, 1975); Stronstad, *Theology*; Menzies, *Empowered*, and Mainville, *L'Esprit*.
[14]See Gunkel, *The Influence of the Holy Spirit* (Philadelphia: Fortress, 1979), esp. 1–71, and on him Turner and Menzies (as at n.2).

Spirit might be discerned behind virtually all Christian witness, not merely in the most blatantly supernatural events of it. By analogy, the Spirit who gave the charismatic *paraklēsis* ('encouragement', 9:31) and joy (4:33; 13:52) and fear of the Lord (5:1–10) which built up the church should also be traced behind the more general community life of the congregations depicted in the summaries (esp. 2:42–47; 4:32–37).[15] Again, in contrast to the *religiongeschichtliche Schule's* assertion that there was little of significance in common between the religious life of Jesus and that of the earliest churches, von Baer (with Büchsel) maintained that for Luke the Spirit was the power of Jesus' life of *sonship* (Lk. 1:35; 3:22), and equally of that of the church.[16] But von Baer agreed that the evidence in favour of these conclusions was relatively fragmentary: i.e. he conceded Luke showed *relatively* little interest in the Spirit's role in the religious renewal of the individual. The Spirit is portrayed first and foremost as charismatic empowering. There have since been those who have deemed the 'little interest' to be effectively none (e.g. Schweizer and Menzies, whose views we have examined above), but the careful study of Haya-Prats (himself rather closer to Gunkel than to von Baer at points) has shown this to be premature.[17] Others (most notably J.D.G. Dunn[18]) have attempted to make new covenant life of sonship by the Spirit (and correlative experience of the kingdom of God) central to Luke's pneumatology, but, as we have seen, this too has required revision.[19]

(5) Luke's pneumatology develops beyond Judaism in giving the Spirit christocentric functions.

If Luke's pneumatology owes much to the Jewish conception of the 'Spirit of prophecy' he goes beyond any usual Jewish ideas (i) in making the Spirit the chief witness to the Christ-event (the charismatic preaching centres on this), and (ii) in casting the exalted Messiah as the one who 'pours out' this Spirit in God's place as his own executive power (Acts 2:33), and as the one who becomes present and known to the disciple *in* the Spirit (e.g. in visionary and other charismatic ex-

[15]*Geist*, 185–92.
[16]*Geist*, 16–20.
[17]*L'Esprit*, ch. 6.
[18]Especially *Baptism*, chs. 2–9.
[19]Dunn himself has subsequently charged Luke with almost complete disregard for the experience of eschatological sonship mediated by the Spirit (*Jesus*, 191). His more recent contributions accept that for Luke the Spirit 'is indeed preeminently the Spirit of prophecy' ('Baptism', 8; cf., earlier, *Jesus*, 189–91).

periences) and extends his influence through them.[20] The 'Spirit of the Lord' has thus effectively become the 'Spirit of Jesus' too (cf. 16:6,7), and Jesus has become significantly identified with 'the Lord' of Joel 2:28–32 [3:1–5 LXX/MT] upon whose name one is to call for salvation (by baptism 'in the name of Jesus Christ' (cf. Acts 2:21,33–36,38,39[21]). Von Baer was careful to note that Luke-Acts does not go as far as to make the Spirit 'the Paraclete' (i.e. the personal presence of Jesus as Advocate/Revealer when Jesus himself is withdrawn through the ascension), nor does Luke present the Spirit quite as clearly as Paul does as the 'Spirit of Christ' who both mediates personal union with the heavenly Lord and radically stamps the believer with his eschatological sonship. But von Baer perceived that Luke has important elements of these more developed conceptions, and several have attempted to tease out further this aspect of Luke's thought.[22]

2. Areas of Continuing Disagreement Concerning Lucan Pneumatology

There is sharpest disagreement on the following (closely related) questions: (i) was the Spirit in Acts Joel's 'Spirit of prophecy' *alone* (or some broader gift based in other Old Testament promises of the Spirit), and what range of charismata and effects are attributable to this gift? (ii) How did Luke relate the Spirit to conversion-initiation? (iii) Was the Spirit for Luke merely a *donum superadditum* of charismatic empower-

---

[20]*Geist*, 39–43; 80–5; 99; 174.

[21]*Geist*, 93–4. cf. G. Stählin, ' "Τὸ πνεῦμα Ιησοῦ" (Apg. 16.7)' in B. Lindars and S.S. Smalley (eds.), *Christ and Spirit in the New Testament* (Cambridge: CUP, 1973), 229–52, and see Ch. 11 below.

[22]cf. Stählin and Turner (as at Ch. 11 below). Mainville (*L'Esprit*, 333 (cf. also 337)) can even describe the Spirit in Acts as 'the presence of Jesus when Jesus is absent', thereby consciously evoking Raymond Brown's own description of the Johannine Paraclete and applying it to the Spirit in Acts (though see the qualification in n.17). G.W. MacRae admits the pneumatology of Acts is the biggest challenge to characterization of Luke-Acts as portraying an 'absentee Christology' ('Whom Heaven Must Receive Until the Time', *Int* 27 (1973), 151–65). Robert O'Toole and others have made a convincing case that it is precisely texts such as Acts 18:10 (with e.g. Lk. 21:15; Acts 2:14–38; 5:31; 9:4–5 (22:7; 26:14), 9:34, etc.) that most truly represent Luke's christology, which is rather one of *soteriological omnipresence,* and the *chief means* of that saving presence is the Spirit (cf. O'Toole, *The Unity of Luke's Theology,* (Wilmington: Glazier, 1984), esp. chs. 2–3; also his essay 'Activity of the Risen Christ in Luke-Acts', *Bib* 62 (1981), 471–98).

ing, or did the Spirit also have soteriological functions? We shall treat these seriatim in the following sections.

II. THE SPIRIT AS THE 'SPIRIT OF PROPHECY' IN ACTS

Does Acts imply that the Spirit given to all Christians is the 'Spirit of prophecy' promised by Joel? Two lines of evidence secure an unequivocally affirmative reply to this question. *First,* the *nature* of the gift of the Spirit promised to Christians in 2:38,39 is clear enough — it is Joel's gift of the Spirit of prophecy. His audience will hardly expect Peter to be speaking of any *other* gift of the Spirit when he has so carefully explained Pentecost in terms of fulfilment of Joel (cf. 2:15–21,33). And when Peter states that all those who are baptized receive the 'gift of the Holy Spirit', what he says continues to refer back to the wording of Joel 2:28–32 [LXX 3:1–5].

> Thus his affirmation that this ἐπαγγελία ('promise'; cf. 2:33) is offered 'to you . . . and to your children' takes up and reaffirms Joel's promise that the Spirit will be poured out 'on your sons and daughters' (2:17c). When Peter then insists the promise is to 'all' called by God (cf. καὶ πᾶσιν: 2:17b) the basis for his claim lies in Joel's assertion, 'I will pour out my Spirit on *all flesh*' (2:28a [3:1a]), and the amplifying phrase τοῖς εἰς μακράν ('to all those who are far off') draws on Joel too (LXX 3:4; MT 3:8)). Finally, the assertion that the gift will be given to everyone 'whom the Lord our God calls to him' alludes to the last words of Joel's oracle (2:32 [3:5b]: 'whomsoever the Lord calls'), not cited earlier by Peter.

Peter thus draws on the wording of Joel's prophecy not merely for the basis of the universality spoken of, but, consequently, for the very nature of the promised gift itself.

Second, in the rest of Acts the Spirit is consistently portrayed as the source of the very gifts Judaism regarded as proto-typical to the 'Spirit of prophecy' (see Ch. 1, above):

(1) The Spirit is thus the author of *revelatory visions* and *dreams*: programmatically at 2:17, but also specifically at Acts 7:55,56 (and Luke would probably trace such vision/dream guidance as 9:10–18; 10:10–20; 16:9,10 and 18:9,10; 22:17,18,21; 23:11 to the Spirit (cf. the specific mention of Spirit in these contexts, 10:19; 16:6,7)[23]).

(2) The Spirit gives *revelatory words* or *instruction* or *guidance*: 1:2; 1:16 (= OT); 4:25 (= OT); 7:51 (= OT); 8:29; 10:19; 11:12,28; 13:2,4; 15:28; 16:6,7; 19:21; 20:22,23; 21:4,11 and 28:25 (= OT).

---

[23]*Contra* Haya-Prats (*L'Esprit*, §4).

(3) The Spirit grants *charismatic wisdom* or *revelatory discernment*: Luke 21:15 and Acts 5:3; 6:3,5,10; 9:31; 13:9 and 16:18.

(4) The Spirit inspires *invasive charismatic praise*, e.g. the tongues on the day of Pentecost: 2:4; 10:46; 19:6, and

(5) the Spirit inspires *charismatic preaching* or *witness*: Acts 1:4,8; 4:8,31; 5:32; 6:10; 9:17 or *charismatic teaching* 9:31 13:52 and 18:25(?) etc. — this is not strictly anticipated in Judaism, but it is an obvious extension of the Jewish concept of the Spirit as the Spirit of prophecy (combining some of the above) and derives from pre-Lucan Christianity.[24]

Along with the specific references to the Baptist's promise (1:5; 11:16) and references to believers receiving this gift of the Spirit (specified explicitly as Joel's gift at 2:17,18,33, 38,39 and as 'the same Spirit' at 10:44,45,47; 11:15; 15:8),[25] *the above include nearly all of the references to the Spirit in the book of Acts.*[26] Luke then evidently regards 'the promise' made to believers to be a christianized version of Joel's 'Spirit of prophecy': (*contra* Dunn and J. Kremer) he does not synthesize some more composite 'promise of the Spirit' by adding other Old Testament prophecies of the eschatological Spirit (such as Ezek. 36) alongside Joel's.[27] In that sense, Acts 2:14–39 is genuinely programmatic for the pneumatology of Acts.

The conclusion that Luke's pneumatology is based in Jewish conceptions of the 'Spirit of prophecy' has become the basis for the claim that Luke could therefore not attribute either miracles or the ethical life of the community to the Spirit (so especially Schweizer and Menzies). These conclusions, however, need to be challenged. As we have seen, they rest on an inadequate account of the Spirit of prophecy in Judaism, and more especially of the Spirit on the anticipated Davidic and related

---

[24]See Turner, 'The Spirit of Prophecy', *NTS* 38 (1992), esp. 68–72, 87–8.

[25]Other references to believers receiving the Spirit are 8:15,16,17,18,19 and 19:2,6.

[26]We are left with only eight occasions that do not immediately fit the categories of gifts we would regard as prototypical of the Spirit of prophecy: (1) Acts 5:3,9 referring to Ananias and Sapphira 'lying to' and 'testing' the Holy Spirit by their deceit; (2) Acts 6:5 and 11:24, ascribing charismatic 'faith' to the Spirit, and 13:52 similarly charismatic 'joy'; (3) 8:39 which speaks of the Spirit snatching Philip up and transporting him away; (4) 10:38, referring to Jesus' own anointing with Spirit and power, and (5) 20:28 where the Spirit is described as appointing overseers. These can all, nevertheless, be understood as pertaining to activities of the Spirit of prophecy: see Turner, *Power*, ch.13, esp. §2.2.

[27]On this point, against Dunn, *Baptism*, 21-22, see R.P. Menzies, 'Luke and the Spirit: a Reply to James Dunn', *JPT* 4 (1994), 115–38, esp. 131–3.

messianic figures. Furthermore, we have noted how the gospels, including Luke's, draw on this traditional portrait of the Messiah of the Spirit, and develop it, especially in the context of New Exodus hopes. Luke himself attributes to the Spirit Jesus' unique eschatological sonship, holiness, messianic wisdom and consecration (1:35 (cf. 2:40–52); 4:1b). He also sees the Spirit as the power by which Jesus accomplished liberating acts (4:14,18–21 (programmatically); 7:21,22; 11:20; Acts 10:38, etc.). If Luke has taken over and even reinforced such Jewish and Jewish-Christian ideas of the Spirit of prophecy on the Messiah, the burden of proof rests on the shoulders of those who claim that Luke's understanding of the Spirit as the 'Spirit of prophecy' would inevitably have precluded his associating the Spirit with the miracles in Acts or with the religious ethical transformation of the community depicted there. We shall revisit this question in section IV.

III. THE GIFT OF THE SPIRIT AND CONVERSION-INITIATION

This has been a major battleground in several wars. Acts has proved to be the Waterloo for those campaigning for a Confirmationist position (that the Pentecostal gift of the Spirit is normally conveyed by laying on of apostolic/episcopal hands subsequent to conversion: so Thornton, Dix, Adler) or a Sacramentalist one (that the Pentecostal Spirit is normally conveyed by the water rite of baptism: so Lampe and Beasley-Murray).[28] The positions advocated at present are: (i) Acts has no consistent norm (but reflects a diversity of sources and/or practices: so, e.g. Quesnel[29]); (ii) the norm is a conversion-initiation pattern in which conversional repentance/faith is crystallized in baptism, and the Spirit is received in connection with the whole process (so Dunn[30]), or (iii) the norm is that the Spirit is given subsequent to conversion and 'salvation' (i.e. as a *donum superadditum*, e.g. of prophetic empowering for mission:

[28]See especially G.W.H. Lampe, *The Seal of the Spirit* (London: SPCK, 1967[2]), and Dunn, *Baptism* (*passim*); *cf.* also Bovon, *Luke*, 229–37 (under the heading 'The Holy Spirit and the Laying on of Hands'). R.M. Price ('Confirmation and Charisma', *Saint Luke's Journal of Theology* 33 (1990), 173–82) argues for a Confirmationist theology of the Spirit in Acts on the ground that the Spirit in Acts is a *donum superadditum*.

[29]M. Quesnel, *Baptisés dans L'Esprit* (Paris: Cerf, 1985), with a good review of previous adherents. Cf. also Haya-Prats and Shepherd. For critique of Quesnel see Turner, *Power*, ch. 12, §2.2.4.

[30]*Baptism*, chs. 4–9; similarly G.T. Montague, 'Pentecostal Fire: Spirit-Baptism in Luke-Acts' in K. McDonnell and G.T. Montague, *Christian Initiation and Baptism in the Holy Spirit* (Collegeville: Liturgical Press, 1991) 22–41.

so Stronstad, Mainville, Menzies). The evidence supports the second of these in so far as (a) 2:38,39 paradigmatically associates the gift of the Spirit with conversional faith and baptism, (b) the only passage which postpones the gift of the Spirit to a point discernibly later than Christian baptism is Acts 8:12–17, and 8:16 implies this was exceptional (the notice would be redundant if the Spirit were *normally* given subsequent to baptism), and (c) the paradigm of 2:38,39 must be assumed for the numerous occasions (before Acts 8 and beyond it; cf. especially 2:41; 8:36–38; 16:15,33; 18:8, etc.) where people are explicitly said to come to faith, or to be baptized, but where reception of the Spirit is not mentioned (i.e. the reader is to assume such conversional faith and baptism is met with the gift of the Spirit unless (as in 8:16) it is stated otherwise).

Acts 19:1–6 has often been taken as a counter-example, but it is probably not. In sharp contrast to Apollos, who was a Spirit-inspired preacher of Jesus although (like the disciples of Jesus) he had experienced only the baptism of John (18:24–28) — if he could still be taught the way 'more accurately' this notice can hardly mean he was resubjected to Christian baptism or topped up with the Spirit[31] — the twelve 'disciples' at Ephesus have *not* heard of the gift of the Spirit, and *are rebaptized*: i.e. Paul treats them as those in the process of conversion.[32] What 'news' do they 'hear' (19:5a) from Paul that becomes grounds for their baptism? It can hardly be that John preached repentance and a coming Messiah (if they had not professed *that*, Paul could hardly have assumed they were true Messianic 'disciples' in the first place); the only other item of information in 19:4 is that *Jesus* is the Messiah they were hoping for. But if that was the *novum* they 'heard', little wonder they were subsequently 'baptized into the Lord Jesus'; they were not yet fully *Christian* disciples. For whatever reason Luke has portrayed them as 'almost' Christians up to 19:4,[33] the point remains that *the Spirit is then granted as usual as part of their conversion-initiation package — no significant 'delay' is implied between 19:5 and 19:6* (and Paul's question in 19:3 presupposes the Spirit is *normally* given in connection with Christian baptism: i.e. where baptism has not led to this gift one must question the baptism).

What does this tell us about the nature of the gift of the Spirit in Acts? Von Baer argued (against Gunkel) that if the Spirit was given *to all* and

---

[31]*Contra* Shepherd, *Function*, 228–9.

[32]These crucial distinctives render improbable Menzies' view that the Ephesian disciples are converts of Apollos, and as fully Christian as he is (see *Development*, 268–77; *Empowered*, 218–25. A similar position is held by H.S. Kim, *Die Geisttaufe des lukanischen Doppelwerks* (Berlin: Lang, 1993), 212–38.

[33]For due criticism of the unlikely explanations of Käsemann, Wilkens and Wolter, see above all C.K. Barrett, 'Apollos and the Twelve Disciples of Ephesus' in W.C. Weinrich (ed.), *The New Testament Age: Essays in Honor of Bo Reicke, Vol I* (Macon: Mercer, 1984), 29–39, and Menzies, *Development*, 268–70.

at conversion then it was unlikely that the gift was conceived of purely as a charismatic empowering.[34] It is to the issues raised by that observation that we now turn.

IV. A *DONUM SUPERADDITUM* OR A SOTERIOLOGICAL NECESSITY?

We have noted (I.(3) above) there is general agreement that the gift of the Spirit in Acts is above all a prophetic empowerment to witness to Jesus. This has usually been interpreted in one of two ways: (i) scholars in the classical Pentecostal tradition (especially Stronstad and Menzies[35]) have inclined to argue that Luke understands the Pentecostal gift to the disciples *in parallel to Jesus' Jordan experience*, and so exclusively[36] as a *donum superadditum* empowering mission (Lk. 4:18-21//Lk. 24:47–49; Acts 1:8; 2:11[37]), and this Pentecostal experience of the disciples has then been taken as paradigmatic for all believers. (ii) Haya-Prats and Mainville have argued for a charismatic endowment serving more wide-ranging (including ecclesiastically orientated) ends.

1. The Spirit Exclusively as Empowerment for Mission?

This interpretation is certainly too narrow to be sustained, and the argument from the parallels with Jesus' case may prove a double-edged sword.[38] To be sure, Luke highlights the gift of the Spirit to the apostles

---

[34]*Geist*, 190–2.

[35]Stronstad, *Theology*, 51–2; Menzies, *Development*, 198–207; *Empowered*, 168–75; but cf. J.B. Shelton, *Mighty in Word and Deed: The Role of the Holy Spirit in Luke-Acts* (Peabody: Hendrickson, 1991), chs. 10–11.

[36]For the 'exclusively' see Stronstad, *Theology*, 12; Menzies, 'Luke and the Spirit,' 119, 138–9.

[37]The parallels Luke provides between Jordan and Pentecost have long been observed: see especially von Baer, *Geist*, 85; Talbert, *Literary Patterns*, 16; Chevallier, 'Luc', 5; Stronstad, *Theology*, ch. 4; L. O'Reilly, *Word and Sign in the Acts of the Apostles* (Rome: PBI, 1987), 29–52; Mainville, *L'Esprit*, 285–6, 291; Menzies, *Development*, 201 (n.2), 206–7.

[38]Dunn, *Baptism*, chs. 3–4, presses the same parallels to prove the disciples only enter the new covenant and eschatological sonship at Pentecost. But the argument from parallels needs careful analysis. The many parallels between Jesus' journey towards suffering in the fifth and final part of Luke and that of Paul in

as an empowering to witness (Lk. 24:47–49; Acts 1:8), but that is because the expansion of the witness is a major plot in Acts, and the twelve (especially Peter) are the leaders in this (at least as far as Acts 15). Similarly, the immediate co-text perhaps focuses the gift of the Spirit to Paul (9:17) as empowering for mission, but if this is so (and it is not explicit) such an emphasis would be perfectly understandable in the light of the fact that it is Paul's mission that will dominate Luke's account from chapter 13 onwards. One hardly need assume, however, that Luke thought the gift was granted these leaders as missionary empowering *alone*. Neither Judaism nor early Christianity prepared for such an idea. Nor would it be comprehensible why Luke should think such a gift *universal* and normatively given at conversion (see III above):

> Luke evidently does not believe that all converts immediately go out to preach like Paul in Damascus (9:20): rather, according to Luke's paradigmatic summary in 2:42–47, they receive instruction, and share in the table fellowship, worship, and communal life of the church. By and large in Jerusalem it is not the company of believers in general but the apostles who preach, work signs, and have 'the ministry of the word of God' (6:2: cf 4:33). In this they are joined by some specially endowed people like Stephen (cf. 6:8,10) and Philip (8:5–40, cf. 'the evangelist' (21:8)), or, on one unusual occasion, by a household of 'friends' of Peter and John (4:23,31). The tale is similar beyond Acts 8. Luke may well have believed a majority of Christians became involved in different types of spoken witness but (perhaps surprisingly) he nowhere explicitly states that the rank-and-file of the church (far less immediate converts) actively spread the word. Rather this seems left to people like Philip, Paul, Barnabas, John Mark, Silas, Timothy, Apollos, i.e. evangelists and their co-workers (of whom no doubt Luke knew far more than he has named: cf. 8:4;[39] 11:19,20, etc.).

Nor, again, is there any suggestion that the Spirit given to the Samaritans, to Cornelius' household or to the Ephesian 'twelve' is ex-

---

(footnote 38 continued)
the fifth and final part of Acts hardly mean their sufferings are of symmetrical theological import. In the case of the Jordan/Pentecost parallels the argument is 'double-edged' because Jesus comes to Jordan as the very impress of the Spirit (1:35) while the disciples have no corresponding experience. One might then argue Pentecost must include not merely an empowerment parallel to Luke 3:22 but also the component of Jesus' experience derived from Luke 1:35 which they lack.

[39] Acts 8:1 generalizes that 'all' were scattered, and 8:4 that 'those who were scattered went about preaching the word', but the latter does not repeat the 'all' of 8:1, and in no way suggests that 'each' preached the word; merely that, as a result of their going out, the word was spread (by some).

clusively an empowerment for mission, and, in fact, Luke does not explicitly associate any of these parties with evangelistic activities of any kind.[40] Finally, this view needs to turn a blind eye to a whole series of pneumatological texts in Acts that clearly have little or nothing to do with missionary empowering, but serve the spiritual life of the church (or of individuals within it). For a consideration of these we must turn above all to Haya-Prats' research.

2. The Spirit as the Charismatic Empowering of the Church

Mainville and Haya-Prats, while recognizing that for Luke the Spirit is above all the driving force of the mission, nevertheless admit this is not the whole story. Most notable amongst the many texts that have virtually no direct evangelistic significance, and, rather, evidently speak of actions of the Spirit for the benefit of the church herself, are 5:3,9 (Ananias and Sapphira's sin is a lying to the Spirit, implying the Spirit monitors the holiness of the church); 6:3 (those endowed with wisdom from the Spirit are appointed to serve tables in the context of a dispute); 11:28 (Agabus' prophecy of famine allows the Antioch church to arrange relief) and 20:28 (the Spirit appoints leaders to the church). A number of other texts relate to purely personal prophecies (e.g. those of warning to Paul in Acts 20:23;21:4,11). Admittedly, some charismata that benefit or direct the church also have secondary missiological significance. As well as clarifying relations between Jews and Gentiles within the church, the decision prompted by the Spirit in Acts 15:28 probably made mission to the Gentiles easier; similarly, churches that live in the fear of the Lord, and the comfort of the Spirit, may expect to attract converts (9:31), just as churches encouraged and challenged by charismatics like Barnabas (11:24) would. And missionaries who by God's grace become 'filled with joy and the Holy Spirit' even when

---

[40]Stronstad, Shelton and Menzies have variously argued that (1) the laying on of hands that bestows the gift (8:17 and 19:6) is an ordination for mission, (2) the gift to Cornelius' household is accompanied by the same prophetic outburst of witness to God's great deeds that served the evangelism of Acts 2, and so marks the Spirit as endowment for evangelism, and (3) the later summaries speak of the growth of the church in Samaria, Caesarea and Ephesus, and so identify the Spirit given to the groups concerned as empowerment for mission. But each of these arguments appears to be special pleading: see M. Turner, ' "Empowerment for Mission"? The Pneumatology of Luke-Acts: An Appreciation and Critique of James B. Shelton's *Mighty in Word and Deed*', *VoxEv* 24 (1994), 103–22, esp. 114–17.

they are rejected (13:52) are undoubtedly thereby refreshed for the next bout of mission. But these are *secondary* missiological *effects*, sometimes suggested by the connections in Luke's narrative; they are not evidently the primary purposes of the charismata in question. Luke, like the rest of Christianity, evidently thought the Spirit was also for the benefit of those in the church, not merely to empower her to draw outsiders into her ranks.

Haya-Prats has also devoted special attention to the question of whether the Spirit has a role in the everyday life of the Christian.[41] Here, however, he tends to agree with Gunkel. Luke considers repentant faith expressed in baptism to bring 'salvation' in the form of forgiveness of sins, and Jesus is 'present' to the community in and through his 'name'. The Spirit is given to those who have received all this, and so as a *donum superadditum*. If the Spirit occasionally fills a person with 'wisdom' (Lk. 21:15; Acts 6:3), 'joy' (13:52; cf. Lk. 10:21) or 'faith' (6:5; 11:24) these are exceptional and powerfully charismatic *intensifications* of ordinary Christian virtues. The Spirit is not required for the ordinary level of Christian faith, joy and wisdom because for Luke these fall within the range of unaided human possibilities. Haya-Prats also then agrees with Gunkel that nothing in the summaries of the church's new life (2:42–47; 4:32–37) is directly attributable to the Spirit, but admits that as these are immediately preceded by the Pentecost and 'Little Pentecost' accounts it is possible Luke understood the Spirit as the inspiration in part of the moral and religious life described in them.[42] This last admission is probably an understatement. The narrative tension of expectation of an 'Israel of the Spirit' is carefully built up from Acts 2:1 to 2:38,39. Yet the summary of conversions and the life of this community (2:40–47) *has not a single mention of the Spirit*. This device requires the reader to resolve the tension with the assumption that it is the unmentioned advent and charismata of the promised Spirit that is responsible for the overall dynamic of the new community. This, of course, might be resisted by those who think the 'Spirit of prophecy' has nothing to do with ethical renewal, but such an assumption appears to rest on a serious distortion of the evidence. In a Jewish environment, 'charismatic wisdom' (the second most common gift attributed to the 'Spirit of prophecy' in Judaism) would precisely be expected to give the dynamic renewed understanding of faith that might then flow into (e.g.) charismatic teaching which addresses others and/or might promote joyful obedience and worship/thanksgiving

---

[41]*L'Esprit*, ch. 6.

[42]*Ibid.*, 156, 162. See the more positive narrative-critical arguments of Shepherd, *Function*, 167, 170–3.

alike in the charismatic and those addressed (cf. already Sir. 39:6 for several of these elements combined).[43] In this light the cases of those described above as 'full of' the Holy Spirit and wisdom, joy or faith should be regarded as exceptional only in degree rather than in the kind of working of the Spirit. And the same Spirit of prophecy would be expected to explain the strong sense of God's (and Christ's) transforming presence in the community. Any Jew hearing Peter's promise of the eschatological 'Spirit of prophecy' (2:38,39) to be granted universally could reasonably expect the Spirit thenceforth to be the power of the community's religious and ethical renewal. I suggest the burden of proof lies on the shoulders of those who claim Luke did not so think.

This raises the question whether Luke implies that this charismatic 'Spirit of prophecy' is simultaneously a soteriological necessity, the power by which Israel's own restoration is wrought.

3. The Spirit as the Charismatic Power of Israel's Restoration?

We have noted that Luke's portrait of the Messiah of the Spirit is set against the background of hopes for Israel's restoration. Luke 1–2 is redolent with hopes for a *Davidic* Messiah who will redeem Israel and transformingly restore her, making her a light to the Gentiles (cf. 1:32–33,35,68–79; 2:25–26,29–35,38). Luke uses traditional material which traced to the Spirit Jesus' to the Spirit conception as the 'holy' Son of God and combined this with an allusion to Isaiah 32:15, and hence to the Spirit as the source of Israel's renewal (1:35). It is probable that the Baptist's promise that the coming one will baptize with Holy Spirit and fire (Lk. 3:16,17) also belongs with this scenario, and develops Jewish reflection on Isaiah 4:4 and 11:1–4. The Baptist himself has sifted Israel in preparation for the Messiah who will finally cleanse Zion through a righteous fiery and purgative rule empowered by the Spirit. For Luke, Jesus' ministry inaugurates this. It is an appeal to all sectors of Israel (including 'the sinners') to participate in the transformation of Israel, and to become a community of reconciliation based in what Borg has called a 'paradigm of mercy',[44] inspired and enabled by God's

---

[43]Cf. also texts in ch. 1, II, §§ 3–4; Philo, *Giants*, 55 and *passim*; *T. Simeon* 4:4; *T. Benj.* 8:1–3, etc.

[44]M.J. Borg, *Conflict, Holiness & Politics in the Teachings of Jesus* (Lewiston: Mellen, 1984).

reconciling presence in liberating power (= the kingdom of God).[45] This, for Luke (like much Judaism), is what 'salvation' is all about: its content is not merely 'forgiveness of sins' and assurance of future bliss (things already presupposed by nomistic Judaism[46]). The divine forgiveness awaited is more specifically the one that will remove the divine chastisement of Israel evinced in her oppressed and sorry estate; and the salvation hoped for is correspondingly a deliverance and messianic rule that frees her to serve God without fear in holiness and righteousness as a community of 'peace' (cf. Lk. 1:68–79).[47] To a limited extent this salvation is made present by Jesus amongst his followers, through his Spirit-empowered acts and teaching (cf. especially 4:18–21),[48] but the events of the Passion precipitate a radical change. For Conzelmann the Passion, of course, means the return of Satan, and

---

[45]For similar conclusions reached by different approaches see e.g. Ben F. Meyer, *The Aims of Jesus*, (London: SCM, 1979); G. Lohfink, *Jesus and Community* (London: SPCK, 1985); cf. also L.D. Hurst, 'Ethics of Jesus', in J.B. Green and S. McKnight (eds.), *Dictionary of Jesus and the Gospels* (Leicester: IVP, 1992), 210–22. These are attempts to discuss the 'historical Jesus' but Luke provides some of the best evidence and builds a similar portrait in his redaction. I.H. Marshall and J.O. York have shown the great degree to which the 'bi-polar reversals' anticipated in the *Magnificat* are seen to be fulfilled in Jesus' ministry and teaching, and in the life of discipleship to which these point (I.H. Marshall, 'The Interpretation of the Magnificat: Luke 1:46–55' in C. Bussmann and W. Radl (eds.), *Der Treue Gottes Trauen* (Freiburg: Herder, 1991), 181–96; J.O. York, *The Last Shall Be First: The Rhetoric of Reversal in Luke* (Sheffield: SAP, 1991). Cf. Turner, *Power*, ch. 11.

[46]Jews were not (as was once thought) 'legalists', who believed in the need to keep every item of the law perfectly, in order to achieve salvation. Essentially most believed God had chosen them and destined them for eternal life *by grace*, and that a Jew would only be barred from the new creation if he or she deliberately revoked the covenant (e.g., by gross unrepented sin). Otherwise repentance, the sacrificial system, the day of atonement, etc. were all there as testimony to God's mercy towards the sinner, and as the divinely appointed means of receiving forgiveness. Jews thus kept the Law as a thankful *response* to God's grace and calling (not in order to earn a place in the redeemed order). This pattern of belief has been called 'nomism' (in deliberate contrast to 'legalism').

[47]Cf. N.T. Wright, *The New Testament and the People of God*, (London: SPCK, 1992), part III (Judaism) and 373–83 on Luke. So also K. Stalder, 'Der Heilige Geist in der lukanischen Ekklesiologie', *Una Sancta* 30 (1975), 287–93. See also Turner, *Power*, chs. 5, §3; 11; 13, and 14, §3.

[48]Conzelmann used the framework of von Baer's three epochs to argue 'salvation' was all but limited to this period; Dunn (*Baptism*, chs. 3–4) used the same framework to argue the disciples only began themselves to experience

a future in which 'salvation' is reduced almost to a memory of the past 'Satan-free' period of the ministry and a hope for the eschaton. *Per contra*, Franklin has rightly observed that Luke 19:11–27; 22:14–30; 23:42,43; 24:49 (etc.) all anticipate that through the Passion God's transforming reign through his messianic king will be *intensified*, rather than weakened. Answering to this, Acts 2:33–36 asserts Jesus' elevation to the supreme place of kingship and power, the throne of David's 'Lord' at God's right hand. This, as both Franklin and Mainville have stressed, is the climax of Luke's christology and soteriology; the fulfilment of the promise in Luke 1:32,33.[49]

But how is this restorative Davidic rule over the house of Jacob (so Lk. 1:32,33) to be implemented from the heavenly throne? And how is the 'salvation' begun by Jesus in the ministry to be continued and intensified amongst the disciples? Luke 24:47–49 and Acts 1:3–8 provide only one possibility: viz. the one means by which Jesus had already inaugurated that salvation; namely the Spirit, now poured out as the Messiah's executive power (Acts 2:33). The same 'Spirit of prophecy' which will enable the Twelve and the community around them to fulfil the destiny of Isaiah 49:6 as a light to the nations (Lk. 24:47), bringing the message of salvation to 'the end of the earth' (Acts 1:8; cf. 13:47), will thus also be the power to raise up Jacob and restore the preserved of Israel (cf. Is. 49:5,6). Accordingly, Luke redactionally identifies 'the promise of the Father' (1:4) with the Baptist's logion; Jesus will now 'baptize' them 'with Holy Spirit' as John promised (1:5 — and the question in 1:6 shows the disciples rightly perceive this concerns the cleansing/restoration of Israel, and so even possibly her promised 'rule' over the nations (cf. Dan. 7)[50]). And this Spirit is to 'come upon them' 'from

---

(footnote 48 continued)
salvation after Pentecost. Against the former see e.g. I.H. Marshall, *Luke: Historian and Theologian* (Carlisle[Exeter]: Paternoster, 1997[1970]); E. Franklin, *Luke: Interpreter of Paul, Critic of Matthew* (Sheffield: SAP, 1994), 13–26 and 249–61. Against the latter, see Turner, 'Jesus and the Spirit', esp. 29–34; Menzies, *Development*, chs. 6, 8 and 9; Turner, *Power*, chs. 9 and 11.

[49] E. Franklin, 'The Ascension and the Eschatology of Luke-Acts', *SJT* 23 (1970) 191–200; *idem, Christ the Lord* (London: SPCK, 1975), 29–41; *idem, Luke*, 249–61. Mainville argues Acts 2:33 is the literary and theological key to the whole of Luke-Acts (*L'Esprit, passim*). Cf. Turner, *Power*, ch. 10.

[50] John's promise evidently cannot be reduced to an assurance the disciples will be empowered to witness and so to sift Israel (as Menzies takes it): the emphatic 'you' (will be baptized) includes *them* (along with the rest of Israel) as the objects of Jesus' messianic purging of Israel. For this broader restorationist view of Luke's concept of John's promise, see Kim, *Geisttaufe*; Turner, *Power*.

on high' (1:8; cf. Lk. 24:49) — a further clear allusion to Isaiah 32:15 (LXX) and to the promise of the restoration of Israel (32:15–20) through the Spirit. In short, the redactional gateway texts into Acts suggest the gift of the Spirit is not merely empowering to witness, but that the varied activities of the Spirit of prophecy in the individual and in the congregation will together also constitute the purging and restoring power of God in the community which effects Israel's transformation/salvation.[51] The latter line of thought is developed at a number of points in Acts.

(1) The Pentecost account (2:1–13) quite deliberately echoes Jewish accounts of the Sinai theophany (it is close to, though not dependent on, Philo's[52]), and Jesus is exalted to God's right hand not merely as the Davidic Messiah, but (as in the Gospel) as the Mosaic Prophet too (cf. also 3:18–23). It is especially as the latter that he ascends on high to receive a gift of foundational importance which he gives to his people (2:33,34; cf. Ex. 19:3; Ps.68:18 (esp. the Targum rendering); Josephus, *Ant.* III.77–78, etc.) at the beginning of a decisive new phase of Israel's existence, and amidst theophanic phenomena strikingly reminiscent of Sinai.[53]

(2) The life of the community depicted in the summaries at Acts 2:42–47 and 4:32–35 matches both the salvation hoped for in Luke 1–2 and the main thrust and goal of Jesus' preaching — an Israel of reconciliation led by the Twelve as a community which is free of oppressors, which without fear joyfully worships God, serving him in holiness and righteousness, and from which

---

[51]See also D.L. Tiede, 'The Exaltation of Jesus and the Restoration of Israel in Acts 1', *HTR* 79 (1986), 278–86; Kim, *Geisttaufe*.

[52]The attempt by Menzies (*Development*, 235–41; *Empowered*, 189–201) to dismiss Moses/Sinai parallels from this scene appears to be somewhat tendentious, for the alternative theophanic parallels he offers lack precisely the most important parallels to Sinai that Acts 2 affords: they do not concern an event on earth before the assembled people of God, nor do they come at a redemptive-historical turning point for Israel, nor do they follow an ascent of Israel's redeemer to God, nor involve miraculous speech reaching all nations. For more balanced assessments see A.J.M. Wedderburn, 'Traditions and Redaction in Acts 2.1–13', *JSNT* 55 (1994), 27-54; Kim, *Geisttaufe*, 157–68, 242, and cf. Turner, *Power*, ch. 10 §1.4.

[53]See J. Dupont, 'Ascension du Christ et don de l'Esprit d'après Actes 2.33', in Lindars and Smalley (eds.), *Christ and Spirit*, 219–28; M. Turner, 'The Spirit of Christ and Christology' in H.H. Rowdon (ed.), *Christ the Lord* (Leicester: IVP, 1982) 168–90, esp. 174–9; *idem, Power*, ch. 10, §§1–2.

poverty and hunger are banished by the caring rich.[54] To what should the sudden emergence of this 'fulfilment' of Jesus' hopes be attributed if not to the Spirit by which he extends his rule over Jacob and purgingly 'baptizes' Zion? There is no need, of course, to assume the Spirit performs such activity *other than* as the 'Spirit of prophecy'.[55] The Spirit experienced in the charismatic teaching of the apostles and other prophetic figures, in the charismatic praise of the community, and in spiritual wisdom granting a joyful grasp of the gospel and its implications (perhaps thereby motivating the caring love for the poor), would together be adequate to explain the evident 'enthusiasm' and the sense of God's transforming presence in the congregation.

(3)   The idea of the 'cleansing' or purging of Israel inherent in the Baptist's promise then emerges most prominently both in the Ananias and Sapphira incident (cf. 5:3,9) and in the Cornelius episode. With respect to the latter, it can be no accident that the one time when the Baptist's promise that Jesus will purge/cleanse Zion with Holy Spirit is 'remembered' is 11:16, in the midst of questions about whether Gentiles can be 'clean' (the focus of Acts 10). Their participation in the Spirit of prophecy shows that Cornelius' household has a part in the 'Israel' the Messiah is cleansing/restoring by the Spirit and thus they are readily admitted to baptism, and Peter can later refer to God having 'cleansed their hearts by faith' (15:9).

> This whole incident, which initially took Peter and the church by surprise, apparently led to some reinterpretation of Israel's hope. In 3:19–26 national restoration of Israel around the Messiah as (together) Abraham's seed was expected eventually to lead to the universalizing of the blessing promised in Gn. 22:18. But in 15:14-18 the argument appears to be that Israel's restoration is in principle complete (merely to be extended further into the diaspora) and accordingly it is the hour for the eschatological influx of Gentiles. The hopes of Luke 1–2 have largely been fulfilled (if in surprising fashion).[56]

---

[54]See D.P. Seccombe, *Possessions and the Poor in Luke-Acts* (Linz: SNTU, 1982), 200–9; York, *Last*, 62. For 'salvation' as participation in the restored community, see Joel B. Green, *The Theology of the Gospel of Luke*, (Cambridge: CUP, 1995); Turner, *Power*, ch. 13.

[55]*Contra*, Shepherd, *Function*, 167, see Turner, *Power*, ch. 13.

[56]Cf. J. Jervell, *Luke and the People of God* (Minneapolis: Augsburg, 1972), especially 41–74. If Luke anticipates some further landslide of Israel to faith — of which there is little sign — it would be into the transformed Israel of the Spirit

To conclude: It is difficult to reduce Luke's 'Spirit of prophecy' to a *donum superadditum*. It is certainly much more than an 'empowering to witness'; the same gifts of the Spirit that fuel the mission (charismatic revelation, wisdom, prophecy, preaching and doxology) also nurture, shape and purify the community, making it a messianic community of 'peace' conforming to the hopes for Israel's restoration. Without this gift there could be no *ongoing* experience of the 'salvation' the disciples experienced in Jesus' ministry, and certainly no deepening of it (something similar would have had to be said of the Samaritans if they had been left by Philip and the apostles without the Spirit granted in 8:17). For Luke the charismatic 'Spirit of prophecy' is very much the power and life of the church, and so probably of the individual too (hence the close association of the gift of the Spirit to conversion-initiation). It is the means by which the heavenly Lord exercises his cleansing and transforming rule over Israel as much as the means by which he uses her as the Isaianic servant to witness his salvation to the end(s) of the earth (1:8; 13:47). In this, Luke's understanding of the Spirit is not so distant from that of either Paul or John as is regularly assumed.[57]

V. CONCLUSION: LUKE'S PNEUMATOLOGY AND THE THEOLOGY OF ACTS

What does Luke's pneumatology tell us about his theological endeavour? His portrayal of the Spirit of prophecy as the charismatic power of Israel's restoration under her Davidic Messiah/Mosaic prophet *appears to be ideologically motivated*. That is, Luke is attempting to explain and so to legitimate the church in the light of her founding moments (and this explains much of the allegedly OT character of his pneumatology[58]). Far from attempting to persuade the reader that the

---

(footnote 56 continued)
he knows in the Church, the one fashioned and ruled by the Messiah on David's throne at God's right hand, not a Temple-and-Torah-centred national Israel ruled by the Messiah seated in Jerusalem. Against those claiming Luke expects a more literal and Zionistic fulfilment of Luke 1–2, see H. Räisänen, 'The Redemption of Israel: A Salvation-Historical Problem in Luke-Acts', in P. Luomanen (ed.), *Luke-Acts: Scandinavian Perspectives* (Göttingen: Vandenhoeck & Ruprecht, 1991), 94–114. Cf. Turner, *Power*, ch. 10 §3, and ch. 13 (*passim*, but esp. §3).

[57] See Turner, 'The Spirit of Prophecy', in Wilson (ed.), *Spirit*, 186–90, for development of this comparison; also A.W.D. Hui, 'The Concept of the Holy Spirit in Ephesians and its Relation to the Pneumatologies of Luke and Paul', unpublished PhD dissertation, Aberdeen 1992, *passim*, for the relation of Luke's pneumatology to Paul's.

[58] So Chevallier, 'Luc', part II.

church finds its true identity when it leaves Israel and Judaism behind (as J.C. O'Neill argued[59]), Luke wishes to maintain she is the fulfilment of the promises to Israel. His exclusion of those who fail to give heed to the Mosaic Prophet from the nation of Israel (3:22,23) and his apparent belief that the promises of Luke 1–2 are largely fulfilled by Acts 15 in *the Post-Pentecost community* supports this, and in addition suggests he writes (like the author of the Fourth Gospel) at a time when Christianity is still actively competing with (hellenistic) Judaism for the claim to be God's 'Israel'.[60] Far less clear is whether Luke also attempts to challenge (e.g.) an institutionalizing church of his own day with an idealized portrayal of her charismatic beginnings. That he believed the 'Spirit of prophecy' was still available to all believers is barely in doubt (cf. Acts 2:39!), and he may have anticipated his account would encourage greater dependence on the Spirit. Only in question is whether there is sufficient evidence to show that Luke knew of a non-charismatic sector of the church which he sought to correct and 'strengthen' (so Kim[61]). The one passage which affords the clearest glimpse of the church of Luke's day (Acts 20:25–35) envisages a number of problems, but a waning of the Spirit does not appear to be amongst them.

---

[59]J.C. O'Neill, *Theology of Acts in its Historical Setting* London, SPCK, 1970²).
[60]Cf. Kim, *Geisttaufe*, 243–4.
[61]The attempt by Kim (*Geisttaufe*, 209–38) to interpret the Ephesian 'twelve' as a cipher for non-charismatic (Markan?) Christian groups of Luke's day is by no means the easiest solution to the difficulties of 18:24-19:6 (on which see above).

Chapter Four

The Spirit in John 1–12

The portrayal of the Spirit in the Fourth Gospel has many interesting points of similarity and dissimilarity with that in Luke-Acts. In both the Spirit is to be understood primarily as a special Christian development of the Jewish understanding of the 'Spirit of prophecy'; in both the Spirit is granted by Jesus himself, beyond the cross and resurrection, and in both the Spirit is given to the disciple as an empowering to witness.[1] Like Luke, John too presents Jesus as the Messiah of the Spirit (based in Isaiah 11:2–4). But, unlike Luke, he nowhere attributes liberating acts of exorcism or healing to the Spirit, and for him the Spirit of prophecy on Jesus is above all understood as the power to *reveal* God, especially in the word of Jesus' teaching and preaching. This is crucial for John because (as we shall see) he regards 'revelation', and the Spirit-enabled wisdom/insight which understands it, as the very means of entering into salvation. In this chapter we shall first briefly examine two passages which explicitly describe Jesus as endowed with the Spirit (1:32–34; 3:34–36), then turn to three discourses (John 3, 4 and 6) which, between them, clarify the relationship between Spirit, word, and saving revelation.

---

[1] On the relation between the Spirit in Luke-Acts and that in John see e.g. W.H. Lofthouse, 'The Holy Spirit in the Acts of the Apostles and in the Fourth Gospel', *ExpT* 52 (1940–41), 334–6; R.T. Stamm, 'Luke-Acts and Three Cardinal Ideas in the Gospel of John', in J.M. Myers, O. Reinherr and H.N. Bream (eds.), *Biblical Studies in Honor of H.C. Alleman* (New York: Augustin, 1960), 170–204; J. McPolin, 'Holy Spirit in Luke and John', *ITQ* 45 (1978), 117–31; M.A. Chevallier, '«Pentecôtes» lucaniennes et «Pentecôtes» johanniques', in J. Delorme and J. Duplacy (eds.), *La Parole de Grâce: Études lucaniennes à la Mémoire d'Augustin George* (Paris: Recherches de Science Religieuse, 1981), 301–14; *idem*, 'Apparentements entre Luc et Jean en matière de pneumatologie', in J.N. Aletti *et al.*, *À Cause de l'Évangile: Études sur les Synoptiques et les Actes* (Paris: Cerf, 1985), 377–408.

I. JESUS ENDOWED WITH THE SPIRIT: JOHN 1:32–34 AND 3:34–36

1. John 1:32–34

John's account jumps from the Prologue, which proclaims Jesus the incarnate Logos who reveals the Father (1:1–18), to the Baptist's testimony concerning Jesus' reception of the Spirit (1:32–34), with no birth or infancy scenes. Käsemann,[2] Schweizer,[3] and others, have claimed John plays down Jesus' endowment with the Spirit, in favour of his own Logos christology — after all, they argue, he who claims to have descended from the Father (as in 3:12,13) barely seems to need the Spirit to supply revelation. To some extent one can see their point, and 3:31,32 comes close to making it explicit when either the evangelist himself or Jesus says:

> The one who comes from above is above all; the one who is of the earth belongs to the earth and speaks about earthly things. The one who comes from heaven is above all. He testifies to what he has seen and heard, yet no one accepts his testimony.

But Felix Porsch and Gary Burge have shown this to be a one-sided presentation of John's evidence.[4] They emphasize that it cannot be without significance that the very first glimpse of Jesus we have in John's Gospel is through the testimony of the Baptist (apparently party to Jesus' vision). And John's witness is that he saw the Spirit descend on the Son and come to 'rest' or 'remain' on him (1:32,33). The language

---

[2]E. Käsemann, *The Testament of Jesus according to John 17* (London: SCM, 1968), 20–6.

[3]*TDNT* 6: 438, 'The path taken by Luke does not satisfy John. He completely abandons the idea of inspiration because this emphasises the distinction between God and Jesus — a distinction which can be overcome only by a third, namely, the Spirit. If the Christ event is really to be understood as the turning-point of the aeons, then everything depends on the fact that the Father Himself, not just a gift of the Father, is genuinely encountered therein. There is thus no reference to the conception of Christ by the Spirit or to His endowment with the Spirit in baptism. . . . The descent of the Spirit on Jesus in 1:33 is simply a proof . . . of the divine sonship of Jesus.'

[4]F. Porsch, *Pneuma und Wort. Ein exegetischer Beitrag zur Pneumatologie des Johannesevangeliums* (Frankfurt: Knecht, 1974); G.M. Burge, *The Anointed Community: The Holy Spirit in the Johannine Community* (Grand Rapids: Eerdmans, 1987), 71,72 and 81–110. The latter has in my view overstated the case for a Spirit christology in John: for criticism, see Max Turner and Gary M. Burge, 'The Anointed Community: A Review and Response', *EvQ* 62 (1990), 253–64, esp. 254–5, 261–3.

here echoes LXX and targum renderings of Isaiah 11:2,[5] and so the Spirit upon Jesus is presented as the endowment of the Davidic Messiah with wisdom, understanding and knowledge of God of the sort we have noted in much intertestamental Judaism (and in Luke 1–2). But in John, as we shall discover, the emphasis is not just on how Jesus *receives* revelation from the Spirit but also on how through the Spirit he *imparts* revelation.

2. John 3:34–36

In 3:34 we are told, 'He whom God has sent speaks the words of God, for he gives the Spirit without measure'. While it is *grammatically* possible, the point can hardly be that Jesus speaks the word of God because *Jesus* gives the Spirit without measure (as Thüsing,[6] Porsch[7] and NRSV take it). It must rather mean 'Jesus utters the words of God *because* God gives *Jesus* the Spirit without measure'. It is possible a deliberate contrast is intended with what is elsewhere understood of the writers of the Old Testament books. Referring to these writers as 'prophets', Rabbi Aha (c.290–330?) is alleged to have stated, 'The Holy Spirit who rests on the prophets, rests on them *only by measure*' — meaning each is allotted his bit to reveal by the Spirit in the writing he gave (*Leviticus Rabbah* 15:2).[8] *John's* point would then be that the *immeasurable* gift of the Spirit (of revelation) *to* Jesus corresponds to the perfection of revelation *through* Jesus — it provides a revelation which *transcends* the Law and the Prophets.[9]

---

[5]See Burge, *Anointed Community*, 53–8. Burge wishes to interpret the verb *menein epi* ('to rest upon') with an intense durative sense (the Spirit came to abide on Jesus *permanently*); but the Baptist can hardly have witnessed the 'permanence' of the Spirit on the Son, and in the lexical cotext of descent as a dove, *menein epi* means simply 'to alight/settle upon'. Undoubtedly John believed the Spirit also 'remained upon him' permanently, but that is not the point here.

[6]W. Thüsing, *Die Erhöhung und Verherrlichung Jesu im Johannesevangelium* (Munster: Aschendorff, 1960), 154–55.

[7]*Pneuma*, 104–105.

[8]This contrasting 'parallel' is clearly too late to aid the Johannine interpreter unless one may assume that an analogous understanding existed earlier.

[9]Cf. Beasley-Murray, 53–4. This would then constitute the second of John's many replacement motifs, in which he makes the bold claim that Jesus, and the revelation he brings, eclipses the main pillars of Judaism. Already in the prologue he has made the point that as incarnate Logos/Wisdom, he and his teaching transcend the Law and definitively reveal the Father in grace and truth

Something like such an understanding would appear then to be confirmed in 3:35b where the result of the Father's love for the Son is that 'he has given all things into his hands'. As at Luke 10:22//Matthew 11:27, this means not that Jesus has been given universal power, but that the totality of *revelation* is given to the Son, whereby he 'utters the words of God' (3:34). 3:36 then draws the natural conclusion: if the fulness of God's revelation is imparted through the Son, then to receive that revelation brings 'life'; correspondingly, to reject it is to reject God, and so to remain under his wrath. It would seem then that John portrays the gift of the Spirit to Jesus at baptism *as the means of his plenary revelation and especially of the power to impart it to others.*

The implications of this are brought out more fully in the major discourses to which we now turn.

II. THE SPIRIT AS THE SOURCE OF SAVING REVELATORY WISDOM IN THE DISCOURSES OF JOHN 1–12

For purposes of clarity in dealing with this theme, we will examine the passages in a different order from that in which they appear in the Fourth Gospel:

(footnote 9 continued)
(1:17,18). Chapter 2 will imply that the revelation in Jesus surpasses the Law as wine betters water, and that Jesus replaces that other major pillar of Judaism, the temple. He is the 'true' temple, the dwelling place of God amongst his people, and the means of their fellowship. Other chapters will follow up this claim; in ch. 3 we learn that *new birth* by the Spirit through belief in the Son replaces natural birth into Israel as the condition for entry to the eschatological blessings of God's reign. In ch. 4 we learn that Jesus' teachings, not the Law, are *living water*, and that *true* worship is in the Spirit mediated through acceptance of his revelation, not merely available at the temple. In ch. 6, Jesus — or specifically his act of giving himself at the cross — is the true *manna* in the wilderness, while, in ch. 7, the Spirit which Christ gives is the *true water* in the wilderness: the eschatological counterparts to the lesser gifts of manna and water enjoyed by Israel in her wanderings. In ch. 8, his day is the joy of Abraham (8:56). And if Judaism claims the Law and her tradition are a lamp to guide people's feet to life, Jesus *is* the *light* and the *life* (chs. 8 and 9), the *way* and the *truth* (ch. 14). He, and not the Jewish leadership, is the fulfilment of God's promise of a *Shepherd* for the flock (ch. 10), and it is in him that the symbol of the *vine*, the national symbol of Israel, truly inheres (ch. 15). Indeed, in him the fulfilment of all OT hope for future life is to be met: for he *is* the *resurrection* and the *life* (11:25).

1. The Offer of 'Living Water': 4:10,13–14

In John 4:10 Jesus rather mysteriously says to the Samaritan woman, 'If you knew the gift of God, and who it is that is saying to you, "Give me a drink", you would have asked him, and he would have given you living water.' The reader quite naturally wishes to know what this 'living water' is that Jesus would have given — a water which (according to 4:13,14) alone truly quenches thirst, and which even 'wells up' like a spring in the believer gushing forth 'to eternal life'.

In Judaism 'living water' is certainly used as a symbol of God's eschatological salvation. The summons to salvation is expressed as the summons to water in Isaiah 55:1, 'Ho, every one who thirsts, come to the waters', and in Zecharaiah 14:8 eschatological salvation is announced in the promise: 'On that day living waters shall flow out from Jerusalem, half of them to the eastern sea and half of them to the western sea; it shall continue in summer as in winter' (and one might compare the similar picture in Ezek. 47:1–12 of the waters flowing out from the eschatological temple). In the context of John's Gospel, which was written to evoke saving belief that leads to 'eternal life' (20:30,31), this mention of 'living water' welling up to eternal life must indeed mean 'salvation'. But that only leads to a further question. In what form is this 'salvation' as dispensed by Jesus to be envisaged?

That question immediately leads back to the recognition that 'living water' is also a traditional Jewish symbol for the gift of the Spirit (cf. Isa. 44:3;[10] 1QS4.21,[11] etc.). That John intends the promise of 'living water' here to be understood as the Spirit is signalled by 4:23: 'The hour is coming *and now is* . . .' when true worshippers worship the Father '*in Spirit* and truth'. And in 7:37–39, John specifically equates the 'living water', which gushes forth in and from the believer (as from the eschatological temple), with the Spirit:

> On the last day of the feast, the great day, Jesus stood up and proclaimed, 'If any one thirst, let him come to me and drink. [38] He who believes in me, as the scripture has said, "Out of his heart shall flow rivers of living water." ' [39] Now this he said about the Spirit, which those who believed in him were to receive; for as yet the Spirit had not been given, because Jesus was not yet glorified.[12]

---

[10]'I will pour water on the thirsty land . . . my Spirit on your offspring'.

[11]'He [God] will pour the Spirit of truth upon him (to cleanse him) of all abomination and falsehood'.

[12]The passage has been taken christologically, by taking vv.37b–38a as a chiasmus:

It would appear, then, to be the saving gift of *Spirit* that Jesus says he would have imparted to the woman (4:10).

But this still leaves the reader with a further obvious question. What sort of saving gift of the Spirit might Jesus have imparted to this woman had she asked him? As 7:39 itself assures, any direct 'bestowal' of the Spirit must await Jesus' glorification through the cross and resurrection. And this qualification is also maintained in the words of 4:23: 'The hour *is coming* . . .' when believers will worship the Father in Spirit and truth. But the same saying also preserves the claim that in some way that future 'hour' had already begun to dawn: 'The hour is coming, *and now is* . . .'. And it is in correspondence with this 'and now is' that Jesus says he would have granted the woman living water had she asked him for it. In that case, however, what manner of 'gift' of living water/Spirit could he possibly here refer to?

The most probable answer comes when we note a further set of Old Testament and Jewish associations connected with Jesus' words: refreshing and life-giving water was also a symbol for divine *wisdom*. Thus, for example, Proverbs 13:14 refers to wisdom as 'a fountain of life'. So too in Isaiah 55:1 (to which we have already referred) the saving waters which the thirsty are invited to drink are God's wisdom and instruction. A similar understanding of wisdom and of God's Law (which supremely expresses it) is found frequently: cf. e.g. Sirach 24:23–29; CD 3.16; 19.34, and *Sipre Deut.* 11.22, §48.[13] In a saying which resonates with John 4:13, Sirach 24:21 has wisdom say: 'Those who eat of me will hunger still; those who drink of me shall thirst for more'. Sirach's point is that those who discover God's wisdom will find it so delicious they will want it in ever increasing supply. John, however, takes the idea a decisive step further, and says the person who drinks the divine wisdom from Jesus is fully satisfied.

This provides the clue to the gift of 'living water' Jesus might impart. It is indeed the Spirit, but the Spirit acting in a particular way – namely,

---

(footnote 12 continued)

If anyone thirst, Let him come to me,

Let him drink, who believes in me

7:38b could then be read to support the invitation by suggesting 'scripture' promises the living waters will flow *from the Messiah* (as the antitype of the rock in the wilderness: Exod. 17:1–6; Ps. 78:15,16, etc.). This view is supported by *inter alios* Beasley-Murray, Brown, Bultmann, Dunn, Painter, and Porsch: see Burge, *Anointed Community* 88–93, who agrees. Attractive though the view is, the arguments against are compelling: see J.B. Cortes, 'Yet Another Look at John 7:37–38', *CBQ* 29 (1967), 75–86; M. Turner, 'The Significance of Receiving the Spirit in John's Gospel', *Vox Ev* 10 (1977), 24–42 (esp. 29–31); Carson, 321–9.

[13] 'As water is life for the world, so are the words of the torah life for the world'.

as the revealer of God's saving wisdom through Jesus' Spirit-imbued teaching (cf. on 6:63 below). Jesus, as Wisdom incarnate,[14] imparts new revelatory wisdom which re-creates a person, and brings 'life'; but he does so precisely as the one to whom the Father has given the Spirit without measure (3:34). And it is this combination, of saving revelatory 'word'/wisdom with the Spirit active in it (and through it), which is experienced by those who truly 'hear' him as the refreshing 'living water' which evokes some measure of worship of God 'in Spirit and truth', even within the period of the ministry itself.

2. The Offer of the True Bread and Drink: John 6:32–58, 60–66

The main part of the discourse in John 6 is a subtle elucidation of the words from Scripture, 'he gave them bread from heaven to eat' (Exod. 16:4,15), offered by Jesus' critical audience as a challenge to him (6:31). The way Jesus responds is similar to some rabbinic midrashic homilies: he first paraphrases the passage (yielding a highly interpretive 'My Father (not Moses) gives (not gave) you the real bread from heaven' (vv.32,3)), then elucidates phrase by phrase.

> *First*, Jesus discusses the true nature of the 'bread God gives' (claiming the manna was only a type of the true bread God gives; Jesus himself is the life-giving bread: 6:32–40).
> *Second*, attention focuses on 'bread from heaven': how can the son of Joseph be 'bread from heaven'? the Jews murmur. And Jesus replies: 6:43–48.
> *Third*, the discourse focuses on 'bread to eat': 6:49–51, 52–58.
> *Finally*, the whole is summarized in a way that recapitulates the opening scripture and paraphrase: 6:57,58.[15]

Also like the midrashim, Jesus elucidates the pentateuchal text with an associated prophetic passage — Isaiah 54–55. Isaiah 54:13, 'All your sons shall be taught by the Lord' is formally quoted at 6:45, while Isaiah 55:1[16] is thematic to the whole discourse, and explains the extension from 'bread' to the otherwise unintroduced topic of refreshing 'drink' in 6:35.

---

[14]The Logos of 1:1–18 so fully matches what Judaism says of wisdom that to speak of the prologue portraying Jesus as 'Wisdom incarnate' is entirely appropriate, if not the full story: see e.g. Brown, Schnackenburg and Beasley-Murray.
[15]See P. Borgen, *Bread From Heaven*, (Leiden: Brill, 1965).
[16]'Ho, everyone who thirsts, come to the waters; and he who has no money, come, buy and eat! Come, buy wine and milk without money and without price. Why do you spend your money for that which is not bread, and your labour for that which does not satisfy?'

Underlying the whole discourse is the rabbinic, and more generally held, assumption (based in Deut. 8:3) that God's gift of manna was symbolic of his intention to give something even more important for 'life' — viz., torah/wisdom. Philo quite explicitly interprets Deuteronomy 8:3 to mean that the manna incident points to God's higher gift of the Law (*Decalogue*, 16–17), and elsewhere he takes the gift of manna as a sign of God's gift of wisdom: cf. *On the Change of Names*, 260:

> And indeed it says 'Behold, I rain upon you bread from heaven' (Exod. 16.4). Of what food can he rightly say that it rained from heaven, save of heavenly wisdom which is sent from above on souls which yearn for virtue by Him who sheds the gift of prudence in rich abundance, whose grace waters the universe . . .? (cf. *Preliminary Studies* 173–4; *Allegorical Interpretations*, 3.162–3).

The view that the heavenly manna is (or is a sign of) wisdom is also traced in the rabbis: *Exodus Rabbah* 25.7 interprets the manna by adducing Proverbs 9:5: 'Come, eat of my bread, and drink of the wine which I have mingled.' Jesus' step from the literal manna of Exodus 16 to the 'true bread from heaven' of 6:32b would (i) be widely anticipated, and (ii) be understood as *introducing the issue of where God's true life-giving instruction or wisdom is to be found*.

Key aspects of the discourse are now readily identified at the following points:

(1) At 6:35b the one who comes to Jesus and believes in him is promised he will 'never hunger or thirst'. As the discourse so far has only mentioned 'bread', this reference to '*thirst*' comes as a surprise. The promise is immediately reminiscent of that of living water in 4:14. The combination evokes Isaiah 55:1. But, more specifically, the 'I am . . .' statement of 6:35a, followed by this invitation in 6:35b quite directly parallels the sequence in Sirach 24. There Wisdom first identifies herself as pre-existent creator, then invites people, 'Come to me you who desire me, eat your fill of my produce' (24:19), and continues 'those who eat me will hunger for more; and those who drink me shall thirst for more' (v.21. Cf. Sir. 15:3, '[Wisdom] will feed him with understanding and give him the water of wisdom to drink'). This is a key to the whole discourse, and shows that *Jesus is describing himself in terms that transcend Wisdom and its embodiment in the Torah.*

(2) 6:51c then provides a second 'key'. Jesus identifies the 'heavenly bread' in question not merely as himself (as at 6:35a) but, more

particularly, as his flesh-for-the-life-of-the-world.[17] Within the wisdom-centred context of the discourse to this point this is not a reference to the eucharistic bread,[18] but to the *death* of Jesus understood as the *supreme revelation of God's wisdom* (cf. 3:14,15). The 'eating' of 6.51b is not literal, but simply a repetition of the 'eating' and 'drinking' metaphor in v.35 which denoted 'believing in' Jesus or 'coming to' Jesus (as at 6:35). In short, *believing in Jesus is supremely believing that the cross-and-exaltation reveals him as God's Son, and God's Wisdom.*

(3) If 6:35 echoes the inviting summons of Wisdom to the hungry to come and eat free bread and to the thirsty to drink refreshing water (or is it milk? or wine? cf. Isa. 55:1), in 6:53-58 the appealing invitation seems suddenly to be swapped for the apparently abhorrent one to feed on flesh and blood (an invitation which might be expected to tempt only the apocalyptic vultures of Ezek. 39:17). Little wonder Bultmann suspected an ecclesiastical glossator! But the point in this strongly sapiential context is rather that the flesh and blood in question correspond to the eating and drinking of heavenly *wisdom* (= 'true bread') in 6:35, and, as there, these things are to be eaten and drunk in the purely metaphorical sense that v.35 identifies as 'coming to' 'believing in' Jesus. More precisely, the 'flesh' and the 'blood' that are to be metaphorically ingested (at 6:53) are simply two different ways of identifying Jesus' *death* as the supreme expression of God's wisdom (as at 6:51c), and the corresponding 'eating' and 'drinking' in question is metaphor for 'taking this in' in the sense of comprehending and living by the ultimate revelation of the cross in authentic faith.

(4) A decisive new stage in the discourse is reached with 6:60-66. Jesus' discourse has left even the disciples scandalized; and now they too begin to 'murmur' (6:61; cf. 6:41). To their situation Jesus offers the open question of 6:62. If they are scandalized by his claim to be the bread come down from heaven, Jesus responds, will seeing him ascend again resolve their doubts? This, of course, is a genuine question; for Jesus will ascend *through the cross*; so, for those without faith, the 'ascent' of Jesus will deepen the scandal of his claim, rather than resolving it.[19]

---

[17]*Contra* RSV which with Sinaiticus joins 'for the life of the world' to the verb 'give', rather than to the noun 'flesh'.

[18]See Lindars on 6:43–51 for the problems with traditional Roman Catholic interpretation in this regard.

[19]Brown and Bornkamm are adamant that Jesus' question relates back to 6:35–50; *not* to the so-called Eucharistic discourse (vv.51–58), which is seen as an

(5)   All this leads to the climax of the discourse: 6:63, 'It is the Spirit
      who gives life; the flesh avails nothing. The words that I have
      spoken to you are Spirit and life.' The assertion in 6:63a that it
      is the Spirit who gives life need not surprise us (see esp. on Jn.
      3, below). More puzzling, at first sight, is 6:63b. Contextually
      this must relate to the 'flesh' which Jesus gives to 'eat' in 6:51c,
      53–58, namely, his death (which will mask his 'ascent' to all but
      those with faith: 6:62!). In that case, to say 'the flesh avails
      nothing' appears to mean that Jesus' incarnational giving of his
      flesh-and-blood at the cross is in itself soteriologically ineffec-
      tive. It is at this point that 6:63a and 6:63c make their crucial
      contribution. That is, the cross itself remains but a stark execu-
      tion unless the *Spirit illumines the event to the individual as God's
      saving wisdom* (so Dunn[20]), and so elicits 'life'. The means by
      which the Spirit accomplishes this is then introduced in 6:63c —
      it is Jesus' own revelatory wisdom/teaching: 'my words are
      Spirit and life'. For John this is largely only a real possibility
      after the 'glorification' of Jesus in the Easter events, and with
      the consequent gift of the Spirit. But, as with the Synoptic Evan-
      gelists, the writer allows that Jesus' hearers at least *began* to
      experience in the ministry the eschatological realities that they
      were more fully to comprehend and enjoy after Jesus' resurrec-
      tion- exaltation. Hence the present tense of 6:63c.[21]

(footnote 19 continued)
editorial insertion. According to them, what scandalizes the disciples is merely
the claim that Jesus is bread from heaven. The further claim that he will give
his flesh for the life of the world, and that people must 'eat' his flesh and 'drink'
his blood — which would have deepened the scandal yet further — is not in
view.
      The problem with Bornkamm's position, however, as Schnackenburg and
C.K. Barrett rightly point out, is that v.63, which is still part of Jesus' answer,
goes on to explain that *'the flesh* is of no avail' (that is, in giving eternal life), and
6:35–50 do not mention the word *'flesh'* at all; while 6:51–58 do so six times. It
would seem to follow that 6.60–63 relate even more directly to 6:51–58 than
they do to 6:35–50. This means the scandal was not merely Jesus' claim to be
bread from heaven, but more precisely that the bread from heaven is his 'flesh'
given in death and that this must somehow be 'appropriated'.
[20]J.D.G. Dunn, 'John VI — A Eucharistic Discourse?' *NTS* 17 (1970–71), 328–38.
[21]For Dunn, the assertion that the Spirit gives life — and that the flesh (of Jesus'
death at Calvary) is of no avail — has to be taken with the statement about
Jesus' ascension. Put together (according to Dunn), John is saying the only thing
that will resolve the scandalous claim in 6:51–58 is the ascension of Jesus (via
the cross) and the gift of the Spirit: 'It is in the believing reception of the Spirit

In the assertion, 'My words are Spirit and life' in 6:63c, then, we encounter a similar claim to that in 4:10–14,23, to the effect that Jesus' revelatory words *are* an experience of the Spirit bringing the divine eschatological wisdom and understanding that leads to 'life'. This claim, of course, goes to the heart of John's soteriology. For John, the fundamental problem of humankind is alienation from God expressed in unbelief, darkness, and ignorance of God. What is needed to overcome it is a Revealer, Light and Knowledge of God — which it is precisely the mission of the Son, empowered by the Spirit, to bring (cf. 8:28; 14:10; 15:22–24). Jesus' revelatory word sets people free (8:31–36); to 'hear' his word (in the full sense) is to experience the Spirit transforming through it and so to taste 'life' (6:63, and the Appendix below on 'Salvation, Revelation and the Death of Jesus in John').

3. Birth 'From Above' and Birth of 'Water and Spirit': John 3

This discourse is without doubt a guide to much which follows. In John 3:3 Jesus asserts that 'no one can see the kingdom of God without being born from above'. NRSV has, I think, rightly translated the Greek word

---

(footnote 21 continued)
of Christ, *the allos paraklētos*, that we eat the flesh and drink the blood of the incarnate Christ' ('John VI', 338). This undoubtedly contains a partial truth, but it does not yet quite do justice to 6:63c, which suggests it is reception of Jesus' Spirit-imbued *word*, rather than reception of the Paraclete *per se*, which is the issue. And according to John, Jesus' words already *'are'* (not merely 'shall be') 'Spirit and life'. 6:63c is most naturally taken to mean that the Spirit on Jesus in the ministry allows already some kind of 'eating' of the bread of life (christocentric God-revealing wisdom) which depends theologically, but not chronologically, on Jesus' giving his flesh and blood at Calvary. It might be possible to find an alternative explanation for 'the words I have spoken to you are "Spirit and life" ' — an interpretation which did not imply a realized eschatology — but such attempts are not invited by John's next words: 'But there are some of you who do not believe': this can only imply John regarded Jesus as accepting that some others *did* believe during the ministry. In the context, this must refer to people who experienced his words as Spirit-and-life, and so came in the ministry to eat of the bread from heaven: indeed, Peter goes on to claim as much: 'Lord . . . you have the words of eternal life; and we have believed, and have come to know you are the Holy One of God.' Cf. the debate between Turner and Burge on the eschatology of the Spirit in '*Anointed Community*', 257–61, 266–7.

anōthen as 'from above' rather than 'anew' or 'again': it is the same word John uses at 3:31 when he says, 'The one who comes from above is above all'. In that case, 'birth from above' is simply a circumlocution for 'birth *from God*', and Jesus' assertion to Nicodemus is that unless *God* generates a person he or she will not experience God's eschatological reign and its benefits. Nicodemus' question in 3:4 is then designed to probe this and elicits Jesus' clarification in 3:5: 'truly, I tell you, no one can enter the kingdom of God without being born of water and Spirit.'

The explanatory 'birth "of water-and-Spirit" ' here is a special construction called a *hendiadys* and must refer to a *unitary* event, a single metaphorical 'birth' accomplished through some sort of combination of water and Spirit. This excludes some quite common explanations of the verse, for example:

(a) it cannot mean, 'You must first be born naturally and later be born spiritually' (taking 'water' either as a euphemism for semen or as the breaking of the waters prior to actual birth) because that separates what John's construction combines.

(b) for the same reason it cannot mean, 'You must be "born from God" by first submitting to John's baptism and subsequently receiving the Spirit.

Those who have seen that the construction points to a unitary event have taken the phrase 'birth "of water-and-Spirit" ' to refer to (post-Easter) Christian baptism. But a problem with that interpretation is that in 3:10 Jesus assumes Nicodemus should be able to understand what he is talking about from his knowledge of Scripture and theology. In so far as the discourses of the Fourth Gospel are also deliberately shaped to break down the middle wall of partition between the historical Jesus and the risen Christ of John's own day, 'Christian baptism' may indeed be the reality in the church to which the evangelist secondarily points. But it is not the immediate meaning in the historical context. If 'birth "of water-and-Spirit" ' is something Jesus expects Nicodemus to understand from his knowledge of Scripture then, as Linda Belleville has shown, the most probable explanation is the promise in Ezekiel 36:25–27.[22]

> I will *sprinkle clean water* upon you, and you shall be clean from all your uncleannesses, and from all your idols I will cleanse you. [26] A new heart I will give you, and a new spirit I will put within you; and I will remove from your body the heart of stone and give you a

---

[22]Belleville, ' "Born of Water and Spirit": John 3:5', *TrinJ* 1 (1980), 125–41.

heart of flesh. [27] I will put *my Spirit* within you, and make you follow my statutes and be careful to observe my ordinances.

In this passage we have a promise of Israel's eschatological cleansing (with water) and of her almost simultaneous transformation through a new creative act of God which results in true filial obedience — i.e. new sonship — which is inspired and maintained by God's indwelling Spirit. The Ezekiel passage does not actually speak of a new '*birth* from God' by water and Spirit, but it is not hard to see how Jesus' language is entirely appropriate. God's act of re-creation which ensures a life of true obedient sonship is effectively a new birth/creation, and such an understanding of Ezekiel's promise was already evidenced in the pre-Christian *Jubilees* 1:23–25:

> . . . and I will *create* in them a holy spirit (cf. Ps. 51:12; Ezek. 36:26) and I will *cleanse* them so that they will not turn away from follow-ing me. . . . And they will do my commandments. And I shall be their *father* and they shall be *sons* to me. And they will be called '*sons* of the living God.

Here the gift of 'new creation' is identified as the gift of 'sonship'.

Nicodemus naturally asks *how* the Spirit is to bring about this act of new creation. Jesus' answer (in 3:12–18) is that it will come about (in parallel with the wilderness story) as people 'look' with authentic faith on the one 'lifted up' in the crucifixion/glorification.

John does not make matters more explicit in this passage, but in the light of what he says elsewhere we may perhaps fill in the 'how' a little more clearly. For John, the cross is the love of the Father for the world revealed in the self-giving of the Son. Not everyone, of course, sees that significance in the crucifixion; such a perspective is only unfolded to the person by the *Spirit's* activity (6:63). That is, when the Spirit acts through the witness to Jesus he enables the hearer to understand the cross and exaltation of Jesus, as the Son's revelation of the Father. And as the person *comes* to such belief this revelation transforms the heart of stone into the responsive heart of flesh. In short, the Johannine salva-tion of 'birth from above' is largely effected through the Spirit's il-lumination of the Christ event as the *divine* event of loving self-revelation. This sort of full Christian 'belief' clearly cannot come about before Jesus is 'glorified' through death, resurrection and the gift of the Spirit. During the ministry, 'belief' in Jesus is thus only partial. But the Spirit-imbued revelatory teaching of Jesus (6:63; 4:10–14,23) al-ready plays a vital function in bringing the disciples *towards* authentic Christian faith.

III. THE SPIRIT AS THE 'SPIRIT OF PROPHECY' IN JOHN 1–12

In the sections we have examined we can readily detect the Jewish understanding that the Spirit (as the 'Spirit of prophecy') gives charismatic revelation, inspired speech and spiritual wisdom/understanding. In and through Jesus who has the revelatory Spirit without measure (3:34), the supreme gift of saving revelatory wisdom is imparted. Undoubtedly John means that the gift of the Spirit to Jesus enables him to give a teaching which is the epitome of divine wisdom. But John wishes to affirm more than that too. He wants to say that *through* Jesus' teaching the Spirit reaches into the hearts of the hearers. So the Spirit on Jesus affects the hearer too. Accordingly, 6:63 tells us that for those who 'hear' his word and 'believe', Jesus' words are themselves an experience of Spirit and life. In the terms of John 4, his Spirit-imbued teaching is 'living water' that will well up to eternal life in the hearer, and already affords him or her some provisional measure of ability to worship in Spirit and in truth. In terms of John 3, the Spirit illuminates the ugly execution at Calvary so that people see it as the decisive revelation of the love of the Father revealed in the self-giving of the Son — and the anticipated effect of this spiritual 'seeing' of authentic belief is the dramatic re-creation of 'birth from above'. A similar point is made in John 6:60–63. All this is to say that people cannot understand the revelation of Jesus objectively given in his ministry or in his death unless the Spirit unfold that revelation to them. And only as the Spirit does so does he bring life.

Here (as at Qumran) it would seem that the 'Spirit of prophecy' has become a soteriologically necessary gift. John appears to be saying a person cannot experience salvation without the revealing activity of the Spirit unfolding the significance of the Christ-event to his or her heart. We shall see this confirmed in the teaching about the Paraclete, which we examine next.

Appendix: Salvation, Revelation and the Death of Jesus in John

We have seen that John very much stresses that Jesus imparts saving revelation: in 1:18 he is the decisive revelation of God; in chapter 3 it is spiritual *understanding* of God's revelation in the Son which brings new birth; in chapter 4 Jesus offers a woman at Samaria 'living water' which is to be understood as 'revelatory wisdom' afforded by the Spirit through the one who has the Spirit without measure (3:34); and in John 6:60–66 it is made clear that Jesus' life and death — which are the epitome of divine wisdom — are of themselves of no avail; only when the word is encountered in the Spirit (i.e. in revelation) does it bring 'life'. All this could suggest that, for John, salvation is by *revelation*. Bultmann was the first to spell out a controversial implication of this, namely: 'The thought of Jesus' death as an atonement for sin has no place in John'.[23] Essentially his case is as follows:

(1) For John, the real plight of man is alienation from God expressed in terms of unbelief, darkness and ignorance of God. These things *are* humankind's sin; they are not merely caused by it. But if that is true, then it follows that what a person needs is not an appeasing sacrifice; but a Revealer, Light, and Knowledge of God.

(2) Jesus provides precisely these things — not through the cross, but through the entirety of his ministry from incarnation to glorification; the cross is simply a final act of obedience, and the stepping-stone to glory.

(3) The one 'work' Jesus has come to do is to *reveal* 'life'. Thus, Jesus is able to offer the best wine, which has been kept to the last (2:1–11) and living water that will quench all thirst and bring the drinker eternal life (4:13–14). More especially Jesus is, and provides, the true bread people need to eat (6:35); the light

---

[23]R. Bultmann, *Theology of the New Testament* (London: SCM, 1952), vol. 2, part 3.

without which they remain in darkness (8:12; 9:5); the resurrection and life without which they are in death (11:25,26); the truth without which they are in sin, falsehood and death (8:21–36; 14:6), and so forth.

According to Bultmann, Jesus can offer these distinctively Johannine things precisely because of the distinctive Johannine christology. John emphasizes Jesus as the Son of Man who (uniquely) descends from heaven (3:13) and reascends 'where he was before' (6:62) through being 'lifted up' (3:13,14). The consequence, as Hultgren puts it, is that 'As Son of Man Jesus is the one who has shared an intimacy with the Father prior to his descent to earth and is therefore able to reveal the Father'. A similar message is announced in the Logos christology of the Prologue, and it is in 'the Son' christology (distinctively emphasized in John) too. The Son is 'sent' by the Father (cf. 3:17; 5:23) and will 'depart' and 'return' to the Father (13:1; 14:12, etc.). The import of this distinctive christological focus is that Jesus uniquely reveals the Father, as is underscored by the repeated theme of Jesus' unity with the Father (10:30,38; 14:8-11), and by the striking affirmations that, for example, 'the Jews' (i.e. unbelievers) do not know him, even if they think they do, because they do not know the Father who sent him (7:27,28); and conversely, and more dramatically, they do not know the Father, because they do not know Jesus (8:19), who alone can reveal him (1:18). The significance of ignorance concerning Jesus is now clear; it entails corresponding ignorance of *God*. And all this means that Jesus is sent, or given, not to die (as in Paul), but to become man, to become the Revealer, and thereby the Saviour of humankind: cf. John 17:3 'This is eternal life, that they know you, the only true God, and Jesus Christ whom you have sent'.

Jesus' one *work* (revelation) is accomplished in a diversity of 'works' which consist of (a) signs and (b) the words of Jesus (8:28; 14:10; 15:22–24) that interpret the signs, and go beyond them. But these signs and teachings all simply point back to Jesus and to his unity with the Father. He does not so much *give* the bread, drink, light, and life of salvation; rather he *is* these things. As Bultmann put it, Jesus' one work is to reveal, but what he reveals is only that he is the Revealer.

(4) In John it is Jesus' revelatory teaching that cleanses and renews the disciples: 'You are all made clean by the word I have spoken to you' (15:3; cf. 13:10; 17:17). Jesus' words are an experience of Spirit and 'life' (6:62); continuing in them frees men and women

from bondage (8:31–34), and the disciples are 'sanctified' or 'consecrated' through the word Jesus has spoken (17:17).

(5) Nowhere does John claim Jesus' death provides an atoning sacrifice — though such an understanding has occasionally mistakenly been read into what John says (1:29; 3:16; 17:9, etc.), and it has further been added by an ecclesiastical glossator at 1 John 1:7; 2:2 and 4:10. And even if these are not glosses, and John has occasionally accidentally presented Jesus' death in traditional terms as an atoning sacrifice, *it would still be a foreign element in his work* — it would not cohere with the writer's own soteriology as emerges clearly from the bulk of the Gospel.

The heart of Bultmann's case, then, is that the genuinely Johannine soteriology has no place for an atoning sacrifice, far less needs one. Salvation is by revelation, yielding new birth in knowledge of God. If we forget for a moment Bultmann's negative statements about the cross, he surely comes very close to the truth. To some extent John sees the Spirit as acting in and through Jesus' teaching, reaching into a person's heart and mind with enlightening wisdom to reveal Jesus and the Father, and thereby to change the heart by dispelling the clouds of disbelief and enthroning God in the believer's life and affections. Is John saying, then, that the Spirit brings people into filial love and obedience for God precisely by 'showing' them the Son? Is this how he thinks people are born again? There is undoubtedly important truth here; but it needs to be modified at three fundamental points.

1. We Cannot Marginalize the Cross in John

J.T. Forestell has convincingly shown that John regards the cross as the supreme moment of the revelation of God in John.[24] Thus John three times deliberately plays on the double meaning of the verb 'lifted up' (*hypsōthēnai*) — it can mean both 'to be crucified' and 'to be exalted': see 3:14,15; 8:28,29 ('When you have lifted up the Son of Man, then you will know that I am, and that I do nothing on my own authority but speak as the Father taught me'), and especially 12:32 ('And I, when I am lifted up from the earth, will draw all men to me'). To this John adds, 'He said this to show by what manner he was to die'; but that only clarifies the double meaning: for the crucifixion itself would hardly *naturally* be

---

[24]J. Forestell, *The Word of the Cross: Salvation as Revelation in the Fourth Gospel* (Rome: PBI, 1974), or, more briefly, A. Hultgren, *Christ and his Benefits* (Philadelphia: Fortress, 1988), ch. 8.

described as 'being lifted up from the earth', nor is it true that at the crucifixion Jesus drew all people to him — both descriptions are more obviously true of Jesus' exaltation and what follows. But the wordplay brings out most forcefully that the cross is itself part of Jesus' exaltation. Similarly, everything in the Gospel moves towards 'the hour' of Jesus' *glorification*. Now while Jesus 'ascension/exaltation' is part of his glorification, the real focus of the 'hour' is the crucifixion. Thus in John's equivalent to the Gethsemane prayer, in 12:27, we hear 'What shall I say, "Father, save me from this hour"? No, for this purpose I have come to this hour.' So when Jesus immediately beforehand says, 'The hour has come for the Son of Man to be glorified', he is talking about his crucifixion (12:23). All this means that the cross, for John, lies at the heart of the revelation that saves; it is the epitome of the divine wisdom revealed (6:51–58; cf. 3:14–16). It cannot be marginalized as Bultmann would have it.

2. We Cannot Remove the Element of Objective Atonement from the Cross

Forestell tries to keep within Bultmann's general thesis by arguing that in John the cross does not objectively atone for sin. The cross is simply the supreme revelation of God's love for us in Jesus; for from the cross we learn that Jesus is willing even to lay down his life for us. It is the revelation of that love that overcomes our unbelief and enmity. Thus are we saved — by revelation, not by any objective atonement.

This fails to satisfy.[25] If Jesus' death did not actually accomplish anything objective, then it is hard to see how it can be said he was laying down his life *for* people at all. And a God who proposed his Son should submit to crucifixion — apparently just so that the horror of his death might draw the more attention — could well be thought to reveal more perversity than love. No, Forestell is right that John sees the cross as the supreme revelation of God's love — but it only makes sense as a revelation of God's love if it is understood as something Jesus *had* to accomplish. As the common explanation of the early church was that Jesus died as an atonement for our sins, and as this is clearly also maintained in the Johannine epistles (1 Jn. 1:7; 2:2; 4:10), that is almost certainly how John's readers will have understood it. John's own reference to Jesus as the Lamb of God who takes away the sins of the world (1:29,32) would encourage such an interpretation right from the beginning of the book.

---

[25]M. Turner, 'Atonement and the Death of Jesus in John — Some Questions to Bultmann and Forestell', *EvQ* 62 (1990), 99–122.

3. The Gift of the Spirit Bringing About New Birth is Only Truly
Granted *After* the Cross (John 7:37–39; 20:22)

If salvation were brought about through Jesus' Spirit-imbued revelation
alone, in John, we would expect him to assert that the Spirit was given,
and new birth commenced, *in* the period of Jesus' ministry. For it was
then, above all, that Jesus gave revelation. Jesus does come very close
to that when he appears to offer the woman in Samaria 'living water'
that will well up to eternal life, and in 4:23 when he asserts that, 'The
hour is coming *and now is* when true worshippers shall worship the
Father in Spirit and in truth'. But John qualifies this with two other
passages, both of which locate the gift of the Spirit only *after* Jesus'
glorification: John 7.37–39 and 20:21,22. With 3:15,16, these passages
essentially shift the decisive moment of 'birth from above' *beyond* the
cross and resurrection.

Conclusion

John truly believes salvation is mediated by revelation. He believes the
Spirit was already reaching the hearts of men and women in Jesus'
ministry, bringing them a taste of what was to come, through Jesus'
Spirit-imbued teaching. But he knows the revelation then was incomplete and so the Spirit could not truly bring life within the time of the
ministry. Accordingly he depicts the disciples as unable to come to
authentic faith and understanding. The revelation Jesus imparts will
come to climactic focus on his own crucifixion and exaltation which at
once deals with sin objectively and at the same time shows what God
is prepared to do to win reconciliation. This complete, the Spirit can
now be given by Jesus. People are then able to come to true authentic
faith; his Spirit-imbued revelation can now take full, deep and transforming hold on their lives. But the Spirit does this precisely by focusing primarily on Jesus' cross and exaltation (3:14–16; 6:51–58). Quite
simply, Bultmann was right in what he asserted, but wrong in what he
denied.

Chapter Five

The Spirit in John 14–16: The Promise of the 'Paraclete'

John 1–12, sometimes called 'the Book of Signs',[1] can be seen as a great downswing of the pendulum of incarnation and revelation. Chapters 13–20 then provide the corresponding upswing of death, resurrection, and exaltation alongside the Father, all of which together John portrays as Jesus' 'glorification'.[2] The turning point is 13:1, '. . . Jesus knew that his hour had come to depart out of this world to the Father.'

To some extent the arrival of this 'hour' has been anticipated at 12:23,27, but there we are concerned with Jesus' last words of public ministry; and we finish on a note of the rejection of Jesus' witness, the lowest point of the pendulum-swing. The Light of the world hides himself from the people (12:36a) who refuse to believe (vv.37–41) or who partly believe, but are afraid to confess their faith (vv.42,43). With chapter 13, Jesus confines his attention to the disciples, and all of the following chapters focus on Jesus' death and exaltation and their consequences. The cross is itself portrayed as part of the upswing (rather than the nadir of Jesus' career) because (in the light of the resurrection) it is seen as the 'lifting up' of the Son of Man which offers the supreme revelation of the love of the Father in the Son, and draws all people to him (cf. 3:14–16; 8:28; 12:32).[3]

Chapters 13–17, appropriately referred to either as 'the farewell discourses' or as 'the testament of Jesus',[4] focus especially on how the

---

[1]C.H. Dodd, *The Interpretation of the Fourth Gospel* (Cambridge: CUP, 1953), 289; R.E. Brown, 1:cxxxviii–cxxxix.

[2]Hence R.E. Brown (*ibid.*) gives these chapters the title 'the Book of Glory'.

[3]For a brief survey of the theme see G.R. Beasley-Murray, *Gospel of Life: Theology in the Fourth Gospel* (Peabody: Hendrickson, 1991), ch. 3, 'The Lifting Up of the Son of Man'.

[4]J. Becker, 'Die Abschiedsreden Jesu im Johannesevangelium', *ZNW* 61 (1971), 215–46; R.W. Paschal, 'The Farewell Prayer of Jesus: A Study of the Gattung and Religious Background of John 17', unpublished PhD dissertation, Cambridge, 1982; E. Bammel, 'The Farewell Discourse of the Evangelist John and its Jewish Heritage', *TynB* 44 (1993), 103–16.

revelatory witness begun by Jesus will be continued to and through the disciples beyond his glorification. It is within this context that we encounter the uniquely Johannine teaching on the Spirit-Paraclete in John 14–16.

I. JESUS PROMISES THE SPIRIT AS 'ANOTHER PARACLETE': THE MEANING OF *PARAKLĒTOS* AND ITS CONCEPTUAL BACKGROUND

In three passages (14:16–26; 15:26,27; 16:7–15) John speaks of a coming gift of the Holy Spirit (14:26), or 'Spirit of Truth' (14:17; 15:26; 16:13: cf. *Jub* 25:14; *T. Jud.* 20:1–5; 1QS 3.18–25), to act as a 'Paraclete' (*paraklētos*: 14:16, 26; 15:26, 16:7). Of the three, it is the term 'Paraclete' that dominates here, and it is this term that is introduced first each time the Spirit is subsequently referred to (14:26; 15:26 and 16:7), so we must investigate its significance.

In Greek the word is formally a passive verbal adjective, 'one called alongside', especially to offer counsel, support or assistance in a court, or in some other potentially adversarial setting. Typically *paraklētoi* intercede on someone's behalf, e.g. to a higher authority, or support their case in juridical or other proceedings, acting as intercessors, mediators, or supporting witnesses. 'Advocate' may thus regularly provide the best translation, providing it is taken in a sufficiently general sense rather than merely to denote a professional legal representative (which was relatively unknown in Jewish and Greek trial procedures),[5] and indeed later Rabbinic Judaism came to use *p^eraqlit* (a loan word) for 'advocate' (cf. *Pirqe Aboth* 4.11). Such a sense would plainly fit 1 John 2:1, but because, however, the functions actually attributed to 'the Paraclete' in John are primarily teaching, revealing and interpreting Jesus to the disciples (with forensic functions only explicit at 15:26; 16:8–11[6]), other meanings of *paraklētos* have been championed. These include,

    (a) 'Comforter' — J.G. Davies argued for such a meaning by effectively deriving *paraklētos* from the verb *parakalein*, 'to

---

[5]While agreeing with K. Grayston ('The Meaning of PARAKLETOS', *JSNT* 13 (1981), 67–82, that *paraklētos* was by no means merely a technical term for a legal functionary in the pre-Christian world, it must nevertheless be said that Grayston plays down the sense of 'advocacy' that is common to most of the examples.

[6]It has occasionally been held against the sense 'advocate' that in these last passages the Spirit is accusatory rather than affording defence, and that this

encourage',[7] — but John does not use the verb at all, and Davies' etymology should prefer an active rather than a passive adjective (*parakalōn* rather than *paraklētos*).

(b) 'Exhorter' — so, roughly, C.K. Barrett, deriving this suggested sense from the related word *paraklēsis* ('exhortation', 'encouragement'), and understanding the Paraclete as the Spirit behind Christian *paraklēsis*.[8] But this faces similar difficulties to those mentioned above.

(c) 'Helper' — Bultmann argued this sense on the basis of somewhat forced linguistic and conceptual association with the multiple 'helpers' that he discovered in Mandean sources.[9] But (i) John speaks of but one Paraclete (on earth with the disciples), not a plurality of them; (ii) arguably the term *yawar*, which Bultmann translated from the Mandean sources as 'helper', rather means 'bearers of (heavenly) light', and (iii) these figures have no forensic (legal) functions in the Mandean literature. The term 'helper' (cf. GNB) could perhaps be argued on the rather different grounds that sponsors/intercessors/mediators afford help, and that the functions of Paraclete are too broad to permit a primarily forensic sense, but this term then suffers the double disadvantage that it loses the evident forensic overtones of 16:8–11, and may inappropriately suggest the inferiority of the Spirit to the disciples.

(d) 'Counsellor' — is the adopted translation of the RSV and NIV, and could find some basis in e.g. Philo, *On Creation*, 23, where the writer speaks of God — without any *paraklētos* (for there was none beside him; God was alone) — making the decision to confer benefits on the creation he was about to bring into being. Here 'advisor' or 'counsellor' is appropriate, and could easily account for the teaching and revealing role attributed to the Spirit in John (14:26; 16:13). But Philo's usage appears to be a relatively unusual 'transferred' sense, and appeal should probably be made to it only when it is clear that *paraklētos cannot* carry its more regular connotation of advocacy of someone's case.

(footnote 6 continued)
requires an active sense rather than the passive one to be inferred from the ending -(*ē*)*tos*. But in Jewish courts (and Greek) the one called as legal assistant or advocate for one party might well (like 'witnesses' in Jewish courts) be expected to adopt a prosecuting role in respect of the opposing party and his or her witnesses.
[7] J.G. Davies, 'The Primary Meaning of Παράκλητος', JTS 4 (1953), 35–8.
[8] C.K. Barrett, 'The Holy Spirit in the Fourth Gospel', *JTS* 1 (1950), 1–15.
[9] Cf. *Theology*, 1:164–83; 2:1–92.

'Advocate' is probably the most secure rendering (and re-adopted by NRSV), though we have yet to explain why John has chosen this term. Those that have accepted the sense 'advocate' have generally found the 'background' in the variety of angelic intercessor defender figures of the Old Testament and intertestamental literature (so Mowinckel and Johansson[10]). Otto Betz advances the more specific thesis that John modelled the Paraclete/Spirit of Truth primarily on Qumran's cosmic dualism (where the 'Spirit of Truth' is in cosmic conflict with the 'Spirit of Error'), but derived the more 'personal' aspects of the Paraclete, in his own portrayal, from Qumran's association of the 'Spirit of Truth' with the great angel Michael, leader of the host of spirits of Light.[11] The discussion is complex (and well reviewed for the English reader by Johnston and Burge[12]), but it needs to be said that to date these background studies (esp. Betz) have largely only succeeded in illuminating various *traits* of John's portrait of the Paraclete, rather than satisfactorily explaining the redactional whole. For that we shall have to examine the main characteristics of John's presentation.

II. THE PARACLETE AS JESUS' SUCCESSOR, SUBSTITUTE AND PRESENCE

Whereas John's picture of the Spirit-Advocate has little substantial background in the history of ideas, it is clearly modelled on *Jesus*. This point is made in two ways. First, it is suggested by Jesus' promise of *'another (allos)* Paraclete (of the same kind)'. The Greek *allos* regularly (not always) means 'another (of the *same* kind)', in contrast to *heteros* 'another (different)'. Second, it is to be inferred from the deliberate parallelism Raymond Brown has noted between what John says about Jesus and what is promised of the Spirit.[13] For example:

(a) both 'come forth'/are 'given'/are 'sent' from the Father into the world (3:16,17; 5:43; 16:27,28; 18:37//14:26; 15:26; 16:7, 8, 13).

---

[10]S. Mowinckel, 'Die Vorstellung des Spätjudentums vom heiligen Geist als Fürsprecher und der johanneische Paraklet', *ZNW* 52 (1933), 97–130. N. Johansson, *Parakletoi* (Lund: Gleerup, 1940).

[11]O. Betz, *Der Paraklet* (Leiden: Brill, 1963).

[12]G. Johnston, *The Spirit-Paraclete in the Gospel of John* (Cambridge: CUP, 1970), ch. 7; Burge, *Anointed Community*, 10–24.

[13]See R.E. Brown, 'The Paraclete in the Fourth Gospel', *NTS* 13 (1966–67), 113–32, or, more briefly, *idem*, 'Appendix V: The Paraclete', in *The Gospel According to Saint John* (2 vols.; London: Chapman, 1971), 1135–44.

(b) both are called 'Holy' (6:69//14:26) and are characterized by 'the Truth' (14:6//14:17; 15:26; 16:13).

(c) if Jesus is the great teacher (cf. 13:13,14), the Paraclete will 'teach you . . . all things' (14:26); and just as the Messiah bears witness to God and reveals all things (4:25,26; cf. 1:18; 3:34–36 etc.) — supremely himself and the Father — so too the Spirit-Advocate will witness to and reveal especially the glorified Son (15:26,27; 16:13,14).

(d) And as Jesus set out to convince and convict the world, which nevertheless did not 'receive' him (1:12 etc.), so too the Spirit-Advocate's task is to convince and convict the world (John 16:8–12), but the world does not receive him either (14:17; 15:18–26[14]).

Such observations indicate that (for John) Jesus and the Spirit-Paraclete are parallel figures, or, at least, have parallel functions. But we can be more precise. The *Sitz-im-Leben* of these parallels (as U.B. Müller has argued[15]) is the usual concern of the Jewish genre 'Farewell Discourses'; namely, to establish how the decisive initiative made by the man of God will be continued beyond his death. *Jesus has acted as the Paraclete so far; the Spirit is to take over that role.* So John portrays the Spirit as replacing Jesus and taking over his 'Paraclete' functions.[16]

But the Paraclete does not come to them merely as a replacement or substitute when Jesus departs. Such a concept is qualified in three ways:

(1) As 14:17e possibly indicates, the disciples already know the Paraclete as 'the Spirit of Truth' they have experienced through Jesus' revelatory wisdom. It is this same Spirit that will indwell them.[17]

(2) More important, the coming Spirit does not merely *replace* Jesus' presence but also mediates the presence of the Father and of the glorified Son to the disciple (14:16–26).

---

[14]See R.E. Brown, 1135 and 1140–1, for similar but more comprehensive lists; cf. also G. Bornkamm, 'Der Paraklet im Johannesevangelium', *Geschichte und Glaube, Gesammelte Aufsätze* (Munich: Kaiser, 1968) vol. 3, 68–89; Burge, *Anointed Community*, 139–42.

[15]U.B. Müller, 'Die Parakletenvorstellung im Johannesevangelium', *ZTK* 71 (1974), 31–78.

[16]For a brief treatment see John Wijngaards, *The Spirit in John* (Wilmington: Glazier, 1988), ch. 9, entitled 'Successor to Jesus'.

[17]Both the textual tradition and the interpretation of 14:17e is, however, in doubt. Beasley-Murray (242–3) reads the verbs in the assertions 'you know him' and 'he lives with you' as proleptic present tenses (for post-Easter possibilities).

Thus, having assured them of the gift of the Spirit in 14:16,17, in v.18 and 19 Jesus promises he will not leave the disciples 'as orphans', but will come to them in such a way that 'the world' will not see him — he will manifest himself to any disciple who loves him (14:21). When the meaning of this is pressed by Judas in 14:22, Jesus reasserts that (if a disciple love him) he *and* the Father will come and make their home with him (14:23). These promises of Jesus' return (with the Father) to the disciples cannot refer to Jesus' 'second coming' (for that event would be a public one the world would indeed see). Nor can Jesus' puzzling words refer to resurrection appearances, for those were not in any way dependent on the love of the disciples. Furthermore, such appearances could not naturally be described as the coming of the Father and the Son to dwell with the disciple (cf. 14:23). As these two affirmations of Jesus' return to the disciples are sandwiched by promises of the Spirit-Paraclete (14:14–17; 14:25,26), and as (in Judaism) the Spirit of prophecy was regarded as the presence of God in revelation, most exegetes infer that it is precisely the promised Spirit that will mediate the presence and self-revelation of Father and Son. Those who deny this (e.g. Beasley-Murray[18]) do not tell us how Christ and the Father are supposed to 'manifest themselves' to the disciple, nor explain (if they can) why John thinks the Spirit need be given at all.

(3) The Spirit is not merely Jesus' substitute, but is also Jesus' own emissary and executive power. That is, he is sent 'in Jesus' name' from the Father (14:26), or, Jesus himself 'sends' him (15:26; 16:7) from the Father.

With these qualifications we may agree at least in part with Raymond Brown that the Paraclete/Advocate is the Holy Spirit in a special role, *namely as the personal presence of Jesus in and with the Christian while Jesus is with the Father*.[19] For John, as for Luke-Acts and Paul, the Spirit is very much the Spirit of Christ.[20]

---

[18]*John*, 258; Cf. *Gospel*, 81–2.

[19]Brown, 1141 (a position which goes back to H. Windisch, *The Spirit-Paraclete in the Fourth Gospel* (Philadelphia: Fortress, 1968), who referred to the Paraclete as the *alter ego* of Jesus). We need not agree, however, with Brown's more provocative conclusion that John has taken the promises of Jesus 'appearing' at the Parousia and collapsed them into a coming in the Spirit instead (because the Parousia hope has failed: Brown, 1141–3). Cf. Burge, *Anointed Community*, 143–47.

[20]See, with different emphases, A.L. Mansure, 'The Relation of the Paraclete to the Spiritual Presence of Jesus in the Fourth Gospel', unpublished PhD dissertation, Boston 1950; Bornkamm, 'Der Paraklet'; E. Bammel, 'Jesus und der Paraklet in Johannes 16', in Lindars and Smalley (eds.), *Christ and Spirit*, 198–217;

III. THE SPIRIT-PARACLETE AS THE DISCIPLES' TEACHER

When Eskil Franck sought a title for his 1985 Uppsala doctoral dissertation on the Paraclete in the Gospel of John — a title which would sum up the main functions of the Paraclete — the title he chose was appropriately *Revelation Taught*.[21] If one is going to describe the Paraclete by his functions, argues Franck, then his is above all the function of Teacher rather than of Comforter, Advocate or whatever else. The basis for this claim is to be found largely in two key passages: John 14:26 and 16:12–15.

The first of these establishes that the Paraclete's task is to remind the disciples of Jesus' teaching and to clarify it to them: 'But the Paraclete, the Holy Spirit, whom the Father will send in my name, he will teach you all things, and bring to your remembrance all that I have said to you.' Dahl has rightly noted that this is a key to John's Gospel.[22] The point is that for all Jesus' teaching within the ministry, the disciples remain still utterly at a loss to comprehend. They are portrayed as unable to see the thrust and significance of what Jesus has been doing and saying. Only with the glorification of Jesus, and the granting of the Spirit, do they 'remember' and understand (cf. 2:22 where this is explicitly stated). Until the Spirit comes, it is as though all is in figures (16:25), not plain speech. That, of course, is part of the reason why, for John, authentic faith is not possible before the cross and exaltation. The Paraclete explains. As Burge aptly comments, at first quoting Mussner:

> Jesus' words 'are not only reproduced by memory but at the same time are unfolded for faith'. The Spirit works not simply mechanically, but interpretatively as well.[23]

But of fundamental importance is to note that what is interpreted is

---

(footnote 20 continued)
J.T. Forestell, 'Jesus and the Paraclete in the Gospel of John', in J. Plevnik (ed.), *Word and Spirit: Essays in Honor of D.M. Stanley* (Willowdale: Regis College, 1975), 151–97; A. Nossol, 'Der Geist als Gegenwart Jesu Christi', in W. Kasper (ed.), *Gegenwart des Geistes* (Freiburg: Herder, 1979), 132–54; Burge, *Anointed Community*, 137–47; J. Ashton, *Understanding the Fourth Gospel* (Oxford: OUP, 1991), 466–70 (positing what is to our mind a false antithesis between the Paraclete as successor and the Paraclete as presence of Christ).
[21] E. Franck, *Revelation Taught: The Paraclete in the Gospel of John* (Lund: Gleerup, 1985).
[22] N.A. Dahl, 'Anamnesis — Memory and Commemoration in Early Christianity', in *Jesus in the Memory of the Early Church* (Minneapolis: Augsburg, 1976, 11–29), 28.
[23] *Anointed Community*, 212.

precisely *Jesus'* revelation. John insists on this historical anchor. The Paraclete's task is not to bring *independent* revelation; first and foremost he explains and draws out the significance of the *historical* revelation.[24]

> For John this is crucial. When the church is beset by all manner of antichrist spirits she must remain in the word she received in the beginning, insists 1 John 2:24. And if the members of the church already have the anointing of the Spirit, and so need no other teachers (1 Jn. 2:27 — it is false teachers with new revelations John has in mind), what the anointing *teaches* is precisely to remain in him and in the word of him they first received.

A similar position, but with a different emphasis, is maintained in the second passage, John 16:12–15, which also serves as John's final comment on the Paraclete. Here the Paraclete is to lead the church into deeper and perhaps further truth:

> [12] I have yet many things to say to you, but you cannot bear them now. [13] When the Spirit of Truth comes, he will guide you into all the truth; for he will not speak on his own authority, but whatever he hears he will speak, and he will declare to you the things that are to come. [14] He will glorify me for he will take what is mine and declare it to you.

This has been taken in some circles as an indication that the Spirit will generate the church's dogma, and in others that the Spirit is concerned to provide prophetic timetables of the End events. But it has to be said that neither is in view. 'The Truth' into which the Spirit guides is *principally the truth Jesus has incarnated and taught*, or things in continuity with it. It clearly refers principally to things that Jesus *would* declare at their last meal together, if only the disciples could take it in (so 16:12). Within the discourse context, what Jesus evidently wished to be able to explain was the fuller significance of his own ministry (in which they had shared), and especially his forthcoming death and glorification. For the disciples had not grasped it fully, and worse, they were not ready so to do. Accordingly it was to be left to the Spirit to reveal those things and explain them later.

All this means, of course, that for John the Spirit's task is primarily to *clarify* to the disciples. It is to deepen their understanding of the truth already essentially revealed. The main task of the Spirit in John is to provide a particular sort of charismatic wisdom: that is, to bring true comprehension of the significance of the historical revelation in Christ. This is confirmed in the statement that the Spirit will not speak of his

---

[24]On this and on the section which follows, see Burge, *Anointed Community*, 211–17; cf. Wijngaards, *Spirit*, ch. 10; Franck, *Revelation*, *passim*.

own authority, but only the things that are Jesus' (16:13). This refers precisely to the things the Father has given the Son to reveal (see 16:15). The perspective is neatly summed up by Felix Porsch:

> Jesus brings the truth, and makes it present through his coming into the world; the Spirit-Paraclete opens up this truth and creates the entrance into it for believers.[25]

Even the reference in the last part of 16:13 to the Spirit as declaring 'the things that are to come' is not primarily to be understood as an affirmation that the Spirit will reveal the *church's* future. We need to remember that from the perspective of Jesus' speech the most important 'things to come' are precisely the events of Jesus' 'glorification' and the clarification of their significance. So it would be *possible* to take this whole piece to say virtually exactly the same as 14:26.[26]

That, however, would almost certainly be to restrict the scope of the saying too tightly. Jesus does, after all, say the Spirit will announce what he *shall* hear (not what he *has* heard), and it would be difficult to restrict 'all the truth' and 'the things to come' to the significance of Jesus' glorification alone, and absolutely nothing else. We would be wise to recognize that for John the *main* function of the Paraclete is to unveil the significance of the Christ-event; but that would probably also include revealing the *consequences* of the Christ-event for the church in different times and places later.

> The Apocalypse would provide a relevant example. Essentially the work shows the import of the exaltation of the Lamb to power (chs. 4–5) for the beleaguered church of John's day. The triumphant Lamb now sits in the throne, and opens the scrolls of destiny, and the seemingly all-powerful tyrannical Roman Empire will suffer eschatological judgement for its blasphemous demand of worship. Only the Lamb, and the church faithful to him, can possibly triumph; and the Son of Man walks in the midst of the churches to strengthen them.

The Spirit that illumines the Christ-event, and reveals Christ and his significance to believers, would naturally also be regarded:

    (1) as the source of *prophetic gifts* (for the Paraclete who gives wisdom that leads to spiritual understanding is evidently a

---

[25]*Pneuma*, 300; cf. H. Schlier, 'Der Heilige Geist als Interpret nach dem Johannesevangelium', in V. Kubina and K. Lehman (eds.), *Der Geist und die Kirche* (Freiburg: Herder, 1980), 165–79.

[26]C.K. Barrett, *ad loc.*, is dubious: he thinks that while 'the things to come' might be read that way from within the frame of reference of the original context, it will not be so read from the *readers'* context.

development of the more generally Jewish concept of the 'Spirit of prophecy'[27]).

(2) as the source of *teaching gifts* in the church (such as John's own).

(3) as the power of the congregations' *worship* in Spirit-and-Truth (cf. 4:24, and note the Paraclete is called the Spirit of Truth (14:17, etc.)) as the Spirit's revelation and illumination of the Christ-event elicits praise and worship, and

(4) as the power of the *new ethical life* of the believer as the Spirit convicts of sin (cf. 16:8), reveals the significance of Jesus' teaching for everyday life, and makes the disciple aware of the presence of the Father and the Son, and enables communion with them.

IV. THE PARACLETE AS 'ADVOCATE' AND THE CHRISTIAN MISSION (JOHN 15:26,27; 16:7–11)

So far we have noted that Jesus promises the Spirit as another Paraclete *like* Jesus, that he is expected to mediate the presence of the Father and the exalted Son, and that this Spirit of Truth would clarify to faith the significance of Jesus' words and deeds. It remains unclear (so far) why the Spirit has been called an *Advocate* at all, and it is not difficult to see why a number of scholars have suggested that such is simply a mistaken translation of the word *paraklētos*. That view, however, fails to take sufficiently seriously John's extensive and polemical presentation of Jesus' ministry and teaching under the metaphor of a cosmic *trial*.[28] It is within this literary setting that the forensic character of the totality of the Spirit's work becomes clear, and the translation 'advocate' (in the sense above) becomes justified, even required.

Within John's 'trial' setting, the issue contested is whether or not Jesus truly is the final manifestation of God, very Son from the Father, whom to know is 'Life' transcending the possibilities offered by

---

[27] For the Spirit and prophecy in the Johannine community, see e.g. the provocative suggestions in M.E. Boring, 'The Influence of Christian Prophecy on the Johannine Portrayal of the Paraclete and Jesus', *NTS* 25 (1978), 113–23; cf. also M.E. Isaacs, 'The Prophetic Spirit in the Fourth Gospel', *HeyJ* 24 (1983), 391–407.

[28] See especially A.E. Harvey, *Jesus on Trial: A Study of the Fourth Gospel*, (London: SPCK, 1976); A.A. Trites, *The New Testament Concept of Witness* (Cambridge: CUP, 1977), 78–124; or, for a briefer review, A. Billington, 'The Paraclete and Mission in the Fourth Gospel', in Antony Billington, Tony Lane and Max Turner (eds.), *Mission and Meaning: Essays presented to Peter Cotterell* (Carlisle: Paternoster, 1995), 90–115 (esp. 95–101).

Judaism (cf. 20:31!). As the sent one, Jesus has a mission to convince 'the world' of God's saving truth, which he incarnates and reveals, and this 'mission' dominates the Gospel (and within 5:31–47 alone Jesus points to five 'witnesses' on his side): he is the chief 'advocate' of the case with which the disciples have become identified. The impending removal of Jesus through cross and exaltation cannot be allowed to leave the disciples 'as orphans'[29] — i.e. without an advocate for their case. (In Judaism, children (and women, usually) could not give evidence in court, their fathers represented them; so an *orphan* is powerless — unless, that is, he or she has some other *advocate*, which is precisely the point here.) Furthermore, neither may the case God has commenced through the advocate Jesus be lost by being reduced to silence through his departure. Rather, the disciples are now 'sent' as Jesus was 'sent' (20:21; cf. 17:17,18), and the Spirit from the heavenly Lord is given to them to take over the earthly Jesus' advocacy of the case (15:26,27; 16:7b–11).[30] It is clarified at 15:26,27 that the Spirit assumes Jesus' role as the chief, and the witness of the disciples is subordinated to his:

> When the Paraclete comes, whom I shall send to you from the Father, even the Spirit of Truth, who proceeds from the Father, he will bear witness to me; [v.27] And you also are witnesses, because you have been with me from the beginning.

The forensic thrust of the Spirit's function as 'advocate' is most explicitly brought out in 16:8–11. 16:8 affirms that when the Paraclete comes he will 'expose', or 'convict',[31] the world with respect to sin, righteousness

---

[29]Correctly NIV, NRSV; RSV's 'desolate' misses the point. Cf. D.E. Holwerda, *The Holy Spirit and Eschatology in the Gospel of John* (Kampen: Kok, 1959), 26–85, esp. 38–48.

[30]There is evidently no tension for John between the ideas of the Spirit being advocate for the disciples and his being advocate for the case of Jesus. The latter is of course the main emphasis, but the disciples have become committed to this case: it is theirs too.

[31]*Elengchein* can mean reprove, shame, convict, blame, resist, interpret, expose, investigate. At 3:20 the evil person comes not to the light lest his evil deeds be 'exposed', and in 8:46 Jesus asks 'which of you can prove me in the wrong', i.e. show me to be a sinner — the only other use. 'Expose' is thus perhaps the most satisfactory translation, but in a sense which comes very close to 'convict'. Curiously, Brown and Porsch have taken this to mean that the Paraclete comforts the *disciples* by exposing to *them* the true sinfulness of the world, the righteousness of Jesus, and the judgement coming on the world (cf. M.F. Berrouard, 'Le Paraclète, défenseur du Christ devant la conscience du croyant (Jean 16,8–11)', *RSPT* 33 (1949), 361–89). But this hardly tallies with the context,

and judgement. This is then spelt out in the rather difficult verses 9–11,[32] which we take to mean:

(a) The Spirit exposes/convicts the world with respect to sin, by pressing the case to the world that its disbelief in Jesus *is really the very essence of* its sin. Such unbelief springs from rejection of God's self-revelation in nature and in his dealings with Israel (inscripturated in the Hebrew Bible), and, more especially in the witness of the disciples to Jesus. It is not merely a matter of ignorance.

(b) The Spirit exposes/convicts the world with respect to *righteousness*. That is, while the world considered Jesus *unrighteous* — and so justly executed — the Spirit presses the case that Jesus' death and his departure from the world was in fact his *exaltation* to the Father's side, and so vindication of Jesus' righteousness.

(c) The Spirit exposes/convicts the world with respect to judgement. That is, he presses the case that the prince of 'the world' stands condemned. It was the evil power whose grip turns men into 'the world' that killed and continues to oppose Christ — but his condemnation is shown in Jesus' vindication.[33]

All this could at first glance suggest the Spirit acts independently of the believer. But this overlooks the fact that the Spirit-Advocate is given *to the disciples* (not merely into the world, alongside them). And the import of the connection of 16:8–11 with 16:12–15 must be observed. The Spirit will convict the world of sin, righteousness and judgement *precisely by revealing the truth, and teaching its significance, to and through the disciples.* 16:8–11 does not mean the Spirit offers *independent* witness;

(footnote 31 continued)
which is a trial before God in which 'the world' stands as the chief opponent. The point is not that the disciples have to be reassured the world is wrong; but that the opposing 'world' needs to be brought to silence and convicted by the witness for Jesus.

[32] The sense is probably best rendered by the JB and NEB (rather than by RSV or NIV): i.e. 'First, about sin — *in that* they refuse to believe in me. Then, about righteousness — *in that* I am going to the Father and you can see me no longer. Finally, about judgement — *in that* the Prince of the World has been condemned'. RSV and NIV have 'because' where other versions have 'in that' — and this obviously leads to an entirely different sense, for which Carson offers the most able defence. Limits of space unfortunately preclude further discussion.

[33] In the above, we come closer to Beasley-Murray, 280–3, (cf. 'Ministry', 76–7), than to the alternatives offered by Brown; Carson; Billington, 'Paraclete', 102–8; and, Burge, *Anointed Community*, 208–10.

John knows of no witness by the Spirit that is not witness *through* the church. But equally, the disciples only give their witness as ones to whom the Spirit has revealed Jesus and the significance of his life, death and resurrection. *It is thus as Teacher and Revealer, that the Spirit will also be 'Paraclete' or Advocate.* In enabling the disciples to understand these things, as Teacher and Revealer, the Spirit provides the believers with the folio for their case against the opposing world. The Revealer functions as the church's advocate both in the support such understanding gives to the believing community and in the powerful witness he enables *through* them to and against the opposing parties.[34]

PRELIMINARY CONCLUSIONS

We must draw together the threads of John's teaching on the Spirit in the next chapter. But three significant conclusions need not await that analysis:

(1) It will be evident the extent to which the teaching concerning the Paraclete is based in the Jewish conception of the Spirit as the 'Spirit of prophecy'. The Paraclete is none other than the Spirit affording both charismatic revelation and the wisdom to be able to integrate this into theology and praxis.

(2) It will simultaneously be clear that the Spirit-Paraclete is more than a *donum superadditum*, a 'second grace' (cf. Ch. 3). (a) In the period after Jesus' ascension the Spirit-Paraclete will be the only way by which the Father and the Son can communicate their presence to the disciples. In a Gospel in which to know the Father in the Son is itself 'eternal life' (cf. 17:3), this can only mean that the Spirit of prophecy is 'soteriologically' necessary. (b) It would appear that the Spirit's illumination (through the gift of charismatic wisdom) is also soteriologically necessary in the sense that it is required for the authentic *understanding* of the gospel which enables re-creation.

(3) At the same time, too, the Spirit-Paraclete is every bit as much 'the driving force of mission' as in Luke-Acts. His very title 'Advocate' reminds us of his central function in this Gospel, namely, to continue the cosmic trial, by providing effective

---

[34]For a similar understanding of the revelatory/teaching functions of the Spirit as part of the Spirit's role as advocate see, e.g. Porsch, *Pneuma*: 222–7; Burge, *Anointed Community*, 37–8; 201–21; Beasley-Murray, *Gospel*, 70–81; Billington, 'Paraclete', 101–2, 110–11.

witness to the Christ-event and to the 'life' of God obtained in communion with the Son. But hereby the antithesis that a number of theologians have driven between the soteriological Spirit in John and the prophetic Spirit of mission in Luke-Acts is unmasked as a false one.

Chapter Six

The Gift of the Spirit to and in the Johannine Church

In this chapter we shall address four questions which take us to the centre of the debate between classic Pentecostals and more traditional evangelicalism. (i) John 20:22 appears, at first sight, to record a gift of the Spirit to the disciples. But was it a real giving of the Spirit, or merely a promise of some future bestowal? If it was indeed a real granting of the Spirit, then, (ii) what was the significance of this gift? Was it the full gift of the Paraclete, or in some way a lesser gift? If it was something less than the full granting of the Paraclete, and the disciples receive the Spirit as Paraclete *beyond* the pages of John's Gospel, (iii) does this mean the disciples have a two-stage experience of the Spirit? And (iv) does that, in turn, imply that Christians in John's church were expected normally to receive the Spirit in two such stages?

I. WAS JOHN 20:22 A GRANTING OF THE SPIRIT BY JESUS?

Conscious of the 'competing' account of Luke-Acts, to the effect that the Spirit was given to the 120 on the day of Pentecost (rather than to a small group of disciples on the evening of Easter Sunday, as John 20:19-23 implies), Theodore of Mopsuestia (c. 350–428) argued that the Johannine passage was not about an actual granting of the Spirit in any way. For him, it was merely an enacted symbolic *promise* of the Spirit which came at Pentecost. The view was condemned by the Council of Constantinople (553), but has been revived with erudition by Don Carson, who argues for the translation 'And with that he breathed, and said, "Receive the Holy Spirit" '.[1] For Carson, Jesus' exhalation was a sign the Spirit will proceed from or through the Son, while the imperative, 'Receive the Holy Spirit' like so many of the imperatives of John,

---

[1]Carson, 652.

has merely future reference.[2] I confess I find this explanation difficult for three reasons.[3]

(1) The verb —ἐμφυσάω (*em-phusaō*) cannot, as far as I am aware, mean simply *'exhale'*; rather, as its roots suggest (*em-* is from the proposition *en*, meaning 'in'), it means 'blow into', 'insufflate' (or perhaps 'blow onto' at Ezek. 21:31[4]). Had John meant simply to say Jesus 'exhaled' he would undoubtedly have used either *ek-phusan* or (less probably) *ekpnein*.

(2) The second reason for doubting Don Carson's interpretation is that the verb John uses was a rare one. It was, however, used in two most memorable passages: in Genesis 2:7, to refer to God breathing the breath of life into Adam, and in Ezekiel 37:9, to refer to the analogous new-creation breathing of the Spirit of life into Israel's dry bones. It is thus not surprising that when Wisdom 15:11 uses the verb it is in what is all but a quotation of Genesis 2:7, as are the occasions in Philo.[5] In short, the very use of the rare verb 'to insufflate' would tend to *evoke* Genesis 2:7 (and the related text in Ezekiel 37:9), and the *acts* of God in which he breathes the breath of life/Spirit into beings.

(3) In Wisdom 15, and in Philo's references to Genesis 2:7, what is 'breathed in' to the first man is not simply 'breath of life' but, more precisely, *divine Spirit*.[6] When John uses the evocative verb ἐνεφύσησεν (*enephusēsen*), and then immediately couples this with the words 'Receive the Holy Spirit', his Jewish readers would surely understand that this was an actual incident of insufflation with the Spirit, comparable with those in the Old Testament and in their own interpretive traditions: i.e. such

[2]See Carson, 649–56, for the details.

[3]Carson's position has been subjected to critical scrutiny by T.R. Hatina, 'John 20,22 in its Eschatological Context: Promise or Fulfilment?', *Bib* 74 (1993), 196–219.

[4]Carson argues Sirach 43:4 uses the verb in question to say the sun 'breathes *out* fiery vapours', but here the majority of texts use the verb *ek-phusan* ('out-breathe').

[5]*The Worse Attacks the Better*, 80; *Allegorical Laws*, 1.33 (cf.37); 3.161; *Creation*, 135; *On Noah's Work as a Planter*, 18, etc.

[6]While Philo knows that what is inbreathed according to the LXX of Gen. 2.7 is *pnoē* ('breath of life'; see *Allegorical Laws*, 1.33, and especially 42), he usually interprets this as divine *pneuma* (*Allegorical Laws*, 1.37; 3.161 (where he actually replaces *pnoē* by *pneuma* in the citation), *On Creation*, 135; *The Worse Attacks*, 80, 83; *On Noah's Work*, 18,24,44).

readers would effectively paraphrase 20:22, 'He breathed the breath of life (into them[7]), saying, "Receive the Holy Spirit" '. We need not, of course, envisage a literal act of insufflating each disciple or a literal breathing out of the Spirit upon them all. The *enephusēsen* may simply represent the narrator's way of expressing the overall theological *significance* of this resurrection appearance, and especially of the effect of Jesus' words, 'Receive the Holy Spirit', understood perhaps as a performative utterance (one bringing about the action described). Whether or not this last suggestion is correct, it seems clear the Evangelist's use of *enephusēsen* was intended to indicate that somehow through the episode Jesus actually *imparted* the Spirit of new creation. We may proceed to our next question.

II. WHAT WAS THE NATURE OF THE GIFT OF THE SPIRIT GRANTED IN JOHN 20:22?

1. The Johannine Pentecost?

If the resurrection appearance with its restoration and recommissioning of the disciples echoes Genesis 2:7 and Ezekiel 37:9, then the gift of the Spirit must, by the same token, be linked with the re-creative Spirit of John 3:3,5: the Spirit who brings new creation 'birth from above' or new 'life', as fulfilment of Ezekiel 36:25–27. This, of course, fits well enough with John 3:14–16 which anticipates that the 'birth from above' will be accomplished only through perceiving the cross with the understanding of faith. It also chimes well with John 6:63–66 and 7:38,39, the latter of which most clearly emphazises that the 'living waters' of the Spirit only begin to burst through from the believer after Jesus' glorification. Accordingly, R.E. Brown's commentary has argued that John has located the *definitive* gift of the Spirit at John 20:22 (and expects no other). This is 'the Johannine Pentecost': here and now the Spirit is given as new birth, as baptism of Spirit, as living waters and as Paraclete. Brown's position has received wide support,[8] and we may briefly rehearse the main arguments:

---

[7]Accordingly Tatian, D, and syr[cur], add the pronoun αυτοις (*autois*, 'them').

[8]Brown's position (2:1022–4, 1036–45) was partially anticipated by (*interalios*) Bernard (1928); Bauer (1933); Archimandrite Cassien, *La Pentecôte johaninique* (Paris: Editeurs Réunis, 1939); Bultmann; C.K. Barrett; C.S. Mann, 'Pentecost, The Spirit, and John', *Theol* 62 (1959), 188–90; Betz, *Paraklet*, 165–9; H. Schlier,

(1) Throughout the Gospel, John has tied the gift of life to the cross and exaltation, and to authentic faith which is only fully possible after these events (cf. Jn. 3; 6; 13:8–10).

(2) John 7:39 specifically ties the gift of the Spirit to Jesus' glorification (i.e. his cross and exaltation), and this connection is dramatized at the cross when the spear-thrust releases blood and water (19:34), echoing the promise that streams of living water (= Spirit) will flow from his midst (7:38[9]).

(3) By 20:19 Jesus' ascension-glorification is accomplished. In John 20:17 Jesus forbids Mary to touch him because he *is ascending* (but has not yet fully ascended) to the Father. But later this process of ascension must be complete, for John has Jesus actually invite Thomas to thrust his hand into his wounds (20:27); so the ascension was probably completed for John between the Sunday morning and evening.[10]

(4) This also tallies with the Paraclete promises; Jesus affirmed that he needed to go away (in death) for the Paraclete to be given (16:7), and this condition too is clearly fulfilled. Thus, according to Brown, Jesus on the resurrection evening gives the Spirit, that brings to life and shall be with the disciples henceforth as another Paraclete.

(5) The Spirit given here is contextually linked with mission (see esp. 20:21 and 20:23), and so must be the Paraclete who (according to Jn. 14–16; esp. 16:8–10) prosecutes Jesus' case through the disciples.

To these, some further arguments have been added since Brown made his case, including:

(*footnote 8 continued*)
'Zum Begriff des Geistes nach dem Johannesevangelium', in J. Blinzer, O. Kuss and F. Mussner (eds.), *Neutestamentliche Aufsätze* (Regensburg: Pustet, 1963), 234–6, and F.M. Braun, *Jean le Théologien* (Paris: Lecoffre, 1966), 225ff. The case is broadly accepted and further developed in different ways by M.A. Chevallier, '«Pentecôtes»', 301–14; Schnackenburg, 321–8; Beasley-Murray, 380–84, and *Gospel*, 79–81; R.W. Lyon, 'John 20:22, Once More', *Asbury Theological Journal* 41 (1988), 73–85; Burge, *Anointed Community*, 114–49, and Hatina, 'John 20,22'.
[9]This of course assumes the 'christocentric' punctuation of 7:37,38 against which we argued above.
[10]See Bultmann, 691.

(6) John 20:22 forms a fitting narrative closure to the Fourth Gospel, and to its prominent theme of the Spirit. As the Gospel opened with an account of creation through the Word (= Jesus: cf. 1:3), so it closes with the new creation brought about by the Word.[11] If in the beginning God breathed the breath of life into Adam, Jesus too, full of the Spirit (3:34; 7:38 (assuming the christocentric punctuation)) imparts the life-giving Spirit from his inner being (20:22[12]). And if, near the beginning of the Gospel, the Baptist announces Jesus as the one who will take away the sins of the world and baptize with Holy Spirit (1:29 (36) and 1:32), John 20:20–23 is about the restoration of the disciples, their being baptized with Spirit, and their related ability to loose the world's sins (or to retain them).[13]

(7) In accordance with the promise that Jesus will not leave the disciples 'as orphans', but grant them the Paraclete (14:16–18), John leaves no chronological gap between Jesus' resurrection-ascension and the coming of the Spirit. Jesus himself fulfils his promise by imparting the Spirit before the completion of his resurrection appearances.[14]

The strengths of this thesis are clear, the more so if one considers that the Gospel originally ended with 20:30,31, and if one refuses prematurely to harmonize John with Acts. Even if one could be sure the writer of the Fourth Gospel knew of Pentecost (and that is often doubted), one might surmise he has brought forward the decisive moment of the gift in order to bring out its theological relationship to Jesus' glorification in death and resurrection-exaltation. One must let John be John, and listen to his distinctive witness, before reflecting on its relationship to the witness of other writers.

That said, however, we need to note that the 'Johannine Pentecost' has problems of its own *from within the Gospel itself.* These start, of course, with the relatively minor consideration that the very term

[11]Hatina observes that the Targum to Ezekiel 37:9 comes close to John 20:22 in that it describes God's *Memra* (Word) as the agent who decrees the giving of the Spirit: so 'John 20,22', 216.

[12]So Burge, *Anointed Community*, 87–98, 137–47.

[13]See J. Swetnam, 'Bestowal of the Spirit in the Fourth Gospel', *Bib* 74 (1993), 556–76. Swetnam, however, bifurcates the gift of the Spirit: at the cross (19:30) the Spirit is given for the discerning of truth, in 20:22 as empowering for the mission that mediates forgiveness. Unfortunately, for John the post-resurrection gift of the Paraclete is necessary to *both.*

[14]Burge, *Anointed Community*, 133, 136–9, 148–9.

'Pentecost' gives too much priority to a Lucan agenda.[15] Much more important, however, are two other considerations: first, the endowment with the Spirit at 20:22 is made *before* the conditions for the promise of the Paraclete, announced in John 14–16, have been completely fulfilled. Second, there is an especially conspicuous absence of any of the distinctively 'Paraclete' activities in the narrative material which follows 20:22,23 (the Spirit does not bring to memory and clarify Jesus' teaching, nor do the disciples bear witness — they fail even to convince Thomas, let alone 'the world'). Let us examine some significant aspects of these two problems in more detail:

(a) Important to Brown's construction is the argument that by 20:19 the glorification is complete, and thus the conditions for the granting of the Spirit are achieved. But is this reading really convincing? It is of course true that the cross and resurrection are part of the glorification in John, but this is only *complete* in the full return to the Father and to the Son's pre-temporal glory (cf. 17:5). That 'ascension' is not completed until Jesus is removed totally from this world into heaven. And while resurrection appearances continue (as in 20:26–29 and ch.21) that process remains incomplete. Jesus' own post-resurrection insistence that he has *not yet* ascended (20:17) would not only tend to confirm the point just made, but also suggest John was pointedly emphasizing that Jesus was neither yet fully 'departed', nor fully 'glorified', and so the condition for the giving of the Spirit in fulness not yet met (cf. 7:39).

> To argue the process must be complete by 20:27 because Jesus allows Thomas to touch him, whilst he had not allowed Mary so to do, appears artificial. Mary is bidden not to 'cling onto' Jesus, because he has not left this world, but shall do so; Thomas to touch his wounds if this alone will bring him to faith. The different instructions arise out of the different needs of the disciples, not out of different stages in Jesus' ascension process.[16]

So the conditions for the coming of the abundance of the Spirit, the arrival of the Paraclete, are as yet unfulfilled: Jesus is not yet *fully* glorified.

(b) Burge's assertion that there is no (Johannine) reason why Jesus

---

[15] As is noted by Brown himself (1039; against Cassien); cf. also Schnackenburg, 3.325–6.

[16] For substantiation and literature see Turner, 'Spirit in John', 28–9, and nn. 38–9.

could not be present at the bestowal of the Spirit-Paraclete entails an unnatural reading of 16:7. While granting that 'send'
(*pempô*) in some contexts might merely carry the sense
'commission' without implying a spatial separation between
'sender' and receivers, the collocation of 'Unless I *depart* . . . the
Paraclete will not come to you; but if I go away, I will *send* him
to you' precisely suggests Jesus will *not* be present at the giving
of the Paraclete. Similar points could be made about the perspective of 14:26 and 15:26. The three sayings taken together evoke
the more general Christian tradition of the sending of the Spirit
from the Father in heaven, with the Son at his right hand (cf.
Acts 2:33; Gal. 4:6, etc.). Unless one had very strong reasons to
the contrary, one would not naturally think of 20:22 as matching
the earlier statements about the sending of the Paraclete from the
Father and from the Son.

(c) A related point is that Brown's hypothesis fails to take real account of the Johannine focus on the character of the Paraclete as
Jesus' *replacement*, and the *substitute* for his presence. The point is
that the Paraclete is the Spirit as the presence of Jesus when Jesus
is in heaven; the Paraclete comes to replace Jesus and to mediate
his presence. But if 20:22 is the giving of the Paraclete, the reader
can only be surprised that Jesus *himself* continues to appear (in
20:26–29 and in ch. 21). From a Johannine perspective, important
aspects of the giving of the Paraclete are *unnecessary* until Jesus
is withdrawn totally into heaven. The other side of the coin is
that appearances of Jesus should be unnecessary when at last the
Paraclete is given. *From the perspective of everything taught in John
14–16, Thomas should be convinced through the Paraclete active in the
disciples.*

(d) It is not surprising, then, that a number of scholars have questioned
whether 20:22 was indeed intended to depict the definitive gift of
the Spirit. Important as the allusion to Genesis 2:7 is, nothing in the
narrative which follows hints that the disciples have at last been
definitively baptized with Spirit (as 1:33 promises), awash with
living waters (as 7:38,39 implies), and empowered by God's own
self-revealing presence as the heavenly Advocate. We do not read
that their hearts burned within them as they came to new understanding (as we do in Luke), nor even that they rejoiced (that is
mentioned *before* the reception of the Spirit, in 20:20). One of the
disciples (Thomas) is not even present with them on this allegedly
'definitive' occasion. When Jesus then appears a week later the disciples are still behind locked doors. And the Johannine traditions in

chapter 21 suggest mildly bemused disciples still in some respects lacking *comprehension*, let alone missionary zeal and purpose. They go back to their old familiar routine — the life of fishing. All this means that in narrative terms there is no evident consequence of the gift at 20:22: no reaction in the disciples, no Paraclete activity through or in them in the following scenes, nor any indication as to whether Thomas received this 'definitive gift'. In brief, in pneumatological terms, John 20–21 is so anticlimactic that a question mark is raised as to whether 20:22 is the sole and definitive gift of the Paraclete and of the 'living waters' promised earlier.

Prominent traits of John's own narrative thus appear to subvert the impression that John 20:22 is the fulfilment of the promises of the Paraclete. It is telling that Schnackenburg (who largely accepts the 'Johannine Pentecost' explanation) is forced to admit, 'the functions which the Paraclete is to take over after Jesus' departure . . . do not yet come into view in 20:22 . . . the effect of the Spirit in the sense of the Paraclete is not yet focused upon'.[17] And for Carson, we may remember, this 'real absence' of the Paraclete was one of the major reasons for taking John 20:22 as a purely symbolic act referring to Pentecost. Others (including Holwerda, Dunn, and Porsch) have felt compelled by this absence of the Paraclete to distinguish the gift of the Spirit in John 20:22 in various ways from the giving of the Spirit as the Paraclete, and to infer that John does not record the latter because it fell beyond the chronological scope of his narrative (as with the other gospels).

2. An Alternative Explanation of John 20:22?

We may leave aside the line of interpretation from Chrysostom to Holwerda which claims John 20:22 is a special gift of the Spirit to the apostles alone, granting them the power to forgive sins. This view faces insurmountable difficulties, not least that it fails to relate the Spirit with the evident new-creation theme implied in the verb *enephusēsen*.[18]

Picking up on the latter allusion to Genesis 2:7 and Ezekiel 37:9, a number of interpreters have developed the kind of contrast Westcott hinted at when he spoke of the paschal gift as a 'new life . . . communicated to them by Christ' which 'was the necessary condition for the descent of the Holy Spirit on the day of Pentecost'.[19] This type of contrast

[17]Schnackenburg, III, 326.
[18]For details and criticism see Turner, 'Spirit in John', 32–3.
[19]Westcott, 295.

has been elucidated by H.M. Ervin and others to support the classical
Pentecostal paradigm that new birth (= John 20) temporally precedes
'baptism in Holy Spirit' (=Acts 2//John 14–16).[20] Even Dunn, whose
work was essentially an attempt to demolish the classical Pentecostal
paradigm, has been prepared to admit that John 20 portrays the apostles'
new creation and that John thought of this as temporally separated from
a later (implied) post- ascension coming of the Paraclete. He differs from
Ervin and other Pentecostal interpreters mainly in his energetic denial
that John would have considered this to provide a normative pattern for
the period *following* Pentecost (see below[21]).

That John intended his reader to understand the event of 20:22 in
terms of eschatological new creation is, in our view, virtually assured
by the allusions to Genesis 2:7/Ezekiel 37:9.[22] The pertinent questions
are how this relates to what has gone before, and, more important, how
it relates to the fulfilment of the Paraclete promises.

(1)   On the first of these issues, we suspect that the tendency (espe-
      cially in Dunn and Burge) to make John 20:22 the decisive es-
      chatological *novum* underestimates the strong element of
      inaugurated eschatology in the period of the ministry itself.[23]
      While granting that John cannot envisage full authentic faith
      until after the glorification of Jesus, we must not overlook the
      fact that John has his own counterpart to the inaugurated es-
      chatology of the Synoptic Gospels. In the latter, the kingdom of
      God is made present in Jesus' ministry, not merely in exorcisms
      and healings, but above all in the self-revealing reconciling love
      of the Father extending even to the despised tax-collectors and

---

[20]H.M. Ervin, *These Are Not Drunken, As Ye Suppose* (Plainfield: Logos, 1968),
25–33; *idem, Spirit-Baptism: A Biblical Investigation* (Peabody: Hendrickson, 1987),
14–21.

[21]Dunn, *Baptism*, ch. 14, esp. 178–82.

[22]M. Wojciechowski, 'Le Don de L'Esprit Saint dans Jean 20.22 selon Tg.Gn 2.7',
NTS 33 (1987), 289–92, does not grant allusions to the creative/re-creative Spirit
here, preferring instead to interpret the references in the light of the targums to
Genesis 2:7, which he believes depict the divine breath not as the source of life,
but rather as that of *word* or *speech*. Accordingly John 20:22 is a promise of
inspired speech: tongues and preaching (so also Lyons, 'John 20:22', 80). But he
is surely mistaken. What is referred to in *Onqelos, Neofiti* and *Pseudo-Jonathan* is
not the gift of 'inspired speech' but the creative impartation of a (human) spirit
capable of speech: i.e. the human capacity to understand and express such understanding (as in Philo).

[23]Cf. Turner, 'Spirit in John', esp. 29–31; Turner and Burge '*Anointed
Community*', 257–61.

sinners. John has his counterpart to this. Jesus' words, which are 'Spirit and life' (6:63) and 'living water' (4:10, 13,14,23), already meet with real faith (if not yet full faith). From the perspective of 6:64, while there is a disciple who does *not* believe, the rest (by implication) do. Accordingly, in 13:10, Jesus can say the disciples *are* cleansed (except Judas) and 15:3 clarifies that they have become 'clean' through the word Jesus has spoken.[24] In the light of this element of inaugurated eschatology, we have argued that the event in 20:22 is better understood as the climax in a *whole process* of life-giving experiences of the Spirit-and-word (through Jesus), extending from the disciples' earliest encounter with the one whose revelatory wisdom is Spirit and life (6:63). By analogy with the understanding of the creation of Adam in Philo and the targums, John 20:22 depicts a final stage of the bringing into being of a new humanity in a climactic re-creative gift of the Spirit which at last secures the authentic 'understanding' (= wisdom) of faith.[25] The resurrection and reconstitution of the people of God from the dry bones of Israel is now in a sense essentially completed (cf. Ezek. 37:9), and the new community is ready to embark on its new life.[26]

(2) The second issue is more delicate. Here we need to avoid two opposed dangers. The first is that of so sharply distinguishing 20:22 from the gift of the Paraclete that we radically bifurcate the Spirit in John, to the point that we have two quite distinct gifts. John may know of many different *experiences* of the Spirit, but (like other NT writers) he only speaks of *one* 'reception' of the gift of the Spirit (7:39; 20:22).[27] And the gift in 20:22 has evident connections with the Paraclete promises, at least in so

---

[24]The language of 'cleansing' chimes with that of 'birth of water and Spirit' in John. 3:5, and its background in Ezekiel 36. Of course, the word in question, at 13:10, is about that washing that will finally be accomplished through the glorification of Jesus (cf. J.D.G. Dunn, 'The Washing of the Disciples' Feet in John 13.1–20', *ZNW* 61 (1970), 247–52); but there is a present component of this effective in and through Jesus' teaching.

[25]Cf. corrected Wojciechowski, above.

[26]Cf. W. Dumbrell, 'The Spirit in John's Gospel', in B.G. Webb (ed.), *Spirit of the Living God* (Homebush West, NSW: Anzea, 1991), 77–94, who largely accepts our earlier account of 20:22, while suggesting I have omitted the corporate dimension inherent in the allusion to Ezekiel 37.

[27]This is a danger into which our earliest writing on John may be felt to have fallen.

far as that the commissioning in 20:21b takes up the dominant theme of the Farewell Discourse, and 20:23 has evident missiological implications (the contacts between 20:19–23 and Luke 24:46–49 have regularly been noted).

The second, and opposing, danger is that of an entire collapse of the Paraclete promises into John 20:22, when, as we have seen, there is evidence the Spirit only substantially *acts* as Paraclete *beyond* the pages of John's narrative.

Porsch (closely followed by Schnackenburg) perhaps proves the most sensitive interpreter when he speaks of John 20:22 as that gift of the Spirit which would later *become* the Paraclete.[28] But even this does not quite express sufficient cohesion between John 20:22 and the later Paraclete activities to avoid a radical bifurcation: e.g. between the Spirit first received as the power of new birth and then received entirely *differently* as the Paraclete. The all-important bridge between the two probably lies (a) in the allusion to Genesis 2:7//Ezekiel 37:9, if that is understood (as in Philo and the targums) as the gift of wisdom/understanding of the Christ-event,[29] and (b) in the connections of 20:22 with the Paraclete tradition through the missiologial allusions in 20:21b and 20:23, just noted. We may elucidate this further in answering the next question.

III. DOES JOHN MEAN THE DISCIPLES HAD A TWO-STAGE EXPERIENCE OF THE SPIRIT?

We may give a qualified affirmative to the question. John appears to see the Spirit active in and 'given' to the disciples as one theological 'gift', but realized in two chronological stages, separated by the completion of Jesus' 'ascension'. First the Spirit, through Jesus, brings the disciples to the new creation life of the resurrected Israel, by imparting spiritual wisdom (in the twofold sense of 'objective' revelation and 'subjective' understanding). This occurs in a long drawn-out *process* which begins in the ministry, but it reaches a climax in the special moment of John 20:22. Second, following that, with the total removal of Jesus from the earthly scene, John envisages the coming of the Spirit as Jesus' replacement: (i) as the means of his continued presence with the disciples, (ii) as the one who teaches about and who illumines the Christ-event, and (iii) as the one who uses (iv) as the basis and means of witness to the

---

[28] *Pneuma*, ch. 2, §1, and 376–77.
[29] So M. Hengel, 'The Old Testament in the Fourth Gospel', *HBT* 12 (1990), 19–41

world. Whether or not the interpreter decides John envisages this 'sending' of the Paraclete as initiated by a distinct single historical experience (such as Pentecost) or whether she prefers to understand it as several such experiences,[30] or even as a 'process' gathering momentum, but with no percetible initial or subsequent 'moments', will depend largely on whether she believes the writer/editor of the Fourth Gospel was aware of the Pentecost tradition. In our view, with the majority of commentators, it is probable that John knew the 'Pentecost' tradition. But that is a subsidiary question.

More important is how the two foci of the one ellipse of the gift of the Spirit are to be related. A line of commentators from Calvin to Hoskyns have referred to the paschal gift as an earnest of Pentecost. But what could such a statement mean? How are the paschal and post-ascension experiences of the Spirit related as one 'reception' or 'gift' of the Spirit? Here we can offer a relatively clear response. *It is the function of the Spirit as author of charismatic wisdom and understanding* (that is, of course, the Spirit acting as the Spirit of prophecy) *that most closely unites John 20:22 and the Paraclete promises into what is theologically 'one' gift,* even if with two (or more) chronological foci. In this perception of the 'Spirit of prophecy' effecting eschatological re-creation of the community, by imparting revelatory and transforming 'wisdom', John comes close to the understanding of the Spirit at Qumran (see above Ch. 1, part II, §3).

IV. DOES JOHN IMPLY THAT THE DISCIPLES' TWO-STAGE EXPERIENCE IS REPEATED IN THE CHURCH?

With Dunn, the answer to this question must be negative. It should be clear that, after the ascension and the giving of the Paraclete, there would not again be the two-stage experience of the Spirit the disciples had. The glorification of Jesus is now complete, and the Spirit given to perform the totality of his expected functions. There would be no parallel means (after the ascension) of the long process of Jesus' teaching ministry. After the ascension of Jesus, it is the Spirit-Paraclete who is given as the revealer-teacher who unfolds the Christ-event, enabling the understanding of the revelation which (in Johannine terms) is 'salvation'. This same Paraclete is the only means of continuing knowledge and deeper understanding of the risen Lord, which, in

---

[30]Cf. Hatina, 'John 20,22', 200–1; 204–6.

Johannine terms, is an on-going experience of 'eternal life' (17:3: cf. Chs. 4 and 5 above): reception of the Spirit-Paraclete is thus a necessary and sufficient condition of eternal life. But precisely in enabling these gifts the Paraclete ensures his support for Christ's case, thereby empowering the disciples' witness, and in doing so functions as the other 'advocate', like Jesus, in the great assize.

Chapter Seven

The Spirit in Paul (1): Questions of Method in Establishing a Pauline Pneumatology

A glance at the various accounts of Paul's teaching on the Spirit shows there is as yet little agreement on how a Pauline theology of the Spirit should be organized.[1] Three factors complicate the problem. *First,* Paul's teaching on the Spirit is largely incidental to his treatment of other questions (even in 1 Cor. 12–14), and this makes it difficult to systematize. *Second,* his teaching is offered in writings that span up to twenty-three years, and as he faces a wide variety of situations. There is reason to believe he worked out his theology in relation to these different situations, and that means it *developed.* In which case, though, we encounter the problem of identifying where, precisely, we locate his 'theology'? *Third,* compared with other writers, Paul creatively relates the Spirit to so *many* themes, that it becomes more difficult to distinguish what is central from what is peripheral. In this chapter we concentrate mainly on the second of these complicating factors. We shall first describe a relatively typical critical 'developmental' scenario (in two of its important variations). Subsequently we shall evaluate the approach.

I. THE CRITICAL DEVELOPMENTAL APPROACHES OF HORN AND MENZIES

Karl Donfried speaks for the majority of New Testament critical scholarship when he maintains:

---

[1]Different analytical/developmental approaches are made by Montague, *Spirit,* chs. 12–19, F.W. Horn, *Das Angeld des Geistes: Studien zur paulinischen Pneumatologie* (Göttingen: Vandenhoeck & Ruprecht, 1992) and Fee, *Presence,* Part 1. These may be contrasted with the radically different thematic presentations of, e.g. E. Schweizer, *TDNT* VI (1968): 415–37; T. Paige, *DPL* 404–13, and Fee, *Presence,* part 2, where the themes examined are still main Pauline categories, and of D. Guthrie, *New Testament Theology,* whose 'themes' derive more from systematic theology.

The proper starting point for the analysis of Pauline thought must be 1 Thessalonians, especially since it contains the key to the theology of the early Paul, and therefore, we would insist, also the key to understanding the theology of the late Paul.[2]

His assumptions, of course, are (i) that 1 Thessalonians is Paul's earliest letter (which he dates as early as 40–44), and (ii) that Paul's 'late' theology can be understood in terms of an unfolding and contextualized development of his earlier ideas (rather than as involving dramatic shifts, and even displacement of the earlier 'centre').

F.W. Horn provides a concise example of such an approach, and we shall examine it first.[3] Then we shall turn to Menzies, who appears to assume a slightly more radical shift.

1. F.W. Horn's Position

Horn divides Paul's pneumatological teaching into three phases.

(1) Early teaching represented by 1 Thessalonians.

Here the Spirit is by and large the 'Spirit of prophecy' functioning in four ways.[4] (i) As empowering Paul's proclamation of the Gospel so that it has impact on the hearers drawing them into persevering faith (1:5,6). (ii) As inspiring joy even in persecution (1:8). (iii) As the source of prophetic utterances in the community which are to be discerned and heeded (5:19–21). And (iv) as God's (ongoing) gift to believers which summons them away 'in sanctification' from their former lives of immorality and dishonesty (4:8). At this stage, the Spirit is still very much the 'Spirit of God', rather than (as in later works) fundamentally christological, e.g. as the 'Spirit of (Jesus) Christ' (Rom. 8:9; Phil.1:19), or 'the Spirit of his [God's] Son' (Gal. 4:6).

---

[2]K.P. Donfried and I.H. Marshall, *The Theology of the Shorter Pauline Letters* (Cambridge: CUP, 1993), 64.

[3]Horn's position is made available to the English reader in his article 'Holy Spirit' in D.N. Freedman (ed.), *The Anchor Bible Dictionary: Volume 3* (New York: Doubleday, 1992), 265–78 (on NT); 271–6 on Paul.

[4]The term is ours, not Horn's, and is justified by two of the main functions ascribed to the Spirit — the empowering of proclamation and prophecy.

(2) Middle period dominated by the dispute with pneumatic enthusiasm represented in 1 Corinthians.

In this phase the Corinthians maintain they already belong primarily to the heavenly/Spirit world (cf. 1 Cor. 4:8), rather than to the world of flesh and blood, through their reception of the Spirit in baptism (1 Cor. 6:11; 12:13). As Gentiles or hellenists they inevitably understand this gift of the indwelling Spirit as a powerful divine *substance*, a very part of the heavenly world, and so already the full arrival of salvation itself, not merely a welcome but unnecessary endowment for prophecy and proclamation in the period of waiting for salvation at the Parousia.[5] According to Horn, Paul takes over their baptismal theology, but refutes their over-realized eschatology. He insists they are *not yet* 'spiritual bodies' belonging to the heavenly sphere (that awaits resurrection, 1 Cor. 15:45–49), and he sharply relativizes glossolalia (which they prize as highest evidence of heavenly/spiritual status, and freedom from constraints) in terms of gifts which 'build up' the historical community on earth (1 Cor. 12–14). Until we become spiritual bodies in the resurrection, Paul argues (against the Corinthian libertinism and individualism), it is especially in the physical body (Paul inserts *sōma* at 6:19), and in the community which is Christ's metaphorical body (1 Cor. 12:12–31), that the spiritual life issuing from the baptismal gift is to be manifest. Nor is this baptismal charism to be separated from the Christ-event: it is no mere heavenly substance, but Christ, the life-giving Spirit (1 Cor. 15:45), that is received. And so to receive the Spirit is to come under Christ's lordship and power.

(3) Late phase dominated by the dispute with Jewish-Christian nomism represented by 2 Corinthians, Galatians, Philippians and Romans.

This is regarded as the most important theological period for Paul's pneumatology, because controversy fires him to make his most distinctive contributions. Over against Judaizing Christians, in 2 Corinthians 3 he claims the Spirit is the Spirit of the New Covenant which displaces the Mosaic Covenant. Life-giving Spirit is thus set in antithesis to death-dealing Torah (2 Cor. 3:6). This Spirit/Torah and Spirit/Letter (*gramma*) antithesis is then extensively developed in Galatians 3–4 and Romans 7–8. Side by side with it, in Galatians 5:13-6:10 and Romans 7–8, he develops his second great distinctive antithesis: between the powers of 'flesh' and 'Spirit'. The Law is hereby portrayed as essentially irrelevant, because humanity's problem is its all-encompassing

---

[5]Cf. Schweizer, *TDNT* VI (1968), 415–16, for an exquisite (if, in my view, utterly misleading) statement of this.

bondage to evil and rebellion which Paul designates as existence according to 'the flesh'. The Law is powerless to overcome the Sin-Flesh alliance (esp. Rom. 7:13-25). The Spirit can (Gal. 5:16,17,19–25; 6:8,9; Rom. 8:1–13) — and so reception of the Spirit becomes both the *necessary* condition for salvation (salvation from existence 'according to the flesh' is impossible without it) and the *sufficient* condition for salvation (because the powerless Law has no contribution to make).

If the pre-Pauline tradition and even perhaps 1 Thessalonians are less than explicit as to whether reception of the gift of the Spirit is *necessary* for salvation, there can be no doubt that by Paul's *late* phase he sees the Spirit as 'the soteriological Spirit'. There is some sort of *development* from Paul's earlier views, and it takes place as Paul works out his pneumatology in the face of different crises in his ministry. The question then becomes whether the 'developments' in question are simply an unfolding of what was already *there* (potentially) at the earlier stages, or whether the development involved is more like the *evolution of an entirely new species*. Horn's view, as we shall see, is consistent with the former. Menzies, *per contra*, has in effect argued for the latter.

2. R.P. Menzies' Position

In his *The Development of Early Christian Pneumatology*, Menzies argues that the Spirit in pre-Pauline pneumatology was *not* necessary for salvation; it was merely an empowering gift of the Spirit of prophecy given to Christians to enable them to serve (especially in the church's mission).[6] According to Menzies, it was Paul's interaction with the sort of teaching in Wisdom of Solomon 9:9–18 (produced probably AD 38–40) that precipitated the change.

The crucial section in Wisdom is 9:17–18:

Who has learned your counsel, unless you have given
   wisdom
and sent the Holy Spirit from on high

---

[6]*Development*, ch.12, is largely an attempt to show there are no pre-Pauline traditions embedded in Paul's letters which made the Spirit soteriologically necessary. He argues with Dunn, against Schweizer, that the flesh/Spirit antithesis in Romans 1:3–4 is not traditional, but Pauline redaction (285–95); against J.S. Vos (*Traditionsgeschichtliche Untersuchungen zur paulinischen Pneumatologie* (Assen: Van Gorcum, 1973), 26–33) that there is nothing pre-Pauline about the references to the Spirit in 1 Cor. 15:44–45; Gal. 5:22,23 or 1 Cor. 6:11, and, again against Vos (*Untersuchungen*, 33–77) that Judaism did not understand the Spirit as the source of eschatological salvation. We may accept his argument with Vos in respect of 1 Cor. 15 and Gal. 5, but not his other points.

And thus the paths of those on earth were set right
and men were taught what pleases you,
and were saved by wisdom.

On Menzies' understanding, this represents a sector of Judaism which
has become profoundly pessimistic about the possibility of humankind
understanding God's will in the Torah and so of being able to live by
it. God must give each the Spirit who enables such an understanding if
they are to be saved at all. This work, according to Menzies, brought
the apostle to recognize that human beings could not understand God's
saving wisdom in Christ without the gift of the Spirit. But without such
an understanding they are doomed, and so the gift of the Spirit becomes soteriologically necessary. According to Menzies, Paul first
elucidates this in 1 Corinthians 2:6–16, and the effect was to produce a
fundamentally new species of pneumatology. The 'Spirit of prophecy'
has evolved into 'the soteriological Spirit'.

II. ASSESSMENT OF THE DEVELOPMENTAL APPROACHES OF HORN AND MENZIES

1. Assessment of F.W. Horn's Position

We shall later clarify some important ways in which we agree with
Horn. But first let us note two different kinds of problem with his
position:

(1) The problem of chronology.

The neat schema of development from an early 1 Thessalonians (41–44 on
Donfried's estimate) to the 'late' Paulines depends on a Pauline chronology which rejects the account of Acts. Acts sets the visit to Thessalonica
in the so-called 'Second Missionary Journey', and this journey cannot
easily be placed before AD 49–50. 1 Thessalonians would then have been
written (from Corinth) in the autumn of AD 50 at the earliest. 1 and 2
Corinthians were written only four or five years later (the latter in Spring
55), and Romans in 57.[7] That does not leave much time (five years instead
of sixteen) for clear 'development', and it may be as easy to speak of Paul
articulating theological themes he had already in essence thought
through, as to suggest every relevant line of his polemic in the letters is a
new contextual 'development'.

---

[7]See e.g. F.F. Bruce, *New Testament History* (London: Nelson, 1969), chs. 24–5;
C.H. Hemer, *The Book of Acts in the Setting of Hellenistic History*, ch. 6 esp.
270–76.

A more serious problem arises with Galatians, however. Horn's developmental thesis requires that the letter's clear flesh/Spirit and Law/Spirit antitheses come late – *after* the two Corinthian letters, that is. But Acts attributes Paul's mission in the Roman province of Galatia to the period of the so-called 'First Missionary Journey', and the description of the Jerusalem visits mentioned in Galatians 2 suggests Galatians may have been written *before* the Apostolic Council of Acts 15 (AD 49?) and so a year or more *before* even 1 Thessalonians.[8] The debate about the date of Galatians is a continuing one. But the arguments for an early dating cannot be dismissed easily, and they inevitably challenge over-confidence in any simple developmental theory, for most of Paul's pneumatology can be found *in nuce* in the letter.[9] This would suggest that perhaps as early as AD 49 (some fifteen years after his Damascus Road experience) he had already developed some of the major lines of pneumatology, and the different situations he faces simply call forth his different emphases. It will be granted that the 'pneumatology' of 1 Thessalonians is less nuanced than that of Galatians, and that could be taken as a powerful argument in favour of Horn's order of the letters, but this kind of argument is suspicious. 1 Thessalonians appears to be a multi-theme 'friendship' letter (like Philippians) treating topics in which pneumatology has no especially privileged place (until 1 Thess. 5:19–21). One cannot help the suspicion that, even if Paul were to have written 1 Thessalonians twenty years later than he did, he might not have found further occasion significantly to develop the pneumatology he expresses in it.[10]

(2) The problem that 1 Thessalonians 4:8 anticipates the later 'developments'.

Even if we bracket off Galatians from the debate, a further problem lies in 1 Thessalonians itself. While the Spirit is most clearly the 'Spirit of prophecy' in 5:19,20, the wording of 1 Thessalonians 4:8 suggests Paul had even at this stage understood the Spirit as the fulfilment of the New Covenant promises of the Spirit in Ezekiel 36–37. 1 Thessalonians 4:8 reads, 'Therefore whoever disregards this [i.e. Paul's call from immorality to holiness], disregards not man but God, who gives his Holy

---

[8] See Hemer, *Book*, chs. 6–7.
[9] For accounts of the Spirit in Galatians, see Fee, *Presence*, ch. 6; Montague, *Spirit*, ch. 16; Dunn, *Baptism*, 106–15 or *idem*, *The Theology of Paul's Letter to the Galatians* (Cambridge: CUP, 1993), 59–63, 104–14, 130–2, 135–6.
[10] By contrast, given the good use Paul has made of the Spirit motif in the Judaizing contexts of 2 Corinthians, Romans and Galatians, we find the pneumatology of the anti-judaizing section in Philippians 3:1–21 amazingly underdeveloped.

Spirit into you.' The rather strange combination of the verb 'to give (the Spirit)' with the final phrase *eis hymas* ('into you') is very rare. It undoubtedly derives from the Greek Old Testament (LXX) rendering of Ezekiel 37:6,14 (cf. 11:19 and 36:26,27) where the sentence 'I will *give* my Spirit *into* you, and you shall live' means 'I will *put* my Spirit *in* you, and you will live'.[11] But if 1 Thessalonians 4:8 reflects Ezekiel 36–37, this in turn implies (as Horn freely admits) that Paul *had already understood the Spirit of prophecy in the congregation as the 'life-giving' re-creative Spirit of Ezekiel's promised New Covenant (see 36:26,27) some time before he came to use that theologoumenon as a powerful weapon in his arguments against the Judaizers in 2 Corinthians 3 and beyond.* In this light, the Spirit/Law antithesis spelt out in 2 Corinthians 3 does not mark a radical new stage or phase in his *pneumatology*; it merely contextualizes the antithesis inherent in Ezekiel 36:26,27 in such a way as to make the Law written in stone irrelevant to salvation promised. It may simply be the lack of any specific Christian Judaizing movement directed against his Thessalonian converts that explains why he does not use the language of justification by faith there, nor elucidate the antitheses he does in 2 Corinthians, Galatians and Romans.

Having criticized some aspects of Horn's account, let us note the possibility of a substantial agreement with him. He may be right when he sees the specific formulation of the great Pauline antitheses (Spirit/flesh, Spirit/letter and Spirit/Torah) as primarily situational and polemical. We have no reason to believe they were part of his expressed theological teaching until he was confronted by the Judaizing that provoked them. What we unfortunately do not know is how early such a Judaizing response may have caused Paul to think along these lines. And if 1 Thessalonians was indeed his earliest letter (which we doubt), the developments were evidently anticipated there.

2. Assessment of R.P. Menzies' Position

According to Menzies, (i) Paul himself was the first to articulate a soteriological pneumatology, (ii) he first did so (in 1 Cor. 2) on the basis of acquaintance with the Wisdom of Solomon (or, the traditions it used),[12] and (iii) this represented a sharp break with earlier Christian tradition. We may note four problems with Menzies' position. Several of these will bring out further agreements we share with Horn.

[11]See Fee, *Presence*, 50–3, for details. Paul uses the same 'into our hearts' in Gal. 4:6 and 2 Cor. 1:22.
[12]Menzies, *Development*, ch. 13.

(1) Paul's soteriological pneumatology antedates 1 Corinthians and is based in Ezekiel 36–37, not Wisdom.

As we have observed above, some years before Paul wrote 1 Corinthians he had already expressed a soteriological pneumatology in 1 Thessalonians 4:8 (and 1:4,5,8), and it was there grounded in Ezekiel (not Wisdom of Solomon).

(2) This soteriological pneumatology probably antedates even Paul.

As we have seen, Menzies attempts to show that no Christians before Paul attributed soteriological functions to the Spirit. But, as Horn has observed, the constancy of certain affirmations, such as 'God has *given us* the Spirit'[13] and 'the Spirit of God dwells in *you*',[14] across the New Testament suggest these are *traditional* formulae. Significantly, they too seem to derive from Ezekiel 11:19; 36:26,27 and 37:6,14. If that is the case, elements of pre-Pauline Christianity appear to have confessed the Spirit as Ezekiel's renewing Spirit of New Covenant life.[15]

Similarly, with other apparently pre-Pauline confessions. Menzies may be right that 1 Corinthians 6:9–11 is not necessarily a baptismal confession,[16] but the wording of 6:11b is odd in its context, and most (including Horn) recognize it as the quotation of a piece of *tradition*.[17] Paul affirms, 'But you were washed, you were sanctified, you were justified in the name of the Lord Jesus Christ and in the Spirit of our God' (cf. Titus 3:5). According to this section, God performs the actions of the three verbs (each complementary ways of referring to what happens in conversion) in the name of Christ and *through* the Spirit. So to the *Spirit's* activity is attributed the washing away of the believer's past, the sanctifying of the person to God, and his or her subjective experience of acquittal of sin. The passage clearly then attributes soteriological significance to the Spirit, and

---

[13] Acts 5:32; 15:8; Rom. 5:5; 11:8; 2 Cor. 1:22; 5:5; 1 Thess. 4:8; 2 Tim. 1:7; 1 Jn. 3:24; 4:13.

[14] 1 Cor. 3:16; 6:19; Rom. 8:9, 11; Eph. 2:21; 1 Pet. 2:5.

[15] We need emphatically to reject Schweizer's view referred to earlier in this chapter. He sees the Spirit in Acts and in the pre-Pauline community as merely 'miraculous powers' that help until the salvation of the Parousia (*TDNT* VI:415–16), and contrasts this with Paul's 'soteriological' understanding of the Spirit grounded in a more general hellenistic understanding of *pneuma* as heavenly substance. The point is rather that the Spirit in the community is Ezekiel's eschatological promise of the new creation of the community through the Spirit's presence and activity.

[16] Menzies, *Development*, 296–300.

[17] See Horn, 'Holy Spirit', 269.

once again it appears to rest in Ezekiel 36:25–27, where the ideas of washing with water, sanctifying, and forgiveness of past sins are brought together.[18]

(3) The connection between 1 Corinthians 2:6–16 and Wisdom 9:17–18 is minimal, rather than decisive.

In the first place, Menzies has probably misinterpreted Wisdom 9 when he thinks it speaks of a gift of the Spirit to each of God's people bringing saving wisdom (as NRSV suggests). This Diaspora writer is rallying Jews against the encroachments of hellenism by asserting that saving wisdom is found only in the Jewish world where God's Spirit has revealed it in the Law and the Prophets.[19] Second, as Fee argues, 1 Corinthians 2 does *not* speak of esoteric wisdom granted by the Spirit (except when the biting irony of 2:12,13 is tragically misunderstood). It speaks rather of the Spirit enabling our comprehension of God's apocalyptic wisdom revealed at the cross. The only place where Paul (or a disciple) connects Spirit and wisdom other than in 1 Corinthians 12:8 (which is too allusive to tell us anything) is Ephesians 1:17, where the writer prays for a Spirit of wisdom and interpretation in the knowledge of God to be given to believers. The background of the language here is Isaiah 11:1,2 and the apocalyptic tradition dependent upon it (e.g. *1 Enoch* 49:2–3; 61:11–12), not Wisdom of Solomon.[20]

(4) Menzies' antithesis between the 'Spirit of prophecy' and the 'soteriological Spirit' is a false one.

The life-giving New Covenant Spirit who draws the believer into holiness in 1 Thessalonians 4:8 is also the 'Spirit of prophecy' who brings prophetic utterance to the community in 1 Thessalonians 5:19,20, and who first brought the disciples to faith through Paul's powerful proclamation of the gospel according to 1:4,5. Similarly, the soteriological

[18]In Ezekiel, it is a metaphorical sprinkling of water that makes clean and sanctifies Israel to God, and brings his forgiveness. Fee attempts to explain the verbs as contextually determined, i.e. 'washed' corresponds to the removal of the filth of the sins just described, 'sanctified' = consecrated to God's new life, and 'justified' echoes the *adikai* of 6:1,7,8. But Paul does not here or elsewhere refer to sins as 'dirt' or 'filth', nor to such being 'washed away' (a verb not found again in Paul).

[19]See Turner, 'The Spirit of Prophecy', *NTS* 38 (1992), 84 n.36.

[20]Against the view Paul depends significantly on Wisdom of Solomon, see Fee, *Presence*, 911–13 (also 93–112 on 1 Cor. 2:6-3:2)

Spirit who washes, sanctifies and acquits the disciple in 1 Corinthians 6:11 is the same Spirit as 'the Spirit of prophecy' who gives the tongues, prophecy, words of wisdom and knowledge, etc. in 1 Corinthians 12:8–10, 14:2 (and 1 Cor. 12–14 and Rom. 12 more generally). As Horn observes, the Spirit remains the Spirit of prophecy throughout the letters: it is one of the three great constants in Paul's pneumatology to appear throughout Paul's letters (the other two being that proclamation of the gospel is wrought by the Spirit and that the gift of the Spirit is paralleled by a pledge to 'walk according to the Spirit'[21]).

More specifically, we may point out that it is precisely in acting *as* the 'Spirit of prophecy' that the Spirit becomes soteriologically *necessary* in 1 Corinthians 2. Paul's point is that those without the Spirit cannot understand God's saving wisdom in the cross. Here, then, it is the Spirit's revelation and illumination that enables authentic Christian faith (1 Cor. 2:9–11). As in Judaism, it is the 'Spirit of prophecy' who reveals; and, as in John, it is Spirit-given revelation that saves. It is precisely through this fusion (as in John) that the 'Spirit of prophecy' becomes soteriologically necessary.

Another reason why Menzies thinks Paul's soteriological Spirit is so fundamentally different from the 'Spirit of prophecy' in Luke-Acts is that he finds it impossible to see how the 'Spirit of prophecy' can have the ethically transforming effect implied in 1 Corinthians 6:11, and in the great antithesis between Spirit and flesh that pervades Galatians 5–6 and Romans 8. But, as we have seen in Judaism, in Acts and in John there is no real problem on this score. The 'Spirit of prophecy' who brings *God's* presence in wisdom and revelation also evokes worship (hence, e.g. the responsive joy of 1 Thess. 1:8), and the wisdom and revelation he brings are not simply neutral facts, data or propositions, but also transforming and sanctifying awareness of God and his will. Hence to live 'according to the Spirit' and as one 'led by the Spirit' (a verb which suggests the revelatory prompting of the Spirit of prophecy) is to live the life of obedient sonship with and before God. Nowhere is this more evident than in Ephesians 3:16–19, where the Spirit of wisdom and revelation prayed for in 1:18 is anticipated to enable such a comprehension of Christ and his love that the receiver will be strengthened in the inner person, and 'filled with the whole fulness of God'. This last clause means to live in total unity with God and completely under his reconciling sovereignty, i.e. in the 'new humanity' ethics of Ephesians 4–6. The revealing and wisdom-enabling

---

[21] Horn, 'Holy Spirit', 275. See J.D.G. Dunn, 'Baptism in the Spirit', 3–27 (27), for a similar argument.

'Spirit of prophecy' is thus also a potent ethically-transforming power.[22]

III. CONCLUSION AND WAY AHEAD

We are not yet in a clear position to offer a critical account of significant *development* in Paul's thought. From the beginning he evinces awareness of the Spirit as the Spirit of prophecy, but connects this with Ezekiel 36–37 in such a way as to make the Spirit of prophecy a soteriological necessity, as was the case in some parts of Judaism, in Acts, in some of the pre-Pauline traditions, and in John. A pneumatology arranged in developmental terms may graphically illustrate Paul's creative contextualization of his basic understanding of the Spirit, but may be misleading if taken as a chronicle of the 'development' of his theology of the Spirit. As a consequence, in the next chapter, we shall deal with the material *thematically*, attempting to highlight characteristically Pauline emphases.

---

[22]We have addressed this problem in 'The Spirit of Prophecy and the Ethical/Religious Life of the Christian Community', in M.W. Wilson (ed.), *Spirit*, 166–90; alternatively, in *Power*, ch. 5.

Chapter Eight

The Spirit in Paul (2): Characteristic Themes

I. THE SPIRIT AS THE SPIRIT OF THE NEW COVENANT AND ISRAEL'S RENEWAL

In one of his earliest letters (1 Thess. 4:8), Paul refers to the gift of the Spirit in terms which unmistakably allude to Ezekiel 36–37. As we have noted, this use of Ezekiel was probably already 'traditional' in Christian circles. We may now examine it, and Paul's use of the tradition, in a little more detail.

1. The Old Testament Promise and Its Interpretation in Judaism and in Pre-Pauline Christianity

In Jeremiah 31:31–34 a new covenant was promised to replace that broken by Israel (leading to the Exile). As with the previous covenant it was addressed to the whole people. But its newness was to consist in three elements:

(1) God's law was to be written on the people's minds and on their hearts, not on tablets of stone (so v.33b–c);

(2) knowledge of God was to be immediate rather than mediated (v.34: 'No longer will a man teach his neighbour . . . saying, "Know the Lord!", because they will all know me, from the least of them to the greatest'), and,

(3) the result would be obedience (contrast 32c).

The exilic prophet, Ezekiel, takes up this promise in chapters 36–37, especially 36:23–28. If he does not actually use Jeremiah's expression 'a new covenant', he nevertheless uses the covenant formulary (36:28, 'You will be my people, and I will be your God'). And the content of the promise matches Jeremiah 31:31–34. It is based in a great event of forgiveness and cleansing (like Jer. 31:34c) and clearly describes an inner transformation and new knowledge of God such as Jeremiah promised. Ezekiel thus says, in 36:26, 'I will give you a new heart and put a new spirit in you; I will remove from you your heart of stone and give you a heart of flesh' — a promise to remove the obdurate nature (heart of stone) and replace it with a responsive one. To this, Ezekiel adds that the consequent obedience of the people to God will be accomplished by the indwelling Spirit of God, v.27: 'I will put my Spirit in you and move you to follow my decrees.'[1]

But the restoration period proved a disappointment, and Jews looked for some deeper eschatological fulfilment of the words of Jeremiah and Ezekiel. *Jubilees* 1.22–25 (second century BC) conflates the prophecies of Ezekiel and Jeremiah and interprets them of Israel's future hope.

> I know their rebellion . . . and they will not obey till they confess their own sin and the sin of their fathers. And after this they will turn to me in all uprightness and with all (their) heart and with all (their) soul [cf. Deut. 6:5; 30:10], and I will circumcize the foreskin of their heart . . .; and I will create in them a holy spirit [Ps. 51:12; cf. Ezek. 36:26], and I will cleanse them (cf. Ezek. 36:25–27a], so that they will not turn away from me from that day unto eternity [Jer. 32:40]. And they will cleave to me and to all my commandments, and will fulfil my commandments [Ezek. 36:27b; Jer. 31:34], and I will be their Father and they will be my children [Jer. 31:9, 20]. And they shall be called children of the living God, and every angel and spirit shall know . . . that these are my children, and that I am their Father in uprightness and righteousness, and that I love them.

For the writer(s) of 1QH 17.25–26; 4Q504.5 and 1QS 4.20–23, these hopes were perhaps already being partly realized in the community. It is along similar lines that early Christian interpreters were to understand the Spirit in the church. If Acts is representative of early pneumatology, it points to a time when the Spirit of prophecy within (mainly) Jewish Christianity was understood as the power of Israel's cleansing and restoration as well as of her witness (see Ch. 3). While the writer of Acts does not himself specifically allude to Ezekiel 36 in this connection, it is not

---

[1]Ezekiel 37 is most naturally understood as a complementary vision concerning the same promise (and this is emphasized by the repeated 'I will give my Spirit into you . . .' (37:14, cf. 37:5, 6, 10), which takes up 36:27 (cf. 11:19)). It is not primarily a prophecy of *literal* eschatological resurrection (although it came to be understood by Jews and Christians to refer to that too), but first and foremost as prophecy of the 'rebirth' of the nation. The 'dead bones' strewn in the wilderness symbolize Israel's 'death' in Exile, cut off from the life-giving God because of her sins (as 37:11 clarifies). In Ezekiel's context the prophecy concerns God's promise to restore the nation to himself and to their land.

difficult to see how other Christians might have made the link, as they perceived the renewing effects of the charismatic Spirit within the community. Paul himself appeals to such a tradition of interpretation, without further comment or explanation, at 1 Thessalonians 4:7,8.

2. The Spirit of the New Covenant in 2 Corinthians 3

To oppose Judaizing influences, Paul takes up this trajectory from the Old Testament promises in a radical and polemically christocentric manner in 2 Corinthians 3:3–18.

(a) In 3:3 he explicitly contrasts his own ministry as one through which the Spirit of God wrote not on tablets of stone, but on human hearts. The positive allusion is to Jeremiah 31 and Ezekiel 36, while the reference to 'tablets of stone' is a polemical allusion to Exodus 34, the other passage which dominates Paul's exposition as far as 3:18.

(b) At 3:6 Paul specifically refers to himself as the servant of a new covenant which is later contrasted with what he calls 'the old covenant' (v.14), read by the Jews.

(c) This new covenant is contrasted as 'a covenant of the Spirit' (v.6) and a 'dispensation of the Spirit' (v.8) over against a covenant consisting in an externally written code of Laws.

(d) While the old covenant and its Law is described as killing (v.6), as bringing death (v.7) and condemnation (v.9), the Spirit of the new is said to bring 'life' (3:6) and righteousness (v.9). And while the old dispensation brought bondage, in the new the Spirit brings freedom (v.17).

(e) The glory that accompanied the giving of the Law of the old covenant was a fading one — the ebb of which was hidden behind the veil Moses wore (v.13 and see Exod. 34:29–35). Indeed the whole old dispensation, according to Paul, was one in which a veil seemed to prevent Israel from truly understanding her Law and from 'seeing' her Lord (vv.14,15). By contrast, the glory of the new covenant entirely transcends that of the old (v.9f). Instead of fading it increases; for believers behold 'the glory' of the Lord (= Christ) with no veil to hide him, and as they do so, Paul claims, they are transformed from one degree of glory to another (3:17,18[2]).

---

[2]For the argument that the 'all of us' of 3:18 refers to believers in general (not merely to the Pauline party of apostolic messengers), and that κατοπτριζόμενοι

(f)   The way an individual transfers from the one state of affairs to the other is indicated in vv.16,17. Just as, according to Exodus 34:34, Moses used to remove the veil when he entered the Lord's presence to speak to him, so now the veil which hides the glory of God in Christ is removed when a person turns to the 'Lord' of Exodus 34:34 — whom Paul identifies (analogically) in vv.16,17 with the Spirit (v.17[3]) In other words, if we drop the imagery, Paul tells us it is by turning to the Spirit, whom believers receive, that the bondage of the Law, and blindness of the old covenant is left behind, and a person enters new covenant existence.[4]

With respect to this 'new covenant' pneumatology we may make three observations:

(1)   The soteriological relevance of the Spirit in Paul's scheme should be clear. The essence of the promised new covenant was that God would put his Spirit in men and women and thereby create in them a new heart and a new obedience, and Paul claims Ezekiel's promise to be fulfilled to believers. This means that for him reception of the Spirit is receiving the indwelling Spirit who 'regenerates' the inner person, bringing 'life', new

---

(footnote 2 continued)
here means 'beholding' (not 'reflecting': *contra*, e.g. L.J. Belleville, *Reflections of Glory. Paul's Polemical Use of the Moses-Doxa Tradition in 2 Corinthians 3.1–18*, (Sheffield: JSOT Press, 1991), esp. 279–81), see Fee, *Presence*, 314–20. N.T. Wright understands the verse to mean all behold the glory of the Spirit's work in the community of Christians: 'Reflected Glory: 2 Corinthians 3:18', in L.D. Hurst and N.T. Wright (eds.), *The Glory of God in the New Testament: Studies in Christology in Memory of George Bradford Caird* (Oxford: Clarendon, 1987), 139–50.

[3]A long line of interpreters from Gunkel to Ingo Hermann (*Kyrios und Pneuma: Studien zur Christologie der paulinischen Hauptbriefe* (Munich: Kösel, 1961), *passim*) have argued the noun phrase 'the Lord' in 3:17a refers to Christ, and that the whole clause ' "the Lord" is the Spirit' identifies the risen Christ and the Spirit. But this misses two points: (1) Paul attempts rather to identify 'the Lord' referred to in the quotation of Exod. 34:34, which he has just cited, (i.e., Yahweh), and (2) in the 2 Cor. co-text, he *applies* the Exodus passage analogically *to the Spirit*. It is this 'identification' which he seeks to secure in 3:17a + b (i.e. in Paul's analogy it is the Spirit who now plays a corresponding role to 'the Lord' of the Exodus passage to whom Moses turns). See J.D.G. Dunn, 'II Corinthians 3.17 — "The Lord is the Spirit" ', *JTS* 21 (1970), 309–20; Belleville, *Reflections*, esp. 255–7.

[4]See e.g. Dunn, *Baptism*, 135–8; Fee, *Presence*, 296–320.

covenant relationship and obedience. This observation enables
us to understand why Paul ties receiving the Spirit so tightly to
conversion.[5] He cannot elucidate receiving the Spirit in terms of
'Confirmation', or some other second blessing, e.g. 'baptism in
the Holy Spirit' (as understood by classical Pentecostals), because for Paul the Spirit is essentially the Spirit of the new
covenant. Without this gift there is no new creation, no new
heart or new spirit, no 'life', and no new covenant relationship.
Which is to say, without the Spirit of the new covenant there is
no Christian existence, in the sense most commonly understand
it, at all.

(2)	Paul's stark covenant/new covenant, Spirit/*gramma* and
Spirit/torah antitheses are part of his distinctive contribution to
New Testament pneumatology.[6] He elucidates them here
against some form of Judaizing opposition, and similarly he
develops them elsewhere as part of his critique of Judaism and
to resist Judaizing influences. It is the Spirit/Torah antithesis
that receives major attention, especially at Galatians 3:1–4:7;
4:29; 5:1–6, 13–24; Romans 7:4–6; 8:1–30 (and cf. Phil. 3:2,3). In
these contexts, the point is made that Torah had proved powerless, in sinful humanity, to enable the 'life' of filial obedience to
which it directs (and so it had become an instrument of condemnation and 'death' instead). *The Spirit alone*, Paul argues, *is
necessary and sufficient to enable this life and obedience* (and reception of the Spirit consequently renders commitment to the
Mosaic covenant soteriologically irrelevant).[7]

(3)	But, at the same time, it should be observed that the pneumatol-
ogy of 2 Corinthians 3 does not represent a move away from
the concept of the 'Spirit of prophecy'. It is thus *the Spirit*, as
'the Lord' of Exodus 34:34, who removes 'the veil' of
misunderstanding that blinds Judaism — and the most natural
explanation of this is that the Spirit achieves such an end
precisely by enabling the kind of wisdom or revelation that

[5]See e.g. Dunn, *Baptism*, chs. 10–13.
[6]On the first, which is only incidental to the passage, see e.g. W.S. Campbell,
'Covenant and New Covenant', in *DPL*, 179–83. For the second see e.g. Rom.
2:29; 7:6.
[7]For a vigorous defence of the sufficiency of the Spirit to enable the 'life' of God
(against those who interpret Gal. 5:16–18 and Rom. 7:13–25 almost to suggest a
present stalemate in the believer between sin and obedience), see Fee, *Presence*,
816–26 and 876–83 (cf. also J.M.G. Barclay, *Obeying the Truth: A Study of Paul's
Ethics in Galatians* (Edinburgh: Clark, 1988), chs. 4 and 6). See below.

yields authentic understanding of the kerygma. This same Spirit is then said to enable an ongoing and transforming 'beholding' of 'the glory of the Lord' (namely Christ: 3:16–18). Both these actions presuppose that the Spirit acts as the revealer and illuminator of the Christ-event (i.e. as the 'Spirit of prophecy') in a way that brings Ezekiel 36 to increasing fulfilment. While 2 Corinthians 3 and John 3 speak in quite different language, the underlying pneumatology, drawing on Ezekiel 36, is remarkably similar. We may now note the corporate and eschatological dimensions of this and related language.

II. THE SPIRIT AS THE SPIRIT OF THE NEW CREATION IN 2 CORINTHIANS 3–5

Already in the Old Testament the giving of a new heart and spirit was regarded as an act of creation: thus, for example, in Psalm 51:10 the penitent cries, 'Create in me a pure heart, O Lord, and put a new and right spirit within me.' Here, the language of creation/new creation, and of a new heart and spirit, is metaphor for individual renewal and restoration to God. Not surprisingly, Judaism was able to take up this language and apply it to individual conversions. Thus in *Joseph and Aseneth*, Joseph prays for the 'conversion' of the beautiful Egyptian Aseneth (whom he cannot marry until she Judaizes), 'Lord God . . . who gave life to all things, and called them from darkness into life, . . . Bless this virgin and renew her by your Spirit, and form her anew by your hidden hand, and make her alive anew by your life' (8:9).

When Paul affirms that, 'If any person is in Christ, there is (or he is) a new creation' (2 Cor. 5:17; cf. Gal. 6:15), we might be tempted to elucidate both this, and the new covenant language of 2 Corinthians 3, along similar lines. As the context of 2 Corinthians 5:17 is a continuation and development of the themes handled in 2 Corinthians 3, it might seem inviting to explain Paul's language of 'new creation' and of the regeneration of God's people promised by Ezekiel, as little more than powerful metaphors for the *individual* inward renewal of heart and spirit by the indwelling Spirit of God. But this proves unsatisfactory for two reasons.[8] *First*, it ignores the predominantly corporate focus of the new covenant promises in the Old Testament. Ezekiel 36–37, for all the prophet's individualism, concerns the re-creation of the

---

[8]See especially A.J.D. Aymer, 'Paul's Understanding of *KAINĒ KTISIS*: Continuity and Discontinuity in Pauline Eschatology', unpublished PhD dissertation, Drew University, 1983, 84–101.

nation as a righteous people, and a similar corporate dimension to new creation language is well brought by e.g. Isaiah 65–66.[9] Paul himself echoes the corporate (ecclesial) dimension of this new covenant/new creation work of the Spirit in God's people in the anti-Judaizing polemic of Philippians 3:2,3 (and cotext), and in the more pastoral contexts of, e.g., 1 Corinthians 12–14 (esp. 12:12–28; 14:12, 26); 2 Corinthians 13:13, Romans 12:4–8, etc. *Second*, in the apocalyptic eschatology of the apocalypses, rabbinic writings and early Christianity, 'new creation' referred either to this national restoration in history, or to the kind of state of affairs which Christians associated with the Parousia (cf. 2 Pet. 3:13 'But in keeping with this promise we are looking forward to a new heaven and a new earth, the home of righteousness': cf. *1 En.* 51:4–5; *2 Bar.* 73–74; Rev. 21–22, etc.). Paul himself appears to have shared the latter view (cf. Rom. 8:18–25), and he has expounded on the theme of his resurrection and new creation hope earlier in the letter (2 Cor. 4:16-5:10). So when Paul speaks of converts as instances of 'new creation', it is probable that he has in mind not only that by the work of the indwelling Spirit they have become new people in heart, spirit and relationship, but also that this new state of affairs was itself the beginning of something much bigger — of cosmic renewal. Each 'conversion' is thus 'new creation' in three dimension: it is undoubtedly individual renewal, but it is also part of the re-creation of 'Israel' as a united people of God in the church,[10] and both of these things are a first instalment of the eschatological new creation.

Given that Paul regards each act of new creation by the Spirit as part of the new creation yet to be consummated, it is entirely natural that he should call the gift of the Spirit a 'downpayment' (*arrabōn*, 2 Cor. 1:22; 5:5; cf. Eph. 1:14), for the activity of the Spirit bringing individual and corporate new creation in the church is in a sense God's giving of the 'first instalment' of the eschatological order, and one which guarantees what is yet to come.[11] Another way Paul expresses the same idea is to speak of believers having 'the first-fruits of the Spirit' (Rom. 8:23); i.e.

---

[9]See especially 65:17,18, which uses the language of the creation of new heavens and new earth as *a way of speaking of* the anticipated transformation of Jerusalem.

[10]This theme is most clearly expounded in Ephesians: see Max Turner, 'Mission and Meaning in Terms of "Unity" in Ephesians', in Antony Billington, Tony Lane and Max Turner (eds.), *Mission and Meaning*, 138–66.

[11]The term ἀρραβών designated the deposit or first instalment of a payment which guaranteed the remainder, and so secured legal claim to the article in question: see e.g. J. Behm, 'ἀρραβών', *TDNT* 1:475; G. Burge, 'First Fruits, Down Payment', *DPL*, 300–1.

their experience of the Spirit is like the 'first-fruits' (*aparchē*) of a harvest in that it guarantees much more to come.[12] In the Romans context, the 'full harvest' to come is the resurrection and the renewed creation.

Similarly, too, the Spirit can be called God's 'seal' (*sphragis*) on his people: i.e. the mark of God's ownership of them and of his intent to redeem them (2 Cor. 1:22 — indeed, here the ideas of first instalment and seal are combined: 'who also sealed us, and put his Spirit in our hearts as a deposit, guaranteeing what is to come'). For Paul, then, the Spirit is very much the power of the age to come — a power proleptically at work in us through the Christ-event; but a power, nevertheless, which orientates our individual and corporate existence towards the End, for which (with creation) we groan in anticipation (Rom. 8:22,23).

Paul, then, reads the promises of new covenant and renewed creation through the spectacles of his Christian modification of the Jewish two-age doctrine. And there is a strong christofocal dimension to this too.

III. THE NEW CREATION 'HUMANITY' AND THE SPIRIT OF CHRIST

The 'new covenant' pneumatology which we have discussed, with its overtones of Ezekiel 36, implies a radical reconstruction of humanity. Conversion-initiation is the death and burial of the people believers once were and the bringing into being of a new kind of humanity, as Romans 5–8 so vividly portrays.

But to be precise, in such 'once/now' passages Paul does not speak in the plural — of the 'people' believers once were and of the new 'men and women' they were becoming. All humankind outside Christ can in a sense for him be seen as one 'man'; for one marked all, and stamped their existence with his character of rebellion and sin — the one man Adam: cf. Romans 5:12–21; 1 Corinthians 15:20–22, 45-49.[13] Accordingly he writes, 'We know that our old man (*ho palaios anthrōpos*) was crucified with him so that the body ruled by sin might be destroyed, and we might no longer be enslaved to sin' (Rom. 6:6; cf. Col. 3:9; Eph. 4:22[14]).

Corresponding with this putting off of 'the old man' (Adam), Paul

---

[12]Cf. A. Sand, 'ἀπαρχή', *EDNT* 1:116–17; Burge, *DPL*, 300–1.

[13]For a brief survey and literature, see L.J. Kreitzer, 'Adam and Christ', *DPL*, 9–15.

[14]Though in the last passage the notion is of the 'type' of humanity, characterized by alienation and its sins.

appears to think of Christian existence not merely as the creation of new 'men' and 'women', but rather of the creation in all believers of one New Man, namely Christ. Hence Paul can say (Gal. 3:27) 'as many of you as have been baptized into Christ have "put on Christ" '; and similarly he instructs the Romans, 'Put on the Lord Jesus Christ, and make no provision for the flesh' (Rom. 13:14). In later Paulines this will be reduced to the simple antithesis between putting off the 'old man' and putting on the New (Col. 3:9,10; Eph. 4:22,24). In this 'new man', that is being 'renewed' in believers, there is no place for the old alienations, e.g. between Greek and Jew, rather 'Christ is all and in all' (Col. 3:10,11[15]). It would seem, thus, that the 'new man' created — the new heart and spirit promised by Ezekiel — turns out in Paul to be little other than 'Christ' in believers. Hence, perhaps, Paul's affirmation, 'I was crucified with Christ, I no longer live, but Christ now lives in me' (Gal. 2:20).

How, more precisely, does the Spirit relate to this? Only in Ephesians 3:16,17 does Paul (or a disciple) explicitly relate the Spirit to the indwelling of Christ in the 'inner person'/'heart'. But two important indications in the earlier letters point in the same direction:

(1) The readiest explanation of Paul's claim in Galatians 2:20, that Christ now lives in and through him, is to be found in the affirmation of Galatians 4:6, that 'Because you are sons, God has sent the Spirit of his Son into our hearts, crying, "Abba! Father" '. The expression 'the Spirit of his Son' (see section VI below) means both the Holy Spirit as the executive power of the exalted Son and, decisively for our point here, the Spirit *that recapitulates Jesus' 'sonship' to God* (expressed, in this context, in terms of his unique filial prayer[16]) *in the disciple*. The latter makes the Spirit the means both of the believers' new covenant sonship and of Christ 'living' in them.[17]

(2) Another crucial passage is Romans 8:9,10. Paul begins with the

---

[15]M. Barth and H. Blanke, *Colossians* (New York: Doubleday, 1994), correctly discern that to translate the *'neos (anthrōpos)'* of Col. 3:10 by 'new nature' (NEB; RSV) or 'new self' (NJB; NRSV) 'short-changes the full intent of this passage', precisely because such renderings fail adequately to bring out the christological force implicit in the expression (411-12). On the Old Man/New Man contrast in Paul, see D.S. Dockery, 'New Nature and Old Nature', *DPL*, 628–9.

[16]On Jesus' *Abba* prayer, see briefly, J.D.G. Dunn, 'Prayer', in *DJG*, 617–25, esp. 618–19.

[17]Some have interpreted 4:6a ('because you are sons') to mean the Galatian believers were already Christians before God sent them the Spirit of his Son. The sending of the Spirit has then been interpreted in a classical Pentecostal

assertion, 'You are not in the flesh, but in the Spirit, if in fact the Spirit of God dwells in you' (8:9a). Here he divides all humankind as to whether they belong to the realm of rebellion, designated 'in the flesh' (see below) or whether they have the indwelling Spirit of the new covenant, bringing obedience, and so can be said to belong to the realm of the Spirit. Paul calls the Spirit 'the Spirit of God' here quite naturally, mirroring the 'my Spirit' of the new covenant promise in Ezekiel 36–37.

More striking, however, is the way Paul elucidates this in the following sentences. In 8:9b he moves directly from speaking of 'the Spirit of God' living in believers (8:9a) to the assertion, 'Anyone who does not have the Spirit of Christ does not belong to him' (8:9b). And he commences his subsequent sentence, 'If, then, Christ is in you . . .' (8:10). It is evident that in 8:9, the two expressions 'the Spirit of God' and 'the Spirit of Christ' are co-referential for the Holy Spirit (cf. also the various other expressions for the divine Spirit in 8:4-6,11,13–16,23–27), but the description of the Spirit as 'the Spirit of Christ' draws attention

---

(footnote 17 continued)
sense; most recently by, e.g. H.D. Hunter (*Spirit-Baptism: A Pentecostal Alternative* (Lanham: UPA, 1983), 35–6) and H.M. Ervin, (*Conversion-Initiation*, 86–8). But as Dunn (*Baptism*, 113–15) has shown, this totally misunderstands Paul's argument and its relationship to its context. Paul can say, 'because you are sons God sends the Spirit of his Son into our hearts' for the simple reason that he is comparing Jewish and Gentile believers before their conversion to Christ with 'sons' in the period of their legal minority, awaiting their inheritance. Experientially such 'sons' are little better off than slaves until the day of their majority/inheritance (4:1-3; cf. 3:23,24). Until then all they have is a promise relating to when they enter their maturity. And Paul's point is that God has now brought his elected sons to their day of majority — he has brought them out of their spiritual minority as Jews or Gentiles into the freedom of adult sonship. Objectively, he has accomplished this through the Christ-event and outpouring of the Spirit; subjectively, it is accomplished in each individual case by the reception of that Spirit experienced as the Spirit of God's Son. As Jesus had known God as 'Abba', so now the Christian experiences God through the gift of the Spirit working as the Spirit of God's Son. This is no second blessing. This gift is the means by which the Christian comes to be related to God as 'Abba', Father: it is nothing less than the matrix of our sonship to God. This conclusion is further assured by the close parallel of Rom. 8:15, where the Spirit is referred to as *the Spirit of adoption* by whom we cry 'Abba! Father!'. It is also telling that the leading Pentecostal NT scholar, Gordon Fee, himself comes to a similar conclusion: see *Presence*, 406–12.

to the Spirit as bringing the presence and activity of the risen Lord into the life of the believer. The connection with 8:10 then gives greater precision to this: if Paul can proceed without explanation from speaking of believers having 'the Spirit of Christ' to 'Christ' being 'in them', one naturally concludes that in this context 'the Spirit of Christ' is none other than the Spirit of God (cf. v.11) experienced as creating in men and women the character and life of Christ. As Fee aptly comments, 'Everything about the argument and the context suggests that "Christ in you" is simply Pauline shorthand for "the Spirit of Christ in you," or perhaps better in this case, "Christ in you by his Spirit" '.[18] Verses 10b–11 then draw the conclusion that if 8:9,10 pertain, then the Spirit [of God] in believers is their guarantee of life and resurrection-redemption.

In sum, the new creation renewal of human existence anticipated by Ezekiel and Jewish tradition is interpreted by Paul as Christ in the believer by the indwelling Spirit. The gift of the Spirit, which is the basis of this, is evidently soteriologically necessary (not a 'second blessing'). We may now turn to the goal of this work in the believer.

IV. THE ESCHATOLOGICAL GOAL OF THE SPIRIT'S WORK: 1 CORINTHIANS 15:42–49

The believers' present experience of Christ in them by the indwelling Spirit is not definitive. For Paul, it is but a faint foretaste of the eschatological goal of the Spirit's work. The goal has already been achieved in and by Christ. For through the resurrection he became what Paul calls a 'spiritual body' (*sōma pneumatikon*: 1 Cor. 15:44,46) — not a body made of spirit (any more than a *sōma psychikon* is made of 'soul' (*psychē*)) but one corresponding to the new creation of the Spirit, and totally reflecting the Spirit's sovereignty. Several points of clarification may be required here:

(1) In the contrast between the *psychikos* and the *pneumatikos*, as in 1 Corinthians 2:14,15, the former adjective refers to 'natural' humanity in contrast to those who have and live by the Spirit.

(2) The use of Genesis 2:7 (LXX) in 1 Corinthians 15:45 articulates the contrast of 15:44–46 as that between the type of body given to the first (human) living being (15:45 = *psychē zōsa* = Adam) as a member of the natural order (hence a

---

[18]Fee, *God's Empowering Presence*, (Peabody: Hendrickson/Carlisle: Paternoster, 1994) 548.

psychikos body), and the type of body belonging to the es-
chatological/resurrection order characterized by the Spirit
(hence a *pneumatikos* body).

(3)   The implication would appear to be that it is *by* the new creation
      act of the Spirit that resurrection takes place,[19] and Paul comes
      close to stating this explicitly in Philippians 3:21 and Romans
      8:11.[20] Such a view would accord well with e.g. *2 Baruch* 21:4;
      23:5, 4 Ezra 6:39–41, and *m. Sota* 9.15,[21] and especially with such
      rabbinic teaching as we find in *Genesis Rabbah* 14.8; 96.5 (some
      MSS); *Exodus Rabbah* 48.4; *Canticles Rabbah* 1.1 §9; *Midr. Ps.* 85.3
      and *Pesiqta Rabbati* 1.6, all of which base the resurrection hope
      on the promise of Ezekiel 37:14, 'I will put my Spirit in you and
      you shall live.'[22] While these rabbinical teachings are late they
      are extremely suggestive: the Paul who builds so much on
      Ezekiel 36:25–27, might readily see a connection between (a) the
      fulfilment of this in the new creation of the Christian com-

---

[19]See M.M.B. Turner, 'The Significance of Spirit-Endowment for Paul', *VoxEv* 9
(1975), 56–69; cf. Dunn, 'Spirit', *NIDNTT* 3, 702; *idem*, 'I Corinthians 15:45 —
Last Adam, Life-giving Spirit', in Lindars and Smalley (eds.), *Christ and Spirit,*
127–42.

[20]Fee, however, denies that Paul attributes resurrection to the Spirit (*Presence,*
808–11). On Romans 8:11b, Fee supports the textual reading of B D F, etc.
(rendering *'because* of his Spirit who dwells in you') rather than that of A C, etc.
(and most modern editions [rendering 'through his Spirit who dwells in you']).
He then interprets the verse to mean, roughly, 'if God's Spirit is in you, then
that is God's guarantee to you that God will raise you to life as he did Jesus':
see *Presence,* 543 n.205. But even if one allowed his textual reading as a possibility, the logic of the guarantee is much more transparent if it is assumed
that it is precisely *through* the Spirit that God accomplishes the act of resurrection (both in Jesus' case and in that of believers). The identification of the Spirit
as 'life' (in the very context of speaking of the body as doomed to death,
because of sin, in v.10) also suggests such a meaning. Horn, by contrast, thinks
the recognition of Jesus' resurrection as the work of the Spirit was the very
basis for the church's claim to have received the eschatological Spirit ('Holy
Spirit', 267; *Angeld*, 91–115), but this cannot be right. There is no early tradition
which specifically attributes resurrection to the Spirit (not even 1 Tim. 3:16, on
which see Fee).

[21]This contains the celebrated saying of Rabbi Phineas ben Jair (c. 200), 'Shun-
ning of sin leads to saintliness, and saintliness leads to [the gift of] the Holy
Spirit, and the Holy Spirit leads to the resurrection of the dead.'

[22]Horn further appeals to 2 Macc. 7:22; *Jos. and As.* 8:9, and the second of the
Eighteen Benedictions. But the former two are not germane (the first refers to the
breath of life, rather than the divine Spirit; the second concerns inner renewal,
not physical resurrection) and the text of the last is insecure.

munity and (b) the Spirit as the basis of the fuller eschatological hope of new creation, through a resurrection like that of Ezekiel 37.[23] Such a connection would make immediate sense of his use of the metaphors 'first fruits' and 'first instalment' in connection with the Spirit (see section II above): as Dunn comments,

> for Paul *the gift of the Spirit is the first part of the redemption of the whole man, the beginning of the process which will end when the believer becomes a spiritual body*, that is, when the man of faith enters into a mode of existence determined solely by the Spirit.[24]

(4) For Paul, seeing the resurrected Jesus was seeing the final goal of all the Spirit's work. For to see the weak and humiliated crucified one resurrected as a glorious *sōma pneumatikon* was to receive a disclosure of the new creation itself and of its principal focus. To see Jesus glorified was to behold the eschatological climax of the Spirit's work in believers: the end of the process the Spirit had only *begun* in them. Accordingly Paul can say, 'Just as we have borne the image of the man of dust (Adam) so we shall (through resurrection) bear the image of the man of heaven (the Last Adam; Christ)' (1 Cor. 15:49). And, 'We await a Saviour, the Lord Jesus Christ, who will transform our lowly bodies into the likeness of his great and glorious body' (Phil. 3:20,21). For Paul, resurrection, and the life it leads to, is the real redemption, liberation, and sonship (Rom. 8:18-24a).[25] By contrast, the new human existence created in believers by the indwelling Spirit is still the barely seen 'inner man' of 2 Corinthians 4. Only at the end will that new creation be revealed in glory in a new body — and then, as Paul asserts in Colossians 3:4, it will be seen that the new life is in turn a manifestation of the resurrected Christ in whom the life of the believer is in the meantime hid.

---

[23]The fullest and most persuasive argument that Paul attributed resurrection to the Spirit is made by D. Müller, 'Geisterfahrung und Totenauferweckung: Untersuchungen zur Totenauferweckung bei Paulus und in den ihm vorgegebenen Überlieferungen', unpublished PhD dissertation, Christian-Albrecht-Universität, Kiel, 1980. Unfortunately, Fee reacts with neither Müller, nor Horn.

[24]*Jesus*, 311 (Dunn's italics), though it may be noted Dunn does not actually state that the Spirit brings about the resurrection body.

[25]See L.J. Kreitzer, 'Resurrection', in *DPL*, 805–12, for survey and literature on the place of resurrection in Paul's hope.

V. THE SPIRIT AS AUTHOR OF THE ESCHATOLOGICAL TENSION BETWEEN THE 'ALREADY' AND THE 'NOT YET' OF CONFORMITY TO CHRIST'S IMAGE

The Spirit who has already begun the new creation in believers is the Spirit who ultimately transforms them into the image of the heavenly man at resurrection (1 Cor. 15:49; Rom. 8:29 and Phil. 3:21). Until then they experience the Spirit as *arrabōn*. Between the initial moment of new creation and its consummation in the future resurrection, Paul anticipates a dynamic process of transformation into the image of Christ (2 Cor. 3:17,18). But this is no simple smooth progress of growth. For all Paul can say about the 'old humanity' being crucified with Christ, and having died with him (Rom. 6:6; Gal. 2:20; Col. 3:9, etc.), the truth is not as clear as the words of 2 Corinthians 5:17 might suggest, with its confident assertion, 'the old has gone; the new has come':

(1) The fact is that, for Paul, believers also continue to share solidarity with Adam — until the resurrection (1 Cor. 15:49). Before that, their lives are still lived in what Paul can call a 'body of death' (Rom. 8:10,13). Death, the fruit of humanity's solidarity with sin in Adam, is still *Christian* experience too.

(2) The promise of new covenant obedience remains incompletely fulfilled. Whereas the man or woman in Christ is no longer under the lordship of 'the flesh' and 'sin', neither are they so free of solidarity with Adam that they do not need constantly to be told to 'put off the old man' (Col. 3:5, 8,9; Eph. 4:22,25–32; 5:3–5), to cease from sin (Rom. 6.12,13 (etc.)). And 1 Corinthians is there to remind any who doubts that these warnings were genuinely needed!

(3) The heart of the problem was the ongoing relationship to 'the flesh' (*sarx*[26]). When Paul uses this with *negative* moral connotations, the term 'flesh' has nothing specifically to do with physicality or sexuality (one does not need a body at all to commit such 'works of the flesh' as idolatry, sorcery, enmities, strife, jealousy, anger, quarrels, dissensions, factions, and envy (Gal. 5:20,21)). Nor is Paul's term 'flesh' well translated in such contexts by 'the sinful nature' (e.g. NIV 1 Cor. 5:5; Gal. 5:13–19; Rom. 7:5; 8:3–13) if this is taken to imply a psychological or real 'component' of our human make-up (in both unbeliever and believer). Paul's contrast between flesh and Spirit rather expres-

---

[26]For the range of meaning of *sarx* in Paul, see e.g. R.J. Erickson, 'Flesh', in *DPL*, 303–6; Fee, *Presence*, 818–19.

ses the *apocalyptic* contrast between a weak human existence *without* God (and so one caught up in the cosmic rebellion of sin), and God's *own* power and strength redemptively at work in humankind.[27] Thus, while Christians still live *in* the flesh (Gal. 2:20; 2 Cor. 4:11) in the morally neutral sense of 'in mortal bodily life', they are indebted not to live 'according to the flesh'; according, that is, to the whole realm of rebellion of which they were once a part. Life 'according to the flesh' is not life according to some anthropological part of me that the Spirit opposes, but the totality of the old human order of existence. For believers, 'the flesh' in the latter sense has been decisively put away, 'crucified', as Galatians 5:24 puts it (like 'the world' of Gal. 6:14).

That said, however, life 'according to the flesh' has by no means been eliminated as a possibility: it remains a potential threat. The Christian is not to allow his or her freedom to become an opportunity for the flesh, warns Paul, in Galatians 5:13. The believer could still 'sow to his own flesh' (Gal. 6:8), and reap consequent destruction. The use of the reflexive pronoun (*heautou*, 'his own') in this last clause implies a serious ongoing potential connection with the old life. The difference between the Christian and the non-Christian is not that the Christian has sloughed off some 'sinful nature', like a dead caterpillar skin, and emerged a beautiful butterfly. Such a change awaits the Parousia. The difference between the Christian and the non-Christian is that the latter is totally determined by *sarx* (rebellious nature), while the Christian has radically distanced herself from it (crucified it) and has the Spirit too. So Paul can write of believers, 'the flesh wars against the Spirit, and the Spirit against the flesh, so that you are not able to do what you wish' (Gal. 5:17). This of course should not be taken to imply a moral stalemate and the inevitability of sin; Paul's point is precisely the opposite. The believer is not 'free' simply to drift as she wishes. She is caught up in a cosmic war, and so she must actively take her side either with the Spirit (leading to life) or with the flesh (leading to destruction[28]). Paul has no doubt that as believers choose for the Spirit, the Spirit enables the new life of righteousness — that is precisely his argument for the sufficiency of the Spirit over against Judaizing claims.[29] But he is aware that conversional 'crucifixion' of the flesh (Gal. 5:24) must

---

[27]For a discussion of the flesh/Spirit dualism in Galatians, see especially Barclay, *Obeying the Truth*, ch. 6; more briefly, Fee, *Presence*, 820–6, 876–83.
[28]See Barclay, *Obeying the Truth*, 110–19.
[29]*Ibid.*, chs. 4–6; Fee, *Presence*, 427–38, 821–2, 876–83.

constantly be renewed. The Christian must fight off the flesh to the death: cf. Rom. 8:13, 'If you by the Spirit put to death the deeds of the body you shall live.'[30]

Just how tough Paul expects the battle to prove depends on one's exegesis of a number of contested passages. Some have deduced from Romans 7:7–25 a very gloomy picture of ethical frustration,[31] but it is improbable this passage refers to Christian existence at all; rather, to Israel's struggle with the Law.[32] At the other extreme, it would be possible to point to Paul's metaphor of 'the fruit of the Spirit' in Galatians 5:22,23 as evidence that he considered the Spirit automatically produced the righteous qualities referred to, and almost without the believer's endeavour. But this would be to misread the passage and its co-text (esp. 5:13,16–18). The first 'fruit' of the Spirit mentioned is 'love', but Paul is aware that love must be striven for in a costly way, and that believers might grow weary and even give up the fight (cf. 5:6,13; 6:4,5,9,10). Such passages indicate that Paul does not conceive of the Spirit as some quasi- magical 'goodness' fluid that wells up into the Christian life without the believer's effort. If the Spirit enlists us in the war against the flesh, he then 'leads us' in the combat (5:18; cf. Rom. 8:13,14), and our responsibility is to 'march in line with the Spirit' (Gal. 5:25). There is no room in the Galatian context for passivity in the Christian life. We are reminded, rather, of Philo's 'prophetic Spirit' who 'leads in every journey of righteousness' (*Giants*, 55), while perhaps leaving the believers struggling to keep up and in formation. As Käsemann sums up the issue:

> The Lord whom we receive in and with our baptism as the Giver of the Spirit, . . . this very Lord urges us on to break through to a service which is perpetually being renewed . . . Only so long as we keep on the pilgrim way and allow ourselves to be recalled daily to the allegiance of Christ, can we abide in the gift which we have received and can it abide, living and powerful, in us.[33]

---

[30]Here, incidentally, the fact that Paul uses the word 'body' where we might expect 'flesh' shows how automatically he associates potential rebellion in sin with pre-resurrection bodily existence.

[31]See, for example, the commentaries by Cranfield and Dunn.

[32]See, e.g. D.J. Moo, 'Israel and Paul in Romans 7:7-12', *NTS* 32 (1986), 122–35; *idem*, *Romans 1–8* (Chicago: Moody, 1991), *ad loc.*

[33]*New Testament Questions of Today* (London: SCM, 1969), 175, as quoted by Barclay, *Obeying the Truth*, 214.

And Paul's widespread use of the *Agōn* (athletic striving) motif
of the Christian life (cf. Phil. 2:12,13; 3:13–16; 1 Cor. 9:24–27; Col
1:28,29, etc.) points in a similar direction.

(4) Solidarity with Adam marks our present existence not only in
death, and the nearness of sin, but also in the partial nature of
our knowledge of God (cf 1 Cor. 13:8–12), and in our continued
experience of suffering (2 Cor. 4–6; 11:21–33; Col. 1:24, etc.).
Christian life is no smooth transformation. It is the jagged
process of the destruction of the 'outer man' and renewal of the
inner: cf. 2 Corinthians 4:10, 'We continually carry about in our
bodies the dying of Jesus (= sufferings) so that the life of Jesus
may be revealed in our mortal bodies.' Paul's account of 'life in
the Spirit' is not dominated by the symbol of the resurrection
alone, but by the cross too. Just as death (for the believer) leads
to resurrection, after the pattern of the Christ-event, so, in
union with Christ through the Spirit, the many lesser 'deaths'
of suffering (cf. 2 Cor. 11:23) lead to corresponding outpourings
of resurrection life in the community (cf. 2 Cor. 1:9; 4:12; Col.
1:24).[34]

VI. THE SPIRIT OF CHRIST

We have already noted that Paul refers to the Spirit as the 'Spirit of
Christ' in Romans 8:9 and as the 'Spirit of his Son' in Galatians 4:6. In
Philippians 1:19, he uses a third related expression, the 'Spirit of Jesus
Christ'. These expressions are capable of being misunderstood in two
opposing ways:

(1) One misunderstanding of them has been to take the genitive as
one of definition, i.e. the Spirit that is (Jesus) Christ. This position usually depends on the assumption (traceable to Gunkel[35])
that Paul makes such an identification explicit at 2 Corinthians
3:17 ('Now the Lord is the Spirit . . .') and at 1 Corinthians 15:45
(understood to mean 'the last Adam became the life-giving

---

[34]On sharing in Christ's sufferings see the excellent short survey in Dunn, *Jesus*,
§55. Useful too is S.J. Hafemann, 'Suffering', in *DPL*, 919–21, but the best study
is his published dissertation, *Suffering and the Spirit: An Exegetical Study of II Cor
2.14-3.3 Within the Context of the Corinthian Correspondence*, (Tübingen: Mohr,
1986).
[35]Gunkel, *The Influence of the Holy Spirit* (Philadelphia: Fortress, 1979), 112–15.

Spirit')[36] For A. Deissmann and W. Bousset,[37] this 'identification' was virtually ontological, and to speak of being (or doing things) 'in Christ' meant the same thing as to speak of being (or performing actions) 'in the Spirit'. More recently the alleged identification has been spelt out primarily in functional rather than ontological terms by Hamilton, Hermann, and Dunn.[38] Each of these writers in different ways wishes to assert that at least *in the disciple's experience* there is no possible distinction between Christ and Spirit.[39]

While it may be right to assert the believer experiences the Spirit as the presence of the risen Lord (see below), we cannot agree that Paul anywhere 'identifies' them. Dunn himself judges Hermann's pivotal text — 2 Corinthians 3:17 — inadmissible evidence for the case, by showing that the statement 'The Lord is the Spirit' identifies the Spirit with 'the Lord' of the Exodus 34 passage, rather than with Christ (see above). Dunn's own case, that Paul nevertheless identifies Christ as the life-giving Holy Spirit at 1 Corinthians 15:45b, fares little better. It is most improbable that the phrase 'a life-giving spirit' refers to the Holy Spirit. We need to remember it is forged as a contrast to the description of Adam in the earlier part of the verse, and as one that accords the greater glory to the resurrection Adam. In 15:45a Adam is described as a *psyche zōsa* (lit. 'living soul').

---

[36]Cf. Dunn, 'I Corinthians 15:45', 139. Gunkel also made appeal to 1 Cor. 6:17, but if this be taken to show Christ=the Spirit it proves too much, for it must simultaneously demonstrate the believer is the Spirit: cf. Fee, *Presence*, 132–4.

[37]A. Deissmann, *Die neutestamentliche Formel 'in Christo Jesu'* (Marburg: Elwert, 1892); W. Bousset, *Kyrios Christos* (originally 1913; ET Nashville: Abingdon, 1970), 154–5, 160–4.

[38]N.G. Hamilton, *The Holy Spirit and Eschatology in Paul*, (Edinburgh: Oliver and Boyd, 1957); Hermann, *Kyrios*; Dunn, 'I Corinthians 15:45'.

[39]Hamilton, *Spirit*, 6; Hermann, *Kyrios*, 140; Dunn, 'I Corinthians 15:45', 139; *idem, Jesus*, 322–3. Hermann's position is actually close to Deissmann's: cf. his statement that *every* saying about Christ must be understood as an affirmation about the Spirit-Christ and *every* action of the risen Lord as worked through the Spirit (*Kyrios*, 141). Dunn, by contrast, asserts that even if Christ and Spirit are indistinguishable in the believer's *experience*, Paul does himself nevertheless distinguish Christ and the Spirit (i.e. on theological grounds rather than experiential ones): cf. *Jesus*, 322–3; *Christology*, 147, where he insists that neither the category 'Spirit (of God)' nor that of '(exalted) Christ' has wholly subsumed the other under it as a subordinate category — so that all we have to deal with now is the Christ-Spirit. 'Christ has a relation to God where the category of Spirit seems to have no clear place' (*ibid.*, cf. 148–9).

For his christological counterpart in v.45b, Paul replaces the adjective 'living' with the more powerful 'life-giving' (to develop the earlier contrast of 1 Corinthians 15:22: 'as all die in Adam . . . so all shall be made alive in Christ'). Similarly, he replaces the anthropological term *psychē* ('soul') with another one with more positive connotations, namely *pneuma*. This choice of term was especially appropriate because he had just previously contrasted the mortal *sōma psychikon* with the resurrection *sōma pneumatikon* (1 Cor. 15:44). The outcome is that his readers would be bound to take the expression 'life-giving spirit' here not as a reference to the Holy Spirit, but as an anthropological counterpart to 45a. What he means may then roughly be paraphrased: The first Adam became a living being belonging to the order of creation; the last Adam became a life-*giving* person of the resurrection order of the Spirit.[40] Neither 2 Corinthians 3:17 nor 1 Corinthians 15:45 thus identifies Christ and the Holy Spirit. Nor does Romans 8:9,10. There is no reason to equate the 'Spirit of Christ' (8:9) with 'Christ in you' (8:10) *simpliciter*; the point is rather that the Spirit of Christ in believers develops 'Christ' in them.[41] The whole thesis of an identification of Christ and the Spirit misses the mark, and we must look elsewhere for the significance of such phrases as 'the Spirit of Christ', and the like.[42]

(2)   A second way to misunderstand these expressions would be to reduce them to mean nothing more than the Spirit of God immanent in believers in the inspiration of Christ-like life in them. This is the (unitarian) position most recently and capably defended by G.W.H. Lampe in his Bampton Lectures.[43] For Lampe, Jesus was neither pre-existent, nor himself personally raised to new life. Rather, God, as Spirit, was uniquely revealed in Jesus' life, ministry, and death, and, subsequently, God began to repeat in believers what he had inspired in Jesus. It was in this sense alone that the Spirit came to the disciple as

---

[40]See Turner, 'Spirit-Endowment for Paul', 61–3; *idem*, 'Spirit and "Divine" Christology', 427–9; G.D. Fee, 'Christology and Pneumatology in Romans 8:9–11 — and Elsewhere: Some Reflections on Paul as a Trinitarian', in Green and Turner (eds.), *Jesus of Nazareth* (Grand Rapids: Eerdmans/Carlisle: Paternoster, 1994) 312–31, esp. 320–2.

[41]See above (part III), and Fee, 'Christology and Pneumatology', 323–6.

[42]See Turner, 'Spirit-Endowment for Paul', 61–5; Fee, 'Christology and Pneumatology', *passim*; Turner, 'Spirit and "Divine" Christology', 424–34.

[43]G.W.H. Lampe, *God As Spirit: The Bampton Lectures* (Oxford: Clarendon, 1977). See esp. ch. 3.

'the Spirit of Jesus Christ'.[44] Without in any way embracing
Lampe's denial of the resurrection, James Dunn has appeared
to approach Lampe's position on the significance of the phrase
'Spirit of Jesus Christ', when he has suggested that Paul (unlike
Luke and John) did not think of the exalted Jesus as 'Lord of the
Spirit', but rather that the Spirit had been 'shaped and charac-
terized by its relationship to Jesus'[45] both through his life lived
as one full of the Spirit, and through his resurrection-exaltation,
Jesus had 'impressed his character and personality on the
Spirit'.[46] Dunn is willing to elucidate the phrase 'Spirit of
Christ' after the analogy of the phrase the 'Spirit of Elijah' (2
Kgs. 2:9,10), and so to mean the Spirit with the character of the
Spirit on Jesus,[47] or, more precisely, the Spirit whose own character has been stamped by the whole Christ-event, and now
impresses that character on the believer. The vital difference
between Dunn's construct and Lampe's is that the Spirit takes
this Christ-character from the crucified and exalted Lord as
well as from the earthly Jesus. But in that case, the term 'Spirit
of Christ' cannot be moulded after the analogy of such rare
phrases in Judaism as the 'Spirit of Elijah' (meaning an endowment of the Spirit of God *like* Elijah's) or the 'Spirit of Moses'
(meaning the Spirit of prophecy on Moses that God shared with
the seventy elders in Num. 11), as Dunn suggests.[48] Neither
Elijah nor Moses 'stamped their character on' or 'gave their
personality to' the Spirit of God. Only one being did this: *Yahweh himself.* The very frequent expressions the 'Spirit of the
LORD' and the 'Spirit of God' meant precisely the self-revealing
presence and power of God. And therein, we suspect, lies
the clue to the real meaning of the Pauline references to the
'Spirit of Christ'. By such expressions he affirms that the Spirit
has become the executive power of the exalted Lord too; the
extension of his person and activity, as well as that of the
Father.[49]

---

[44]See Lampe, *God*, 114, for his definition of the Christ-Spirit.
[45]*Christology*, 145.
[46]J.D.G. Dunn, 'Jesus — Flesh and Spirit: An Exposition of Romans I.3–4', *JTS*
24 (1973), 40–68 (59); cf. his epigram, 'if the Spirit [in the ministry] gave Jesus
his power, Jesus gave the Spirit his personality'; cf. *Jesus*, 325.
[47]J.D.G. Dunn, *The Partings of the Ways* (London: SCM, 1991), 201.
[48]For the rare instances of these in Judaism see Turner, 'Spirit and "Divine"
Christology', 443.
[49]*Ibid'*, 424–34, for a defence of this.

In conclusion, when Paul speaks of the 'Spirit of (Jesus) Christ' or of the 'Spirit of his Son', Paul neither strictly identifies Christ and the Spirit, nor does he *merely* mean that the Spirit bears the character of Jesus' sonship and impresses it on the believer, though that was certainly part of his meaning in Romans 8:9,10 and Galatians 4:6. Such a meaning is, however, only a corollary of the more primary force of the expressions, and does not explain Philippians 1:19.[50] To say the Spirit is the 'Spirit of (Jesus) Christ', or the 'Spirit of his Son' is to affirm that the Spirit is Christ's executive power, and self-revealing presence. It is to affirm, in other words, that *the Spirit relates to the exalted Christ in the same way that the Spirit was earlier considered to be related to Yahweh by such expressions as the 'Spirit of the Lord' or the 'Spirit of God'*. It is not just a matter of the Spirit creating Christ in us, or reproducing Jesus' sonship in us (important as this is). As significantly, Paul can speak of the Spirit as (e.g.) 'the Spirit of Jesus Christ' (Phil. 1:19) because, since the resurrection, Jesus himself has been *giving* this 'life' (cf. 1 Cor. 15:45), *distributing* the church's spiritual gifts and ministries (1 Cor. 12:5; Eph. 4:8–11), and *making his own Lordship and presence felt through the Spirit.* As N.G. Hamilton put it:

> The Spirit so effectively performs his office of communicating to men the benefits of the risen Christ that for all intents and purposes of faith the Lord Himself is present bestowing grace on his own. The Spirit portrays the Lord so well that we lose sight of the Spirit and are conscious of the Lord only.[51]

In the co-text of Philippians 1:19 it is not Christ-like character which Paul expects to receive through the 'Spirit of Jesus Christ'; it is rather fellowship (*through* the Spirit) with Christ himself who suffered, and the support of him who now has the power to sustain all things. The Spirit of Christ as the Spirit who proceeds now *from* Christ, as from the Father, is at the heart of Paul's whole 'Christ-mysticism', with its lively sense of unity with the risen Lord, and of the same Lord himself addressing the believer (e.g. 2 Cor. 12:8,9), and promoting the quality of life in his people that he himself had lived out (e.g. 1 Thess. 3:12).

VII. CONCLUSION

We have yet to investigate an important dimension of Paul's pneumatology, namely the corporate dimension of the Spirit's work in

---

[50]*Ibid.*, 432.
[51]*Spirit*, 6.

and through spiritual gifts amongst the community (see Ch. 15). But we may already state some important conclusions. The gift of the Spirit for Paul is manifestly the power of the believers' salvation, 'the absolutely essential constituent of the whole Christian life'.[52] Christian 'life' begins by the Spirit (2 Cor. 3; Gal. 3:3–5), is sustained by the Spirit in the fight against 'the flesh' (Gal. 3 and 5–6; Rom. 8) and in the renewed 'fellowship' of the community (Phil. 2:1; 2 Cor. 13:13) as one body (cf. 1 Cor. 12; Rom. 12), and it will be consummated in the Spirit (1 Cor. 15), who is the 'first instalment' of the believers' resurrection life. There are certainly distinctive Pauline emphases not found elsewhere in Luke-Acts or John. But, for all that, the Spirit is still recognizable as a theologically developed version of the 'Spirit of prophecy' we met in those other works. Above all, Paul sees the Spirit as the self-revealing presence of God in Christ. We have noted this lies at the heart of 1 Corinthians 2:7–16 and Ephesians 3:16–19 (see Ch. 7 above), and similarly at 2 Corinthians. 3:16–18. In each, the Spirit enables the revelation and/or wisdom to understand the Christ-event, and this understanding is itself perceived to be transformatory. The main Pauline Spirit/flesh antithesis has, of course, been understood to entail a different manner of working of the Spirit — an infusion of ethical empowering at a level other than the conscious — but, as we have seen, Paul's language of being 'led' by the Spirit, and of our responsibility to 'keep in line with the Spirit' suggests rather the prophetic Spirit which guides and inclines. This need not mean Paul envisaged each concrete ethical decision to elicit an immediate revelation or prompting of the Spirit (though he may have believed this played a significant part in some Christian decisions); the Spirit could 'lead' as effectively through the preaching and teaching of godly leaders, and through the illumination of the gospel in accumulated gifts of wisdom and understanding. But all such actions fall within the boundaries of the Spirit as the Spirit of prophecy. Nor need one go further afield to explain the love of God poured into believers' hearts (e.g. Rom. 5:5); the witness of the Spirit to the believer's 'sonship' (e.g. Rom. 8:15,16); the so-called 'fruits of the Spirit' (Gal. 5:22,23 (cf. 5:25)) — all of which could be understood as different manifestations of spiritual wisdom — and the various forms of Spirit-prompted prayer and praise that abound. The only activity of the Spirit described by Paul which falls outside what one might normally expect of the 'Spirit of prophecy' is resurrection by the Spirit (if indeed that is part of Paul's teaching).

---

[52]Fee, *Presence*, 898 (cf. 896–8).

Chapter Nine

Towards Biblical and Systematic Theology

So far we have given an analytic account of the gift of the Spirit in three major New Testament writers, Luke, John and Paul. The programme has been essentially descriptive and historical. We have not allowed our knowledge of (e.g.) Luke's account of 'Pentecost' to provide the answer to the question of when John considered the gift of the Spirit to have been given; nor have we permitted Paul's much fuller teaching on the Spirit to inform our account of Luke's theology of the Spirit. We have sought to penetrate the conceptual 'world' of each writer on his own terms, and to describe their respective pneumatologies almost exclusively in relation to the events, processes and themes each independently portrays, and against the Old Testament and Jewish 'backgrounds' each evokes. It is methodologically appropriate to proceed in this fashion, even if we believe that Luke knew more of Paul's (and possibly John's) theology than he indicates. We need to let each give his own account of the Spirit in the life of the church, and listen with care to its arrangement and harmonies, before we ask questions about how the three accounts might give a theology to the church which follows.[1]

Given that we have heard the separate voices, however, how do we proceed towards a 'theology' of the Spirit? Is such a construct significant, and does it have an appropriate place in a University course? These are, of course, questions which have been vigorously debated from Gabler's day to the present. In this chapter we shall briefly survey that debate, and highlight the issues that will guide us forwards.

---

[1] If, instead, we play all three together, before hearing them separately, we risk not hearing them at all. It might be argued, *per contra*, that one best hears three separate parts combined in the one symphony, rather than listening to them separately. But I would wish to suggest that Luke, John and Paul were not offering 'parts' to be played with each other, but each their own variations of

I. THE ATTEMPT TO SEPARATE 'BIBLICAL THEOLOGY' FROM 'DOGMATIC THEOLOGY'

There is a sense in which any systematic or dogmatic theology which looks to the Bible as providing some kind of norm might be called a 'biblical theology'. But in 1787 J.P. Gabler gave his famous Altdorf inaugural lecture under the title, 'An oration on the proper distinction between biblical and dogmatic theology and the specific objectives of each'. For Gabler, true biblical theology was first and foremost a *descriptive* study of the beliefs and practices of the individual biblical authors in their respective historical settings. Dogmatic theology, by contrast, was the *normative* or *prescriptive* teaching of the church informed by (*inter alia*) biblical, historical and philosophical considerations.[2] The call for a divide between biblical theology and dogmatic theology appealed to different sectors for quite different reasons. Pietists were able to rally to it as a call to permit the biblical writers the sort of serious hearing that might allow Scripture to reform the rigid proof-texting scholastic Protestantism of the day. But in the liberal and rationalistic climate of the time it also came to be heard (somewhat against Gabler's own intentions[3]) as a charter for an *independent* biblical theology.[4] Writing just over a century later, in 1897, Wrede could contend so-called 'New Testament theology' (when it was done properly!) was a purely historical discipline freed from the shackles of dogma and of the concern for ecclesial relevance.[5]

The period from Gabler to Wrede saw revolutionary changes in the

---

[2]Morgan translates Gabler's distinction thus: NT theology, unlike dogmatics, has 'a historical character in that it hangs on what the sacred writers thought about divine things; dogmatic theology, on the other hand, bears a didactic character in that it teaches what every theologian through his use of reason philosophizes about divine things' (R. Morgan, *The Nature of New Testament Theology* (London: SCM, 1973), 3).

[3]As is now increasingly recognized, Gabler anticipated an intermediate form of 'biblical theology' which would provide a bridge towards dogmatic theology. He distinguished between what he called 'true biblical theology' — the historical and descriptive task just outlined — and 'pure biblical theology' which would extract timeless theological universals from the rubble of historically constrained opinions: see C.H.H. Scobie, 'The Challenge of Biblical Theology', *TynB* 42 (1991), 31–61, esp. 49ff.

[4]See Scobie, 'Challenge', 38–40; H. Räisänen, *Beyond New Testament Theology*, (London: SCM, 1990), part I; B.S. Childs, *Biblical Theology of the Old and New Testaments* (London: SCM, 1992), ch. 1; *idem*, *Biblical Theology in Crisis* (Philadelphia: Fortress, 1970).

[5]For an English translation of W. Wrede's essay, see 'The Task and Methods of "New Testament Theology" ' in Morgan, *Nature*, 68–116.

biblical disciplines. Released from its relationship to dogmatic theology, biblical theology came close to deconstructing itself. Its central assumption — that the two Testaments formed one Bible — was evidently a later *ecclesial* one, while, as Gabler had intimated, a primarily descriptive discipline was bound to divide relatively sharply between Old and New Testament theologies.[6] In addition, the diversity between the writings contained in either Testament appeared so great as to make it unclear whether it was truly justifiable to speak either of an Old Testament or of a New Testament 'theology'. The proclamation of Jesus, the opposed positions of early Jewish Christianity (that, e.g. of Peter and James, on the one hand, and of Paul, on the other), and the more catholic tendencies of the later writings were all perceived to have radically different soteriologies and ecclesiologies.[7] For F.C. Baur the real 'theology' between them was to be found precisely in the move towards the (Hegelian) synthesis provided by Luke-Acts, Ephesians, etc.

While this issue of the emerging diversity discovered by 'historical' research was undoubtedly of central import, Wrede had two further quarrels with the term 'New Testament theology'. Following Gabler and others, he contended (against B. Weiss and H.J. Holtzmann) that the key term 'theology' was inappropriate for the subject matter. The biblical writings expressed rather the differing faith, hopes and practices of a variety of religious movements: with the possible exception of Paul (for whom his theology was his religion and *vice versa*), these writings were not primarily expressions of 'theology' or 'doctrine' as much as of the broader notion of 'religion'. Furthermore, from the perspective of a historical and descriptive discipline, rather than a prescriptive one, there was no reason to set the New Testament apart from other religious writings in the Judaeo-Christian tradition. Scholarship had long since largely abandoned the view that a doctrine of inspiration conferred some special distinct quality on the canonical writings, and without it they were not intrinsically distinguishable from those of the apocrypha, the pseudepigrapha, the apostolic Fathers, and so forth.

---

[6]The first clear instance was the separate publication by G.L. Bauer of his *Theologie des alten Testaments* (Leipzig: Weygand, 1796) and his four volumes of *Biblische Theologie des Neuen Testaments* (Leipzig: Weygand, 1800–02).
[7]See, e.g. J.D.G. Dunn, *Unity and Diversity in the New Testament: An Enquiry into the Character of Earliest Christianity* (London: SCM, 1977); J. Reumann, *Variety and Unity in New Testament Thought*, (Oxford: OUP, 1991); but cf. D.A. Carson, 'Unity and Diversity in the New Testament: The Possibility of Systematic Theology' in D.A. Carson and J.D. Woodbridge (eds.), *Scripture and Truth* (Leicester: IVP, 1983), 65–95; G.E. Ladd, *A Theology of the New Testament* (revised edition, ed. D.A. Hagner, Grand Rapids: Eerdmans, 1993), ch. 46.

To be sure, some were of greater quality, some of less, but as Wrede put it, no New Testament writing was born with the predicate 'canonical' attached — which was merely an ecclesial decision of the early Fathers which brought together things that did not belong together, and kept apart things that did belong together.[8] Amongst the things kept apart that belonged together, in Wrede's perception, was the collateral study of other religions of the Graeco-Roman period (especially Judaism), which in his view so heavily influenced emerging forms of Christianity. Finally, Wrede insisted that such important elements of Paul's teaching as, e.g., his view of 'justification by faith' came neither from his Judaism, nor from heaven (whether in the Damascus Road chris-tophany or some other revelation), but emerged within the historical contingencies of his Gentile mission, and was fashioned in the debates with Judaizers that this provoked. All this meant that, for Wrede, 'New Testament theology' was something of a mirage. The real task was to write a history of early Christian religion within the broader religious setting of the Graeco-Roman world. Wrede died before he could carry out the task, but other members of what came to be called the *Religionsgeschichtliche Schule* carried the programme forward, especially Bousset, Gunkel and Reitzenstein, and J. Weiss's unfinished and post-humously published *History of Primitive Christianity* perhaps came closest to providing the encyclopaedic work Wrede had envisaged.[9]

If we jump almost one more century to H. Räisänen's (1990) *Beyond New Testament Theology*, we encounter the fruits of Wrede's thinking, but with some of its implications more clearly spelt out. According to Räisänen, 'New Testament theology' is not a fit subject for the University's curriculum, only for the Seminary's. The assumption ap-pears to be that the University, or Academy, studies subjects in which 'knowledge' is gained in the form of discovery of facts and the develop-ment of theories on the basis of neutral critical argument. Such facts, theories and arguments are genuinely in the public domain. That is, they are open to all; they do not rest on prior acceptance of a belief-system. To speak of 'New Testament theology', however, assumes the purely eccl-esial confession that some twenty-seven apparently disparate documents have a special coherence and authority, and so deserve to be treated separately from other religious writings of the time. To speak of them as providing the basis for a 'theology' is once again an issue of the church's dogma. The Seminary and Bible College are thus the fitting place for such subjects, not the Academy. The nearest we can get in the University

[8]See Wrede's essay in Morgan, *Nature*, 70.
[9](London: Macmillan, 1937). The German original, *Das Urchristentum*, appeared in 1917.

setting might be a 'history of early Christian thought', but that would not give privileged place to (say) the canonical Gospels over against the Gnostic ones, nor to the Pauline letters over those attributed to Barnabas, Clement, or Ignatius. And, one suspects, such a course would usually be taught on equal terms alongside similar courses on Judaism and other Graeco-Roman religions. That Räisänen's is by no means a lone voice can be seen from the increasing trend towards departments of religion rather than of theology in British and North American universities.

II. 'THEOLOGY' DEFENDED

There can be no doubt that the goals and methods of biblical studies were decisively revolutionized by Wrede. But his insistence that the academic study of early Christian religious ideas was a purely historical endeavour, that could be isolated from dogma, was open to obvious criticism. That criticism came most robustly from Adolf Schlatter in 1909.[10] Schlatter was careful enough an historian to accept that there was considerable development in the New Testament, and that significant points of Wrede's programme were correct. But he judged the attempt to disengage historical study of the writings from the interests of dogmatics was neither desirable nor possible. He rightly saw that 'dogmatics' was itself a critical discipline vitally interested in that history and considerably shaped by it — '[a] person can only become clear about the course of his own life by seeing the past as it exercises its power upon us'.[11] As important, Schlatter also saw (much more clearly than most of his contemporaries) that the allegedly neutral historian, who attempts to marshal the 'significant' events and to elucidate the important 'developments' in the religious thought of earliest Christianity, can himself do so only on the basis of some *presupposed understanding of the nature of the world and, more specifically, of the subject matter in question* — but this pre-understanding amounts to nothing less than an unacknowledged and unarticulated 'dogma'.[12]

---

[10]For ET of Schlatter's essay, see 'The Theology of the New Testament and Dogmatics', in Morgan, *Nature*, 117–66.
[11]See Schlatter in Morgan, *Nature*, 119.
[12]Schlatter, in Morgan, *Nature*, especially 125–8. Of course, those who think of 'dogmatics' merely as the contents of some of the older systematic theologies — i.e. as an ordered arrangement of theological themes (e.g. the nature of God, nature of Man, redemption, church, and eschatology) — will not fully appreciate Schlatter's point. By dogmatics, he means a discipline which potentially engages with every aspect of a person's world-view, but especially with its ultimate concerns. On this understanding atheism and Deism are dogma or theologies as much as Christian theology.

And Schlatter perceived that in the case of Wrede, and many of his contemporaries, the 'dogma' in question was strongly anti-ecclesiastical, historically reductionist and (in its very search for a detached stance) profoundly resistant to the claims of New Testament writings. There simply was no safe, dogma-free neutral historical ground from which to pursue Wrede's enquiry: the two disciplines, if potentially distinguishable (and each a guardian against the excesses of the other), were nevertheless interdependent at every stage.

Today we have moved beyond the 'naive realism' of the Enlightenment's over-confident belief in the neutral objectivity of human critical analysis (though aspects of Räisänen's quest suggests he and others might still be trapped there), and we have gone through the depressing modern and postmodern reactions retreating into phenomenalism, and despair of any ability to arrive at reliable critical judgements concerning events or entities outside the knowing self.[13] Hopefully we are beginning to emerge into a period of critical realism, which avoids these opposing dangers.[14] Wright defines this critical realism over against opposed dangers of positivism and phenomenalism as

> a way of describing the process of 'knowing' that acknowledges the *reality of the thing known, as something other than the knower* (hence 'realism'), while also fully acknowledging that the only access we have to this reality lies along the spiralling path of *appropriate dialogue or conversation between the knower and the thing known* (hence 'critical').[15]

Within such an epistemological programme (and given two scholars with otherwise similar knowledge of the first century world and critical powers), the inquirer who has struggled with the substance and method of philosophical and systematic theology (whether Christian or atheist) is liable to make more nuanced judgements concerning Paul's theology (or religious ideas) than the colleague whose 'theology' is largely the critically unexamined one of his own pre-understanding. Once having established a critical distance, the former inquirer is liable to be far more capable of 'appropriate dialogue' with Paul than the latter.[16]

---

[13]For a sparkling analysis see N.T. Wright, *New Testament,* parts I and II.

[14]See B.F. Meyer, *Critical Realism and the New Testament* (Allison Park: Pickwick, 1989).

[15]N.T. Wright, *New Testament,* 35.

[16]Compare Wright, *New Testament,* 137: 'Biblical studies needs theology, because only with theological tools can historical exegesis get at what the characters in the history were thinking, planning, aiming to do.'

Three other points in the Wrede/Räisänen criticism of New Testament theology may now briefly be addressed.[17] First, the charge that the New Testament writings concern religion rather than theology is surely a red herring. It was, of course, a helpful counterbalance against those types of New Testament theology in which every incidental phrase in the New Testament was examined in detail as a theological proposition.[18] But what people say and do in the performance of their 'religion' itself tells much about the gods in whom they believe, their view of humanity, of creation, of culture, and so forth. And these are the substance of all 'theologies', whether Christian or not, and whether critical or not. Räisänen's own preference for concentrating on 'religious thought' rather than 'religion' is all but indistinguishable from 'theology'.

Second, the concentration on the 'canonical' works can be justified on grounds other than a doctrine of inspiration. For the most part the writings in question were widely accepted by the church as 'apostolic' and of primary importance well before final agreement on the exact bounds of the canon.[19] From then on these works became definitional for Christianity and its developing theology. On these grounds alone one could justify both the primacy of place given them in any critical Christian theology, and the special discipline of New Testament studies devoted to them. I do not pretend that when it comes to the construction of a theology for today a moderate critic will give the *same* weight to these documents as will a conservative, who perhaps holds the traditional authorships and a doctrine of plenary inspiration of Scripture. Indeed, he or she might choose only to make substantial use of some of the writings (e.g. the 'major witnesses'), rather than all. My point is the simpler one that, this notwithstanding, such moderate (or not so moderate) critics may still justify a lively interest in 'New Testament' theology; indeed, notable such theologies have been produced by (*inter alios*) R. Bultmann, W.G. Kümmel and L. Goppelt.[20]

Third, the evident ecclesial or confessional interest involved in the

---

[17]For a recent searching criticism of their essentially modernist enterprise, see A.K.M. Adam, *Making Sense of New Testament Theology* (Macon: MercerUP, 1995), chs. 5–6.

[18]For examples, see Wrede, in Morgan, *Nature*, 73–80.

[19]The fact that much critical opinion attributes a few of the writings to later disciples of the apostolic bands need not affect this considerably (provided the discipleship in question is seen as 'close').

[20]Bultmann, *Theology*; W.G. Kümmel, *The Theology of the New Testament*, (London: SCM, 1975); L. Goppelt, *Theology of the New Testament*, (Grand Rapids: Eerdmans, 1981–82).

writing of these works does not mean that they (or their more dogmatic counterparts) should be banished from the Academy to the Seminary. Some, of course, will indeed largely find their home in the latter, either because they are directed to too narrow a sector of the church or because they are insufficiently critical in method, or both. But Räisänen's suggestion that because 'New Testament theology' is confessional it should be done in the Seminary rather than in the Academy fails on two counts. In the first place it fails to recognize the degree to which all academic study concerned with ultimate issues proceeds from different (and competing) types of (largely confessional) world-view. There are no 'neutral' observation posts, and the search for the view from nowhere leads us nowhere.[21] Then, too, good works of theology are often written not merely to serve the community of believers, but more especially to offer a significant challenge to important aspects of the world-views competing in the public arena of the Academy.[22] Both in its proclamation, and in its consequent analysis of culture, Christianity is essentially a public venture, not a private one.

Of course Räisänen might fairly respond that he himself envisages a whole second phase of academic reflection on the contribution of early Christian ideas to the humanities that could find a place in the Academy, but that the writing of New Testament theologies does not belong to this. His point is partly that the actualizing or interpretation phase should not be confused with the exegetical one: the former belongs to the twentieth-century setting, not to the first, and is to be discussed within the academic disciplines which analyse today's world. He is thus particularly critical of those New Testament theologies (e.g. Bultmann and Goppelt) that seek most strongly to break down the middle wall of partition between the first century and the present. But while the criticism is apposite if that interest swamps the exegesis, or structures the endeavour in a way that is foreign to the material, any serious attempt to elucidate the thought of the New Testament writers can only come about as a twentieth-century interpreter strives to give that thought coherence and depth. The product will inevitably then be

---

[21] I take the latter claim from Trevor Hart, *Faith Thinking: The Dynamics of Christian Theology* (London: SPCK, 1995), 69 (concluding his chapter entitled 'Admiring the View from Nowhere').

[22] See Hart, *Faith*, chs. 4–5. The title of the latter — Theology as Passionate Quest for Public Truth — indicates his own position. See also N.T. Wright, *New Testament*, ch. 5. Amongst recent theological works that offer serious analysis of alternative worldviews see e.g. Alistair McFadyen's, *The Call to Personhood* (Cambridge: CUP, 1990) or Colin Gunton's, *The One, the Three and the Many* (Cambridge: CUP, 1993).

laden with potential 'significance' (at least for the interpreter who sympathizes with NT writers). Rather than looking at this as a regrettable intrusion we should recognize that New Testament theologies may draw out for us such answers to the ultimate questions as the New Testament writers affirmed to be implicit in the Christ-event and in the rise of the church to which it led (or to have been revealed concerning them). They thus offer the opportunity to see whether at the foundational moment of the Christian world-view there is a coherent, credible and significant affirmation — something worthy of subsequent theological reflection both in the Academy and in the Seminary.[23] New Testament theology and dogmatic (or systematic) theology have their place in both institutions.

III. TOWARDS BIBLICAL AND SYSTEMATIC THEOLOGY

As we stated at the beginning of this chapter, we have so far deliberately kept the pneumatologies of Luke, Paul and John apart. It is now reasonable to ask concerning their relations to each other. We could ask this first at a descriptive level: to what extent do the three offer a united and coherent view of the Spirit? Is there a genuine 'New Testament' theology of the Spirit, or is the diversity such that we can only speak of quite different witnesses concerning early Christian pneumatology? Subsequently we could ask whether it is possible to speak of a broader 'biblical theology' of the Spirit that gives due weight to the contribution of the various Old Testament writings. To raise such a possibility is obviously to treat what is primarily a 'confessional' question, but that should not put it entirely outside the interest of the Academy, for whether or not the two Testaments speak in harmony has significance for an assessment of the Christian world-view. Then, third, we might ask how such New Testament or biblical theologies of the Spirit relate to the theological construals of the church, yesterday and today. This is the task approached in different ways by historical theology, systematic theology and dogmatic theology.[24] To answer any of these questions satisfactorily would take a monograph, but constraints of space permit only the following brief remarks:

---

[23]See N.T. Wright, *New Testament*, ch. 5.

[24]'Historical theology' is the largely descriptive discipline which elucidates (*inter alia*) (1) trajectories of Christian thought, whether on some specific theme (e.g., 'law and grace') or more globally, (2) the thinking of one or more specific contributors either on a particular theme (e.g. 'Luther, Zwingli and Calvin on the Lord's Supper'), or more globally (e.g. *Calvin's Theology*), etc.

(1) Whether we are asking about New Testament theology, biblical theology or systematic theology, we need to be aware that for some these are purely descriptive disciplines, while for others they are also (in varying degrees) prescriptive or normative. For Christians within the conservative evangelical wing of Protestantism, Old and New Testament theologies are potentially of greatest importance, because for such believers the Scriptures from which these theologies are drawn are still regarded as the infallibly inspired word of God. Within such a construal the text itself becomes the very revelation of God and so the real 'subject matter' of theological inquiry (a factor which may partly explain the preference for commentaries rather than theological monographs within this sector). A danger of such an approach to the New Testament can be its failure to take adequate account of the fact that this revelation was given in and through human agents who were explaining or celebrating the implications of the Christ-event *contextually*. Inability to recognize the extent to which, e.g., Paul's 'theology' was itself partly (others might say substantially) developed in the process of his considered response to particular pastoral crises may encourage a corresponding failure to expect any further worthwhile

---

(footnote 24 continued)

'Dogmatic theology' is the critically argued but nevertheless confessional study of what should be considered normative for Christian belief on some specific issue (such as 'Trinity', 'Revelation', or 'Sacraments'), or whole range of issues, in the light of (1) the biblical witness, (2) the tradition of the church (and the history of polemics between them), (3) critical knowledge in other disciplines (philosophy, empirical theology, sociology, natural sciences, etc.), and (4) personal and ecclesial experience. Different scholars will give varying weightings to the four elements here.

'Systematic theology' is used in ways that largely overlap with either 'historical theology' (especially where scholars prefer a descriptive discipline to a prescriptive one) or 'dogmatic theology' (where they have a more prescriptive bent). Schleiermacher's dogmatics (*The Christian Faith*) is primarily a work of philosophical theology, with little weight given to the biblical witness; by contrast, Wayne Grudem's recent *Systematic Theology* is better described by his subtitle (*An Introduction to Biblical Doctrine*), while nevertheless including some contribution from historical theology, and ecclesial experience (especially in pneumatology). The adjective 'systematic' would normally draw attention to the fact that the subject material examined is studied in respect of its internal and logical relationship of sub-themes, and/or in relation to other adjacent themes (e.g. 'the relation of belief in the immortality of the soul to views of eternal judgment'), or overall collections of them.

theological development *beyond* the New Testament, as the church attempted to answer new questions not faced in Scripture. The post-reformation slogan '*sola Scriptura*' can then be misunderstood to mean not merely that Scripture is the final authority or norm for Christian belief, but that there can be no other significant source or resource for Christian understanding (neither reason, nor the teaching office of the church, or whatever).[25] While it is by no means true that all evangelicals have fallen into such traps, the dangers are real enough.

(2) As we have indicated, the term 'biblical theology' has been used of a range of descriptive and prescriptive kinds of study. The term itself sharply raises the question of the relation of the Testaments. That question has been answered in essentially four ways:[26] (a) the New Testament alone is normative Scripture (so many from Marcion to F. Delitzsch and A. von Harnack); (b) the New Testament is the essential Bible, the Old its foreword and presupposition (so, roughly, Schleiermacher and Bultmann[27] — not to mention most evangelicalism, if one is to judge by its *usage* of the Old Testament); (c) the Old Testament is the essential Bible, with the New as its theological appendix (A. van Ruler[28]), and (d) the Old and New Testaments are together equally one Bible (W. Vischer,[29] D.L. Baker, B.S. Childs). Of these, arguably only (d) represents an 'orthodox' confession, but that in turn raises the question *how* the two can possibly be called 'one Bible' in a sense that does not effectively reduce what is being claimed either to option (b) or, less probably, to option (c). What is it that unites these very different looking collections, while at the same time giving an equal place to each?

---

[25]For criticism of such a position see A.N.S. Lane, '*Sola Scriptura*? Making Sense of a Post-Reformation Slogan' in P.E. Satterthwaite and D.F. Wright (eds.), *A Pathway into Holy Scripture* (Grand Rapids: Eerdmans, 1994), 297–327; also R. Lints, *The Fabric of Theology: A Prolegomenon to Evangelical Theology* (Grand Rapids: Eerdmans, 1993), ch. 4.

[26]These positions are fully described in D.L. Baker, *Two Testaments, One Bible: A Study of the Theological Relationship between the Old and New Testaments*, (Leicester: Apollos, 1991[2]).

[27]Especially his essays, 'The Significance of the Old Testament for Christian Faith' (1933) and 'Prophecy and Fulfilment' (1949). For a critical account of Bultmann's position see Baker, *Testaments*, 67–83.

[28]A. van Ruler, *The Christian Church and the Old Testament*, (ET: Grand Rapids: Eerdmans, 1966) (German original, 1955).

[29]ET *The Witness of the Old Testament to Christ* (London: Lutterworth, 1949).

For Wilhelm Vischer, as with the Fathers, 'Christ' was the uniting centre of the Old Testament and of the New. As an Old Testament scholar, of course, Vischer was fully aware that the Old Testament has relatively few explicit messianic prophecies.[30] What he meant by calling 'Christ' the centre of the Old Testament was rather that the whole pattern of Israel's experience and institutions pointed forward typologically to Christ, while the New Testament pointed back to him in a more directly referential way. Both Testaments, according to Vischer, are thus equally *witness* to Christ, but they bear that witness in quite different fashions: they are like antiphonal choirs, with Christ at the centre. Extending something like this sort of approach, Brevard Childs argues for a similar symmetry between the different witnesses of the diverse Old and New Testament writings to the nature of God, creation, covenant, Christ's lordship, reconciliation, law and gospel, old and new humanity, God's rule, and ethics. In this light, 'biblical theology' is the study of the inner unity of the two testaments on key themes. Or, to be more precise, its real subject matter is not 'themes' or the text, it is the divine realities to which the two sets of texts bear their different witness.[31] For, ultimately, 'to remain on the textual level is to miss the key which unites the dissident voices into a harmonious whole. Rather Biblical Theology attempts to hear the different voices in relation to the divine reality to which they point in such diverse ways.'[32]

It will immediately be clear that this is a 'prescriptive' account of the nature of biblical theology. But Childs' approach has three strengths over many of its rivals. First, it proceeds from careful descriptive (historical) exegetical and critical reflection on most of the canon. Childs is attuned to the diversity not merely between the Old and New Testament collections, but between the individual writings of each (he has written substantial introductions to both testaments[33]), and he resolutely

---

[30]These are, however, more numerous and more coherent than is sometimes alleged: see P.E. Satterthwaite, R.S. Hess, and G.J. Wenham (eds.), *The Lord's Anointed: Interpretation of Old Testament Messianic Texts* (Carlisle: Paternoster, 1995).

[31]Childs, *Biblical Theology of the Old and New Testaments*, esp. 80–90.

[32]*Ibid.*, 85.

[33]B.S. Childs, *Introduction to the Old Testament as Scripture*, (London: SCM, 1979); *idem, The New Testament as Canon: An Introduction* (London: SCM, 1984). He has also written a major commentary on Exodus (in which he has related the vari-

refuses the temptation to flatland harmonization at the textual level. Second, his canonical approach looks for 'deep structure' unity, and in a multiplicity of key themes. In this way he offers a more convincing account of the unity of the two testaments than those which seek to explain it by some single 'central' motif (whether covenant, or salvation-history, or whatever). Third, while his emphasis on the divine 'witness' of the individual writings (combined with his determined 'canonical' approach) does justice to the principle of *sola Scriptura*, by taking his integrating point as the 'divine reality' to which the Scriptures witness *he opens up the whole discipline of biblical theology to the insights of systematic theology and of empirical theology.*[34]

(3) It is approximately along these lines that we will venture 'towards biblical and systematic theology'. We shall certainly not attempt to give full separate accounts of the Spirit from the perspective of the distinct disciplines,[35] nor will the shape of what follows exactly match Childs' endeavour. We shall look rather for the kind of mediating biblical theology that expresses the contribution of the Old Testament/New Testament witness to a fuller systematics. A number of scholars (from Gabler himself to Childs) have in different ways insisted on some second and essentially prescriptive phase of what they meant by 'biblical theology': the critical weighing and assessment of the

---

(footnote 33 continued)
ous aspects of the task of *theological* exegesis) and a theology of the OT as Scripture under the title *Old Testament Theology in a Canonical Context* (London: SCM, 1985).

[34]Empirical theology is the careful observation of reality (events or processes in the world, including states of perception) and critical reflection on the implication of the findings for theology. Typically such a study might test competing descriptions about the practice and psychological experience of prophecy (drawn from exegetical or theoretical considerations, or based in a narrow and anecdotal analysis) by mounting a careful field study of the phenomenon across several church groups. The caution of Ottmar Fuchs is well taken: 'without observing reality . . . there is no theology, let alone practical theology. The less one observes, so much less can one claim to accomplish good theological work' ('Charismatic Prophecy and Innovation', *JET* 8 (1995) 89–95).

[35]For a more comprehensive account of the relations between the two, see e.g. I.H. Marshall, 'Climbing Ropes, Ellipses and Symphonies: The Relation between Biblical and Systematic Theology', in Satterthwaite and D.F. Wright (eds.), *Pathway*, 199–219, and D.A. Carson, 'Current Issues in Biblical Theology: A New Testament Perspective' *BBR* 5 (1995), 17–41.

diverse witnesses and the attempt to articulate their potential contribution to systematic and dogmatic theology. The scope and purpose of the resulting dialogue between such mediating biblical theology (or, in this case, New Testament theology) and dogmatic theology is well expressed by Dunn:

> On the one hand, they are *not* the same. . . . Dogmatic theology . . . must . . . range wider, to embrace not only historical theology but also themes and issues not raised by or within the New Testament. On the other hand, . . . since the New Testament itself must be part of the subject matter of dogmatic theology, New Testament theology is in effect a sub-section of dogmatic theology. But because of the canonical force of the New Testament it also follows that New Testament theology must exercise some sort of check or control within the wider discipline. Dogmatic theology is a wider dialogue than New Testament theology, but where dogmatic theology relates to issues on which New Testament theology has a say, it follows that New Testament theology must be allowed to play its normative role in that wider dialogue.[36]

It is this kind of dialogue we envisage, even though we shall present it largely from the New Testament end. We shall attempt to move from our descriptive accounts of the pneumatology of Luke, John and Paul to a more prescriptive mode, and one informed by relations with the other dialogue partners, systematic and dogmatic theology. In the two chapters that immediately follow we shall move towards such an account of the 'gift of the Spirit' and of the relation of the Spirit to God and to Christ. Then, in the remainder of this book, we shall examine the biblical witness concerning spiritual 'charismata' in the church and assess its relationship to claims to similar phenomena in the church today.

---

[36]J.D.G. Dunn and J.P. Mackey, *New Testament Theology in Dialogue* (London: SPCK, 1987), 25–6 (and see the whole discussion, 1–26).

Chapter Ten

Towards a Biblical and Systematic Theology of 'the Gift of the Spirit' to Believers

In Chapters 2–8 we offered an analytic account of the gift of the Spirit in three major New Testament writers, Luke, John and Paul, and noted that each can be regarded as a development of the kind of Jewish views of the 'Spirit of prophecy' described in Chapter 1. The account was essentially descriptive and historical, much in line with what would be anticipated by those from Wrede to Räisänen, who consider such to be the only legitimate goal of academic New Testament enquiry. In this chapter we press the further questions of whether there is a coherent New Testament 'theology' of the gift of the Spirit to believers, and how it might relate to a biblical theology and systematic theology of the Spirit. In part I, we shall begin by noting the diversity between Luke's writings and those of Paul and John. We will then examine whether this diversity is best explained in terms of two separate types of gift of the Spirit (one in conversion, then a subsequent one for empowering), or simply as different emphases concerning the actions of the gift of the Spirit fundamentally given in conversion-initiation. In the whole of this section we shall conduct the inquiry as far as possible from within a first century horizon. In part II we shall then move to more modern considerations.

I. TOWARDS A NEW TESTAMENT THEOLOGY OF THE GIFT OF THE SPIRIT

1. Diversity in New Testament Pneumatology of the Gift of the Spirit

We are confronted most sharply with the problem of diversity in the relation of the Lucan witness to that of Paul and John. Gunkel, Schweizer, Haya-Prats, Stronstad and Menzies have each argued that for Luke the gift of the Spirit is simply some special charismatic empowering, e.g. for witness, while in Paul and John the gift of the Spirit to the individual is essential to create and to sustain Christian 'life' in any form. Of the scholars concerned, Stronstad and Menzies are perhaps of special interest as they are otherwise biblically conservative. Yet they both wish to maintain that Luke's theology of the gift of the Spirit is sharply distinct from that of Paul. Menzies, in particular, argues Luke did not know Paul's letters and evidently did not know much about his theology either.[1] He points out that while the cross is central to Paul's soteriology, it is not so in Luke-Acts, not even in the teaching he attributes to Paul. Similarly, Luke shows no hint in Paul's speeches of any awareness of Paul's soteriological Spirit. Faced with this difference of presentation, it would be possible to harmonize Luke and Paul, as Lampe does, by suggesting that Luke holds essentially the same soteriological pneumatology but lays a 'special emphasis' on the charismatic/prophetic dimension of the Spirit's activity. But Menzies rejects such a possibility. He claims Luke's narrative actually *excludes* the soteriological dimension from the gift of the Spirit, always making the gift of the Spirit *subsequent* to reception of salvation.[2] His theology is thus genuinely independent of Paul's.

> Luke describes the gift of the Spirit *exclusively* in charismatic (or, more specifically, in prophetic terms) as the source of power for effective witness. Luke's narrative, then, reflects more than simply a different agenda or emphasis: Luke's pneumatology is *different* from — although *complementary* to — that of Paul.[3]

When facing the relation of such assertions to the question of biblical authority, Menzies appeals to Howard Marshall's article on 'Theological Criticism':[4]

> Marshall points out that a conservative doctrine of Scripture assumes that 'Scripture as a whole is harmonious.' However, he notes that this assumption does not rule out theological differences between various biblical authors. Rather, it suggests that the differences which do exist are 'differences in harmonious development rather than irreconcilable contradictions'. I would suggest therefore that a high view of Scripture demands, not that Luke and Paul have the same pneumatological perspective, but rather that Luke's distinctive theology is ultimately reconcilable with that of Paul, and that

---

[1]Menzies, *Empowered*, 241–2.

[2]*Ibid.*, 237 (citing Lk. 11:13; Acts 8:4–17 and 19:1–7, i.e. to show the Spirit is only given to those who are already saved). This is all said in the context of a whole chapter (12) entitled 'The Issue of Subsequence'.

[3]*Ibid.*, 237–8.

[4]I.H. Marshall, 'An Evangelical Approach to "Theological Criticism" ', *Themelios* 13 (1988), 79–85.

both perspectives can be seen as contributing to a process of harmonious development.[5]

In principle this is correct. We must indeed listen to Luke in the totality and integrity of his witness to pneumatology (and its relationship to soteriology, etc.), without prematurely fusing his horizons with Paul's. The first task of prescriptive New Testament theology is then to elucidate how the different witnesses of Luke, Paul and John cohere.

2. Coherence Attempted through a Two-Stage Model of Spirit Reception (Menzies)

I do not understand precisely how Dr Menzies expects to articulate the coherence between Luke's view of the gift of the Spirit and that of Paul and John. Several aspects of his discussion, however, strongly suggest he is thinking largely in terms of a simple addition: i.e. believers first, at conversion, receive the Spirit as the regenerating soteriological Spirit of sonship, and new covenant life (as Paul and John agree), then at some point subsequently they receive the Lucan 'Spirit of prophecy' as an experientially distinct empowering for mission.[6] According to Menzies, the inception of this latter gift is normatively (and, given the nature of the gift, very appropriately) marked by some outburst of glossolalia.[7] This is a clear two-stage pneumatology, and Menzies explicitly resists Gordon Fee's attempt to scrap the classical Pentecostal doctrine of 'subsequence'.[8] Menzies fears that doing so would effectively collapse Luke's distinctive gift of the Spirit of prophecy into the Pauline/Johannine gift of the soteriological Spirit at conversion. This, he argues, would diminish expectation of the Spirit's separate empowering for mission and effectively eliminate the Pentecostal contribution to the church. The doctrine of subsequence, he asserts, 'articulates a conviction crucial for Pentecostal theology and practice: Spirit-baptism, in the Pentecostal sense, is distinct (at least logically, if not chronologically) from conversion'.[9] This last assertion is, of course, a consideration from contemporary pastoral theology rather than from the discipline of New Testament studies, and we shall have to examine it later.

---

[5] Menzies, *Empowered*, 240.
[6] Cf. Menzies' description of Luke-Acts as indicating 'a separate level of Spirit empowerment subsequent to regeneration' (*Empowered*, 252). Menzies suggests that Paul sees the gifts of 1 Cor.12:8–10 as the result of a distinct second gift of the Spirit (See 'Spirit-Baptism'). But Paul clarifies no such distinction.
[7] *Ibid.*, ch. 13.
[8] *Ibid.*, ch. 12. Gordon Fee is himself a Pentecostal.
[9] *Ibid.*, 236.

3. Problems with Two-Stage Solutions

Menzies' position is a sophisticated defence of the classical Pentecostal position, but it is worth noting that two-stage views are held outside that tradition in many parts of the Charismatic movement,[10] and, too, by some in traditional Episcopalian denominations who use similar arguments to support the sacrament of Confirmation.[11] Closest to Menzies' own position (but coming from an entirely different churchmanship) is the Episcopalian Charismatic, Robert M. Price.[12] Price, like Menzies, also sharply distinguishes Paul's soteriological pneumatology from Luke's empowering one, but he regards the Pauline gift as granted in baptism, while assigning the Lucan one to the sacrament of Confirmation. Before we launch into the difficulties with such views, we may begin by noting that for both Menzies and Price this two-stage solution is very much a theological construct. It arises from the attempt to harmonize Paul and Luke from outside their own horizons. As Menzies and Price would be the first to agree, neither Luke nor Paul (nor any other NT writers) themselves envisage two distinct types of giving of the Spirit to Christians (at least, not after Pentecost).[13] Of course, Luke knows of times where people are filled anew with the Spirit (as at Acts 4:31, etc.), but this is always as a refreshing experience of the same gift of the Spirit of prophecy already earlier received. It is not theologically a distinct or 'different' giving of the Spirit.

In reaching an assessment of such a theology we need to bear the following points in mind:

(1) Menzies' argument would probably only work if what Luke envisaged by the 'gift of the Spirit' involved quite *distinct* activities of the Spirit from those implied in Paul's understanding of the gift of the Spirit at conversion. What Luke meant by the 'gift of the Spirit' could then in principle be 'added' to the believer who had already experienced what Paul meant by having received the gift of the Spirit.

---

[10]See H.I. Lederle, *Treasures Old and New: Interpretations of 'Spirit-Baptism' in the Charismatic Renewal Movement* (Peabody: Hendrickson, 1988), chs. 2–3.
[11]See Dunn, *Baptism, passim.*
[12]R.M. Price, 'Confirmation', 173–182.
[13]See Price's explicit remarks: he claims the two different pneumatologies of Paul and Luke, 'cannot and should not be forcibly harmonized *exegetically*, but they can quite easily be harmonized *theologically*. We might synthesize both Paul and Luke by saying that the indwelling Spirit is received in water baptism, but the empowerment of the Spirit is received subsequently in confirmation by the imposition of hands.' ('Confirmation', 181).

We allowed for such a view in our earlier work by arguing that the phrase 'to receive the (gift of the) Spirit' means simply the commencement of a *specific nexus* of activities of the Spirit in a person.[14] The onset of a new nexus of activities in an individual might then readily be referred to as a second reception of the Spirit. We drew attention to the case of Jesus, who in a sense received the Spirit in Luke 1:35, but subsequently further 'received' the Spirit (beginning entirely new sets of activities) in Luke 3:21,22 and at Acts 2:33. This kind of usage opened the door to two possibilities: (a) that Luke, Paul and John might individually use the language of 'receiving' the Spirit to denote different sets of activity of the Spirit, and so may relate Spirit-reception to conversion-initiation in fundamentally different ways without contradicting each other, and (b) that each of these writers might have envisaged *several* (different) 'receptions' of the Spirit by any one believer, at different stages, and each for a different function (e.g. the conversional gift and a subsequent one of empowering for ministry). Menzies invokes the first of these possibilities, and W. Atkinson both of them.[15]

The fact is, however, that Paul's conception of the gift of the Spirit is simply *broader* than Luke's, *while nevertheless containing everything that Luke implies*. The one gift of the Spirit to the Christian at conversion is God's empowering presence which brings not only sonship and new creation life but also the different charismata of the Spirit of prophecy such as those outlined in 1 Corinthians 12–14 and Romans 12. These include the very gifts of wisdom, revelation and various types of inspired speech which are prototypical to Luke's conception of the 'Spirit of prophecy', and which were undoubtedly experienced by Paul as part of his empowering for mission (cf. 1 Thess. 1:5;

---

[14]Turner, 'Luke and the Spirit: Studies in the Significance of Receiving the Spirit in Luke-Acts', unpublished PhD dissertation, Cambridge, 1980, 35–40; *idem*, 'Spirit Endowment in Luke-Acts: Some Linguistic Considerations', *VoxEv* 12 (1981), 55–60; *idem*, 'Spirit in John', 24–6.

[15]See W. Atkinson, 'Pentecostal Responses to Dunn's *Baptism in the Holy Spirit*: Pauline Responses', *JPT* 7 (1995) 49–72, esp. 64–6. Atkinson (himself a Pentecostal) notes that Luke's use of Spirit-endowment language differs in form and function from Paul's, and that (despite the second possibility) in fact each NT writer only speaks of one Spirit-reception by any believer. Nevertheless, he contends there was nothing in the way of their speaking of individuals receiving the Spirit several times, and this may offer a comfortable way *for us* to achieve coherence between the writings (see esp. 70). Indeed (*contra* the impression given by Dunn that Pentecostals used Spirit-reception only for post-conversional Spirit-baptism) much Pentecostalism did in fact distinguish the regenerative gift of the Spirit from the empowering gift.

Rom. 15:18,19, etc.). Paul's comprehensive understanding of the
gift of the Spirit granted to Christians at conversion does not
leave anything for Luke's to 'add'. Of course, Paul does not
think that each convert receives all the giftings he or she will
ever receive at conversion. In 1 Corinthians 14 he urges some to
seek the charism of interpretation (14:13), and even more to seek
the charism of prophecy (14:1, etc.). But the point remains that
he expects them to receive these things through the sovereign
activity of the one Spirit which they received in conversion (1
Cor. 12:13): *he does not suggest they should seek some second giving of
the Spirit before they might be granted such charismata.*[16] In other
words, by failing to articulate any theologically distinct second
gift of the Spirit, Paul has done the very thing Menzies chides Fee
for doing with Acts. Paul has effectively rubbed out the possibility of any sharp distinction (if such ever existed) between
charismatic pneumatology and soteriological pneumatology.

(2) One certainly cannot use Luke to *impose* such a distinction on a
reading of Paul, as though Luke's effort might bring theological
nuance to Paul, and clarify for us that Paul must really have
'meant' to teach something like a doctrine of subsequence, even
if he never expressed it quite clearly enough. Some (though not

---

[16]Contra Menzies, 'Spirit-Baptism', in Ma and Menzies (eds.), *Pentecostalism in
Context* (Sheffield; SAP, 1997), 48–59. A number of Pentecostal scholars have
attempted to read Paul's words ἐν ἑνὶ πνεύματι ἡμεῖς πάντες εἰς ἓν σῶμα
ἐβαπτίσθημεν ('in/by one Spirit we were immersed into the one body') as a
reference to Spirit-baptism in the classical Pentecostal sense (so, most recently,
H.D. Hunter, *Spirit-Baptism*, 39–42), but there is no hint of such a view in Paul
(see Fee, *Presence*, 178–82). Other Pentecostals, e.g. H.M. Ervin, *Conversion-Initiation and the Baptism is the Holy Spirit: A Critique of James D.G. Dunn* Baptism in
the Holy Spirit (Peabody: Hendrickson, 1984) have been persuaded by Dunn
that 12:13a refers to conversion, but have pressed the words of 12:13c, καὶ
πάντες ἐν πνεῦμα ἐποτίσθημεν ('and we were all caused to drink the one Spirit')
to refer to subsequent Spirit-baptism. But it is easier to take 12:13c as piece of
parallelism to 12:13a, and so to refer to conversion-initiation reception of the
Spirit (see Fee, *ad loc*, and W. Atkinson, 'Pentecostal Responses', esp. 51–2, 55–6,
57–9). Even if it were taken to refer to subsequent experiences of the Spirit,
there is no indication that some *distinct* gift of empowering is intended rather
than repeated experiences of the same gift of the Spirit received in conversion-
initiation. Fee himself claims, 'Paul has none of our hang-ups over whether a
Spirit person can "receive the Spirit" ' (so *Presence*, 741 (on Phil. 1:19: cf. 388 (on
Gal. 3:5), 52 (on 1 Thess. 4:8), and 720-2 (on Eph. 5:18)), but he does not mean
by this that Paul gives any hint of a second distinct gift of the Spirit as a *donum
superadditum*. He means rather that the Spirit is the key to all aspects of Christian life, and that believers continually experience 'ongoing appropriations' (cf.
864) of the initial gift.

Menzies or Price) have tried to argue that such a doctrine of subsequence lies behind Galatians 4:6 and 1 Corinthians 12:13, but only at the expense of misunderstanding the co-text and Paul's argument.[17] As Gordon Fee has shown, such attempts are merely the reading into the text of vested interests, not critical exegesis. Both texts imply activities of the Spirit subsequent to conversion, but these are ongoing activities of the one Spirit received in conversion, not subtle references to a subsequent and theologically distinct granting of the Spirit.

(3)   Nor can we harmonize in this way at the higher level of New Testament theology, e.g. by suggesting Luke's witness theologically demarcates an area which Paul's pneumatology accidentally left undifferentiated; the difference between the activities of the Spirit which enable new creation and ordinary Christian living and those, dependent on the Spirit as the 'Spirit of prophecy', which empower for mission. As we have seen in Chapters 7 and 8, for Paul it is precisely the wisdom-granting revelatory Spirit — that is, the Spirit *as the 'Spirit of prophecy'* — who enables the understanding of the cross that leads to conversion and continuing authentic faith (Gal. 3:1–5; 1 Cor. 2:10–14; 2 Cor. 3:16–18; 4:13; Eph. 3:16–19). It is as this same 'Spirit of prophecy' that the Spirit communicates the presence and guidance of the Father and the risen Lord. It is as the same 'Spirit of prophecy' again that the Spirit 'leads' the Christian in the new life of sonship and in the fight against the flesh (Rom. 8; Gal. 4–6). If this is so, however, we must ask what it could possibly mean to insist a believer needs to receive a second different, theologically distinct, gift of the Spirit in order to serve in the church and in God's mission. If it is by the wisdom and revealing power of the 'Spirit of prophecy' that the Christian receives these soteriological benefits, then surely the same 'Spirit of prophecy' would be expected to afford the wisdom, revelation and inspired speech that would enable service in the church and in God's mission. Of course, it could be said that in the one case the Spirit acts primarily for the benefit of the believer herself and in the other he acts *through* the believer primarily for the benefit of others. But this is surely an irrelevant distinction when at bottom it comes down to the same 'Spirit of prophecy' functioning through the same prototypical gifts in both cases.

---

[17]See e.g. Ervin, *Conversion-Initiation*, 86–8 (on Gal 4:6, and quite misunderstanding Dunn's subtle but convincing exegesis) and 101–2. For critique of Ervin, see W. Atkinson, 'Pentecostal Responses', 53–7: cf. also the previous note.

Indeed, this observation may explain why it is so natural for Paul (in 1 Cor. 12–14) to trace the charisms which enable service and mission back to the one Spirit given in conversion, even when he must have been aware that some of the charisms were only actually experienced some time after conversion. The same observation would also suggest we should attempt to establish coherence between Paul, Luke and John on the basis of a single giving of the Spirit (at conversion) rather than a double one. It should be duly noted that this is a theological and prescriptive argument, not simply a descriptive or exegetical one.

4. Coherence Attempted through a One-Stage Model of Spirit Reception

We have suggested that a one-stage model is inherent to Paul because the one gift of the 'Spirit of prophecy' serves both soteriological and empowering purposes through essentially the same prototypical gifts. It should immediately be clear that the same applies to John. We have seen that for John 'salvation' and 'new birth/creation' are brought about through revelation and revelatory wisdom, and that the Spirit performs these soteriological functions by enabling a person to understand the cross as the glorification of the Son, and the supreme revelation of God's saving love for the world (cf. John 3). The Spirit-Paraclete also brings the self-manifesting presence of the Father and the Son to live with the disciples (14:15–28), and this communion is 'life' itself (cf. 17:3). Further, we have noted, the same Spirit-Paraclete empowers the mission of the church by unfolding the significance of the Christ-event to the community of believers and leading them further into the truth (15:26,27; 16:7–15). All these functions of the Spirit are unified in the underlying concept of the Spirit as the 'Spirit of prophecy' who imparts wisdom and revelation.[18] We should thus expect that after Pentecost the one (necessary) reception of the Spirit as Paraclete in conversion would mediate all envisaged soteriological and subsequent empowering functions. John does not anticipate two *distinct* gifts of the Spirit to Christians after the ascension, and his theology of the Spirit leaves no rationale for such. In that sense John and Paul stand together.

What about Luke? Does he really offer a different paradigm? On exegetical grounds, we have suggested not. To be sure, as with John, there are complexities in relating the pre-Pentecost experience of the disciples with what Luke envisages beyond Jesus' ascension. But *after*

---

[18]See 'Holy Spirit', in *DJG* 347–51, and the literature there (or Chs. 5–6 above).

Pentecost the issues are relatively clear. First, as we have seen, Luke expects the 'Spirit of prophecy' to be given at conversion-initiation (paradigmatically at Acts 2:38,39). The Samaritans are his only real exception, and he *indicates* they are exceptional (8:16). There are not sufficient grounds here for Menzies' doctrine of subsequence (far less for the form of it which Price proposes, namely 'Confirmation' following years after baptism). Luke's purpose to provide an account of the expansion of Christianity certainly explains his emphasis on the 'Spirit of prophecy' as 'empowering' for mission, but we have seen he does not think of it exclusively in such terms. He also understands the 'Spirit of prophecy' as the power by which the risen Lord 'baptizes (= purifies)' Israel, restoringly transforming her as a community of the new covenant, and as a light to the Gentiles (1:3–8; 2:1–13,41–47, etc.). For Luke too, soteriological functions and empowering functions are granted through the one gift of the 'Spirit of prophecy' at conversion, even if the latter are sovereignly distributed, and may only come to expression later in the Christian life. It is not that Luke offers a theologically distinct conception of the gift of the Spirit; rather, he offers essentially the same theology, but articulates it less fully (as with so many other areas of his 'theology').

We conclude that for each of our three major witnesses, the gift of the Spirit to believers affords the whole experiential dimension of the Christian life, which is *essentially* charismatic in nature. The gift is granted in the complex of conversion- initiation. The prototypical activities of the 'Spirit of prophecy' which believers receive — revelation, wisdom and understanding, and invasive speech — together enable the dynamic and transforming presence of God in and through the community. These charismata operate at individual and corporate levels, enabling a life-giving, joyful understanding of (and ability to apply) the gospel, impelling and enabling different services to others in the church, and driving and empowering the mission to proclaim the good news.

Whereas the way was open for the New Testament writers to speak of believers after Easter experiencing two (or more) quite distinct gifts of the Spirit (one for new covenant life and sonship, a subsequent one of empowering for ministry), this option was not pursued. We should not take this to mean that each believer 'got it all' at conversion. Both Luke and Paul anticipate a succession of further fresh experiences of the Spirit, whether in the multiplicity of individual moments of charismatic expression, or at the commencement of new phases of ministry (cf. 1 Tim. 4:14; 2 Tim. 1:7), or the refreshment of these (cf. 2 Tim. 1:7).[19]

---

[19]On Paul's view, see especially Fee, *Presence*, 864, and Ch. 15.

Luke can use the language 'filled with the Spirit' and 'full of the Spirit' both to designate such charismatic 'moments' (e.g. Lk. 1:41,67; Acts 2:4; 4:8,31; 7:55; 13:9) and to denote occasional longer-term endowments for ministry (Lk. 1:15; 4:1; Acts 9:17).[20] But neither Luke nor Paul uses 'to receive (the gift of) the Holy Spirit' of some definite second experience — they use such expressions only in connection with the conversion-initation complex. Nor does either have any other linguistic expression (whether 'baptize in Holy Spirit' or 'fill with/full of the Holy Spirit') to designate entry to some clearly demarcated 'second blessing' realm available to all. Indeed, where Luke (diff. Paul[21]) refers to people 'full of' the Spirit, this is rather his way of speaking of people marked by an *unusually* intense presence and activity of the Spirit. There is simply no clear exegetical evidence to suggest that Luke, Paul or John envisaged the possibility that there were in the post-Easter church two classes of Christians, distinguished by whether or not they had received the Pentecost gift of the Spirit. That there could be any 'believers' who lacked the new Christian 'Spirit of prophecy' was strictly an exceptional and anomalous possibility (as Acts 8 indicates), because this gift (with the charismata it afforded), was at the heart of the new life of salvation, service and mission.

II. TOWARDS A SYSTEMATIC THEOLOGY OF THE GIFT OF THE SPIRIT TO CHRISTIANS

In this section we shall not attempt to formulate a 'systematic theology' of the gift of the Spirit to believers (which would necessitate considerable repetition of what has gone before), but briefly consider the appropriation of our New Testament conclusions in the light of some broader and more contemporary considerations.

---

[20]For Luke's complex and subtle (but primarily phenomenological) use of 'fill with/full of', see Turner, *Power*, appendix to ch. 6.

[21]Paul's only use of 'fulness' language in connection with the Spirit comes in Eph. 5:18. Here (as the references to wisdom (5:15) and 'the will of the Lord' (5:17), and the stereotypical contrast with foolishness (5:17) and drunkenness (5:18), imply) it is an injunction to live fully in the wisdom the Spirit grants — a wisdom which (as in Sir. 39:6) yields in doxology, but also in a new Christian lifestyle of mutual submission. Grammatically the imperative 'be filled' of 5:18 governs all the participles in 5:19–21, and the section 5:22-6:9 which depends on the last participle 'being subject (to one another)' in v.21.

1. The Spirit in Relation to the Immanence and Transcendence of God

In many of the older churches (Catholic, Orthodox and Protestant), the Spirit has largely been understood as the immanence of God in the church. That is to say, baptism and confirmation, the very existence of the congregation, the reading and exposition of the word, the congregation's intercession, doxology and celebration of the eucharist, together with the disciplined Christian life, are all understood as sustained *by* the Spirit and as themselves the evidence *of* the Spirit amongst God's people, even when, alas, there is little or no immediate *sense* of the Spirit in these things. As sinful humanity in quest of autonomy from God, we are ever in danger of attempting to tame and to institutionalize the Spirit. By contrast, the Pentecostal and Charismatic movements have correctly perceived that, by and large, the activities of the Spirit in Luke-Acts *are a matter of immediate perception*; the *self-manifesting* presence of God. Activities are characterized as of the Spirit largely when they break out beyond merely human possibilities. The Spirit in Acts marks the transcendence of God: (a) 'over and against' the community in the sense that he announces judgments that instil the fear of the Lord (e.g. Acts 5:1–11) and in so far as the Spirit's initiatives constantly break through the merely human expectations, and guide the church in directions to which she was innately resistant (e.g. the move to the Gentiles), and (b) irrupting charismatically *through* believers to address and fortify the community and to empower its proclamation to outsiders. In this respect Luke's picture resonates most strongly with the Old Testament emphasis on the charismatic Spirit, and sensitizes us to similar features in Paul that we might otherwise have been prone to read in terms of God's immanence in the community.[22] We need not doubt that there are aspects of New Testament pneumatology which are suggestive of God's immanence in the church (as e.g. divine presence and wisdom), and which have been too easily ignored by Pentecostals and Charismatics, but these movements have recalled us to a healthy respect for the Spirit's transcendence, and an expectation of his intervention.

The New Testament writings also pose a challenge to those dogmatic pneumatologies which extend the immanence of God in the Spirit beyond the church into the world and into inanimate creation.[23] We

---

[22]On Luke's contribution in this respect, and the challenge it poses to an over-formalized church, see Turner, *Power*, ch. 14, §5.1.

[23]For the most recent (and creative) attempt, see J. Moltmann, *The Spirit of Life: A Universal Affirmation* (London: SCM, 1992). But this needs to be read with his *The Church in the Power of the Spirit* (London: SCM, 1975) to avoid misunderstanding.

may entirely applaud (e.g.) Moltmann's criticism of earlier pneumatologies for restricting the Spirit's activity to the ecclesiastical institutions or to the inner devotional life of the human soul. He is surely right that the Spirit comes to special expression in the full-bodied fellowship of whole human beings which imitates the joyful fellowship within the divine trinity. Nevertheless, the strong restriction of 'the gift of the Spirit' to *believers*, combined with the strange silence of the New Testament concerning the Spirit in creation,[24] must question (more sharply than Moltmann and Rahner allow) how we relate all this to the world that does not acknowledge Christ.[25]

2. The Weakness of Classical Pentecostal and Neo- Pentecostal Two-Stage Pneumatologies[26]

Modern contributions to the debate appear increasingly to support the view that we cannot split the giving of the Spirit into two distinct successive stages. In this respect it is significant that notable Pentecostal leaders, including their foremost New Testament scholar, Gordon Fee, have abandoned the classical Pentecostal paradigm of subsequence and initial evidence.[27] It is also significant that most of those attempting to restate the classical Pentecostal model (including Donald Basham, Dennis Bennett, Roger Stronstad, J. Rodman Williams, Howard Ervin and Robert Menzies) still largely depend on the exegetically suspicious arguments (i) that Jesus' Jordan empowering is prototypical of a later anointing for empowering alone, (ii) that the experience of the disciples (believing at Easter, but receiving the Spirit at Pentecost) is paradig-

---

[24]Cf. M.A. Chevallier, 'Sur un Silence du Nouveau Testament: L'Esprit de Dieu à l'Oeuvre dans le Cosmos et l'Humanité', *NTS* 33 (1987), 344–69.

[25]It is notable that the review articles in *JPT* 4 (1994) by M. Stibbe (5–16), P. Kuzmic (17–24), F.D. Macchia (25–33; and *idem*, 'The Spirit and Life: A Further response to Jürgen Moltmann', *JPT* 5 (1994), 121–7) and S.K.H. Chan (35–40) each, in different ways, suggests Moltmann has overplayed the immanence of God in the Spirit and played down too much the Spirit as God's transcendence.

[26]Following Bittlinger and Lederle, I use the term 'classical Pentecostal' for the traditional positions of the major Pentecostal denominations, and 'neo-Pentecostal' for the similar strongly two-stage pneumatologies of those in the various Charismatic Renewal movements. The latter adopt varying positions on the questions of 'conditions' for reception of Spirit-baptism, and on whether glossolalia is a necessary 'initial evidence'. See Lederle, *Treasures*, chs. 2–3, for the typology.

[27]For other notables including W. Hollenweger, C. Krust, L. Steiner, R. Spittler, and for Fee's own position, see e.g. Lederle, *Treasures*, 27–32.

matic, and (iii) that Acts 8 is paradigmatic.[28] There is further a marked
failure to be able to distinguish how the work of the Spirit in conversion-initiation and everyday discipleship differs (theologically) from
the work of the Spirit in the alleged second stage of Spirit-baptism.

The sharpest distinction is that offered by the earliest Pentecostals
(and forcefully restated by Menzies), namely that the distinctively Pentecostal Spirit is vocational empowering for witness. But (after Pentecost) Luke connects this gift of the Spirit with the
conversion-initiation, not with some more mature stage of the
believers' spiritual journey, and, in any case, his account fails to give
the impression that all Christians are empowered as missionaries. More
important, as we have seen, the 'empowering' envisaged depends largely on *the same gifts of wisdom, revelation, and inspired speech* that make
possible the presence and direction of Christ to the individual and to
the community in the life of salvation. This type of distinction between
the initial giving of the Spirit and subsequent Spirit-baptism thus dis-
solves. The same observation renders unintelligible the view that
(second-stage) 'Spirit-baptism' enables the believer for the first time to
experience the Spirit's charismata: it is only in and through the experience of various charismata that the believer becomes aware of
Christ at all.

It is not surprising that others have interpreted 'Spirit-baptism' more
ambiguously as some sort of *intensification* of the conversional gift (e.g.
a deeper more experiential relationship with the Lord, and one that
empowers for service to the church and in witness to the world). But
this kind of approach does not support a rigid two-stage theology of
the Spirit as easily as it does some other paradigms that we shall examine later. In the first place, it hinges on an almost intractable abstrac-
tion (what level of Spirit-experience belongs to the conversional gift,
and what to Spirit-baptism?). Second, this difficulty threatens to make
it incoherent to speak of the second experience as a theologically *distinct* gift and reception of the Spirit, and promotes impossible attempts
to rationalize it.[29] And while this paradigm clearly suggests we should
find two distinct types of Christian, it faces the problems of (a) the lack

---

[28]See the critique by Lederle, *Treasures*, 55–66, and by Turner (above, Chs. 2–3,
or *idem, Power, passim*).
[29]See Lederle, *Treasures*, 73–96. Impossible solutions include the attempt by,
e.g., H. Horton and D. Prince to argue that the conversional gift is a working of
the Spirit from outside the person, while Spirit-baptism is an internal work (this
pneumatological topography flies in the face of OT and NT usage: the Spirit can
be said to be 'upon' or 'in' Jesus, and others, and even to 'clothe himself with
Gideon' (and others), without the slightest functional difference (see Turner,
'Spirit Endowment', 47–8)).

of evidence that any single New Testament writer speaks of two successive gifts of the Spirit to post-Easter believers, (b) the lack of any clear
empirical difference between the quality of Christian discipleship
before and after 'Spirit-baptism' for a *considerable sector* of those involved, and (c) the lack of material evidence that Christians in traditional churches are necessarily less spiritual or less gifted (over a wide
range of gifts) than those in Pentecostal and Charismatic ones (of
course, it is always easy to compare best with worst to support the
argument in either direction!). Finally, explanations of 'Spirit-baptism'
in terms of 'intensification' of the conversional gift fail to explain how
this allegedly 'second-blessing' gift differs from *subsequent* intensifying
occasions of renewal in the Spirit.

3. The Weakness of Primarily 'Sacramental' Accounts of the Gift of the Spirit

Given the notorious difficulty of making sense of the difference between first and second receptions of the Spirit in terms of some sort of
unspecified 'intensification' of the former in the latter, and given the
difficulty of accommodating the Pentecostal paradigm to the conversion-initiation theologies of most denominational churches, it is not
surprising that many (including Cardinal Suenens, Kilian McDonnell,
René Laurentin, Simon Tugwell and John Gunstone) have attempted to
interpret 'pentecostal' experiences as the later 'flowering' or 'release' of
the gift of the Spirit granted in baptism (or Confirmation).[30] This
paradigm shares some of the problems just elucidated, but in addition,
as Lederle points out,

> There is a sense of unreality in telling someone who has just had a
> powerful renewal experience that theologically nothing has hap-
> pened at that particular time or that the Holy Spirit did not come in
> any new way at all, and that all that transpired was that the Spirit,
> received at baptism, was experientially 'released' . . . I have suc-
> cumbed to the temptation to describe this as the 'time bomb' theory
> thereby expressing, perhaps, more a Reformed impatience . . . with
> the constant preoccupation of many High Church theologians with
> the sacraments than with anything else.[31]

---

[30]For Sacramental interpretations of Spirit-baptism, see Lederle, *Treasures*, ch. 3.
[31]*Ibid.*, 223.

4. The Strength of 'Integrative' Accounts of Spirit-Baptism

The remaining diverse approaches to Charismatic renewal identified by Lederle's survey in one way or another attempt to integrate their charismatic experiences with the historic Christian faith *without* appeal either to a classical Pentecostal (two-stage) model or to a sacramental one. Amongst the most theologically nuanced and sophisticated attempts are those of Arnold Bittlinger, Heribert Mühlen, Francis Sullivan, and Henry Lederle himself.[32]

The main 'integrative' views all interpret Charismatic experience (whether a crisis experience or not) as renewing, ongoing and extending experiences or appropriations of the one gift of the Spirit given to all Christians in conversion-initiation. These views differ from more traditional forms of Christianity in their vivid expectation of God's intervention in and though the church in miraculous gifts, including tongues, prophecy and healing. But they differ too from, e.g. classical Pentecostalism in a number of important ways, recognizing the following significant points:

(a) The dynamic spiritual life which Pentecostalism rooted in a second-stage Spirit-baptism is widely found outside those sectors of the Charismatic movement which adopt two-stage paradigms.

(b) Such charismata as healing and prophetic words are encountered in Christian movements that do not necessarily claim any type of 'Spirit-baptism' experience as a gateway to them (and may not even describe themselves as Charismatic renewal movements), while, equally, other believers may grow slowly into a Pentecostal spirituality, and use of varied charismata, without any crisis experience. In other words, what Pentecostals understand as a subsequent 'baptism in Spirit' does not in practice appear to be in any way 'necessary' for 'charismatic' life.

(c) For some believers there has been an important 'moment' of the

---

[32]*Ibid.*, ch. 4, outlines some fifteen slightly differing approaches, including those mentioned here. Some are noticeably less successful than others, because, for example, they portray the experience of charismatic renewal as the final stage of Christian initiation (thereby creating the anomaly of large numbers of Christians whose conversion-initiation is incomplete because they have not yet experienced some immediate charismatic event such as tongues or prophecy). Amongst these we might include the quite different positions of oneness Pentecostals, David Watson *One in the Spirit*, (London: Hodder, 1973), and David Pawson, *The Normal Christian Birth* (London: Hodder, 1989). For Lederle's own variation on the 'integrative' approach, in more detail, see *Treasures*, ch. 5, (esp. 227–40).

Spirit, experienced subsequent to conversion, beyond which they came to experience one or several of the types of gift described in 1 Corinthians 12:8-10, but it is difficult to find anything approaching a normative pattern to such experiences — e.g. whether the 'moment' is attended by tongues, or some other inspired speech, or none. All one may say is that there is a correlation between what a person expects of God and what he or she experiences of him.

(d) There is no sharp distinction between the charismata described in 1 Corinthians 12:8–10 and other less dramatic experiences of new spiritual understanding, teaching, etc., found widely both inside and outside churches professing a two-stage pneumatology. Furthermore, many (e.g.) traditional Evangelicals clearly have the Spirit's 'power to witness',[33] while eschewing anything approaching a Pentecostal or Charismatic Renewal interpretation of their gifting.

(e) Those who have had a crisis 'Spirit-baptism' of some kind, beyond conversion, may have further, sometimes more dramatic, experiences of empowering, but this does not provide the basis for Pentecostal theologies of third, fourth and fifth stage 'receptions' of the Spirit.[34] By the same token, a 'second-blessing' experience does not theologically entail or guarantee a fixed *two*-stage pneumatology. Combining points (c)–(e), if, in practice, there is no single 'normal' second-blessing experience, and if such experiences do not provide the gateway to any sharply distinctive spiritual gifts or empowerings that are not found amongst (e.g.) more traditional Evangelicals (except, perhaps, tongues themselves), then we do not have the empirical grounds for a rigidly two-stage paradigm of Spirit-reception. 'Pentecostal' experiences are then better explained as single events within a potentially multiple-occasion *series* of renewal or empowering

---

[33]Traditional evangelicalism is chosen as the group with which to compare Pentecostals because in most other respects its beliefs and practices are closest to those of Pentecostals.

[34]To be sure, F.A. Sullivan, *Charisms and Charismatic Renewal: A Biblical and Theological Study* (Dublin: Gill and Macmillan, 1982) allows the believer may experience several givings and receivings of the Spirit, but he bases this in Aquinas's understanding that each mission of a divine Person is a becoming present in a new activity or relationship, rather than a movement to a place where he was not before. But this distinction cannot support a classical Pentecostal two-stage pneumatology without also subverting it by introducing the possibility of a multitude of further 'comings' of the Spirit to the believer.

experiences of the one gift of the Spirit granted in conversion-initiation.

(f) The biblical language of Spirit-baptism is best explained as referring to the corporate initiation of the church provided by Pentecost, and for subsequent conversion-initiation experiences of the Spirit (including what follows these).

Lederle thus claims the 'experiential or charismatic dimension of the life and faith of Christians is characteristic of all forms of vibrant Christianity.'[35] It comes to expression not merely in the sort of gifts indicated in 1 Corinthians 12:8–10, but also in joyful celebration and fellowship, trusting prayer, prophetic witness, spiritual teaching, obedient and sacrificial acts of service, etc. An experience of receiving tongues, or some other charism, accompanied by, for example, a heightened sense of the presence of God, does not mark entry into some different realm of the Spirit, or some theologically distinct new reception of the Spirit, but is simply part and parcel of the all-encompassing work of renewal and re-creation which the believer experiences, in a variety of fruit and charisms, from the beginning of Christian life. What Pentecostals experienced as a second-stage 'Spirit-baptism' should thus be understood as just one of potentially many 'growth experiences' in the charismatic Spirit given in conversion-initiation rather than the normative mode of entry to some decisively new realm of the Spirit.

5. Alleged Practical and Pastoral Weaknesses of a Unitary Model of Spirit-Reception

Does a unitary model of Spirit-reception threaten to diminish the expectation of spiritual empowering in the church, and its missionary orientation? This is what Menzies fears. Let us make three comments.

(1) It is clear that Paul anticipated a lively 'charismatic' church, in which every area of Christian life and ministry was deeply shaped by experiential awareness of the Spirit. Yet apparently he felt no need to elucidate any second-blessing theology in order to undergird and strengthen this. It is his vision of the church as a body continually open to the Spirit and regularly experiencing God's intervention in varieties of gifts — combined with his own pastoral example, oversight and encouragement — which seems to have maintained this enthusiastic expectation and experience.

Contemporary comparison may be illustrative. Evidently, to

---

[35]*Treasures*, 227.

hold before believers the promise of a second blessing, with clear
initial evidence, has driven many from complacency over their
own lack of spiritual experience to a search for some direct encounter with God in power. But there is dead formalism in the
post-'baptism in the Spirit' sector of the Pentecostal and Charismatic church too. An experience of the Spirit and glossolalia
alone can easily lead to the complacency of 'having arrived'. It is
the general vision of the church as an ongoing charismatic body
— and careful pastoral oversight and encouragement — that is
more likely to avoid formalism than a two-stage paradigm of
Spirit-reception. As we have noted, many sectors of the Charismatic movement — and even a small but influential group of
leaders and teachers within the traditional Pentecostal
denominations — maintain a lively charismatic spirituality
without any second-blessing theology.[36]

(2) Similarly, there is no reason to tie missionary orientation and
zeal to a second-blessing theology. Paul's churches appear to
have grown rapidly without his expressing the view that the
Spirit is granted to each as an empowering for witness. The
strongest *theological* link between the Spirit and mission is forged
by John, not Luke. For John the primary task of the Spirit as
Advocate is to press Jesus' case in the cosmic trial against all
unbelief. Yet the Spirit is expected to do this through the gift of
the Spirit-Paraclete leading the church into the truth incarnate in
Christ, and so making her a community of love which reflects
the love between the Father and the Son. From such a community the word of witness becomes manifest with convicting
power. That is, John does not attach this mission-orientation of
the church to any second distinct gift of the Spirit, but to the
Spirit-Paraclete given to all Christians in conversion.

Again modern parallels are illustrative. Many sectors of the
traditional Evangelical (and other allegedly 'non-charismatic')
churches have a thriving commitment to mission, while some
sectors of the Charismatic movement have become inward-look-
ing, despite a traditional Pentecostal 'theology' of the Spirit. I am
not aware that a critical case can be made that churches with a
second grace pneumatology derived from Luke are inevitably
more liable to be involved in mission than those which have a
unitary theology of Spirit-reception.

(3) If, as we have argued, a Christianized version of the concept of
the 'Spirit of prophecy' lies at the heart of the New Testament

---

[36]See *ibid.*, chs. 3–4, for numerous examples.

conception of the gift of the Spirit, then the gift of the Spirit to Christians at conversion is transparently the means of the whole charismatic/experiential dimension of Christian existence. As Fee has so tellingly shown with respect to Paul, the Spirit is its dynamic and life. Wherever the Father or the Son are 'felt' — whether in prayer, or in worship, or in the fellowship of love, or through teaching, or in prophesyings or tongues — they are perceived in and through variegated forms and combinations of the prototypical gifts of the Spirit of prophecy: wisdom, revelatory insight or inspired speech.

It is conventional in many circles to classify Charismatic and 'non-charismatic' churches on the basis of whether they experience tongues, prophecy and healing. But this is far too narrow a basis, obscuring the much wider range of gifts that flow from the Spirit as the Spirit of prophecy. Many traditional evangelical churches which deny the validity of these gifts are still deeply spiritual churches. In such churches the charismatic Spirit of prophecy enlivens and directs the church through other gifts, granting illumination of Scripture in preaching, wisdom and understanding in Bible study; a deep sense of God's presence and guidance in corporate and individual prayer, and so forth. These are all manifestations of the same Spirit of prophecy that gives glossolalia and prophecy in the so-called Charismatic churches. There are perhaps churches that are all but dead, and in which, alas, one never senses anything that transcends ordinary human possibilities with an awareness of God. But wherever God *is* sensed, he is made known only in and through the Spirit of prophecy. All authentic Christian church life — life that mediates the presence and power of God in a variety of ways — is charismatic in its truest sense. The gifts and manifestations of the Spirit of prophecy which unite the so-called charismatic and non-charismatic evangelical churches (and others too) are more numerous and perhaps more significant than the ones that unfortunately divide them.[37]

---

[37]For a fuller discussion of this see Turner, *Power*, ch. 14, §5.2 (D).

Chapter Eleven

Towards Trinitarian Pneumatology — Perspectives from Pentecost

It has become almost a cliché to assert that there is no explicit theology of trinity in the Bible. The assertion is, of course, correct: it is not clear that the New Testament writers agreed that Father, Son and Spirit were one God in three persons, far less that they considered them to be co-eternally so. An important question is rather whether the theology of the two testaments is *implicitly* trinitarian. Does what is said of Father, Son and Spirit require us to go beyond what the New Testament writers themselves asserted (and thought) to anything approaching more specifically trinitarian formulations? If that is the case, trinitarianism might be said to be an aspect of *prescriptive* New Testament theology, even if it cannot be discovered by purely *descriptive* New Testament theology.

As is well known, the faith of the Old Testament, and of the Judaism in which Christianity was born, was monotheistic in the exclusive sense. It was only reflection on the revelation of God in Christ which first led believers towards an *inclusive* monotheism, but this initially took a largely binitarian rather than strictly trinitarian shape. Attention naturally focused on the ministry, death, and resurrection-exaltation of Jesus, and the implications of these. Such reflection led to the explicit christological confession of Jesus' unity with God as the 'one Lord' of creation and redemption (cf. Acts 2:33–38; 1 Cor. 8:6; Phil. 2:6, 9,10; Col. 1:15–20; Heb. 1:2,3; Jn. 1:1–18, etc.). Worship came to be offered to Jesus,[1] and even the very title 'God' referred to him (Heb. 1:8; Jn. 1:1,18 (some MSS); 20:28; 1 Jn. 5:20; Rom. 9:5; Tit. 2:13 and 2 Pet. 1:1).[2] No such

---

[1] For the christological significance of this, see e.g. L. Hurtado, *One God, One Lord* (London: SCM, 1988), 11–15 and ch.5. J.D.G. Dunn argues Hurtado has overemphasized the 'worship' of Jesus (see *Partings*, 203–6), but his corrective probably goes too far in the opposite direction.

[2] Some of these are disputed: for discussion, see M.J. Harris, *Jesus as God: The New Testament Use of Theos in Reference to Jesus* (Grand Rapids: Baker, 1992).

attention, however, was paid to the Spirit. This has led some to conclude that, as far the New Testament witness goes, earliest Christian monotheism was properly binitarian rather than trinitarian.[3]

But there is important evidence pointing in a more specifically trinitarian direction. Young and Ford, for example, have suggested that the cardinal 'grammatical' rule of (post New Testament) trinitarianism is: 'always identify God through Father, Son and Holy Spirit, and intend this even when only one is mentioned.'[4] Paul, they then say, writes according to this rule, even if he does not provide an analysis of the grammar: 'his gospel exerted a pressure on his talk of God which he himself did not analyse but which is consonant with a [trinitarian] differentiation and relationality in God.'[5] We shall have more to say on the trinitarian shape of Paul's pneumatology (and that of other NT writers) later. What I wish to explore more specifically in what follows is what I consider to be the essentially trinitarian implications of Pentecost, or, more precisely, of Jesus' resurrection-exaltation giving of the Spirit. I shall argue that this event not only provides what is perhaps the firmest basis for the New Testament's divine christology (i.e. a christology that breaches traditional Jewish exclusive monotheism), but also gives pneumatology a strong push in a trinitarian direction. The argument may crudely be stated thus: (i) for Judaism, the expression 'the Spirit of the Lord' is a way of speaking of Yahweh *himself* (in action); (ii) in the light of this, the claim that Jesus 'sends' the Spirit must be seen as an *exclusively* divine function (unlike, e.g., creation, or pronouncing forgiveness of sins, which could readily be thought of as delegated to a divine agent), and, (iii), the divine Spirit was necessarily now differentiated to some extent from Yahweh (or the previous claim would amount to a blasphemous assertion that the exalted Jesus in some sense became 'Lord' over the Father himself).

I. THE SPIRIT IN JUDAISM

Judaism, in the tradition of the Old Testament, was monotheistic in the exclusive sense: i.e., there was only *one* figure on the throne in heaven. When the mystic Elisha b. Abujah spoke of '*two* Powers' in heaven (3 *Enoch* 16:2–4, *b. Hag.* 15a) he was immediately pronounced apostate. To

---

[3]Cf. C.F.D. Moule, 'The New Testament and the Trinity', *ExpT* 88 (1976–77), 16–20; idem, *The Holy Spirit* (London: Mowbrays, 1978), ch. 4.

[4]F. Young and D.F. Ford, *Meaning and Truth in 2 Corinthians* (London: SPCK, 1987), 257.

[5]*Ibid*, 257 (and cf. 255–60).

be sure there were occasional individuals and groups who toyed the idea of some plurality within the one God, but they were disregarded as speculative, misled or worse.[6] However close Judaism may have drawn to hypostatizing an angelic being or a divine attribute, at no point does a hypostatization of the God's *Spirit* come into question.[7] God's Spirit is always rather the extension of God's *own* personality, vitality and power, the very 'breath of his mouth' (Job 33:4; 34:14; Ps. 33:6; Wis. 11:20, etc.), not a second divine personal being. The 'Spirit of the Lord' is, in other words, a way of speaking of God himself, present and active: 'Spirit' is virtually synechdoche for 'God'. For this reason, the Spirit can readily be personified. Isaiah 63:10, for example, tells us that the wilderness generation 'rebelled, and grieved God's Holy Spirit'. But this (as the next line indicates) was simply a way of saying they grieved God himself, who was present in and through his Spirit. Indeed, this kind of personification of the Spirit in rabbinic Judaism occasionally goes even beyond that encountered anywhere in the New Testament, at least in the violence of the personal language used: as Abelson points out, the Spirit not only quotes Scripture, 'It also cries. It

---

[6]The aggressive stance of the rabbis may indicate that there was lively controversy over mediators within certain sectors of Judaism, and this can be traced back at least to Philo's time if not before (A.F. Segal, *Two Powers in Heaven* (Leiden: Brill, 1977), *passim*). Proverbs 8 and 9:1 strongly personify the figure of Wisdom (cf. Sir. 24; Wis. 10); Philo, while considering himself a monotheist, seems all but to make a divine hypostasis of the λόγος (*On Dreams* 1. 62–6; 230–3: cf. Segal, *Powers*, 161ff.); and in the (only slightly later) apocalyptists, God's chief executive angels (e.g. Yaoel in *Apoc. Abr.* 17; Eremiel in *Apoc. Zeph.* 6; and the chief angel in *Jos. and Asen.* ch. 14) can be described in exalted terms directly reminiscent of the majestic theophany in Ezekiel 1. Nevertheless, Christopher Rowland concludes, 'Whether we can yet speak of this angel being a second power in the heavenly world must be doubted' (*The Open Heaven* (London: SPCK, 1982), 111), and L. Hurtado, *One Lord*, gives an even more emphatically negative verdict on all claims that Judaism admitted any sort of 'second power'. More recently, Hayman and Barker have argued that in several strands of Judaism the supreme angel was a divine being (a belief derived from the allegedly ancient view that the High God (El Elyon) had several 'sons', of whom one was Yahweh): see P. Hayman, 'Monotheism — A Misused Word in Jewish Studies?', *JJS* 42 (1991), 1–15; M. Barker, *The Great Angel: A Study of Israel's Second God* (London: SPCK, 1992). But these provocative attempts appear eccentric: cf. J.D.G. Dunn, 'The Making of Christology — Evolution or Unfolding?', in Green and Turner (eds.), *Jesus of Nazareth*, 437–52 (esp. 444–7).
[7]See Max Turner, 'Spirit and "Divine" Christology', in Green and Turner (eds.), *Jesus of Nazareth*, 413–36 (esp. 422–3), and J.D.G. Dunn, *Christology*, 129–36.

holds dialogue with God, or some person. It pleads. It laments and weeps; it rejoices and comforts.'[8] But it would be entirely inappropriate to argue from this that rabbinic Judaism (or any other sector of Judaism for that matter) had come to think of the Spirit as an independent hypostasis distinct from Yahweh. Such language is simply figurative speech. Neither the Old Testament nor Judaism were binitarian in their view of the Spirit.

It is for this reason that it is quite inadequate, methodologically, to build a case for the divine personhood of the Spirit in the New Testament from those places where the Spirit is said 'to teach' (Lk. 12:12); 'to give utterance' (Acts 2:4); 'to say' (Acts 8:29; cf. 1:16; 10:19; 11:12; 13:2; 20:23; 21:4; 28:25); 'to send' (Acts 13:4); 'to forbid' (Acts 16:6); 'to appoint as overseer' (Acts 20:28), or whatever. All these could simply be shorthand for '*God*, as Spirit (or 'by his Spirit'), said . . .', etc.

II. THE OUTPOURING OF THE SPIRIT AS TRINITARIAN DISCLOSURE

Within his ministry, according to the Gospels, Jesus made certain exalted claims, including the claim to pre-exist Abraham, to forgive sins, to inaugurate the kingdom of God, to be one with the Father, to be the eschatological Son of Man and judge of humanity, and to be the one who would sit at God's right hand. Christologically important as these claims are, none of them requires any more than that the speaker be an exalted divine agent. In other words, various of these claims could be made by some angels, by other heavenly beings, or even by humans exalted to heaven (like Enoch, Elijah and Abel[9]). But the outpouring of the Spirit by the exalted Jesus constitutes a disclosure of a different kind, for here Jesus is depicted as exercising some sort of lordship over the divine Spirit. This is particularly remarkable because, as we have seen, the Spirit is understood in Judaism as God himself in action, or the extension of his *own* personal power and vitality (as opposed to his use of agents, like angels). It is this claim that Jesus pours out the Spirit that I argue (elsewhere) is one of the most important roots of 'divine'

---

[8]A. Abelson, *The Immanence of God in Rabbinic Judaism* (London: Hermon, 1969 [originally 1912]), 225. Cf. D. Hill, *Greek Words*, 223. For other examples, see Turner, 'Spirit and "Divine" Christology', in Green and Turner (eds.), *Jesus of Nazareth*, 422.
[9]See Hurtado, *One Lord*, chs. 2–4.

christology in the New Testament.[10] We shall first briefly note the main witness to this disclosure, that of Luke, John and Paul.

1. The Evidence of Luke-Acts

As we saw in Chapter 3, Peter's Pentecost speech interprets Jesus' ascension as his enthronement at God's right hand; the Messiah now begins the eternal rule from the throne of David, as promised in Luke 1:32,33. As the climax to his speech, Peter concludes, in 2:36, 'Therefore let all the house of Israel know that God has made him Lord and Messiah, this Jesus whom you crucified.' How were all Israel (not to mention Luke's readers) to know this? They could hardly themselves see Jesus there; and the fact that he was taken up into the heavenlies did not itself imply that he would thenceforth rule from there (for the same was by no means necessarily always concluded of other figures, exalted to heaven, such as Enoch, Moses and Elijah). The required 'evidence' is offered in 2:33, where Peter claims that it is *Jesus* who poured out the gifts of the Spirit that first drew the crowd's attention. The questioning bystanders, of course, would need to take this latter affirmation on trust. That it was Jesus himself who poured out God's Spirit would at that stage have been no more 'visible' than his session at God's right hand. But Luke's readers were in a different situation; they were in a much better position to reflect on the christofocal experience of the Spirit in the church and to understand that the Spirit of God had become 'the Spirit of Jesus' too (cf. Acts 16:7[11]).

The christological implications of this are relatively clear for Luke. In Acts 2:17, Luke redactionally stresses that *God* (in Joel) promised, 'I will pour out my Spirit on all flesh'. None would be surprised at that, for, as we have said, in Judaism God's Spirit is his very *own* 'life', power and vitality. God *alone* can act through his Spirit, because his Spirit is *himself* in action. For a Jew, it would not make sense to speak of someone else — someone *other* than God — pouring out God's Spirit and exercising his own lordship over and through the Spirit. That would imply that the person concerned had come to preside over and direct God's own self-revealing vitality. And yet, this is exactly what Peter, in effect, claims on behalf of Jesus. Not '*God* has poured out this which

---

[10]Turner, 'The Spirit of Christ and Christology' in Rowdon (ed.), *Christ*, 168–90; more fully Turner, 'Spirit and "Divine" Christology', 413–36.

[11]See Ch. 3, IV, §3, and Turner, *Power*, ch. 10.

you see and hear'; but, having received executive power to administer Joel's promise, *Jesus* 'has poured out this which you see and hear.' This implies nothing less than that Jesus has become in some sense 'Lord of the Spirit', as indeed Luke 24:49 anticipated ('See, *I* am sending upon you the promise of the Father [*scil.* the Spirit]'). Accordingly, as we go through Acts it appears that the Spirit is the self-manifesting and empowering presence of both the Father and the Son (the 'power' by which Jesus exercises his rule from the Davidic throne). In christological terms, Luke virtually identifies Jesus as one 'Lord' with the Lord God of Joel 2:28–32.[12]

2. The Evidence of John's Gospel

We have observed (Ch. 5) how John portrays the Paraclete as the abiding self-manifesting presence of Jesus and the Father with the disciple, after Jesus has been exalted to the Father's side (cf. 14:16–26). The fundamental 'work' of the Spirit-Paraclete is to direct the disciples into the truth about Jesus and to glorify him (16:13–15; cf. 14:26). These are of course remarkable claims. One certainly could not imagine any Jew speaking of the Spirit bringing the presence of the Father and Moses (as if on equal terms) to Jews on earth. But perhaps even more remarkable are two further passages in John's Farewell Discourses. In 15:26 Jesus states, 'When the Advocate comes, whom *I* will send to you from the Father, the Spirit of Truth who comes from the Father, he will testify on my behalf' (cf. 14:26). Similarly, in John 16:7, he says, 'But if I go, *I* will send him to you'. Here, as in the similar passages in Luke-Acts, Jesus is clearly somehow envisaged as Lord of God's Spirit and the Spirit, in turn, serves christocentric goals. In other words, God's Spirit is portrayed not merely as the executive power of the Father, but as that of the exalted Lord as well.

3. The Evidence of Paul's Letters

Paul's pneumatology is similar in this respect.[13] Essentially he regards the post-resurrection gift of the Spirit as 'an ambassador acting on behalf of both God and Christ, and thus as the power of Christ exercising

---

[12]For the argument in detail, see Turner, *Power*, chs. 10, 11 (§2), 13 (§3), and the articles cited above.

[13]See Ch. 8 above, (esp. part VI), and, at greater length, Turner, 'Spirit and "Divine" Christology', 424–34.

his lordship in the church'.[14] In the light of this, such expressions as 'the Spirit of Christ' (Rom. 8:9), 'the Spirit of his Son' (Gal. 4:6), and 'the Spirit of Jesus Christ' (Phil. 1:19) should be understood after the analogy of the expressions 'the Spirit of God' or 'the Spirit of the Lord'. That is, they 'were used to express the belief that the Spirit acted on behalf of God and of Christ, and under the sovereignty of both',[15] not merely to suggest that through the resurrection-exaltation the Spirit had (in one way or another) taken on the 'character' of Christ and impresses it on believers. While the latter is undoubtedly part of what Paul means, Dunn accepts that this christifying of the Spirit still also implies that Jesus somehow 'took over the Spirit . . . and became Lord of the Spirit'.[16]

4. Trinitarian Theological Consequences

We have argued that the claims made in these passages were reflected in the churches' experience of Christ through the Spirit, and that the claims themselves entail a fully divine christology. That is, these claims go beyond anything Judaism could assert of a mere creature, however exalted. One can immediately see how God might be thought ready to delegate certain intrinsically divine functions to exalted agents, e.g. granting to Abel the right of eschatological judgment and forgiveness of sins (so *Testament of Abraham* 12–13). Delegating to a divinely empowered agent even such functions as creation is conceivable, within Judaism, because the agent remains under God's lordship. But Jesus' 'lordship' over and through the Spirit is a quite different matter, precisely because it appears to accord Jesus a lordship *within God himself*, i.e. over the Spirit which is his own personal presence in action. To that extent the claim that Jesus is Lord of the Spirit implies at least a binitarian theology: the outpouring of God's Spirit by Jesus entails that the Father and the Son are together one God. We shall not elucidate this further here,[17] but turn our attention to the implications for pneumatology.

We suggest that Jesus' exaltation-lordship over the Spirit also

---

[14]Turner, 'Spirit of Christ and Christology', in Rowdon (ed.), *Christ*, 188.
[15]*Ibid.*
[16]J.D.G. Dunn, 'Jesus — Flesh and Spirit, 40–68 (68). His later writings seemed to turn back on this, but see Turner, 'Spirit and "Divine" Christology', 424–34, esp. 429–30.
[17]Cf. Turner, 'Spirit and "Divine" Christology', esp. 419–424.

probably implies a distinct divine personhood in the Spirit. There appear to be only two alternatives to such a possibility, and neither of them is inviting.

(1) It would be possible to suppose that Christians retained the Jewish understanding that to speak of 'the Spirit' is nothing more than to speak of the Father's own personal vitality and 'life' in action (almost after the analogy of the relation between a human 'person' and his or her 'spirit'). It would not be difficult to understand how the exalted Lord could then be understood to be so united with the Father, that the Son's presence and sovereignty might be felt on earth through the activity of the Spirit of the Father. But such a view would encounter fierce problems with the assertions to the effect that Jesus exerts some degree of lordship over the Spirit. It cannot account, in other words, for Jesus' 'I will send him to you' (Jn. 16:7; cf. Lk. 24:49; Jn. 14:26; 15:26). If this means Jesus will send the 'Spirit' which is nothing other than the Father himself in action, then we verge on a blasphemous assertion that Jesus has become Lord over the Father — a blasphemy only mildly mitigated by the covering assertion that Jesus will send this Spirit 'from' the Father (15:26). In short, the more strongly we identify God's Spirit with the Father (in action), the more theologically eccentric it becomes to speak of Jesus' lordship of the Spirit, or of the Spirit as 'the Spirit of Jesus Christ', or of the Father sending 'the Spirit *of his Son*' (Gal. 4:6). We need some theological 'space', or 'distance', between the Father and the Spirit before we can listen to these affirmations with any degree of theological comfort. Indeed, the 'sending' of the Spirit by the Son 'from the Father' (15:26) itself implies some kind of differentiation of the Spirit from the Father.

(2) One way to provide such 'space' would be to suppose a revision in the early Christian understanding of pneumatology, of a kind which hypostatized the Spirit and demoted him into an agent acting on God's behalf. This 'spirit' would need to be at once a personal, and, at the same time, a potentially omnipresent agent, to account both for the functions the Spirit is said to perform (saying; teaching; appointing elders; sending; distributing gifts as he wills; interceding, etc.[18]) and his simultaneous

---

[18]For a list of the 'personal' activities attributed to the Spirit in Luke-Acts, see Turner, *Power*, ch. 2, §1; for a similar list in Paul, see Fee, *Presence*, 829–31; for John, see below, and for a more wide-ranging, but less detailed list, see A.W. Wainwright, *The Trinity in the New Testament* (London: SPCK, 1962), 200–4.

activity in believers across the then known world. But it might at least be possible to imagine that Christians came to think of the Spirit as some supreme divine agent; one, nevertheless, that was not himself divine, but merely 'filled' with God (e.g. like Metatron in *3 Enoch*). Within such a revised pneumatology, both the Father and the Son could be thought to relate to disciples through this one especially powerful S/spirit.

A major problem facing such a proposal is that it does not appear to have been an option in the first-century Jewish setting. Whereas God's wisdom, righteousness, name, etc. may have been hypostatized, God's Spirit was never so. The reason for this was that Spirit was too tightly bound up with God's *own* activity — himself in action. Indeed, the term 'the Spirit of the Lord' is used in connection with divine activities precisely to *contrast* those activities as performed by God himself *instead* of being performed through divine agents. And, more decisively, in the New Testament too the term 'Spirit of God' retains the sense 'God as Spirit', rather than meaning the mighty spirit-creature who acts as God's agent. Thus, for example, to lie to the Holy Spirit (Acts 5:3) is directly equated with lying *to God* (Acts 5:4) in a way that would not follow if the Spirit were merely akin to the mighty God-like angels Yaoel (*Apocalypse of Abraham*, chs. 10 and 14) or Eremiel (of *Apocalypse of Zephaniah*, ch. 6) or the Enochian 'little Yahweh', Metatron (*3 Enoch*).

Of course it would be *possible* to imagine the emergence of a new conception of divine agent, which combined the omnipresence of the *sophia/pneuma* of Wisdom of Solomon with a deep personhood that enabled the agent fully to mediate the self-manifesting presence and activity of God, and Christ, to believers, but we have no evidence of such a development within the New Testament. Rather, in 1 Corinthians 2:10,11, when Paul wishes to explain how the Spirit of God alone knows the mind and thoughts of God, his analogy is with how the human spirit alone knows that person's own deepest thoughts: i.e., God's Spirit comes from within God and is God; the Spirit is not some other (and lower) being investigating God. This passage thus witnesses to the unity of the Spirit with God, while simultaneously distinguishing the Spirit to some extent from the Father and the Son.

Our first two explanatory options thus fail us, and the final consideration points instead to a third way, one that approaches trinitarianism. It would be natural enough for Jewish Christians to maintain their pre-

Christian commitment to the full divine nature of the Spirit. In the light of Jesus' exaltation-lordship over the Spirit, however, they would need to distance the Spirit from the Father in some way, in order to avoid speaking of the Son sending the Father. In all this it would also be natural for them to continue to affirm the divine personhood of the Spirit. Judaism, of course, had understood this experience of personhood in the Spirit simply as the extension of the Father's own personhood. But as the Spirit became theologically differentiated from the Father, by Christ's commissioning of the Spirit, it may have become natural to assume the Spirit too shared in divine personhood. This would then readily explain how the Spirit was able to mediate the Father and the Son to believers. In other words, it would be natural for the Spirit increasingly to become perceived as a locus of personhood within God, but one *other* than the Father and the Son. One can see strong hints of this in Paul at, e.g., 1 Corinthians 2:10,11; 12:5–7; 2 Corinthians 3:17–18; 13:13; Romans 8:26,27, and in the whole trinitarian 'shape' of the rest of Paul's pneumatology.[19] One also has the evidence of Matthew 28:19 (baptism in the *one* name of Father, Son and Spirit is no casual triad, but suggests the Spirit has the same being as the Father and the Son), but perhaps the divine personhood of the Spirit is most conspicuous in John 14–16, to which we now turn.

5. Trinitarian Pneumatology in John 14–16?

Traditionally, the argument for a trinitarian understanding of the Spirit in John 14-16 has centred on two aspects: (1) the masculine pronoun *autos* = 'he' (16:7), and the masculine demonstrative adjective *ekeinos* = 'that one' (14:26; 15:26; 16:8,13,14) are used in reference to the Spirit. (2) The Spirit is said to perform personal functions: 'teaching' (14:26); 'bearing witness' (15:26); 'convicting the world' (16:8); 'leading into all truth' (16:13); 'speaking not of himself, but what he hears' (16:13b) and 'glorifying Christ' (16:14).

---

[19]See G.D. Fee, 'Christology and Pneumatology, 312–31; similarly, Fee, *Presence*, ch. 13. Fee correctly argues that the Spirit is personal, and distinct from the Father, yet the Spirit remains the 'Spirit of God' (and the presence of God in Christians: 843–5), primarily related to the *Father* (*Presence*, 829–36), and, as such, is clearly *not* identified with the risen Lord (831–4, 837–8: *contra* Gunkel, Hermann, Berkhof, Dunn, *et al.*), even if the Spirit is *also* (but much more rarely) referred to as the 'Spirit of Christ' (837–8). This pattern is intrinsically trinitarian (839–42).

These two arguments are not as secure as one might wish. The masculine pronoun was virtually forced on the writer to agree in gender with *ho paraklētos*, a masculine noun. And in 14:17 the *neuter* pronoun is used, not the masculine. As for the allegedly personal functions, it has to be admitted that, taken individually, the themes of the Spirit teaching, giving revelation, leading, bearing witness, etc. do not go beyond the Old Testament perspective. Even, e.g. the Scriptures are said to 'bear witness' to Jesus (5:39), but we are not expected to assume they are thereby identified as a fourth member of the Godhead.

The most convincing examples suggesting the Spirit is coming to be thought of as a divine person come from 16:13,14. Here the disciples are told (in v.13) that the Spirit will not speak of his own, but only what he hears in the heavenly places. And v.14 clarifies, 'He will glorify me, because he will take what is mine and declare it to you.' One might be tempted to explain all this (as one does the Jewish examples) merely as vivid personification, but three considerations make this improbable.

(1) In the first place the *extended* personification (frequent and compatible incidences over three chapters) points in the direction of a departure from traditional Jewish personifications of the Spirit.

(2) Perhaps the strongest indication that John's thinking moves beyond the Old Testament view of the Spirit (i.e. that the Spirit is merely the mode of Yahweh's presence) is his whole presentation of the Paraclete as a *parallel figure to Jesus* in the relationships sustained to the Father and Son, to the disciple, and to the world (see Ch. 5). Arguably, this requires that John views the Spirit as a divine figure who relates to the Father and to the exalted Son after the analogy of Jesus' relation to the Father in the ministry.

(3) Important too is the consideration that in the theology of the Fourth Gospel, the Son glorifies the Father, and the Father the Son: they do not glorify *themselves*. When it is then said that the Spirit will *not* glorify himself, but the Son, the Spirit is being portrayed as a separate Person (16:13,14). Either that, or (if the Spirit is merely an extension of Christ's personality) Christ is, in the final analysis, glorifying *himself*.[20] The Spirit enables the Johannine community to confess Jesus, and worship the Father, but he is distinct from both — no mere extension of their personality. This is clear from the fact that the community neither worships nor confesses him. Paradoxically, he reveals himself as

---

[20]For this argument, see T. Smail, *The Giving Gift: The Holy Spirit in Person* (London: Hodder, 1988), 51–3, 84–7.

a distinct Person, precisely in being what Smail calls 'the Person without a Face'.[21]

III. CONCLUSION

Jesus' exaltation gift of the Spirit 'from the Father' provides a real basis for something approaching a trinitarian account of God. To what extent the New Testament writers entirely grasped the significance of this is not clear. But its significance for theology today is considerable. It stands as a major obstacle to Unitarian theologies, such as Lampe's,[22] which remove the risen Christ and collapse the Spirit into God, and to Spirit christologies, such as that of Berkhof and others,[23] which collapse the Spirit into Christ and finish with functional binitarianism.[24]

---

[21]This is the title (and substance) of Smail, *Gift*, ch. 2. His title owes something to Yves Congar, *I Believe in the Holy Spirit* (London: Chapman, 1983), vol. 3, 5.

[22]G.W.H. Lampe, *God*.

[23]H. Berkhof, *The Doctrine of the Holy Spirit* (London: Epworth, 1965).

[24]For an accessible but penetrating modern theology of the Spirit, see Smail, *Gift*.

PART II
SPIRITUAL GIFTS IN THE NEW TESTAMENT CHURCH AND TODAY

Introductory Remarks

In this second part of our work we shall examine the subject of 'spiritual gifts'. We shall look at the place of such gifts in the life of the New Testament church, and raise questions about how they correspond to phenomena in the church today.

At the outset, however, we must recognize a fundamental terminological problem. What do we mean when we talk about 'spiritual gifts'? We need to recognize that the term is a vague one, and that some Christian writers have used it much more broadly than others. If we take as our starting point the twentieth-century end of the hermeneutical question we immediately encounter problems of denotation. What activities or processes in the world external to language do we signify when we speak of 'spiritual gifts'? The answer depends to a considerable extent on the speaker. For W.R. Jones — to judge by the title and contents of his essay in a handbook of Pentecostal doctrine — there are just nine gifts.[1] They are set out in 1 Corinthians 12:8–10 (viz. word of wisdom, word of knowledge, discerning of spirits, 'faith', working of miracles, gifts of healing, prophecy, tongues and interpretation), and Jones would readily point you to phenomena in his church which (he would claim) were denotata of these nine specified gifts (i.e. the things denoted by the nine terms). Presumably *only* the types of events he describes qualify for the designation 'gifts of the Spirit'. Jones' position is not untypical of popular writing in Pentecostal and Charismatic circles. Effectively the range of phenomena labelled 'charismata' or 'spiritual gifts' in such circles and elsewhere is often reduced to the spectacular manifestations — especially healing, prophecy and tongues — and this (as Congar puts it[2]) 'even by deservedly respected authors' varying from Leo XIII to A. Kuyper and B.B. Warfield.[3]

---

[1] In P.S. Brewster (ed.), *Pentecostal Doctrine* (Cheltenham: Brewster, 1976), 47–62; cf. 95–112.

[2] Y.J.M. Congar, *I Believe,* vol 2, 162.

[3] *Most recently T.R. Edgar's polemically anti-charismatic work, Miraculous Gifts,* (New Jersey: Loiseaux, 1983), 14.

At the other extreme today we find writers who give such a broad sense to the expressions 'spiritual gifts' or 'charismata' that it is barely possible to think of any event which belongs properly to the life of the Christian which could not legitimately be called a denotatum of the terms. E. Käsemann's essay on ministry in the early church clearly tends in this direction.[4] Extending the notion of 'spiritual gifts' even beyond Käsemann's usage we may note the position of K. Rahner, E. Dussel and J. Moltmann.[5] For them the charisms of the Spirit cannot be exhausted within the confines of the church, nor within those of other religions, but are also envinced in the world, e.g. in the rise of secular heroes fighting for the cause of justice, etc. *Any* experience of existential 'grace' is an experience and gift of the Spirit. Thus not only are all outside the church deemed 'anonymous Christians' (Rahner), but they have become 'anonymous Charismatics' to boot.[6] Here we have moved — albeit on theological grounds — to a whole realm of activities best classified under Max Weber's sociologically-orientated concept of charisma (itself a secularization of Sohm's[7]).

So we have a problem right at the outset: what exactly are we talking *about* when we speak of 'spiritual gifts'? The problem is, of course, not merely one of defining the limits of the class: at the root of that difficulty is the problem of giving what is called a semantic stereotype of 'spiritual gifts': that is, a list of typical characteristics of the things to which the expression is correctly applied.

Can we avoid the problem by pressing the question back to the first-century end of the hermeneutical question, and asking what the New Testament means by 'spiritual gifts'? This looks attractive at first, but on closer examination we find that the new route is dogged by problems of its own. The simple fact is that the New Testament writers were not native speakers of English and consequently do not use the phrase 'spiritual gifts' at all. So we are reduced to trying to find what language the individual New Testament writers use to denote the closest *equivalents* of our concept(s) of 'spiritual gifts'. That, of course, means the agenda is fixed at the twentieth-century end of the hermeneutical question again — only with the hope that some 'merging of the horizons' might take a creative place in the process.

---

[4]E. Käsemann, *Essays on New Testament Themes* (London: SCM, 1964), 63–94; cf. his *Questions*, 188–95.

[5]K. Rahner, *The Spirit in the Church* (London: Burns and Oates, 1979), especially the first essay; E. Dussel, 'The Differentiation of Charisma', *Concilium* 109 (1978), 38–55; Moltmann, *Spirit of Life*.

[6]A perceptive jibe made by Mark Stibbe in his review of Moltmann (see above).

[7]R. Laurentin, 'Charisms: Terminological Precision', *Concilium* 109 (1978), 3–12.

How then may we proceed? Whereas it may be all but impossible to provide a full semantic stereotype of 'spiritual gifts' in general, we have no problem whatever in identifying a few 'prototypical'[8] examples. On virtually any modern theological definition of 'spiritual gifts' the phenomena Paul denotes by the list in 1 Corinthians 12:8–10 are definitely individually prototypes of what we call 'spiritual gifts'. Of these, three are of particular interest to present day debates between Pentecostal and Charismatic churches on the one side and more traditional (and especially cessationist) Protestantism on the other; namely, the gifts of prophecy, tongues and healing. We shall examine the New Testament witness concerning these individually in Chapters 12, 13 and 14. In Chapter 15 we return to the more general discussion of whether we can identify a Pauline concept of 'spiritual gifts' from 1 Corinthians 12:8–10 and elsewhere, and how extensive such a class might be, and its relation to, e.g., 'natural gifts', 'leadership gifts', and 'fruits of the Spirit'. In other words, we shall discuss in broad terms the place of 'spiritual gifts' in the theology of Paul and in the life of the Pauline community.[9]

With this behind us we turn our attention towards the question of relevance for today. Chapter 16 examines the cessationist position, and enquires to what extent its appeal to Scripture itself for such a position can be justified. Chapters 17 onwards consider to what extent one can find modern valid counterparts to New Testament gifts of tongues, prophecy and healing, and our final chapter turns to more general questions of the place of 'spiritual gifts' in the life of the church today.

---

[8]I use the term here as in lexical semantics: a 'prototype' of a predicate is a thing-in-the world (object, activity, event, etc.) which is held to be typical of the kind of thing (object, activity, event, etc.) which can be denoted by the predicate.

[9]Constraints of space require this exclusive concentration on Paul; for the place of charismata of the Spirit in Luke-Acts, see Chs. 2–3 and the sections on Luke-Acts in Chs. 12–14, or, more fully, *Power.*

Chapter Twelve

Prophecy in the New Testament

Most readers will come to this chapter aware of lively debates within the church about the nature of biblical prophecy and its significance for today. Thus, for example, from within the Reformed Evangelical circle, J.I. Packer virtually identifies biblical prophecy with contemporary preaching when he says:

> The essence of the prophetic ministry was forthtelling God's present word to his people, and this regularly meant application of revealed truth rather than augmentation of it. As Old Testament prophets preached the law and recalled Israel to face God's covenant claim on their obedience . . . so it appears that New Testament prophets preached the gospel . . . for conversion, edification and encouragement . . . By parity of reasoning, therefore, any verbal enforcement of biblical teaching as it applies to one's present hearers may probably be called prophecy today, for that in truth is what it is.[1]

Others, however, see a sharp distinction between biblical prophecy and preaching, yet still remain deeply divided on the nature and duration of New Testament prophecy. A long- traditional cessationist view has been carefully expressed by F.D. Farnell in his 1980 doctoral dissertation, submitted at Dallas Theological Seminary,[2] and much of his argument has been made available for a wider audience in four long articles in *Bibliotheca Sacra* (1992–1993[3]). Farnell's case, in essence, is that 'prophecy' is a certain sort of revelatory speech, namely speech which

---

[1] J.I. Packer, *Keep in Step with the Spirit* (Leicester: IVP, 1984), 215.
[2] 'The New Testament Prophetic Gift: Its Nature and Duration, unpublished DTh dissertation, Dallas Theological Seminary, 1980.
[3] F.D. Farnell, 'The Current Debate About New Testament Prophecy', *BSac* 149 (1992), 277–303; *idem*, 'The Gift of Prophecy in the Old and New Testaments', *BSac* 149 (1992), 387–410; *idem*, 'Does the New Testament Teach Two Prophetic Gifts?', *BSac* 150 (1993), 62–88; *idem*, 'When Will the Gift of Prophecy Cease?', *BSac* 150 (1993), 171–202. For a similar position, see K.L. Gentry, *The Charismatic Gift of Prophecy* (Memphis: Footstool Publications, 1986 and 1989[2]). References are to the latter edition.

is *fully* inspired by God's Spirit and therefore totally true and totally authoritative (a 'definition' he merely adopts from R.L. Saucy[4]). It was given to establish and elucidate 'the truth' of God revealed in history, supremely in the Christ-event, and, with the completion of the all-sufficient biblical revelation, prophecy ceased. He thus quotes with full approval this statement from C.C. Ryrie on New Testament prophecy:

> The gift of prophecy included receiving a message directly from God through special revelation, being guided in declaring it to the people, and having it authenticated in some way by God himself. . . . This . . . was a gift limited in its need and use, for it was needed during the writing of the New Testament and its usefulness ceased when the books were completed.[5]

Farnell's work is largely an elucidation of this view, and his basic *argument* for it is that a tissue of parallels of language and ideas establishes that New Testament prophecy is the same in nature and function as the prophecy with which we are familiar from the Old Testament canonical prophets. As Joel 2 looks forward to the eschatological gift of prophecy, so Acts 2 claims it is fulfilled in the church of the apostles.

Traditional Pentecostals and Evangelical Charismatics represent a third position. While distinguishing prophecy from preaching, they also distinguish infallible apostolic teaching and writing from ordinary congregational prophecy, which for them carries much less authority. In this they receive scholarly support from the work of Wayne Grudem.[6]

On Old Testament prophecy, Grudem's recent position differs only little from Farnell's. But he thinks the intertestamental writers introduced a new weaker concept of 'prophecy'. While prophecy was still the reception and subsequent transmission of spontaneous and divinely originating revelation,[7] in Philo and Josephus that could mean as little as having a flash of divinely given knowledge about a person or situation, or being given insight or discernment from God. This (and his research on 1 Cor. 14) led Grudem to suggest there were *two* distinct *types* of prophecy in the New Testament. In the apostles was restored the fully authoritative prophecy of the Old Testament type; but

---

[4]'Gift of Prophecy', 387 n.1.
[5]C.C. Ryrie, *The Holy Spirit* (Chicago: Moody, 1965), 86.
[6]Grudem's Cambridge PhD was published in America with the title *The Gift of Prophecy in 1 Corinthians* (Washington: UPA, 1982; henceforth *Gift*), and he has released a more popular version called *The Gift of Prophecy* (Eastbourne: Kingsway, 1988; henceforth *Prophecy*).
[7]*Gift*, 135–42.

amongst the congregation more generally was the weaker type we meet in the intertestamental literature. The former gave the foundational revelation which became inscripturated as the New Testament — and ceased with the passing of the apostolic circle. The weaker type of prophecy had little to do with providing 'doctrine', but served the needs of upbuilding and direction of the church, or individuals, often in particulars on which Scripture had nothing to say, and (Grudem would add) this latter type of prophecy did not pass away. It is alive in many churches today. We might well describe this second type of prophecy in the words of the subtitle of one of his chapters on New Testament prophecy outside the apostolic circle. Here he sums it up as, 'Speaking merely human words to report something God brings to mind'.[8] For Grudem, prophecy today is this mixed gift: divine insight or revelation, but potentially fallibly received and interpreted by the one who prophesies.

These three twentieth-century views are each to some extent based in historical considerations, but they clearly set out from ecclesial and theological agendas (especially those concerning the authority of Scripture) and (with the exception of Grudem's earlier exegetical volume) pay rather scant respect to the historical and linguistic considerations of what was meant by prophecy in the first-century world. But it is here we must begin if we are to achieve an adequate foundation.

I. NEW TESTAMENT PROPHECY IN ITS FIRST-CENTURY SETTING

The most complete and most nuanced historical surveys of prophetism in the New Testament, and its conceptual hinterland, are those provided by David Aune's *Prophecy in Early Christianity and the Ancient Mediterranean World*, and Christopher Forbes' *Prophecy and Inspired Speech in Early Christianity and its Hellenistic Environment*.[9] From their work it emerges that we may provide a single simple stereotype of what is meant by 'prophecy' (or 'to prophesy') in the New Testament. Essentially, prophecy was a type of oracular speech: that is, *it was an intelligible verbal message believed to originate with God, and to be communicated through an inspired human intermediary*.[10]

We need to note five things about this provisional 'definition':

---

[8] *Prophecy*, ch. 4.
[9] (Exeter: Paternoster, 1983), and (Tübingen: Mohr, 1995), respectively.
[10] Aune, *Prophecy*, 339. Cf. Forbes, *Prophecy*, 219.

(1) We have referred to it as a 'stereotype' — which is a technical term borrowed from semantics; it means a description of what would be regarded as the *typical* member of the class. The 'stereotype' of a 'stool' (contrasting it with chair, sofa, etc.) is that it is a seat with three or four legs and no back or arms. It would no doubt be possible to find what we would be prepared to call a stool that had only one leg, plus or minus a short back and even something like arms; but we would say such stools were not 'typical' of the genre. Our stereotype of 'prophecy' governs what is taken as typical, not the less usual features.

(2) In terms of lexical semantics, the New Testament usage of *prophētēs* ('prophet') cognates is much closer to the LXX than to contemporary hellenistic Greek. For the latter, the noun 'prophecy' (*prophēteia*) did not mean inspired speech, but either the period of tenure of the office of prophet, or the office itself. The corresponding verb, *prophēteuein* ('to prophesy'), meant to fulfil the office of prophet. *Prophētēs* (fem. *prophētis*) itself in the Classical period denoted one of three things, all related to the etymological sense 'spokesperson' or 'announcer': (a) a cult official (not necessarily himself inspired) who mediated the oracles of the diviner (*mantis*) to others; (b) the diviner him/herself in his/her capacity as the one who declares the god's will, and (c) an official spokesman of some more general kind. Within the hellenistic period the term came to be used additionally of Egyptian priests with little oracular function, and for honorary and financial executive officers of the cult of Apollo, and 'nothing requires us to believe that inspiration was believed to be a defining quality of προφῆται.'[11] The use of this word-group by the LXX for the phenomena of prophetism in the Old Testament is thus slightly surprising (except of shrine/temple oracular prophets). Most Old Testament 'prophecy' was oracular speech in the sense provisionally defined above, and for which the more natural Greek equivalent would be μαντική (*mantikē*).

(3) Within septuagintal and New Testament usage, *prophēteuein* ('to prophesy') and *prophēteia* ('prophecy') stereotypically apply to oracular *speech-activities* as opposed to other forms of natural divination (e.g. the use of lots, or visions while sleeping in the oracle precincts) or technical divination, in which the god's will was determined through the manner of flight of birds, the rustling of leaves in a sacred grove, the internal state of sacrificial

---

[11]Forbes, *Prophecy*, 199: cf. chs. 5 and 8 for extensive justification of this summary.

animals, the interpretation of dreams or portents, etc.[12] (These other types of divination were in fact much more common to Graeco-Roman prophetism than oracular speech.) Prophecies might be written down (and, within the biblical tradition, even become 'Scripture'), but that was not necessarily typical of the concept.

(4) Stereotypically 'prophecy' (and its equivalent *mantikē*) was *intelligible* speech, which differentiates it from other types of inspired speech including, e.g., 'tongues'.

> According to many scholars, in the early phase of its history the Delphic oracle (the *promantis*) spoke ecstatically and *un*intelligibly, but it was then the duty of the oracle's 'prophet' to *interpret* the utterance into an intelligible form (and poetic metre). This reconstruction has been shown to be unconvincing at all points by Fontenrose and Forbes, who have argued the inspired *promantis* spoke intelligbly and was herself responsible for the final form of the oracle.[13] Either way the point remains that the final form of the 'prophecy' was itself intelligible. To say this, of course, does not preclude that prophetic oracles were regularly cryptic, laden with metaphor, vague and ambiguous: when Croesus of Lydia (560-546 BC) inquired of the Delphic oracle whether he should advance against Cyrus or not, he took comfort in the response that if he sent an army against the Persians he would destroy a great empire. Ironically it turned out to be his own (Herodotus, i.53). But the point remains, such oracles were *linguistically* intelligible, not ecstatic gibberish.

(5) Stereotypically (within the Judaeo-Christian tradition) prophecy was a distinct message, the content of which was believed to come from God by direct inspiration, and the same applies for Graeco-Roman forms of oracular speech. The content of the message was often short and usually situationally specific:

> Thus when the Cnidians had difficulty in digging a canal, and inquired of Delphi, they received the oracular response:
> 'The isthmus neither fence with towers nor dig through for Zeus had made it an island, had he so desired.' (Herodotus i. 174[14]).
> Similarly, Lucian reports the following prescriptive oracle given by Glykon-Asklepios to an inquirer (Sacerdos): 'Do not trust Lepidus,

---

[12]'Natural' divination meant the apprehending of the god's will or guidance through direct contact or immediate inspiration, and contrasts with 'technical' divination which required learned skills and lore.

[13]J. Fontenrose, *The Delphic Oracle*, (Berkeley: University of California Press, 1978); Forbes, *Prophecy*, chs 5. and 8.

[14]Aune, *Prophecy*, 59.

for a dismal fate follows' (Lucian, *Alexander* 43[15]), and Philostratus narrates the following mixed oracular beatitude as given to Cypselus:

'Happy is the man who comes down to my temple
Cypselus son of Eëtes, renowned king of Corinth,
he and his sons, but not his sons' sons' (*Apollonius*, i.10).[16]

This makes what the ancients understood by 'prophecy' intrinsically different from what we usually mean by 'preaching' or religious 'teaching' (though many oracles contained instructional material).

> Teaching or preaching are types of what we call 'expository discourse'. Expository discourses are any type of discourse where a man or woman seeks to explain some concept or set of ideas, himself or herself largely controlling both the content and arrangement of the material (e.g. a political speech, a talk on metallurgy, or a description of how to mend a puncture). 'Teaching' or 'preaching' is the teacher's prepared explanation of a revelation *already given* in Scripture or tradition. Prophecy is the relating of a revelation given directly by God, and its content and organization is typically regarded as more directly and situationally inspired by God.

Of course, there were modulations on the stereotype we have just advanced, not least in a Judaism and a Jewish Christianity that looked back especially to the Old Testament. We turn now to examine this in a little more detail.

1. Prophecy in the Old Testament and Intertestamental Period.

It is not difficult to see how the wide variety of Old Testament and intertestamental prophecy largely fits the stereotype advanced above. Old Testament prophecy was not basically concerned with giving detailed prediction about things to come centuries later, nor with providing fresh revelation of dogma, new general or particular truths of theology. On the whole, prophecy was understood as Israel's God showing his people his *immediate* will for them. Amos' prophecies (reign of Uzziah (783-42 BC)), for example, basically warn Judah and Israel of judgement on the nation. The nation at the time believed it was bound to be blessed of God, because it was God's chosen people, and

---

[15]See Aune, *Prophecy*, 59.
[16]For numerous examples of Graeco-Roman prophetic oracles, see Aune, *Prophecy*, chs. 2–3.

God would not deal with their sin in the same way as he would with the nations'. Amos declared rather (2:6–8),

Thus says the Lord:

'For the three transgressions of Israel
and for four, I will not revoke the punishment
because they sell the righteous for silver
and the needy for a pair of sandals —
they who trample the head of the poor into the dust of the earth, and
push the afflicted out of the way;
father and son go in to the same girl
so that my holy name is profaned;
they lay themselves down beside every altar
on garments taken in pledge;
and in the House of their God they drink wine bought with fines
they imposed.'

Speaking on Yahweh's behalf, Amos warns that if the nation does not repent, God will descend in judgement. Israel will be devoured by the sword, and scattered in exile. Only a tattered remnant will be left. Similarly, as God's spokesman, Hosea explains that the divine judgement coming upon Israel issues from Yahweh's jealous divine love, and is his attempt to turn her away from her religious harlotry, her social injustice, and warring oppression of Judah. Through Isaiah and his disciples, God is heard to promise he will restore his exiled people, and bring them gloriously back to the land, etc.

In short, of central importance to Israel's conception of the prophets was that they were *God's mouthpiece to the people.* Accordingly, God says to Jeremiah, 'I have put my words in your mouth' (1:9). Correspondingly, we regularly read statements of the type, 'the Lord . . . sent a message by the prophet Nathan (to David)' (2 Sam. 12:25). In such circumstances, the words of the prophet are regarded as God's very words.

Prophecy was thereby one of the three guardians of the covenant; the others being the Law taught by the priests, and the cultus administrated by them. From the perspective of the Old Testament writers and compilers, prophets (along with some leaders, kings and priests) alone had the Spirit of God. If the people were to know the will of God (beyond that which was written in the Law, or alongside it, complementing it, and showing which parts of its message at present related to the specific circumstances of the nation), it had to be through them. Their prophecy is often regarded as a largely black or white matter. If they spoke true prophecy the words of the prophet are understood as the very words of God — hence the messenger formula: 'Thus says the Lord, "I will . . . " ' This was to be understood as a claim to speak directly for God. To disobey the prophet was then to disobey God himself (Deut. 18:19). But, by the same token, no one was allowed to make this claim idly. If prophets *claimed* to speak for God, and their words proved not to be true, they were to be put to death (Deut. 18:20–22). These observations highlight the potential seriousness of prophecy within the religious economy, and may also suggest that the prophet could know relatively clearly what was coming from God and what was not. That is, the prophetic revelation is assumed to come sharply and distinctly. If we are to judge by the example of Ezekiel, the prophet typically received his revelations and the content of his oracles in full some time *before* he delivered them to the people; it was perhaps only rarely a matter of *immediately* inspired speech or 'invasive' prophecy.

If what we have said so far is the general picture, let us immediately recognize that it needs the following four qualifications:

(1) Alongside the non-invasive type of prophecy indicated, there appears to have been a compulsive charismatic sort of prophesying which consisted in some kind of invasively inspired worship rather than specifically oracular intelligible speech: see especially 1 Samuel 10:5,6,10–12; 19:20–24. *Targum Jonathan* to the passages concerned takes each occasion to denote (semi-ecstatic) charismatic songs of praise; whether this is true or not (and the context of musical accompaniment in 1 Sam. 10 favours the interpretation; cf. 1 Chr. 25:1–7), the point remains that these occasions do not envisage oracles carefully delivered by prophets to targeted individuals, and the NRSV translation, 'they will be in a prophetic frenzy', may more closely match the discernible features of the passages (the verb *tsalach*, 'come mightily upon', used with the Spirit at 10:6 and 10:10, is the same as that used to denote the powerful rush of the Spirit upon Samson at Jdg. 14:6,19, etc.). The same may apply to the seventy elders who 'prophesied' spontaneously when the Spirit came upon them in Numbers 11:25,26. In terms of our earlier typology of the charismata regularly attributed to the 'Spirit of prophecy', in Chapter 1, these are occasions of 'invasively inspired charismatic praise or worship'.

(2) Similarly, these and other passages remind us there were 'prophets' and 'prophecy' in ancient Israel *other* than the canonical prophets. In both passages in 1 Samuel we meet a whole guild of 'prophets'. With these we may compare the company of fifty prophets, called the 'sons of the prophets', who come to

Elisha in 2 Kings 2, (cf. 1 Kgs. 20:35) etc., and the various individuals David sets aside to prophesy with the lyre, harp and cymbal in 1 Chronicles 25:1–7. In this last instance, the 'prophecy' in question appears to be charismatic worship within the liturgical service of Israel. Thus of Jeduthun it is specifically noted it was his gift that 'he prophesied with the lyre in thanksgiving and praise to the Lord' (25:3).

(3) Not all prophecy was addressed to *the nation*. In addition to inspired doxological speech apparently addressed *to God*, oracles were also delivered to *individuals* concerning their purely personal affairs before God. An obvious case is that of the old prophet at Bethel who announces imminent judgement on the man of God who has disobediently broken his journey home (1 Kgs. 13:20,21). And in the context of 1 Samuel 10, which we have just alluded to, we need to remember that young Saul and his companion first approached Samuel as a prophet, hoping that *as a seer* he would be able to reveal to them the whereabouts of their missing donkeys (9:3–10). Here it is evidently expected that Samuel will be able to provide a response oracle when questioned about a purely practical matter. In this passage we have a close parallel to the frequent Greek phenomenon of consulting the oracle for immediate advice on family and business matters (Should I marry X? May I trust Y? Shall I recover from disease Z? etc. For similar solicited oracles, see e.g. 2 Kgs. 1:2; 8:7–15, etc).

(4) Parts of the Old Testament witness indicate an awareness that the *mediated* knowledge of God afforded by the prophets is not the ideal. The ideal is rather that *all* should have the Spirit (cf. Jer. 31:33,34; Ezek. 36:25–27 and Joel 2:28–32). The vision is of a future in which all God's people know him, and know his will, immediately and charismatically, through the Spirit of prophecy given to the individual rather than through occasional national prophets.

The intertestamental period has widely been considered a period of the withdrawal of prophecy from Israel, and appeal in support of this 'dogma' of a 'Spirit-less' and 'prophet-less' period has regularly been made to 1 Maccabees 4:46; 9:27; 14:41; Josephus, *Against Apion*, 1.37–41; *2 Baruch* 85:3, *Prayer of Azariah* 15, and especially to *Tosefta Sotah* 13.2–4, with its assertion that 'When Haggai, Zechariah, and Malachi, the last of the prophets, died, the Holy Spirit ceased in [from] Israel'.[17] It now

---

[17]Horn, *Angeld*, 26–32; Farnell, 'Gift of Prophecy', 387–90.

seems probable, however, that these texts have been largely misunderstood.[18] J.R. Levison has pointed out that *Tosefta Sotah* chapters
10–15 are replete with parallel statements of the sort 'when Rabbi
Joshua died, men of counsel ceased, and reflection ended in Israel' (*t.
Sot.* 15.3), and that such statements mean little more than that the death
of the persons concerned deprived Israel of their great gifts. These
generous rhetorical exaggerations should hardly be pressed literally to
mean a universal and permanent cessation of the gifts concerned (unless this is explicitly claimed). *Tosefta Sotah* 13.2 laments the loss of the
powerful presence of the Spirit that the deaths of Haggai, Zechariah
and Malachi entailed, but does not imply a long-term or ubiquitous
absence of the Spirit. Indeed this very passage (13.3,4) goes on to speak
of Hillel and Samuel the Small as two upon whom the Spirit rested
even if the rest of the generation were unworthy of the honour.[19] In
fact, such numerous claims to prophetic revelations were made in this
'intertestamental' period that even scholars who hold to the dogma of
the cessation of the Spirit are forced to rethink or modify it,[20] and some
of the most important of the claims are made in the very writings appealed to for the doctrine that the Spirit was withdrawn from Israel
(Josephus and the Rabbis). There is an all-too-apparent tension between
the assertions of the cessation of the Spirit/prophecy and continuing
claims to prophecy. Grudem (following a lead from H.A. Wolfson, Gutt-
man, Hill and others) attempted to explain this tension in terms of the
appearance of a lesser form of prophecy:

> There was thought to be no more prophecy of the OT type, which
> possessed an absolute divine authority extending to the very words of
> the prophet; at the same time, the occurrence of occasional revelatory
> phenomena was readily acknowledged. This secondary type of
> phenomenon may sometimes have been called 'prophecy', and it may
> have been thought to possess some kind of 'divine authority of general
> content', but it was always understood that it did not possess the kind
> of absolute divine authority . . . [of the] prophecies of the OT.[21]

---

[18]See Aune, *Prophecy*, 103–6; F.E. Greenspahn, 'Why Prophecy Ceased', *JBL* 108
(1989), 37–49 (esp. 38–40), and esp. Levison (below).

[19]See J.R. Levison, 'Did the Spirit withdraw from Israel? An Evaluation of the
earliest Jewish Data', *NTS* 43 (1997), 35–57.

[20]See R. Meyer, *Der Prophet aus Galiläa* (Darmstadt: WB, 1970 [orig. 1940]), 45–
60; *idem*, '*E*', *TDNT* VI:812–28; D. Hill, *New Testament Prophecy* (London: MMS,
1979), 21–43; Grudem, *Gift*, 27-32, or Aune, *Prophecy*, 103–52, for examples.

[21]*Gift*, 26. For Hill, the interstestamental form is largely charismatic exegesis
and/or foretelling, rather than addition of new prophecies or 'the direct and
xxx

But Grudem's reference to prophecy 'of the OT type' with 'absolute divine authority' clearly presupposes that the ~~inscripturated~~ prophecies of Old Testament *canonical* prophets were some sort of 'norm' for prophecy, whereas we have seen there was much prophecy in Israel where the question of verbal inerrancy was irrelevant.[22] One suspects Grudem (as others) illegitimately combines elements of his doctrine of Scripture with his analysis of prophetic phenomenology — a point to which we shall need to return in Chapter 16. In short, while the 'intertestamental' period may not have produced prophetic figures of the calibre of the canonical prophets, prophecy was by no means extinct. Harnack could even claim that 'prophecy was in luxuriant bloom, and . . . prophets were numerous, and secured both adherents and readers.'[23] If this perhaps exaggerates, and so misleads, it is nevertheless much closer to the truth than claims concerning the 'cessation' of prophecy in the period. Even Josephus (cf. *War* 3.351–4, 400–2; *Life*, 42[24]) and Philo counted themselves amongst those who received charismatic revelations and gave significant prophecy,[25] and Philo appears potentially to extend the ability to every just person (*Who is the Heir*, 259–60).

The prophecies of the 'intertestamental' period vary in form and content, but usually recognizably fit the stereotype advanced above. Thus, for example, we may take that of one Jesus ben Hananiah, uttered four years before the disastrous war with Rome, and effectively repeated as 'Woe to Jerusalem' until the prophet was himself killed during the final stages of the Roman siege of the city (AD 70):

A cry from the east
a cry from the west

(footnote 21 continued)
immediate address from the "council of the Lord" in themessenger form "Thus says the Lord" ' (*Prophecy*, 41, commenting on the Teacher of Righteousness at Qumran, but his comment reflects his understanding of a far broader position: cf. 21–31, 33–43).

[22] In his earlier *Gift* he evinces much fuller awareness of this: see esp. 33–42.

[23] A. Harnack, *The Mission and Expansion of Christianity in the First Three Centuries*, vol. 1, 332 (quoted by Grudem, *Gift*, 24). Cf. Aune's judgment that prophecy was 'alive and well', though in a form considerably different from that of classical OT prophecy (*Prophecy*, 104: and note his own quotation of Sandmel's conclusion that outside the rabbis 'the view that prophecy had ended simply did not exist').

[24] See J. Blenkinsopp, 'Prophecy and Priesthood in Josephus', *JJS* 25 (1974), 239–62.

[25] On Philo, see (e.g.) Aune, *Prophecy*, 147–51.

a cry from the four winds
A cry against Jerusalem and the temple
a cry against the bridegroom and the bride
a voice against all the people (Josephus, *War* 6.301).

There is no mistaking this for anything but oracular speech. Similarly,
when Jewish writers *attribute* prophecies to figures within ancient Israel, they are usually stereotypical cases of messages from God, immediately revealed to inspired human intermediaries, and subsequently
(or coincidentally) related to others.[26] They are not 'expository
discourses' of the type noted above. Where we come closest to the latter
— in the 'prophetic' expositions of the Teacher of Righteousness at
Qumran — the exposition is achieved only through 'revelation' of
'mysteries' that could not possibly be discerned by any normal reading
of the passages in question (cf. 1QpHab 7.1–5), and it is not given as
prophecies, but as teaching.[27]

2. Correlation with Pauline and Lucan usage of 'Prophecy' and 'to Prophesy' for Ecclesial Forms of Inspired Speech

Prophecy in the New Testament church has been the subject of many
works, the most significant of which are those by E. Fascher; E.
Cothonet; T.M. Crone; G. Dautzenberg; U. Müller; J. Panagopoulos; E.E.
Ellis; D. Hill; W. Grudem; D.E. Aune; M.E. Boring; T.W. Gillespie, and
C. Forbes.[28] Though we shall come across the claim that by 'prophecy'
Paul means charismatic preaching (see part II, §4, below), a brief survey
of linguistic uses suggests continuity with the stereotype above.

---

[26]Aune, *Prophecy*, 112–21 and 148–150, discusses instances in Apocalyptic, Philo
and 'Pseudo-Philo' (i.e. *Biblical Antiquities*), but the phenomenon is widespread.
[27]For Daniel, the Teacher of Righteousness, the Essenes and Josephus, as charismatic interpreters of Scripture, sometimes involving prophecies, see e.g. R.
Meyer, *TDNT* VI:819–21. Similarly it is possible that Josephus understood his
own *Antiquities* as 'prophecy', in the sense of inspired record of God's dealings
with Israel, and after the analogy of regarding the biblical histories as (in a
loose sense) 'prophecy' (because regarded as granted by the Holy Spirit).
[28]E. Fascher, ΠΡΟΦΗΤΗΣ, (Giessen: Töppelmann, 1927); É. Cothonet,
'Prophétisme dans le Nouveau Testament', *DBSupp* VIII, 1222–1337; G.
Friedrich, 'προφήτης', *TDNT* VI:828–61; T.M. Crone, *Early Christian Prophecy*
(Baltimore: St Mary's UP, 1973); G. Dautzenberg, *Urchristliche Prophetie*, (Stut-
tgart: Kohlhammer, 1975); U. B. Müller, *Prophetie und Predigt im Neuen Testament*,
(Gütersloh: Mohn, 1975); J. Panagopoulos (ed.), *Prophetic Vocation in the New
Testament and Today* (Leiden: Brill, 1977); E.E. Ellis, *Prophecy and Hermeneutic in*

(1) *Prophēteuein* ('to prophesy') is used of ecclesial inspired speech on some 21 occasions (Gospel parallels excluded). In a number of instances it is simply unclear what type of speech is intended, because the context gives too few clues (Mt. 7:22; Acts 21:9; Rev. 10:11, 11:3[29]). In one tradition (Lk. 22:64//Mt. 26:68, cf. Mk. 14:65) Jesus, blindfolded, is struck, and goaded 'to prophesy' who has hit him. This is a clear if unusual case of oracular utterance, for here prophecy means utterance on the basis of an immediate revelation (of the identity of the assailant). The two remaining instances in the gospel tradition bear the same meaning (Lk. 1:67 and John 11:51). In the former, Zechariah is said to be filled with the Spirit and to 'prophesy' the Benedictus which follows, combining an oracle blessing God for salvation (1:68–75) with a recognition oracle concerning the Baptist and his future role (1:76–79). In John 11:51 it is a case of the High Priest (unconsciously) uttering a short (and ironic) oracular statement concerning the meaning of Jesus' death. All the occasions before and outside Paul thus conform to the stereotype. The Pauline references all fall within 1 Corinthians: (11:4,5; 13:9; 14:1,3,4,5 (*bis*),24,31,39), and we may presume the first two relate to the same phenomenon as is discussed in more detail in chapters 12–14. The nature of the phenomenon in question is most clearly inferred from 1 Corinthians 14:29–31: 'Two or three prophets should speak and the others should weigh carefully what is said. And if a revelation comes to someone who is sitting down, the first should stop. For you can all prophesy in turn so that everyone may be instructed and encouraged.' As Grudem elucidates (at length), for Paul, 'to prophesy' is essentially to receive and subsequently to communicate some spontaneous, divinely given *apokalypsis*.[30] A similar picture emerges in the remaining New Testament occurrences which come from Acts.

(footnote 28 continued)
Early Christianity: New Testament Essays (Tübingen: Mohr, 1978); D. Hill, *Prophecy*; Grudem, *Gift*; idem, *Prophecy*; Aune, *Prophecy*; M.E. Boring, *The Continuing Voice: Christian Prophecy and the Gospel Tradition* (Louisville: Westminster/John Knox, 1991); T.W. Gillespie, *The First Theologians: A Study in Early Christian Prophecy* (Grand Rapids: Eerdmans, 1994), and Forbes, *Prophecy*.
[29]The allusions to Isaiah and Ezekiel in the Revelation contexts, however, suggest oracular speech, and this conforms with the whole cotext.
[30]Cf. Grudem, *Gift*, 115–43, esp. 139–42. A similar definition is advanced by J. Panagopoulos, 'Die urchristliche Prophetie: Ihr Character und ihre Funktion', in Panagopoulos (ed.), *Vocation*, 1–32: 'The prophetic word is mediated or given directly through revelation, in particular through a dream, vision, hearing or

Acts 2:17,18, quoting Joel, states that Israel's sons and daughters will prophesy (17b and 18b) because God will reveal things to them in dreams and visions — the assumption (in accord with most Old Testament and much intertestamental literature)[31] is that prophecy is the declaring of a revelatory experience received by such means. In Acts 19:6 Luke describes an outpouring of the Spirit on twelve 'disciples' at Ephesus with the words 'they began to speak in tongues and prophesy'. In this instance, 'prophesy' probably does not have the sense 'to report a revelation (word, vision or dream) received', but the more general 'to speak while under the invasive influence of the Spirit'. The precedents for that type of 'prophecy' are to be found in 1 Samuel 19:20–24; 10:5–13; Numbers 11:24–30, etc.[32] What is not clear is whether the particle *kai* ('and') of Acts 19:6 is epexegetic (thereby identifying the speaking in tongues as a form of 'prophecy'[33]) or (more probably) simply conjoining. Either way we have a slightly different sense to that which Paul uses in the situation confronting him at Corinth, but a clearly related one.[34] Just what other phenomena Luke might have been willing to denote by *prophēteuein* we shall need to discuss below.

(2) *Prophēteia* ('prophecy'). There are ten New Testament references to *prophēteia* as some forms of ecclesial inspired speech (Rom.

(footnote 30 continued)
direct revelation of the Lord, an angel, or some other organ of communication; the prophet [merely] receives it . . . and hands it on . . . The prophets cannot speak such prophetic words of themselves alone, but only where and when God wills' (27; cf. 2 Pet. 1:21). Cf. also Dunn, *Jesus*, 228.

[31]Cf. Dautzenberg, *Prophetie*, pt.1.

[32]Grudem, *Gift*, 33–37.

[33]Haya-Prats (*L'Esprit*, 24) argues this would be consistent with general Greek usage, but see C. Forbes, 'Early Inspired Speech and Hellenist Popular Religion', *NovT* 28 (1986), 257–70. Forbes himself denies that there is precedent in Greek prophetism for such a connection, but nevertheless believes Luke makes it — largely on the grounds that he thinks Peter's Pentecost speech explains the immediately preceding glossolalia as 'prophecy' by appeal to Joel's promise (Forbes, *Prophecy*, 219–21, and 252–3 n.2). But his own position fails to see that Peter's use of Joel merely claims the one hundred and twenty had received the 'Spirit of prophecy'. The latter explains the glossolalia without formally identifying it as itself 'prophecy'.

[34]Aune, *Prophecy* 199, follows N.J. Engelsen in saying Paul was the first to separate the two phenomena (tongues and prophecy), and this on situational grounds: cf. Crone, *Prophecy*, 219–22.

12:6; 1 Cor. 12:10; 13:2, 8; 14:6,22; 1 Thess. 5:20; 1 Tim. 1:18; 4:14, and Rev. 11:6), and a further five to the Apocalypse as a 'book of prophecy' (a collection of revelatory oracles plus other material).[35] The reference in 1 Timothy 4:14 implies some kind of recognition/commissioning oracle (accompanying laying on of hands) which announced (and effected) God's empowering of Timothy at his consecration for service. 1:18 more specifically implies accompanying directive and/or predictive revelations. The occurrences in 1 Corinthians clearly refer to the same phenomenon of oracular speech indicated above by the verb 'to prophesy' in 1 Corinthians 14:29–31. The uses in Romans 12:6 and 1 Thessalonians 5:20 are sufficient closely parallel in co-textual traits to require no special comment. In short, all the Pauline reference to *prophēteia* are most readily explained as oracular speech.

(3) *Prophētēs* 'prophet' is evidently semantically related to *prophēteuein*. But the relationship is complex. Josephus and Philo considered themselves to speak prophecies but were reticent to designate themselves 'prophets'. On the other hand, in the Greek world a *prophētēs* could be a 'spokesman' for the god, even if he did not utter any oracles, and evidently a similar development took place in Judaism. Millinerian leader-prophets such as Theudas (AD 44–46), 'the Egyptian' (some time between 52–60) and others, who collected bands of followers in the wilderness, and promised God would begin redemption there with a display of signs, were 'prophets' more because they styled themselves typologically on Moses and Joshua, as sign-working deliverers, than for provision of prophetic oracles as such.[36] And when the New Testament uses the term 'false prophet(s)', the people in view appear to be charismatic leader-teachers rather than those who prophesy (cf. Mk. 13:22; Lk. 6:26; Mt. 7:15; 2 Pet. 2:1). The questions are then (a) whether Luke and Paul use *prophētēs* of anyone who utters a 'prophecy' (or,

---

[35]The only exception is the reference to the 'Spirit of prophecy' in Rev 19:10.

[36]See Aune, *Prophecy*, 124–6; P.W. Barnett, 'The Jewish Sign Prophets — A.D. 40–70: Their Intentions and Origin', *NTS* 27 (1980–81), 681–97; R.A. Horsley, 'Popular Prophetic Movements at the Time of Jesus: Their Principal Features and Social Origins', *JSNT* 26 (1986), 3–27; *idem*, ' "Like One of the Prophets of Old": Two Types of Popular Prophets at the Time of Jesus', *CBQ* 47 (1985), 435–63, esp. 454–61. Horsley places John the Baptist and Jesus amongst 'oracular prophets', rather than with 'prophets who led movements', but in these two cases the distinction tends to break down.

instead, restrict the use of the title 'prophet' in some way), and
(b) whether 'prophet' language or imagery is used of those who
do not prophesy. We shall return to these questions more fully
later, here merely noting (with respect to (a)) that Grudem may
be right to argue that Paul can use the terms *both* ways (cf. 1
Cor. 14:31,32), but usually restricted his application of the noun
'prophet' in a manner that involved both subjective factors (cf.
1 Cor. 14:37: 'If anyone considers himself to be a prophet . . .')
and *informal* recognition by the church.[37]

II. THE NEW TESTAMENT CONCEPTS OF PROPHECY

We move now from discussion of word-usage to the concept(s) signified
by the *propheteuein* word-group. What can we discern about the nature of
New Testament prophecy beyond what we have said above? The essence
of prophecy in Paul, we have noted, is the declaration of a revelation
imparted by a spiritual agent (God, or Jesus, in the Spirit, in the case of
'true' prophets/ prophecies[38]). Seven major points require elucidation:

1. The Psychology of Prophecy[39]

The question whether New Testament prophecy was an 'ecstatic'
phenomenon has regularly been raised. It is commonly held that
Graeco-Roman oracular speech was ecstatic, while the Jewish and
Christian counterparts were not. This antithesis rests on a caricature of
the former (based in a minimal proportion of the evidence),[40] on a
failure to recognise ecstaticism in the biblical tradition,[41] and on a confusion between philosophical/ theological and behavioural meanings of
'ecstasy'.[42] In Graeco-Roman discussions of prophetism, the interest in

---

[37]Grudem, *Gift*, ch. 4, esp. 231.

[38]Not by 'angels' as Ellis supposes: see Grudem, *Gift*, 120–2.

[39]Cf. Grudem, *Gift*, ch. 2 onwards.

[40]*Contra*, e.g., H. Bacht, 'Wahres und falsches Prophetentum', *Bib* 32 (1951),
237–62), see Aune, *Prophecy*, 230–1 and *passim*, but especially Forbes, *Prophecy*,
chs. 5, 8 and (esp.) 11.

[41]See R. Wilson, 'Prophecy and Ecstasy: A Re-examination', *JBL* 98 (1979), 321–
37.

[42]'Ecstasy is much too vague a term to employ unless it be abundantly qualified
to make clear that there are many degrees of it, ranging from mild dissociation
to extreme uncontrollable rapture', C.G. Williams, 'Glossolalia as a Religious
Phenomenon: "Tongues" at Corinth and Pentecost', *Rel* 5 (1975), 16–32 (21);
idem, Tongues of the Spirit: A Study of Pentecostal Glossolalia and Related Phenomena
(Cardiff: UWP, 1981), ch. 1.

ekstasis/mania (being 'outside oneself') is primarily on the *means* by which the oracle comes, i.e. that it is by the eclipse of the human mind by the divine persona as the controlling power over speech. Philo captures the point well (and shows his debt to (e.g.) Plato's *Phaedrus* 244a–245c, *Timaeus* 71, and *Ion* 533d–534e) when he says:

> This is what regularly befalls the fellowship of prophets. The [human] mind is evicted at the arrival of the divine Spirit, but when that departs the mind returns to its tenancy. Mortal and immortal may not share the same home. And therefore the setting of reason and the darkness which surrounds it produce ecstasy and divine mania. (*Who is the Heir of Divine Things* 265; cf. *Special Laws* 4.49[43])

And what he means by this is not that the prophet necessarily becomes unconscious or displays what a twentieth-century observer might mean by 'frenzy' and 'mania', but that the prophet's speech is now entirely under the inspiration of God. The point is not that the prophet loses consciousness, merely that his or her mind does not contribute to the speech event. As he continues,

> For indeed the prophet, even when he seems to be speaking, really holds his peace, and his organs of speech, mouth and tongue, are wholly in the employ of Another, to shew forth what he wills. Unseen by us that Other beats on the chords with the skill of a master-hand and makes them instruments of sweet music, laden with every harmony. (266)

When, however, the term 'ecstasy' is used by moderns it typically denotes a psychological state — and this varying from a mild altered state of consciousness to entire loss of awareness of surroundings and of voluntary control. Those engaged in sociological and anthropological disciplines prefer the terminology '(possession) trance' to 'ecstasy' in order to focus this psychological/behavioural aspect. Here the word 'trance' is used 'to account for alterations or discontinuity in consciousness, awareness, personality, or other aspects of psychological

---

[43]'For no pronouncement of a prophet is ever his own; he is an interpreter prompted by Another in all his utterances, when knowing not what he does he is filled with inspiration as the reason withdraws and surrenders the citadel of the soul to a new visitor and tenant, the divine Spirit, which plays upon the vocal organism and dictates the words which clearly express its prophetic message.'

functioning' produced by the inspiration,[44] and varying in force from 'controlled' trance to 'uncontrolled'.

Even in the passages just referred to there is little clear evidence that Philo's *ekstasis* or *mania* included the loss of perception of surroundings, of voluntary behaviour and of self-awareness which marks 'uncontrolled trance'. Furthermore, he was certainly aware of forms of prophecy in which the prophet, fully conscious, hears and interprets words spoken by God, and other forms in which, under inspiration, the prophet may ask questions of God and receive the answers (cf. *Life of Moses* 2.188–92[45]). This is not simply Philo being truer to his Jewish heritage (strong forms of 'trance' were relatively rare to the record of Jewish prophecy); Plutarch (AD 60–130), too, argues that the later (non-poetic) forms of prophecy at Delphi are to be explained as an inspiration and revelations given by the god, but apprehended and articulated through the human perception of the non-poetic prophetess (*On the Pythian Oracle*, 397c, 404–5; *contrast*, *On the Failure of Oracles*, 432). While it is *possible* Graeco-Roman prophetism gave a greater prominence to *ekstasis*, and this was more often regarded as accompanied by the stronger forms of possession trance (especially in the earlier discussions), these features were by no means widespread to Graeco-Roman prophetism, nor unknown in Jewish and later Christian prophecy (especially that of the *Didache* and Montanism[46]).

But what of the form(s) of prophecy we encounter in Luke-Acts and

---

[44]Erika Bourguignon, *Possession* (San Francisco: Chandler and Sharp, 1976), 9 (the term 'possession' here is used to denote inspiration by an alien S/spirit, and stands in contrast to 'shamanism' in which the practitioner's own 'spirit' travels 'out of the body' to other scenes/events). For similar usage within sociology, see I.M. Lewis, *Ecstatic Religion: An Anthropological Study of Spirit Possession and Shamanism*, (London: Routledge, 1989[2] (first ed., Baltimore, 1971); R. Wilson, 'Prophecy and Ecstasy', 324–8.

[45]See D. Winston, 'Two Types of Mosaic Prophecy according to Philo', *JSP* 2 (1989), 49–67; J.R. Levison, 'Two Types of Ecstatic Prophecy according to Philo', *Studia Philonica Annual* 6 (1994), 83–9. The latter agrees with Winston that (according to Philo) Moses experiences ' "a milder form of ecstatic prophecy" which preserves rather than displaces his human abilities' (86). Cf. also his conclusion to *Life of Moses* 2.188–91: here 'Inspiration does not interrupt the natural process which begins with Moses' emotional response; on the contrary, Moses is not, like Balaam and the other prophets, a mindless channel for God, but speaks, like God, out of his own person, with his motions and mind intact.' Aune may also be right when he observes that Philo's description of the prophetic state as '*sober* intoxication' (*Creation* 70–71) implies continuing awareness throughout the experience (*Prophecy*, 150).

[46]See the fuller discussion in Callan, 'Prophecy', 128–36, 138–9.

Paul? N. Engelsen argued that early Christian prophecy was a strongly ecstatic phenomenon, on the grounds that Paul was the first to distinguish what (for Engelsen) was evidently ecstatic and incomprehensible glossolalia from intelligible prophecy (see Ch. 13 below). But Grudem, Aune, Callan and Forbes are probably right to deduce from 1 Corinthians that Paul did not anticipate 'ecstatic' or strongly entranced types of *prophecy* (not even behind 1 Cor. 12:3[47]), but at the most 'controlled' prophetic 'trance'.[48] On the one hand, the revelation that comes to the prophet is distinct and compelling, such that the prophet may (wrongly in Paul's opinion) feel he could not resist the Spirit (1 Cor. 14:32), or (rightly in Paul's view) that he must be given almost immediate hearing if the revelation comes to him during worship (1 Cor. 14:30). On the other hand, the one prophesying is sufficiently aware of his surroundings to be able to bring his speech to a close when another signals he has received an immediate revelation (1 Cor. 14:30).[49] Furthermore, in contrast to the one who receives a revelation in the meeting itself, those who are required to give way to the latter appear to be people who have received the content of their prophecy *before* coming to the meeting. In such a case the speech event itself might not have been attended by any altered state of consciousness (similarly with OT prophets who often received the content of their oracles days or more before communicating them). In the New Testament, the most plausible cases of prophetic speech marked by strong experience of 'trance' are Acts 10:45,46 and Acts 19:6, where the dramatic outpouring of the Spirit occasions invasive charismatic doxology, mixing tongues with prophetic praise.[50] But there is no reason to believe these extraordinary conversional experiences were the norm, and even here there is little reason to assume the phenomena were uncontrollable after their immediate inception, or that the converts experienced significant loss of self-awareness, or of consciousness of their external circumstances.

The strength and sharpness of the revelation experienced in prophecy probably also varied widely. At one extreme we have the powerful visionary experiences of Paul, e.g. in Acts 10:10; 22:17 and 2 Cor. 12,

---

[47]Grudem, *Gift*, 150–77 (esp. 155–72); K.S. Hemphill, 'The Pauline Concept of Charisma: A Situational and Developmental Approach', PhD dissertation, Cambridge, 1977, 69–72.

[48]Aune, *Prophecy*, 19–21. Cf. the similar verdict reached by G. Friedrich, *TDNT* VI:851. Forbes thinks even this goes too far (*Prophecy*, chs. 9–10).

[49]Cf. Callan, 'Prophecy', 127.

[50]Cf. Acts 10:10; 11:5; 22:17; but these are not associated with prophecy as such.

etc.[51] (though not all such led to prophecy), or of John in the Apocalypse (note John characterizes his work as *prophecy*: Rev. 1:3; 22:18,19); at the other extreme *apokalyptein* ('to reveal') can be used even of the firm conviction gradually etched on the mind (e.g. Phil. 3:15). The verb is neutral with respect to the strength and clarity of the revelation.[52]

2. The Content of Prophetic Speech

This seems to have been wide-ranging. It includes anything from specific directions to churches concerning personnel (Acts 13:2,3), the solution for disputes (Acts 15:28,32?), specific guidance and assurance given to missionaries (e.g. Acts 16:6–13;18:10), and warning of famine (Acts 11:28), to prediction of Paul's personal fate (Acts 20:23; 21:4,11). It should be noted that each of these instances involves the necessity of God's revealing particularistic knowledge — not merely general principles that could be deduced, for example, by illuminated reading of the Torah, or from the gospel tradition, or from apostolic *didache*. The prophetic analysis of the seven churches in Revelation 2–3 points in the same direction. Paul, too, assumes that the same particularistic knowledge will be imparted when he says the outsider will be convicted, for God (through Corinthian prophesying) will reveal the secrets of his heart (1 Cor. 14:25). What is envisaged here is the laying bare of personal information which the outsider is convinced only God could have revealed (as in Jn. 4:16–19[53]).

But it is unlikely that Paul would have placed prophecy in such a privileged position (prophets second to apostles; prophecy the highest gift to which the Corinthians could aspire: 1 Cor. 12:28,29;14:1 etc.) unless prophetic *apokalypsis* went further than this, and involved the impartation of theological 'mysteries' (cf. 1 Cor. 13:2[54]). Aune uses five criteria to identify prophetic oracles in the New Testament, all or most of which should be satisfied before a passage is recognized as 'prophecy'.[55] Thus prophecy may be suspected if a saying or speech is: (i) attributed to a supernatural being; (ii) consists of prediction or

---

[51]A.T. Lincoln, "'Paul the Visionary": The Setting and Significance of the Rapture to Paradise in II Corinthians XII.1–10', *NTS* 25 (1979), 204–20. But cf. M.D. Goulder, 'Vision and Knowledge', *JSNT* 56 (1994), 53–71, who argues the visionary of 2 Cor. 12:2–5 was not Paul, who disclaimed such visions.
[52]Grudem, *Gift*, 134–6.
[53]E. Best, 'Prophets and Preachers', *SJT* 12 (1959), 129–50, 146ff.
[54]Dautzenberg, *Prophetie*, ch. 4.
[55]*Prophecy*, 247–8; 317–18.

involves special knowledge; (iii) introduced or concluded by formul..,.,
which in other contexts are marks of prophetic diction; (iv) prefixed by
a statement of the inspiration of the speaker; (v) does not sit easily in
the literary context.

Using these criteria, Aune discovers some 59 prophecies embedded
in the New Testament (e.g. Gal. 5:21; 1 Thess. 3:4; 4:2–6,16,17; 2 Thess.
3:6,10,12; 1 Cor. 14:37,38; 15:51,52; 2 Cor. 12:9; Rom. 11:25,26, and 1 Tim.
4:1–3 from amongst the 'Paulines').[56] The types of oracle include:

- (a) *oracles of assurance* (e.g. Acts 18:9; 23:11; 27:23,24; 2 Cor. 12:9,
  etc.);
- (b) *prescriptive oracles* (e.g. Gal. 5:21; Acts 13:2; 21:4; 2 Thess. 3:6,
  etc.);
- (c) *announcements of salvation* (Rev. 14:13; 19:9, etc.);
- (d) *announcements of judgement* (Acts 13:9–11; 1 Cor. 14:37,38; Gal.
  1:8,9);
- (e) *legitimation oracles* (e.g. 1 Cor. 12:3) — and including *self-commen-
  dation oracles* (Rev. 1:8,17), and
- (f) *eschatological theophany oracles* (Rom. 11:25,26; 1 Cor. 15:51,52; 1
  Thess. 4:16,17, etc.).

Clearly the last of these — and for that matter the previous three types
— are 'doctrinal' in nature.[57]

It should be obvious by now that the form and content of early
Christian prophecy was exceedingly varied, and parallels can be found
to some forms in non-prophetic speech. This observation prompts
Aune to his conclusion: 'the distinctive feature of prophetic speech was
not so much its *content* or *form*, but its (direct) *supernatural origin*.'[58]

3. The Purpose(s) of Prophecy

On this it is commonplace to begin with Paul's statement in 1 Corinthians 14:3 (cf. v.31) that prophecy is for the edification, exhortation and
consolation of the congregation. Two points must be remembered however. Firstly, Paul does not offer this proposition as a sufficient condition of the predicate *prophēteia*. It is not: forms of speech other than
prophecy serve the same purpose, such as words of wisdom and

---

[56]*Prophecy*, ch.10 and 441, n.47, for a list of 107 oracles including those from
Didache, Hermas, Ignatius, Odes of Solomon, and other early Christian writings.
[57]*Prophecy*, chs. 10,12.
[58]*Ibid.*, 338.

knowledge (1 Cor. 12:8), tongues (when interpreted), homily, exposition and teaching. These alternatives may be highly charismatic too; but that does not make them 'prophecy'.[59] Secondly, Paul's statement in 14:3 need not even be a *necessary* condition of *prophēteuein* — he may merely have thought it would usually characterize congregational prophecy. Certainly 1 Corinthians 14:3 should not be used to marginalize prophecy given to individuals outside the framework of the assembly of the congregation (as, e.g. Agabus to Paul in Acts 21:11[60]). More precisely, the function of prophecy can to some extent be read off the forms of prophetic speech identified: oracles of assurance, salvation, judgment, legitimation, prescription and eschatological theophany, etc. These activities of God in the congregation serve as a sign (cf. 1 Cor. 14:22) to his people: a sign of blessing indicating that he is with them; that he knows them intimately; that he knows what dangers beset them; that he has them in his hand, leads them and instructs them. It is a sign that may be transparent, too, to the unbeliever (vv. 24,25).

4. Does Prophecy Denote Charismatic Exegesis, Preaching or Teaching?

It need not be doubted that prophecies had didactic and prescriptive elements (see above[61]), nor that those who rose to be recognized as 'prophets' in the early church were leaders who were able to preach and to teach (cf. Acts 15:32). But it is quite another matter to assert that inspired preaching, exegesis or teachings are actually (wholly or in part) what the New Testament *means* by prophecy. Warnings against such misunderstanding, which are especially prevalent in Reformed circles, have been given by (*inter multos alios*) Best[62] and Grudem.[63] But the positive case has recently been reasserted by Cothonet, Ellis, Hill, Müller, Boring and Gillespie.[64] Their position rests, however, on dubious arguments:

---

[59]See esp. Grudem, *Gift*, 181–5.

[60]Aune, *Prophecy*, 195ff., 211ff.

[61]See, however, Grudem, *Gift*, 185, on *manthanō* ('to teach') in 1 Cor. 14:32.

[62]'Prophets', *passim*.

[63]*Gift*, 139–44.

[64]E. Cothonet, 'Les Prophètes chrétiens comme Exégètes charismatiques de l'Écriture', in Panagopoulos (ed.), *Vocation*, 77–107; D. Hill, 'Christian Prophets as Teachers or Instructors in the Church', in Panagopoulos (ed.), *Vocation*, 108–30; Ellis, *Prophecy*, pt. 2; Gillespie, *Theologians*, *passim*.

(1) The position is antecedently unlikely. After all, prophecy in Judaism was stereotypically *oracular* speech.[65] Furthermore, the belief was held in some rabbinic quarters that significant *prophecy* had ceased; now there were *sages* and *scribes* instead (*Baba Batra* 122ab; cf. *Seder Olam Rabbah* 30[66]). Where such statements were made, the point was precisely that God no longer speaks directly, *but by Scripture* interpreted and expounded. Where such statements were denied, and the continuation of prophecy maintained, it was usually as the declaration of knowledge imparted directly to the speaker from a supernatural source (e.g. Josephus' dream-prophecy of Vespasian's election as Emperor; cf. also that of Johanan ben Zakkai) — albeit sometimes then read back into Scripture (as in *Wars* 3.351–4[67]). As Romans 12:6–8 includes prophecy, teaching, and exhortation in a list intended to illustrate *diverse* gifts, it is probable the old and widespread distinction between prophecy and various forms of expository discourse held for Paul too: similarly in 1 Corinthians 12:8–10, 28,29 (where prophets and teachers are distinguished), and 14:6,26. Charismatic *teaching* probably included exposition that related Scripture and tradition to the immediate needs of a congregation, while prophecy primarily denoted the declaration by a person of material revealed to him or to her *directly* by the supernatural source, rather than mediated through consideration of Scripture.

(2) Ellis argues that there are occasions in the New Testament where midrashic exegesis is accompanied by the formula 'says the Lord', and that the latter is a claim to prophetic knowledge by the exegete (e.g. the use of Deut. 32:35 in Rom. 12:19). But this has been severely criticized by Aune.[68] In response he argues: (a) the same phenomena in *Barnabas* are explained by the writer not as *prophecy* but as *teaching*. (b) The *legei kyrios* ('the Lord says') formula is not a claim to inspired speech (and anyway never used in prophetic speech) but simply identifies God as the speaker of the Old Testament passage under consideration. (c) There is no material (historical) connection between such 'implicit midrash' and early Christian prophecy as such. No evidence connects charismatic exegesis with prophets, while

---

[65] Aune, *Prophecy*, ch. 2.

[66] See Grudem (*Gift*, 21ff.) and Aune (*Prophecy*, ch. 5) for full treatment and literature.

[67] Aune, *Prophecy*, 141–3, 144–6.

[68] *Ibid.*, 343–5: cf. also Forbes, *Prophecy*, 225–37.

such teaching would naturally be expected of 'teachers' (and may occasionally have been given by 'prophets', but then as 'teaching' not as 'prophecy').

(3)   Those who argue for the equation of prophecy with preaching or teaching usually argue from the paraenetic function of Old Testament prophecy to the conclusion that New Testament paraenesis (= ethical exhortation) is therefore prophetic. Müller refines this, building on the reference to prophecy as accomplishing exhortation (1 Cor. 14:3), and pointing to the substantial paraenetic force of the prophecies to the churches in Revelation 2–3.[69] He then (like Aune) tries to uncover prophetic passages, but from the paraenetic sections of Paul's letters. This whole approach, however, overlooks the fact that paraenesis is not a *distinctive* feature of Old or New Testament prophecy as such, but common to a variety of genres: the Sermon on the Mount, as presented in Matthew 5–7, is clearly understood by the redactor as a type of 'exhortation speech', but it is not a 'prophecy'. Similarly, there are notable examples of 'prophecy' which do not involve challenge to repentance or exhortation: e.g. Agabus' prophecies of famine in Judea and Paul's impending fate in Jerusalem. As indicated above, 1 Corinthians 14:3 is not an adequate guide to the distinctive character of 'prophecy'.[70]

(4)   The most subtle and extended argument of the case has been made by T.W. Gillespie. His fundamental arguments are:

(i)   Paul's injunction in 14:29,30 that the prophet should draw his or her speech to a close if another receives a revelation, combined with his restriction on the number of prophecies to just two or three, indicates they were lengthy discourses.[71]

(ii)   The criterion for testing prophecy in 1 Thessalonians 5:20 and Romans 12:6 is 'the analogy of the Faith' — which he thinks means 'by the traditioned faith of the gospel' — and concludes, 'The logical inference is that, for Paul at least, prophecy was a form of gospel proclamation. . . . What the early Christian prophets were doing when they were prophesying is that they were proclaiming the gospel'.[72]

---

[69]U.B. Müller, *Prophetie*, 47–108.
[70]Similarly J. Reiling, 'Prophecy, the Spirit and the Church', in Panagopoulos (ed.), *Vocation*, 58–76, who refers to 1 Cor. 14:3 as 'deceptive' in this respect (69). Cf. also Crone, *Prophecy*, 213.
[71]Gillespie, *Theologians*, 24–25 (extending Müller's points).
[72]*Ibid.*, 63.

(iii) The content of prophecy is identified by 1 Corinthians 14:3 as upbuilding, exhortation (*paraklēsis*) and comfort (*paramythia*), and so *preaching*. Gillespie is aware that Reiling and Crone have opposed this, noting that tongues too (if interpreted) 'edifies' the church (14:5), and that 'to build up' is too broad a concept to aid in defining the prophet's role (similarly 'exhortation' and 'comfort'). But he dismisses the sceptics: these are the very terms Paul regularly uses to describe proclamation acts.[73] In Romans 15:20 (cf. 1:15), *oikodomein* and *euangelizesthai* are even used interchangeably (when the latter is directed to Christians). Both 'laying the foundation' and 'building on it' 'are therefore metaphors for the key term *euangelizesthai*. . . . The terms *oikodomein/ oikodomē* thus designate the *creatio continua* of the church through the preaching of the gospel to the church.' Prophesying is then said to meet the test of 14:26 ('Let all things be done for building up'), 'because, as an act of proclamation, it effects *oikodomē* (v.3) through an articulation of the one gospel that alone creates and builds up the church'.[74]

(iv) 1 Corinthians 2:6–16, concerning Paul's kerygma (= [initial] proclamation of the Christian message) and his subsequent teaching as inspired expressions of God's wisdom, has strong terminological and thematic connections with the discussion of prophecy in 1 Corinthians 12–14. The theme of 2:6–16 is thus prophecy even if the terminology is not used,[75] and Paul styles his apostolic ministry in the image of the Old Testament prophets.

(v) 1 Corinthians 15 continues the theme of chapters 12–14. It is an example of Paul's own conception of prophecy, and a critique of the Corinthian prophetic word that 'there is no resurrection of the dead' (15:12b). For Paul, Christian prophecy 'was (1) an exposition of the kerygma in terms of its intrinsic divine wisdom, (2) effected by the revelatory activity of the Spirit [cf. vv.51,52] within an ecclesial context, (3) expressed in extended discourse that included exposition of Scripture and logical argumentation, and (4) subjected to material criticism.'[76]

---

[73]*Theologians*, 142–50.
[74]*Ibid.*, 144.
[75]*Ibid.*, 165–98.
[76]*Ibid.*, 237.

Taking his points seriatim:

(i)   Paul's restriction to two or three prophecies tells us little
      about their length, for he makes the same restriction on
      tongues and interpretation (14:27), and these are usually
      understood to have been relatively short utterances. The
      point, in respect of both, is that time for judgement and
      reflection is required. Furthermore, Paul's willingness al-
      most to equate the *combination* of tongues and interpreta-
      tion with prophecy (14:5,27–31) might suggest the
      prophecy he has in view is not primarily argued proclama-
      tion, but oracular speech (even if this may have been fol-
      lowed by an element of interpretation and 'application' of
      the prophecy).

(ii) It is more probable that Romans 12:6 should be taken as an
      amplification of v.3, and 'has to do with prophesying ac-
      cording to the faith that has been apportioned to those with
      the prophetic gift.'[77] But even if we allow 'the faith' of 12:6
      as an objective genitive, the conclusion Gillespie draws is
      not a logical one. That prophecy (like *any* Christian activity)
      should be judged *by* the traditioned faith of the gospel does
      not mean it *is itself* a verbal proclamation of the gospel.

(iii) It need not be doubted that Paul considered both prophecy
      and charismatic preaching quintessentially to 'build up', to
      exhort, and to encourage. But one simply cannot for that
      reason formally equate preaching with prophecy. The same
      argument would require that Paul equated interpreted
      glossolalia as 'preaching' (for 14:5 speaks of this combina-
      tion 'building up' the church; cf. 14:26b, where the 'all
      things' listed in 14:25a are expected to accomplish the
      same). In addition, according to 14:4 the one who speaks in
      tongues *without* interpretation 'builds up' him/herself; but
      we should not deduce from that that Paul considered glos-
      solalia to be a 'preaching of the gospel' to oneself.

(iv) That Paul saw an analogy between prophecy and other
      forms of inspired speech, including Spirit- empowered
      preaching and teaching, need not be doubted. The percep-
      tion of such an analogy was probably widespread, and we
      have already noted how Philo, while discussing Moses'
      legislation on the Sabbath, draws out the analogy between
      inspired wisdom discourse and prophecy on the grounds

---

[77]See Fee, *Presence*, 604–11 (609).

that the mind 'could not have made so straight an aim if there were not also the divine Spirit guiding it to the truth itself' (*Life of Moses* 2.265). But for Philo such wisdom discourse is merely 'akin to prophecy'; he does not make the mistake of identifying the two. Similarly, while Paul can compare his apostolic commission to that of Old Testament prophets, and while he also almost certainly himself uttered prophecies, he never uses the words 'to prophesy' or 'prophecy' in reference to his proclamation of the gospel.

(v) 1 Corinthians 15 continues to deal with the problems of a (gnosticizing) spiritual enthusiasm, the various aspects of which Paul has addressed throughout the letter. There are therefore material connections between chapters 12–14 and chapter 15. But there is insufficient evidence to justify the claim that the *theme* of chapter 15 is still 'prophecy', and even less to support the view that Paul regarded the whole chapter as Pauline 'prophecy' in response to an alleged Corinthian prophetic word in 15:12b.[78] While there is a measure of consensus that 1 Corinthians 15:50–52 may incorporate what was originally a prophecy,[79] there is no need to extend the oracle to vv.53–58 merely because vv.54b–56 imply charismatic exegesis of Isaiah 25:8 and Hosea 13:14 (as Gillespie claims), for such exegesis of Old Testament texts is commonplace to Paul's teaching. 1 Corinthians 15 is better classified as 'spiritual teaching informed by prophecy/revelation (and by other factors)' than as 'prophecy' *simpliciter*.

We would not wish to claim that it is impossible Paul ever used the word 'prophecy' to denote something wider than oracular speech, and the advice in 1 Corinthians 14:30 may imply an element of narrative, or

---

[78]If Paul thought of 15:12b ('There is no resurrection from the dead') as an inspired utterance at all (of which he gives no indication), he is more likely to have classified it (along with claims such as 'all things are lawful to me' (6:12); 'all possess knowledge' (8:1); 'no idol in the world really exists' (8:4)) as mistaken Corinthian words of 'knowledge' or of 'wisdom'. Or, more correctly, the kernel saying together with the accompanying explanation and application might constitute a 'word of knowledge/wisdom', and such 'words' may well have been differentiated from 'prophecy' by the higher proportion of 'expository discourse' which marked them.
[79]See, e.g. U.B. Müller, *Prophetie*, 224–5; Aune, *Prophecy*, 250–1; H. Merklein, 'Der Theologe als Prophet: Zur Funktion prophetischen Redens im theologischen Diskurs des Paulus', *NTS* 38 (1992), 402–29 (416–18).

explanation, or application, beyond the 'prophecy proper' (which may, or may not, have been regarded as part of the 'prophesying'). But the burden of proof seems to rest with those who wish to claim that charismatic preaching and exegesis were normal aspects of *prophecy* rather than of *teaching*. Gillespie's definition of (Pauline) prophecy (as at point (v) above) would actually *exclude* from the classification 'prophecy' such 'obvious' cases of the phenomenon (from a broad first- century perspective) as Agabus' oracle of famine in Judea and of Paul's impending fate.

5. Were All Regarded as Able to Prophesy?

We can be certain that in Paul's view not all were prophets: the form of the question in 1 Corinthians 12:29 ensures that. But it has usually been argued that Paul, and others in the New Testament, reserved the honoured title 'prophet' for the recognized *specialist* in prophecy, especially for those who were also charismatic leader figures, while allowing that all at Corinth might prophesy one-by-one (1 Cor. 14:31).[80] To this is often added the further argument that, in Luke, the gift of the Spirit described and promised in Acts 2 is Joel's promise of the Spirit of prophecy. Ergo, it is all too often concluded, each Christian is a prophet, or, at least, can prophesy.[81] But the latter conclusion is insecure because, as we have seen, the 'Spirit of prophecy' in Luke's view gave a broader range of gifts than merely prophecy (including glossolalia, dreams, visions, words of guidance, wisdom, power in evangelizing and pastoral preaching), so prophecy as such was perhaps not guaranteed to all. As for the Pauline evidence, Aune has pointed out that 'all may prophesy one-by-one' (v.31) could simply denote the 'prophets' of v.29, in which case there is no suggestion that prophecy was universal. However, it is probably better, with Grudem, to take a middle position. Prophets are the tested specialists and leading figures; but the whole congregation may (even should) *seek* prophecy (1 Cor. 14:1,5,39). None is excluded *a priori*, even if God will not in fact distribute any one gift to all (1 Cor. 12:14–30[82]). Indeed, in the weaker sense Grudem attributes to *prophēteuein* (the relating of something God brings to mind), *all* might on different occasions be expected to 'prophesy'.

---

[80]Cf. Dunn, *Jesus*, 171–2, 281; Reiling in Panagopoulos (ed.), *Vocation*, 67–8.
[81]Most recently, Forbes, *Prophecy*, 219–21, 252–3.
[82]Grudem, *Gift*, 235ff. Cf. Forbes, *Prophecy*, 250–65, arguing the 'two or three' permitted to prophesy in 14:29 are the elitist prophets, while Paul himself extends the opportunity of prophecy to 'all' in 14:31.

6. The Authority and Limitations of New Testament Prophecy

We have noted that Grudem, following the lead of Guy, Friedrich and others, considered the mantle of authoritative prophecy (effectively with the word-for-word inspiration of the prophetic messenger oracles) to have transferred from the canonical prophets to the *apostles*,[83] while arguing that the more general congregational sort of prophecy we encounter in 1 Thessalonians 5, 1 Corinthians 12–14 and Romans 12, carried only the authority of general content, and was parallel to the revelatory phenomena in early Judaism with its consciousness of the withdrawal of true prophecy — a weaker sort of prophecy with a lesser authority.[84]

The evidence on which Grudem bases this construct includes the following: (i) many aspects of Paul's apostolic self-consciousness closely parallel that of Old Testament prophets.[85] (ii) Paul relativizes the authority of Corinthian prophets and subordinates them to his (1 Cor. 14:37,38). (iii) John — an apostle — claims divine authority of actual words for the Apocalypse (Rev. 22:18). (iv) Paul knows that *congregational* prophecy, by contrast, is sometimes so unprepossessing that prophecy as a whole is in danger of being despised (1 Thess. 5:19,20). (v) Both at Thessalonica and at Corinth he demands that congregational prophecy be *evaluated*[86] — not that it just be accepted totally as true prophecy or rejected totally as false prophecy (as in the Old Testament, according to Grudem). The presupposition is that any one New Testament prophetic oracle is expected to be *mixed* in quality, and the wheat must be separated from the chaff. The one prophesying may genuinely have received something from God (albeit often indistinctly), but the 'vision' is partial, limited in perspective, and prone to wrong interpretation by the speaker even as he declares it (1 Cor. 13:9,12).

> Thus in Acts, Grudem notes, Agabus prophesies to Paul, 'Thus says the Holy Spirit, "This is the way the Jews in Jerusalem will bind the man who owns this belt, and will give him over into the hands of the Gentiles"' (21:11). As Grudem notes, Paul did go to Jerusalem, and he did finish up in the hands of the Gentiles — but it was not the Jews who handed him over. The Romans actually rescued him from a Jewish mob intent on killing him (see Acts 22–23). The prophecies in Acts 21:4 seem even less on target. According to Luke,

---

[83]Grudem, *Gift*, ch. 1, esp. 43–54; similarly, D. Hill, *Prophecy*, e.g. 116.
[84]Grudem, *Gift*, 21ff., 54–73.
[85]See J.M. Myers and E.D. Freed, 'Is Paul also among the Prophets?'; *Int* 20 (1966), 40–53; Grudem, *Gift*, 43–49, and, above all, K.O. Sandnes, *Paul — One of the Prophets?* (Tübingen: Mohr, 1991).
[86]For this sense of *diakrinō* (*contra* Dautzenberg), see Grudem, *Gift*, 58–9, 263–88.

'through the Spirit' certain disciples 'tried to tell Paul *not* to go up to Jerusalem'. It seems the Spirit had shown them (like many others (20:23)) the fate that awaits Paul there; but they had wrongly inferred that he should not go to Jerusalem, and had *included* that as derived from the Spirit too. Paul knows otherwise; that it *is* God's will he go on to Jerusalem (19:21; 20:22,23). The prophetic utterances thus have a very mixed quality. They were not all black or white, but varying shades of grey. Now it is possible that Grudem has made too much of the Agabus example (for Paul in Acts 28:17 does actually describe himself as having been bound in Jerusalem and 'given over into the hands of the Romans', in what seems a conscious allusion to the wording of the prophecy), but 21:4 is more convincing, and tallies with what we find in Paul too.

Paul's advice in 1 Corinthians 14:30,31 that one prophesying should give way to another with more immediate revelation, so that (s)he may prophesy, is hardly understandable if 'to prophesy' means the giving of God's very words.[87] The assumption is rather of some measure of human description, interpretation, and perhaps application, that could be rounded off sharply, but voluntarily, if God brought a fresh revelation at the time of the meeting.

Similarly, according to 1 Corinthians 14:29, the *prophecies* are to be *sifted*. The Greek word for the latter, *diakrinō*, implies separating and evaluating more readily than the straightforward choice between whether the prophecy is simply wholly true or false (for which *krinō* would be a more obvious choice): cf. 1 Thessalonians 5:21. Paul's advice then is quite different (*contra* Farnell) from the Old Testament practice which involved Israel testing whether she was listening to a true prophet or a false one. Here, clearly, it is not a matter of deciding whether it is *true* prophecy or *false* prophecy, and then stoning the prophet (or at least exorcising her) in the latter case. It is a matter of deciding what is from God, and how it applies, and of separating this from what is merely human inference. Indeed, the human element and human error appears to have been so apparent that in 1 Thessalonians 5:19,20 Paul has to warn the congregation, 'Do not *despise* prophecies, but *test everything*; hold fast to what is good.'

Arguably, then, prophecy in the New Testament is thus a mixed phenomenon.

The presentation of Grudem's case is oversimplified, but we suspect that Grudem too, has occasionally himself over- schematized the evidence:

(1) With respect to the first two points, we need to note they appear to be misdirected. Karl Sandnes, more than any other, has explored the great extent to which Paul regarded himself as a counterpart to the canonical prophets. But he also correctly em-

---

[87]*Contra* Farnell, 'Two Prophetic Gifts?', 62–88, who argues that all 'true' NT prophecy was inspired to a level of verbal inerrancy commensurate with OT canonical prophecies.

phasizes the differences. The full weight of Paul's 'prophetic' authority lies behind his *gospel*, grounded in the Christ-event and his Damascus Road Revelation (cf. Gal. 1:12–17; 2 Cor. 3–4) — *that*, for him, is what carries complete authority. He is willing to anathematize those who preach a different gospel, and he is willing to subordinate puffed-up prophets to it (1 Cor. 14:37). But Paul does not maintain that his whole teaching and writing consists in a long procession of fully authoritative prophetic oracles (even though they may contain some), and correspondingly he argues and explains his position as a father to children, rather than warning his readers on every issue of the curses on those who disobey God's prophet! All that Paul says is consistent with his believing he has, rather, full 'authority of general content' (i.e. it has a true propositional structure), but nowhere does he suggest that he is claiming 'divine authority of actual words'.[88] And this sharp distinction of Grudem's is itself suspect: semantically it is not necessarily the surface structure of the *wording* of a communication that is of primary significance, but rather the *semantic structure of the propositions* it contains and entails that is of first importance. Divine 'authority of general content' could thus be as significant as 'authority of actual words'.

One suspects that Grudem wishes to accord Paul 'the divine authority of actual words' in order to secure the inerrancy of what he says in its inscripturated form. Farnell explicitly advocates such a position — for him all authentic New Testament prophecies had to be inerrant in order to guarantee the Church reliable teaching and to enable the writers of Scripture to give infallible revelation.[89] But this entirely unhistorical approach confuses the issues. The Pauline letters are not 'prophecies', but apostolic teaching; and the gift of prophecy was in any case not needed in order to write what came to be acknowledged as New Testament Scriptures (cf. the Gospels and Acts, etc.).

(2) The third and following points also fail to support the sharp

---

[88]Sandnes, *Paul*; cf. Dunn, *Jesus*, 47 (who claims that, for Paul, his authority was the authority of the gospel itself as it was revealed to him in the Damascus Road christophany); cf. J.C. Beker, *Paul the Apostle* (Edinburgh: Clark, 1980); cf. S. Kim, *The Origin of Paul's Gospel* (Tübingen: Mohr, 1981). Paul's references to 'my gospel' do not necessitate the belief that Paul claimed divine authority of actual words (*contra* Grudem). It is the general structure of his gospel that he hereby denotes.
[89]See especially Farnell, 'When will the Gift of Prophecy Cease?', 171–202.

distinction between apostolic prophecy and that elsewhere. While the Apocalypse perhaps comes closest to the claim of verbal inspiration (cf. 22:19), it needs to be noted that the claim to authority here is made in the name of *prophecy* (1:3; 22:7,18,19), not explicitly in that of *apostolicity*.[90] This (together with the above observations) suggests that there was no *sharp* distinction between apostolic prophecy and the prophesyings of others. Rather, we may suspect a spectrum of authority of charisma extending from apostolic speech and prophecy (backed by apostolic commission) at one extreme, to vague and barely profitable attempts at oracular speech such as brought 'prophecy' as a whole into question at Thessalonica (1 Thess. 5:19,20) at the other. Prophetic speech might fall anywhere on the spectrum, so the task of evaluation fell to the congregation.[91] In the final analysis Paul does not say that all New Testament prophets see through a glass darkly while apostles see clearly: the apostles' prophecy, too, is *ek merous* and *en ainigmati* (1 Cor. 13:9,12).[92]

(3)   The New Testament nowhere suggests that the Spirit of the canonical prophets has now returned, but merely to the apostles — thus dividing all other persons or charismata off, and levelling them down with the sort of phenomena professed by early Judaism in its consciousness that the Spirit had largely been withdrawn (Acts 2:17–38). Farnell and Gentry, indeed, attempt to argue that Peter's use of the Joel citation (in Acts 2) signifies the return of the full revelatory power of the Old Testament canonical prophets, now distributed to the apostles and prophets to ensure a comparably trustworthy New Testament revelation.[93] But such a claim entirely misunderstands the intertestamental interpretation of Joel's promise, and fails to take

---

[90]See the critique of Aune, *Prophecy*, 206–8.
[91]On the importance of congregational discernment for Paul, see e.g. J.D.G. Dunn, 'Discernment of Spirits — A Neglected Gift', in W. Harrington (ed.), *Witness to the Spirit* (Dublin: Irish Biblical Association, 1979) 79–96; *idem*, 'The Responsible Congregation (I Co. 14:26–40)', in L. de Lorenzi (ed.), *Charisma und Agape (1 Ko 10–14)* (Rome: PBI, 1983), 201–36; cf. J. Martucci, 'Diakrisis pneumatōn (I Co. 12, 10)', *EgTh* 9 (1978), 465–71; J. Gnilka, 'La Relation entre la Responsibilité Communautaire et l'Autorité Ministérielle d'après le NT, en tenant Compte Spécialement du "Corpus Paulinum" ', in L. de Lorenzi (ed.), *Paul de Tarse* (Rome: PBI, 1979), 455–70; Forbes, *Prophecy*, 265–70.
[92]As Grudem himself notes, *Gift*, 53–4, 49, n.100.
[93]See Farnell, 'Gift of Prophecy', 388–93.

account of the fact that Peter promises this gift to *all* believers (2:38,39: cf. Chs. 1 and 3 above).[94]

Whilst we are unhappy about the way Grudem phrases his contrasts, we fully accept that he has put his finger on an important issue, and that Paul indeed relativizes the authority of prophetic communications in the church. We shall discuss the temporal limits Paul places on prophecy later (ch.16). We now pass briefly to the question of the role of prophecy within New Testament theologizing.

7. The Contribution of Prophecy in the Development of New Testament 'Theology'

For all the importance Paul appears to place on 'prophets' and prophecy in 1 Corinthians 12–14 (cf. Rom. 12 and Eph. 3–4), we are left very unclear as to their contribution to the development of 'theology' in the earliest church. A complicating factor is that Paul may have given such an apparently elevated place to 'prophets' without that necessarily meaning that he prized them mainly for their prophecies as such (he may have appreciated equally the associated leadership and teaching ministries of these notable men of God).

For those writing from a cessationist position the question of the contribution of prophecy is easily answered. Prophecy was foundational for New Testament Theology because it was given *primarily* in order to provide the theological revelations which alone could furnish a 'sufficient Scripture'; if there was other prophecy it was only to guide the churches in matters that arose because the canon was as yet incomplete.[95] (And, of course, with the completion of the canon the charisma became redundant.) To support this, appeal is made especially to Ephesians 2:20 and 3:5.[96] Thus, according to Gaffin, while Ephesians 4:11 clarifies that the earlier-mentioned prophets are not merely the same as the apostles (cf. also 1 Cor. 12:28), 2:20 and 3:5 nevertheless show the fundamental role of prophecy by including the prophets in a hendiadys that concerns their foundational part in the elucidation of the gospel mystery. He then takes the arbitrary step of insisting 2:20 be given a governing role in the

---

[94]Gentry is forced to explain away Peter's universalizing as pure hyperbole (*Gift*, 7).

[95]See, for example, R.B. Gaffin, *Perspectives on Pentecost: Studies in New Testament Teaching on the Gifts of the Holy Spirit* (Phillipsburg: Presbyterian and Reformed, 1979), esp. 99–100. Compare Farnell, 'When Will the Gift of Prophecy Cease?', 171–202 (esp. 174–9).

[96]Cf. Gaffin, *Perspectives*, 93–102.

interpretation of prophecy as it is not merely *ad hoc*: 'Ephesians 2:20 makes a generalization that covers *all* other New Testament statements on prophecy.'[97] This inevitably leads him to reject the view that 1 Corinthians 14 implies a lesser form of prophecy: such a view

> distinguishes between canonical revelation for the whole church and private revelations for individual believers . . . between . . . what is 'necessary for salvation' and revelations that "go beyond" the Bible and bear on individual life situations, needs, and concerns. Such an understanding of revelation is in irreconcilable conflict with what the Bible itself shows to be the covenantal, redemptive-historical character of *all* revelation. [97] Scripture leaves no place for privatized, localized revelations for specific individual needs and circumstances. [98][98]

In order to justify this last assertion, Gaffin 'deals with' the Agabus prophecies.[99] In Acts 11.28, we are told, the prophecy is given to cement the newly established foundational bond of fellowship within the church between Jew and Gentile (i.e. Greeks in Antioch with Jews in Jerusalem), while in 21:10,11 the prophecy is no individual matter: rather, it 'concerns the unfolding of Paul's apostolic ministry to the Gentiles (cf. 20:23)'. But these treatments of the Agabus prophecies simply highlight the degree of special pleading involved in this kind of hypothesis. Luke does not imply the church in Antioch had anything but a small group of Gentiles at the stage in view in 11:28,29 (the majority would have been hellenistic Jews); consequently he says nothing about cementing unity between Jewish and Gentile churches by such means. And Acts 21:10,11 does not unfold any significant theology concerning Paul's apostolic ministry (far less one 'necessary for salvation'); it remains a personal prophecy (like so many in OT and intertestamental Judaism) even if it pertains to a leader of the church. As we have seen, the view that *all* authentic biblical prophecy is concerned with theological revelation of national and covenantal importance cannot be supported by any examination of the Old Testament materials.

We may return to the claims made in respect of Ephesians 2:20. The most we can say in Gaffin's favour is that the text concerned indicates *one* of the functions that prophecy fulfilled. And we should not press it to mean more than the co-text of Ephesians 3:2–13 implies, namely that the apostles, together with prophets, provided the 'foundation' of the church in the sense that they established that the Gentiles were thence-

---

[97]*Ibid.*, 96 (my italics).
[98]*Ibid.*, 97–8.
[99]*Ibid.*, 99.

forth made co-heirs together in a single new body which epitomized and revealed the cosmic reconciliation of all things begun in Christ.[100] The letter is not concerned to elucidate some more general affirmation of the role of prophecy in the development of theology. As for the view that prophecy elsewhere in the New Testament was exclusively concerned with providing soteriologically necessary revelation, we should surely resist the implied picture of witnesses feverishly attempting to record, from the multitude prophesying in the manifold congregations, 'revelations' which they might convey hot-foot to their nearest apostolic 'centre' for possible inclusion in the forthcoming 'Holy Scriptures'.

We need to come back to the more serious question of the influence of revelatory prophecies on the development of theology. We have noted that Paul regards the fundamental determination of the gospel as built in to the commission of the apostles (Gal. 1–2, etc.). There is relatively little in Paul's theology that cannot be explained as a deduction from his Damascus Road experience, and from his commission as apostle to the Gentiles,[101] once his rabbinic background, his early knowledge of the kerygma (which led him to persecute the church), and his growing knowledge of the tradition in the church are taken into consideration. Most of Paul's 'theology' is his reflective articulation of the Christ-event, and of his commission to the Gentiles, into different circumstances. For this the gift of charismatic wisdom may have been more significant than that of prophecy. In so far as we can detect the presence or influence of prophecies in Paul they pertain largely to occasional details of the eschatological programme (the mystery of Israel's hardening and salvation (Rom. 11:25,26) the awakening transformation of the living and the dead (1 Cor. 15:51,52; 1 Thess. 4:15–17), conditions excluding entrance to the kingdom of God (Gal. 5:21, etc.), a word of assurance (2 Cor. 12:9), a warning of persecution (1 Thess. 3:4), and perhaps some occasional ethical warnings (1 Thess. 4:2-6; 2 Thess. 3:6,10,12)). With the exception of the eschatological prophecies, the rest are pastoral 'words' which articulate already known theology to specific circumstances, rather than offering new theological revelation. The kerygmatic revelation/tradition is thus the touchstone for most else: it provides the test of the revelatory *charismata*, not vice versa. Indeed, although Paul's wording in Ephesians 2:20, and his ranking of prophets second only to apostles in 1 Corinthians 12:28, may suggest that the prophetic word of some established prophets contributed to the laying down of precedents, norms and traditions in the

---

[100]Cf. M. Turner, 'Mission', in Billington, Lane, and Turner (eds.), *Mission and Meaning*, 138–66.
[101]Cf. Kim, *Origin*, *passim*, and those noted at n.88 above.

church (an activity which ultimately marginalized the prophets), Paul nevertheless clearly subordinates the authority of the prophetic phenomena at Corinth to his own (cf. 14:37). He does not feel able to allow the Corinthian prophets to decide the agenda for worship, but specifies how they are to operate, and he further relativizes their authority by demanding congregational sifting of their utterances. It would seem that Paul did not regard the Corinthians' practice of the revelatory gifts, which he describes in 1 Corinthians 12:8–10, as of primary significance in the shaping of theological structures. Their purpose seems more intended to have been to operate within the rough confines of the gospel and of apostolic teaching — either to illuminate these, or to elucidate their personal significance and application. In addition, he may have expected prophecies to give direction in situations where neither Scripture, nor gospel, nor tradition could do so, or to set particular Corinthian events, practices or spiritual states in heavenly perspective. Through such prophecies the risen Lord might be expected to reveal how he perceived the church's condition in general and in particular, and to give it spiritual direction.

The Apocalypse may appear to twentieth-century readers to be one great theological revelation; but this is misleading. The impression is created mainly because we are so unfamiliar with this sort of literature. In fact, the seven letters to the churches, with which it commences, are prophetic spiritual diagnoses of those congregations (not the elucidation of theological revelation). And the rest is not so much revelation of many new things (many Jews already held the sequence of woes, fall of Satan, Millennium, tree of life, etc.), but a disclosure of how Christ and his death and exaltation to God's throne are central to it all. As for the remaining New Testament writings, they claim themselves neither to be 'prophecy' nor even to have been written with substantial aid from the gift of prophecy.

Altogether there is little evidence that prophecy played a major part in the development of theology, rather than in the more specific guidance and pastoral oversight of the congregations.[102]

---

[102]This applies too to the claim that the gospel tradition was augmented by post-resurrection 'prophecies' from the risen Lord fed back into the Jesus tradition. Against the claims of Bultmann and Käsemann in this regard, see the criticisms of D. Hill, 'On the Evidence for the Creative Role of Christian Prophets', *NTS* 20 (1974), 262–74; J.D.G. Dunn, 'Prophetic "I"-Sayings and the Jesus Tradition: The Importance of Testing Prophetic Utterances Within Early Christianity', *NTS* 24 (1977–78), 175–98. M.E. Boring has attempted to salvage the Bultmann/Käsemann argument, but against him see the stringent criticism of Aune, *Prophecy*, ch. 9, and Gillespie, *Theologians*, 11–20. Gillespie's own position that the prophets were the first Christian theologians depends too much on his identification of prophecy with charismatic preaching (see §2.4 above).

Chapter Thirteen

Tongues in the New Testament

The phenomenon of 'tongues' is mentioned in only two books of the New Testament: Acts and 1 Corinthians. Yet it has attracted considerable scholarly attention. The mainstream New Testament contributions are largely interested in the religious 'background' to the New Testament phenomenon, and particularly in the question of why tongues appears only to have surfaced as a 'live congregational issue' in Corinth, and how Paul responded to it.[1] Here the consensus view is that glossolalia was not common in the church, and that it is best understood against the more general, especially hellenistic, phenomena of ecstatic (and so unintelligible) speech. At the fringes of this scholarship, however, various contributions tackle the subject either in relation to Pentecostal arguments concerning 'initial evidence', or as cessationist

---

[1]On the NT phenomena of tongues see especially: E. Lombard, *De la Glossolalie chez les premiers Chrétiens* (Lausanne: Bridel, 1910); J. Behm, 'γλῶσσα', *TDNT* I:719–27; J.G. Davies, 'Pentecost and Glossolalia', *JTS* 3 (1952), 228–31; F.W. Beare, 'Speaking with Tongues: A Critical Survey of the New Testament Evidence', *JBL* 83 (1964), 229–46; S.D. Currie, '"Speaking in Tongues": Early Evidence Outside the New Testament Bearing on *"Glossais Lalein"* ', *Int* 19 (1965), 274–94; R.J. Banks and G. Moon, 'Speaking in Tongues: A New Survey of New Testament Evidence', *Churchman* 80 (1966), 278–94; R.H. Gundry, '"Ecstatic Utterance" (NEB)?', *JTS* 17 (1966), 299–307; J.P.M. Sweet, 'A Sign for Unbelievers: Paul's Attitude to Glossolalia', *NTS* 13 (1967), 240–57; Engelsen, 'Glossolalia and other forms of Inspired Speech according to 1 Corinthians 12–14', unpublished PhD dissertation, Yale University, 1970; M.D. Smith, 'Glossolalia and Other Spiritual Gifts in a New Testament Perspective', *Int* 28 (1974), 307–20; E. Best, 'The Interpretation of Tongues', *SJT* 28 (1975), 45–62; Dunn, *Jesus*, esp. 148–52; 242–6; C.G. Williams, 'Glossolalia as a Religious Phenomenon: "Tongues" at Corinth and Pentecost', *Rel* 5 (1975), 16–32; R.A. Harrisville, 'Speaking in Tongues: A Lexicographical Study', *CBQ* 38 (1976), 35–48; K. Stendahl, 'Glossolalia and the Charismatic Movement' in J. Jervell and W.A. Meeks (eds.), *God's Christ and His People: Studies in Honour of Nils Alstrup Dahl* (Oslo: Univeritetsforlaget, 1977), 122–31; T.W. Gillespie, 'A Pattern of Prophetic Speech in First Corinthians', *JBL* 97 (1978), 74–98; W. Grudem, '1 Corinthians 14:20–25: Prophecy and Tongues as Signs of God's Attitude', *WTJ* 41 (1979), 381–96; B.C. Johanson, 'Tongues, a Sign for Unbelievers?: A Structural

attempts to establish glossolalia as a 'sign' gift unique to the apostolic age, and quite different from modern glossolalia. Of the latter we shall note two distinct approaches: (i) the attempt by Edgar[2] to argue that New Testament tongues were miraculous foreign languages given to open up unbelievers to the gospel, and (ii) the attempt by Gaffin to argue that the function of (interpreted) tongues (alongside prophecy) was to provide the church's necessary revelation (before the completion of the canon), and (when uninterpreted) as a sign against unbelieving Israel at the inauguration of the new covenant.[3] In this chapter we shall inquire what Luke and Paul meant by *glōssais lalein* ('to speak in tongues'), i.e. what kind of phenomena such language is intended to denote, and what part they anticipated this to play in Christian 'life'. Then we shall consider the wider issues of alleged parallels and theological significance.

I. TONGUES IN ACTS

1. Acts 2:1–13

There is no doubt that Luke considers the Pentecost phenomenon, which he designates as *heterais glōssais lalein* ('to speak with other tongues'), to be *xenolalia*, that is, the speaking of actual foreign languages.[4] Not only is this suggested *prima facie* by the word *glōssa*, especially qualified by *hetera* ('other'), but it is further demanded in v.6, where it is said of the crowd of diaspora pilgrims that 'they each heard

---

(footnote 1 continued)
and Exegetical Study of 1 Corinthians xiv.20–25', *NTS* 25 (1979), 180–203; A.C. Thiselton, 'The "Interpretation" of Tongues: A New Suggestion in the Light of Greek Usage in Philo and Josephus', *JTS* 30 (1979), 15–36; C.G. Williams, *Tongues*; W.E. Mills, *A Theological/Exegetical Approach to Glossolalia*, (London: Univ. Press of America, 1985); Carson, *Showing the Spirit* (Grand Rapids: Baker, 1987 and Carlisle: Paternoster, 1995), esp. 77–88, 100–118, 138–58; G. Theissen, *Psychological Aspects of Pauline Theology* (Edinburgh: Clark, 1987), 267–342; C.M. Robeck Jr., 'Tongues', *DPL*, 939–43; Fee, *Presence*, esp. 172–4; 184–9; 145–56; 193–204; 214–51; 889–90; Gillespie, *Theologians*, ch.4; J.F.M. Smit, 'Tongues and Prophecy: Deciphering 1 Cor 14:22', *Bib* 75 (1994), 175–90, and Forbes, *Prophecy*, chs. 2–7.
[2]*Gifts*, esp. 110–94.
[3]Gaffin, *Perspectives*, ch. 4, §C, and ch. 5, §D.
[4]For the terminology, see N. Bloch-Hoell, *The Pentecostal Movement* (London: Allen and Unwin, 1964), 142–3; C.G. Williams, *Tongues*, prefers *xenoglossia*. Both use these in distinction from 'glossolalia' by which they mean ordinary non-cognitive, lexically non-communicative utterances.

in their own dialect' (*tē(i) idia(i) dialektō(i)*; cf. vv.8 and 11). This cannot be taken as specifying a miracle of hearing rather than one of speech.[5] We may not seriously doubt that Luke attributed the fundamental charisma in this process to the activity of God in the one hundred and twenty *believers*. He would not wish to suggest that the apostolic band merely prattled incomprehensibly, while God worked the yet greater miracle of interpretation of tongues in the *un*believers. No substantial problem is created for this view by the fact that some in the crowd comment 'they are filled with new wine' (v.13).[6] Luke envisages a very large crowd indeed by the time that Peter speaks his explanation (cf. 2:41); certainly not all will have understood the full variety of 'dialects' Luke reports as having been spoken (vv.8–11[7]); and some could be expected to have heard nothing intelligible at all.[8] Of course, one should not try artificially to harmonize Luke's details, but nor should one unnecessarily make a fool of him when one can plausibly explain how he may have viewed the scene.

What is the content of the 'tongues' speech? Here it is worth noting that Luke simply designates it *ta megalia tou theou* (v. 11; 'the greatnesses of God' or 'the mighty deeds of God'). His use of the related verbal form (*megalunō*) in 10:46 and 19:17, where simply praise to God is meant, suggests that the tongues in Acts 2 are not to be construed as an evangelistic communication as such: indeed the tongues-speeches taken by themselves only lead observers (sympathetic and otherwise) to questions and to confusion. It is Peter's *preaching* which communicates the gospel. This conclusion is further supported by the observation that Judaism might readily anticipate invasive charismatic praise at the inception of the Spirit of prophecy.[9]

---

[5] See Kremer, *Pfingstbericht und Pfingstgeschehen: Eine Exegetische Untersuchung zu Apg 2:1–13* (Stuttgart: KBW, 1973) 120–6. Jenny Everts, 'Tongues or Languages? Contextual Consistency in the Translation of Acts 2', *JPT* 4 (1994), 71–80, is the latest to argue Acts 2 refers to miraculous hearing by the crowd, but while that might be argued for the pre-Lucan tradition (cf. Mills, *Approach*, 54–70), Luke himself subverts such a reading (see Mills, *Approach*, 62,92,101–5).

[6] *Contra*, e.g. Dunn, *Jesus*, 149.

[7] Cf. Marshall, *Acts*, 70–1.

[8] The *heis hekastos* ('each one') of vv. 6, 8 need not be pressed to mean everyone in the crowd heard their own language/dialect. Gundry ('Ecstatic Utterance', 304) and Edgar (*Gifts*, 126) argue that Luke means the visiting foreigners heard their vernacular, while to the Palestinians it was all gibberish. Cf. also K. Haacker, 'Das Pfingstwunder als exegetisches Problem', in O. Böcher and K. Haacker (eds.), *Verborum Veritas* (Wuppertal: Brockhaus, 1970), 125–31.

[9] See Ch. 1 above, and my argument with Menzies on this point in *Power*, ch. 10, §1.2.

2. The Rest of Acts

On two further occasions Luke specifically records incidents of tongues: Acts 10:46 and 19:6. In Caesarea, Peter and his companions recognize that Cornelius has received the Spirit of prophecy, as at Pentecost,
'for they heard them speaking with tongues and exalting God' (10:46).
Similarly in Acts 19:6, with the outpouring of the Spirit upon the twelve
erstwhile disciples of John the Baptist, 'they began to speak with tongues and prophesy'. On neither occasion is there any suggestion to the
effect that the tongues were languages actually recognized by any of
the hearers.[10] We are not told *how* Peter concluded they were genuinely
speaking with tongues (rather than gibberish) — Luke assumes that the
context of God's action in the whole proceedings leading up to this
point, and the evident parallels with the Pentecost experience, are sufficient guarantee. Nor is there any suggestion here that tongues serve
any kind of evangelistic function: there are no unbelieving bystanders
to be startled into belief by these outbursts, on either occasion.

What is less clear concerning these accounts is whether the exalting
of God (10:46) or prophesying (19:6) is assumed to be the *content* of the
tongues speech or (more probably) related phenomena experienced in
the same event. If Luke envisaged readers who were Jews, or God-
fearers with a knowledge of Judaism, he would anticipate them to expect invasive charismatic praise in one's own tongue much more than
in an unintelligible one. The narrative at 10:46 may then be intended to
suggest a *mixture* of the two types of invasive charismatic praise, rather
than simply identifying them. A similar observation could be made
with respect to the twinning of glossolalia with prophesying at 19:6.

Beyond this we can only note Luke's rather surprising silence. He
indicates no knowledge of glossolalia as a phenomenon occurring *after*
initial reception of the Spirit: there is nothing in Acts to match the
congregational phenomenon of tongues, described by Paul in 1 Corinthians 12-14, or the private practice of it anticipated there. But his account of the expansion of Christianity is perhaps too selective for us to
be able to draw any significant conclusions from this, especially as his
'summaries' of church life (2:42–47; 4:32-37 and 5:12–16) are so
restricted.

---

[10]Edgar, *Gifts*, 132, supposes they were, on the grounds that Peter later says
Cornelius received the same gift 'as he gave us' (Acts 11:17): but this refers to
the gift of the Spirit of prophecy, not to xenolalia as such.

3. Did Luke Regard Tongues as a *Normative* Initial Evidence of Receiving the Spirit?

An affirmative answer has been defended recently by Menzies, who argues that Luke anticipated *all* Christians would receive this manifestation as the entirely appropriate sign of their reception of the 'Spirit of prophecy'.[11] Against this we have argued:[12]

(a) if (with Menzies) appeal is made to a Jewish understanding of the 'Spirit of prophecy', then the inception of such a gift would not necessarily, or even usually, be attended by any specific external 'manifestations'.

(b) that such manifestation would be anticipated only on occasions of powerful or significant irruptions of the Spirit, or where some sort of 'attestation' was necessary or clearly desirable.

(c) that this last consideration fully accounts for (i) the tongues at Pentecost, (ii) the parallel glossolalia at Caesarea (this could be considered God's most appropriate demonstration of his entirely unexpected extension of the Pentecost gift of the Spirit to Gentile believers), (iii) the unspecified manifestation at Acts 8:18, which marks the extension of the Pentecost gift to the 'outsider' Samaritans, and (iv) the occasion at Ephesus, where the question of Spirit-reception (or rather lack of it) had been the issue.[13] In all other occasions of conversions described (even where these are related in some detail, as in the cases, e.g., of the Ethiopian (8:26–40) and Paul (9:1–19), there is no allusion to any form of invasive charismatic speech.

(d) the expectation of 'initial evidence' otherwise only makes sense if the gift of the Spirit is thought of as a second- blessing subsequent to conversion, but Luke considers the Spirit the means of God's presence in salvation and anticipates the gift usually to be given in conversion- initiation. The powerful experience of the gospel, the response of commitment, and the joy these evoked would then themselves normally be taken as evidence of Spirit-

---

[11]*Empowered*, ch. 13: see also Jon Ruthven, *On the Cessation of the Charismata: The Protestant Polemic on Postbiblical Miracles* (Sheffield: SAP, 1993), 207–12.

[12]*Power*, ch. 10, §1.2, and more ecpecially, ch. 12, § 2.5, (D).

[13]There are also two other important Lucan sub-themes at work here: Luke wishes to portray Ephesus as the climax of Paul's mission, and the place where he worked with unusual power (cf. 19:11), and he also uses it as a closure for his theme of the Baptist's promise the Messiah will baptize in Holy Spirit (which makes it particularly fitting that these disciples of the Baptist receive the fulfilment of his promise in a powerful way).

reception (unless evidence of lack of the Spirit emerged subsequently).

(e) Jewish Christians would certainly not expect xenolalia as the
specific indication of Spirit-reception (rather than, e.g., invasive
prophecy, or invasive doxology, in the recipient's mother
tongue), where attestation was expected at all. Nor do the
descriptions in 10:46 and 19:6 necessarily imply that *each* person
receiving the Spirit manifested initial evidence of some kind
(Luke's 'all's could generalize of the group), far less that *each*
spoke in tongues (Luke probably means some experienced invasive praise or prophecy while others spoke in tongues).

In brief, Luke considered invasive charismatic praise (whether in
'tongues' or in the recipient's own language) occasionally to mark conversional Spirit-reception. But the case that he thought this was regular
is unconvincing, and that he thought it 'normative' is beyond
demonstration.[14]

4. Preliminary Conclusions

Luke clearly considers the tongues at Pentecost to be xenolalia. Contrary to the common claim, however, there is no evidence he thinks
glōssais lalein generally served an evangelistic purpose. Certainly he
never suggests, in the twenty-six chapters that follow the Pentecost
account, that xenolalia was ever identified as recognized languages
again, nor that they played any part in evangelism.[15] Consequently,
two major and oft-repeated objections to Lucan historicity on the issue
of tongues — namely that Paul does not think of tongues as evangelistic, nor does he think of them as intelligible — simply fall to the
ground. It is reasonable to assume Luke considered the Pentecostal
recognition of xenolalia, and the positive effect of this, to be a unique
and providential sign marking the beginning of the age of the Spirit of
prophecy: one that was not repeated exactly elsewhere. From the

---

[14]Here I must concur with G.D. Fee, *Gospel and Spirit: Issues in New Testament
Hermeneutics* (Peabody: Hendrickson, 1991), chs. 6 and 7; Larry W. Hurtado,
'Normal, but Not a Norm: Initial Evidence and the New Testament', in G.B.
McGee (ed.), *Initial Evidence: Historical and Biblical Perspectives on the Pentecostal
Doctrine of Spirit Baptism* (Peabody: Hendrickson, 1991), 189–201, and J. Ramsey
Michaels, 'Evidences of the Spirit, or the Spirit as Evidence? Some Non-
Pentecostal Reflections', in the same volume (202–18).

[15]*Contra* Edgar (*Gifts*, 198ff), who sees the purpose of tongues as a 'sign-gift' to
soften people up for evangelism.

evidence we have it would not even be possible to be sure that Luke thought *all* tongues-speech was xenolalia as opposed to some wider concept of tongues-speech (cf. Paul's *genē glōssōn* 'different kinds of tongues'; 1 Cor. 12:10)

II. PAUL'S VIEW OF 'TONGUES'

1. Denotation

What does Paul imagine *glōssē(i)* (or *glōssais*) *lalein* to denote? Most commentators, following H. Leisegang, draw parallels between 1 Corinthians 12–14 and the allegedly ecstatic utterance of the Pythia at Delphi, or Dionysiac *enthysiasmos* (though Crone and Forbes have shown that the parallels are not nearly as close as is usually thought).[16] The more discerning writers at least make a sharp distinction between how the Corinthians may have viewed tongues speech and how Paul himself viewed it.[17] In Paul's view the *glōssai* are *languages*, not merely ecstatic shouts and pre-cognitive mumblings.[18] This is the normal meaning of *glōssa*, and none of the parallels brought forward by Behm[19] or Bauer-Arndt-Gingrich shows that *glōssa* means ecstatic non-cognitive utterance, however riddling and 'dark' the speech denoted by *glōssa* in the parallels may have been thought to be.[20] Thiselton notes that, in Philo, *hermēneuein* compounds can mean 'put into speech', rather than 'translate' or 'interpret'. From this observation he infers that when Paul speaks of *hermēneia glōssōn* he means the putting into words of (presumably) non-cognitive 'tongues'.[21] But this is unconvincing. To be sure, one can put into (intelligible) words (*hermēneuein*) one's thoughts (etc.). But collocated with *glōssē(i) lalein*, *hermēneuein* would more naturally mean 'translate' or, more broadly, 'interpret'.[22] This is in keeping with the fact that Paul can make an immediate parallel (not merely an il-

---

[16]Crone, *Prophecy*, ch. 1 and 220–21; Forbes, *Prophecy*, chs. 2–7.

[17]So Dunn, *Jesus*, though it must be stated that such claims as 'the conclusion becomes almost inescapable: glossolalia as practised in . . . Corinth was a form of ecstatic utterance — sounds, cries, words uttered in a state of spiritual ecstasy' (243) are methodologically unjustified.

[18]Against the view Paul could have conceived of glossolalia in these latter ways, see Forbes, *Prophecy*, 53–72 (whose view at most significant points below is very similar to our own).

[19]*TDNT* I:719–27.

[20]See Edgar, *Gifts*, 110–21; Forbes, *Prophecy*, 60–4.

[21]Thiselton, 'Interpretation', 15–36.

[22]For a fuller case against Thiselton, see Forbes, *Prophecy*, 65–72.

lustration) between *glōssais lalein* and the *heteroglōssoi* (foreign languages) of Isaiah 28:11 (1 Cor. 14:21,22). It is further in keeping with his ranking of the phenomenon as a spiritual gift (1 Cor. 12:8–10:28), the right use of which he mildly encourages (1 Cor. 14:5), personally experiences, and is thankful for (1 Cor. 14:18).

Was it human languages or angelic languages — 'tongues of angels' (1 Cor. 13:1) — that Paul had in mind?[23] Dunn thinks Gundry is wrong to identify the languages as earthly ones.[24] He contends, firstly, that the 'tongues of men' in 13:1 are inspired speech in the vernacular (ranging from preaching to prophesying) and contrast with angelic tongues speech. Secondly, he argues, the subject matter is 'mysteries' (13:2) — eschatological secrets known only in heaven — so the language used will be the language of heaven. Thirdly, Paul could only *compare* tongues with the effect of speaking in foreign languages (14:10,11,16, 19–25) if he thought tongues were not human languages.[25] But none of these arguments is conclusive:

(1) In 14:10,11, Paul could be pointing to the obvious consequences in the secular realm of what the Corinthians fail to see in the spiritual, without contrasting the types of language as such: they are proud of their 'tongues' which others do not understand; Paul points out how close they come to being ridiculed as 'barbarians' rather than exalted as 'spirituals'.

(2) There is no reason to accept that mysteries spoken in the Spirit must be in a heavenly tongue, as Paul will declare at least one heavenly mystery in Greek just one chapter further on in the letter (1 Cor. 15:51,52), and indeed his initial preaching centred on the 'mystery' of the gospel (2:1,7; 4:1)!

(3) If Paul thought all tongues were angelic he is unlikely to have maintained they belong only to our pre- resurrection 'childhood' (1 Cor. 13:11) and will pass away.[26] Given this, however, we need not reject that Paul thought some types of 'tongue' (cf. *genē glōssōn*; 12:10) were angelic (as, e.g., in *Test. Job* 48–50; *Apoc. Zeph.* 8, though on these see below[27]).

---

[23]We may dismiss as entirely incredible the view that the tongues in question are *learned* foreign languages, and that the problem in Corinth is demonstrations of these skills. See Forbes, *Prophecy*, 57, n.28.

[24]Dunn, *Jesus*, 243–4 (against Gundry, 'Ecstatic Utterance', *passim*).

[25]*Ibid.*, 244; C.G. Williams, *Tongues*, ch. 2 (against Gundry, 'Ecstatic Utterance', 306).

[26]So, e.g., Thiselton, 'Interpretation', 32.

[27]Or perhaps it was the Corinthians who thought they spoke with angelic tongues: cf. Hemphill, 'Concept', 123.

Further arguments have been brought against the conclusion that Paul envisaged actual languages, but each of them is very shaky. (i) Why, it is asked, do we not have more ancient reports of tongues being recognized? But this question seems to rest on the misunderstanding that Luke expected xenolalia to be recognized and thus to prepare for evangelism. (ii) Why, it is asked, do Irenaeus and Celsus regard tongues as babbling or 'lalling' if it was a widespread belief in the early church that *glōssais lalein* was xenolalia? The answer here would appear to be that the passages Currie[28] and Thiselton[29] use to substantiate this (*Adv. Haer* 3. xiii; *Adv. Celsus* 7. ix) are not about *glōssais lalein* at all; they are about the production of incoherent *prophetic* speech (incoherent, that is, not because the individual words are unintelligible, but because they are riddling, cryptic or simply vague — a common criticism of unsolicited oracles in the ancient world[30]). (iii) Why, it is asked, would Paul be so disparaging as he is in 1 Corinthians 12–14 if he thought tongues were a true language miracle? In this connection Thiselton quotes a series of scholars who regard Paul as disparaging of tongues and ends by quoting Best: 'Paul would hardly . . . have criticized it since it would have been so useful in evangelism and certainly could not have been described as speech to God alone'.[31] Yet again we meet the misunderstanding concerning the relationship of tongues to evangelism. But more broadly the answer has to be given that Paul is not critical of tongues *per se*[32] — he practises it himself abundantly, is thankful for it (1 Cor. 14:18) and encourages it (14:5[33]) — what he is against, and criticizes heavily, is the domination of the *assembly* by *uninterpreted* tongues.

We conclude that Paul probably thought of tongues-speech as xenolalia and (possibly) heavenly languages. If he had any contact with the sort of tradition embedded in Acts 2 — which is not improbable — this would have confirmed his view.

2. The Purpose of Tongues in Paul

Though Paul does not explicitly say why God has given the gift of tongues, he does, in passing, indicate several ways in which it functions.

---

[28]'Speaking', 290.

[29]'Interpretation', 29.

[30]Aune, *Prophecy*, 51, etc. See especially Forbes' detailed treatment of the passage in *Adv. Celsus* (*Prophecy*, 165–8).

[31]Best, 'Interpretation', 47.

[32]Hemphill, 'Concept', 123; Fee, *Presence*, 889–90.

[33]*Contra* Hemphill, 'Concept', 127, the positive approbation of tongues in 5a cannot be emptied *entirely* by appeal to its rhetorical function with respect to 5b.

(1) Tongues as signs?

In 1 Corinthians 14:22, Paul states: 'So tongues are a sign not to believers, but to unbelievers; while prophecy is a sign not to unbelievers but to believers.' This would almost make sense as a straightforward statement if Paul had Lucan Pentecostal xenolalia as his model: we would then approach the claim that Paul thought of xenolalia as a convincing sign-gift and primary aid to evangelism. In fact, Edgar, having rejected all alternative exegeses, says, with some naiveté: 'This view alone has no problems'![34] But if all Paul had to say on the subject was that tongues was an evangelistic sign-gift (and Edgar insists that this is the one and only purpose of tongues) why does it take him three very difficult chapters to say so? If it is not really a gift for the assembly *at all*,[35] why does God allow it in the assembly? And, more pertinently, why does God give a spiritual gift of 'interpretation of tongues' (12:10), which *ex hypothesi* is unnecessary — for tongues are not intended for the congregation but to startle pagans (who will know the languages) into belief? And why does Paul, in this context, expect precisely that outsiders will *not* understand the tongues (unless perhaps there be interpretation), but will either confess or complain 'you rave' (v.23)? Not surprisingly, most commentators have suspected Paul of more subtle rhetoric and irony than Edgar imagines.

Aware that Paul in verses 23–25 seems to reverse what he states in verse 22, Johanson argues that verse 22 is actually a rhetorical question in which Paul sums up the views of the Corinthian enthusiasts whom he opposes.[36] They magnify tongues because they (wrongly) regard it as an apologetic-evangelistic gift. Rather more probable is the interpretation of W. Grudem, taking up and developing earlier discussion (e.g. by Sweet[37]). Grudem argues that the word *sēmeion* has a double connotation in the LXX: it can mark a 'sign' either of God's blessing on his covenant people and/or of his judgement on unbelievers. In Isaiah 28:11 the point is that Israel have not listened to God when he spoke clearly so he will now speak through the foreign language of an invading army. Paul is alluding to this, and making capital out of it, when he tells the Corinthians not to speak in tongues (without interpretation); for that way of God's speaking would be inappropriate — certainly not an evangelistic aid (for they will say 'you rave'), but rather a sign of judgement (God refuses to speak in anything but a foreign

---

[34]*Gifts*, 202, and see 201–13.
[35]*Ibid.*, 199.
[36]'Tongues', 193ff.
[37]Grudem, 'Prophecy', *passim*; *Gift*, 185–201.

and incomprehensible language). Prophecy, on the other hand, precisely because (in contrast to tongues) it is God's self-revealing and communicating presence, is a sign of his blessing of his people. The convicted outsider can see this and says, 'Truly God is amongst you' (v.25[38]). If Grudem's interpretation is along the right lines, then Paul does not claim tongues on their own to be a positive sign to unbelievers at all (though if they were interpreted or recognized — a situation Paul does not envisage — he would no doubt attribute to them a positive value). In Grudem's view, tongues may mistakenly be made to function as a sign to unbelievers, but then only as a negative one. Paul, for his part, does not think this is their proper purpose, and so he prescribes that they be used only with interpretation, when they may approximate the positive sign value of prophecy. We may thus exclude the view that Paul thought of tongues as primarily intended for the outsider (nor is this view especially encouraged by the late ending in Mark 16:15–17, on which Edgar dangerously builds so much). It is worth noting that Paul's argument seems convoluted here because essentially he only introduces the Old Testament quotation to make the polemical point (over against Corinthian boasting in tongues)[39] that, as far as the Old Testament sheds any light on the issue, (uninterpreted) tongues are not a sign of God's especial blessing of his people, but his judgement on unbelief. It may be noted that this somewhat *ad hoc* use of Isaiah 28:11 (and in a context where the unbelievers in question are almost certainly Gentiles) does not support Gaffin's view that Paul considered (uninterpreted) glossolalia primarily as a sign against unbelief *in Israel*, and there is no evidence to support such a view elsewhere.[40] But if tongues are not really to be exercised as a sign to unbelievers, nor as a sign to believers, what are tongues for?

(2) *For the building up of the church?*

Paul is so adamant that tongues on their own do not edify the church that not a few of his interpreters have argued that he wished to suppress the phenomenon — at least in the assembly. This neglects the fact

---

[38]Forbes argues that Paul thinks of prophecy as a sign for believers primarily because it evokes this confession from the believer and so points to the eschatological fulfilment of Isa. 45:14 and Zech. 8:23 (*Prophecy*, 179–81). But the two senses are complementary.

[39]Hemphill, 'Concept', 141.

[40]Gaffin, *Perspectives*, 103–6. Against him, see Edgar, *Gifts*, 204–6 (cf. n. 31 for those who held such a belief before Gaffin) and Grudem in Grieg and Springer (eds.), *Kingdom*, 71–4.

that Paul specifically states that the tongues-speaker utters 'mysteries' (14:2), and clearly allows that tongues with interpretation is as useful to the up-building of the church as prophecy (1 Cor. 14:5c).[41] If it must be tongues *or* intelligible speech, Paul would have only the latter (14:19); but that is not the choice. Interpretation is intelligible speech, so tongues, interpreted, can be expected in the public worship (1 Cor. 14:25), and commended if in moderation (14:27,28,39). But the reservations noted still suggest we have yet to put our finger on what Paul regards as the main purpose of tongues.

(3) Tongues as an aid to private devotion?

This, the usual explanation given by Pentecostals, Charismatics and, for that matter, by most New Testament scholars,[42] has been vigorously denied by Edgar, who insists: (i) that such a view contradicts the 'sign' purpose stated in 1 Corinthians 14:22; Mark 16:15–17 and implicit in Acts 2:1–13. (ii) A private gift would not be for the edification of the church and makes it unique. (iii) Such a gift would be self-centred.[43] (iv) If the gift of tongues could edify it would surely be given to all.[44] (v) If the purpose is private devotion directed to God, why should there be a gift of interpretation?[45] (vi) Anyway, Paul says that tongues do not edify the believer; his or her mind remains fallow.[46] (vii) It is clear that in 1 Corinthians 14:2 using a gift to speak 'only to God' is equivalent to 'speaking into the air' (14:9[47]); it is, for Paul, a negative concept, not something to be exercised. (viii) In 14:14–16 Paul discourages praying with the Spirit alone (which is not tongues anyway) and urges praying with the mind also.[48]

---

[41]Forbes curiously charges that I exclude interpretation from my account of tongues, and so fail to give adequate account of the public revelatory role Paul anticipates for (interpreted) tongues (*Prophecy*, 97 n.56). He may be right on the latter, but it is not because I excluded 'interpretation'. The whole paragraph above (§2.2) is taken from the earlier essay with only minor alterations. For Forbes' more positive position, see *Prophecy*, 94–7.

[42]For Pentecostals, see W.J. Hollenweger, *The Pentecostals* (London: SCM, 1972), 342; for Charismatics, see e.g. M. Poloma, *The Charismatic Movement: Is There a New Pentecost?* (Boston: Twayne, 1982), 50ff. For NT scholars, see (e.g.) Robeck, *DPL*, 941; Fee, *Presence*; Forbes, *Prophecy*, 92–3.

[43]*Gifts*, 173.

[44]*Ibid.*

[45]*Ibid.*, 176.

[46]*Ibid.*, 178–81.

[47]*Ibid.*, 188–9.

[48]*Ibid.*, 192ff.

We take these points seriatim:

(1) There is no contradiction between tongues viewed as an aid in devotion and what is said in 1 Corinthians 14:22; Mark 16:15–17 and Acts 2:1–13, unless one arbitrarily asserts tongues may only have one function (i.e. to provide a convincingly miraculous 'sign' to unbelievers). Edgar does just this, but he is inconsistent here for he is forced to admit that Acts 10:46 and 19:6 do not denote sign-gifts of evangelistic import.[49] Edgar is wrong in giving exclusive place, or even primary place, to the function of tongues stated in the long ending of Mark and implied in Acts 2: in doing this he almost certainly misrepresents Paul.

(2) As exercised in the church, with interpretation, the gift does edify. And, if used privately to build up the individual, this also (albeit indirectly) edifies the church.[50] But the notion that no gift could possibly be given to benefit the receiver/user (rather than the church (s)he serves) is quite arbitrary (cf. Rom. 8:26,27) and fails to see that all the other gifts build up the endowed as well (though not exclusively).

(3) As doxological speech, or prayer, one would anticipate the gift would be better described as 'God-centred' than 'self-centred'.

(4) If tongues is merely one gift amongst many, by which an endowed person might be built up, then the person who has not received the gift is not thereby necessarily impoverished.

(5) On Edgar's view it should be an anomaly that the gift of interpretation is required at all: but on the view presented above the speaker who has tongues and interpretation will not only edify the church more, but also edify himself more (it may be noted that Paul assumes that it is the tongues-speaker who should interpret usually, vv.5, 13[51]).

(6) Edgar's antithesis is false; Paul allows that spiritual activity not

---

[49]*Ibid.*, 176.

[50]For discussion, see, e.g., Hemphill, 'Concept', §44.

[51]Correctly, Thiselton, 'Interpretation', 32–3. Edgar curiously assumes this situation would be exceptional (*Gifts*, 193). V. Budgen advances the curious thesis that 'tongues' were understood fully by the speaker (*The Charismatics and the Word of God*, Welwyn: Evangelical Press, 1985, 47–54). But then why should the glossolalist need to pray for the miraculous gift of interpretation (14:13; cf. 12:10,30), or be silent if there is none with this gift of interpretation (14:28)? Budgen's answer is that such a gift is needed in order to give a precise and accurate rendering of God's words. But this is extravagent special pleading: could not the congregation be edified by something less — e.g. by the glossolalist's paraphrase of the content of his message?

cognitively recognized by the practitioner may nevertheless edify him or her (cf. Rom. 8:26).

(7) To be sure, Paul bans the phenomenon (if uninterpreted) from the assembly; but he fully recognizes that it is genuinely a *speaking to God* (14:2,28) — the problem for the assembly is that unless interpreted it is 'only to God'. It is correct of Edgar to say that Paul does not hereby positively advocate private devotional tongues; but what Paul says nevertheless entails that he considered it an appropriate use.[52] Later, however, in 1 Corinthians 14:28, Paul commands that if *glōssai* are not interpreted the speaker should then be silent in church; he should speak rather 'to himself and to God'. As it is improbable that Paul is counselling private use of tongues in church when another is ministering, this seems to be a positive injunction to private use.[53]

(8) Praying and singing with the Spirit are almost certainly tongues (or, at least, not forms of speech understood by the speaker) else the contrast with prayer 'with the mind' (*tō(i) noi*) makes contextually less sense. This is confirmed by the contrast *en glōssē(i)/tō(i) noi lalein* in verse 19.[54] However much we agree with Edgar that Paul encourages prayer 'with the mind also', he clearly recognizes as valid a form of prayer that is not with the mind, but is merely *glōssē(i)* ('with a tongue'; 14:14).

We conclude that Paul saw a variety of functions to be fulfilled by tongues-speech, including a doxological and simultaneously revelatory role to the congregation (when accompanied by interpretation), but he possibly saw its *major* role to be a private one.

3. Did Paul Expect All to Speak with Tongues?

In 1 Corinthians 12:30 this question is put in a form which clearly indicates that Paul expected a negative answer. But it has been maintained by traditional Pentecostalism that this expected 'no' only relates to speaking in tongues in the assembled church. Private tongues was virtually universal (almost all having been 'baptized in the Spirit').[55]

---

[52]Hemphill, 'Concept', 126, n.258.

[53]*Ibid.*, 149.

[54]So Dunn, *Jesus*, 245; Hemphill, 'Concept', 135–36.

[55]Cf. D.J. Bennett, 'The Gifts of the Holy Spirit', in M.P. Hamilton (ed.), *The Charismatic Movement* (Grand Rapids: Eerdmans, 1975), 18–19; Menzies can even claim, 'Paul affirms that *every Christian may — and indeed should be edified*

This appears to be special pleading: are apostles only apostles in the assembled church, etc. (12:28a)? And if not, how were the Corinthians to perceive that in 12:28b Paul was referring only to 'assembly' gifts rather than ordinary 'tongues'? And if there were a special and distinct inspiration for 'assembly' tongues how was it going wrong at Corinth? Why did not Paul simply tell them not to use their ordinary tongues in the assembly, but only speak in church if under the special charisma, etc.? In fact, Paul makes no such distinction and offers no such obvious advice: for him tongues may be of different kinds, but the distinction of type is not between private and assembly speech.

III. GENERAL CONSIDERATIONS

Having provided an overview of glossolalia in Acts and 1 Corinthians, we may now briefly face two more general but related issues concerning the nature of the gift.

1. The Religious 'Background' of Glossolalia

We began by noting that the consensus of New Testament scholarship is that glossolalia was simply a Christian variant of a more general phenomenon of ecstatic unintelligible speech in hellenistic antiquity, and that it is the influence of this 'background' at Corinth that gave rise to the particular problems with tongues that Paul addresses.[56] This, of course, must assume the absence of a 'Jewish' explanation, and Harrisville has argued this should be our first port of call, if only because the collocation 'to speak with (other) tongues' cannot be found elsewhere. He posits a possible background for glossolalia in a Jewish apocalypticism which did not distinguish between unintelligible ecstatic speech and glossolalia.[57] But the crucial evidence is lacking. In the first place the texts which Harrisville cites as evidence of ecstatic

---

(footnote 55 continued)
through the private manifestation of tongues' (his italics; *Empowered*, 248). On what is this based? It is on the (unargued) assumption that 1 Cor. 14:5 ('Now I would like all of you to speak in tongues, but even more to prophesy') should be taken as an actual possibility rather than as the rhetorical and concessionary statement of an unrealizable ideal (as at 1 Cor. 7:7).

[56]For a critical review of scholarship, see Forbes, *Prophecy*, ch. 2.

[57]'Speaking in Tongues', 42–7.

and unintelligible speech (*1 Enoch* 40; 71:11 and *Martyrdom of Isaiah* 5:14)[58] in fact show no hint of *unintelligibility* at all, even if *1 Enoch* 71:11 is powerfully charismatic (and the reference to *Mart. Isa.* 5:18 is in any case irrelevant as it is clearly part of the Christian redaction of the work).[59] The only passage of potential interest cited by Harrisville is *Testament of Job* 48–50, where Job's three daughters don heavenly charismatic sashes that transform them and enable them to praise God with hymns in angelic languages. Unfortunately, these chapters appear to be part of an addition to the Jewish work, and it is probable they are from a Christian or Gnostic hand.[60] The only other work germane to the question is *Apocalypse of Zephaniah* 8, where the seer prays with the angels, knowing their language, but here it is neither clearly a charismatic phenomenon, nor is it unintelligible to the speaker (and once again the matter of dating is problematic).

For failure of a clear Jewish background to the phenomenon, it is not surprising that a majority have turned to hellenism for the explanation. If the latter does not explain the initial outbreak in Jerusalem, Luke's record may be doubted, or one may appeal to a more general religious background of ecstaticism.[61] The case for a hellenistic background, it is felt, is clearest in 1 Corinthians, especially in the parallel between unintelligible glossolalia that requires interpretation, and the need for the ecstatic unintelligible utterances of the Delphic priestess to be interpreted by the prophet. But this alleged parallel breaks down, Forbes contends, at every point:[62] (i) the evidence the Delphic priestess was frenzied is slender, and essentially boils down to a couple of passages in Plutarch (*Moralia*, 759 b and 763 a) which are in any case contradicted elsewhere by the same author (437 d). (ii) The allied claim she must have produced 'incoherent babbling' then falls to the ground, and is in any case entirely inconsistent with the explicit statements to the effect that (in the Classical period) she herself produced the oracles in verse, even if this was no longer always the case later. But even then, Plutarch and Strabo contend, what was rendered into verse by others was *prose* (not incoherent babbling). (iii) This versification was not undertaken by

[58]'Speaking in Tongues', 47.
[59]The same criticism is made by Forbes, *Prophecy*, 182–3.
[60]R.P. Spittler, in his introduction to the work in *OTP* 1: 833–4, argues chs. 46–53 are a Montanist addition, but see the criticism by Forbes, *Prophecy*, 183–6.
[61]The latter is adopted by Mills, *Approach*, esp. 12–20, 54–70 (arguing Luke has turned an event of ecstatic response to the Spirit, issuing in emotional groaning and occasional snippets of speech, into one of fluent foreign languages).
[62]*Prophecy*, ch. 5.

the *prophētēs* but by 'poets', and neither their task nor that of the
'prophet' were regarded as conducted under inspiration. If the result
was 'unintelligible' and needed elucidation by the 'prophet' it was because it was cryptic, riddling or vague, not because it was linguistically
unintelligible. In short, if the Delphic oracle was 'inspired' (*entheos*),
'ecstatic' and 'manic', this, for the ancients, did not necessarily mean
loss of consciousness or verbal coherence.

Casting the net more widely, Forbes makes a case for the following:

(1) At no other cult centres does the inspiration or *ekstasis* lead to
linguistic unintelligibility (the norm expected was poetic oracles).

(2) The frenzied speech associated with the Mystery Religions
(specifically the cults of Cybele or Dionysus) afford no suitable
parallel to tongues — here the frenzy was typically induced by
(*inter alia*) wine, frenzied dancing and other forms of violent
physical activity, rhythmic shouts of invocation and acclamation, etc., on which our Christian sources are virtually silent,
and the charismatic speech was mainly invocation and ejacula-
tive acclamation, not oracular.[63]

(3) Nor can one find adequate parallels in magical circles (the lists
of supposed divine names that have been claimed as a parallel
to unintelligible tongues were a means of invocation intended
to lead to the state of inspiration, or possession: they were not
charismatic speech issuing from such a state), or other types of
popular hellenistic religion.[64]

The outcome of Forbes' detailed research is that there was no
widespread hellenistic phenomenon of ecstatic and linguistically incoherent speech to provide a background for the Corinthian problems.
Christian glossolalia was thus something of a religious novum (at least
as far as the movement itself would have been aware), and the Corinthians probably learned of it from Paul. The *problem* at Corinth is more
likely then to be explained in terms of elitist prophets prizing a gift they
knew to have been important for the Jerusalem apostles and for Paul
himself (cf. 1 Cor. 14:18). Forbes' analysis clears the air for a brief discussion of our next question.

2. Were New Testament 'Tongues' Ecstatic?

Much indeed depends on what is meant by ecstatic; and many New
Testament scholars use the term with little knowledge of sociological,

[63]See *Ibid.*, ch. 6.
[64]See *Ibid.*, ch. 7.

anthropological or psychological typologies of ecstasy.[65] In practice we do not know much about the psychological state of New Testament tongues speech. Those who speak of it as ecstatic utterance tend either wrongly to assume that *glōssais lalein* belongs with a range of inspired-speech phenomena in non-Christian religions of antiquity, which they assume were unintelligible and 'ecstatic', or they assume that New Testament tongues speech is identical with reports of ecstatic glossolalia today without paying attention to the far greater stream of modern tongues speech which is definitely non-ecstatic. Certainly, when modern New Testament scholars maintain that New Testament tongues speech was *compelled* speech, they contradict Paul who assumes it was not: 1 Corinthians 14:28. For Paul, tongues was neither more nor less 'ecstatic' than prophecy (on which see our discussion in Ch. 12, §2.4[66]).

IV. CONCLUSIONS

In brief, both Luke and Paul regarded glossolalia as invasive charismatic praise in languages unknown to the speaker. Neither views it as a special evangelistic sign-miracle. Neither thinks of it as a temporary sign specifically against *Israel's* unbelief at the inauguration of the new covenant. That tongues should function as a judgement sign at all, for Paul, would follow only from *misuse* of the gift (i.e. failure to interpret it). Certainly neither thinks that tongues were given to identify the apostles as repositories of infallible doctrine. A positive 'sign' value of tongues may be deduced for Luke from the Pentecost story. This account, which echoes Jewish Sinai traditions,[67] presents the event as an eschatological theophany marking the powerful new beginning of Israel's transformation. Tongues might then be understood in Luke-Acts as a distinctive sign of God's eschatological renewing presence,[68] and there are hints that Luke (or the tradition before him) may also have understood tongues as a sign of God's reunification of language and people, a reversal of the alienation of Babel.[69] But Luke does not make the latter explicit, and within his narrative the sign function of

---

[65]See Williams, *Tongues*, ch. 1, cf. 30. With some justification Forbes can complain, ' "Ecstasy" is one of the most misused terms in the vocabulary of New Testament scholarship in our area' (*Prophecy*, 53 (and 53–6 generally)).

[66]So correctly Engelsen, 'Glossolalia', 204.

[67]This judgement has been disputed, but should not be: see Turner, *Power*, ch. 10.

[68]See F.D. Macchia, 'Sighs', 47–73, esp. 55–60.

[69]Cf. J.G. Davies, 'Pentecost and Glossolalia', *JTS* 3 (1952), 228–31.

tongues is primarily as an indication of God's restoring presence and of the joy it brings. More specifically, Luke sees tongues as a distinctive (but not universal) sign of the messianic outpouring of the Spirit of prophecy which restores and transforms Israel.[70]

Like Luke, Paul does not expound a positive 'sign' value of tongues, only speaking of its possible negative function as a sign of judgement if it is used without interpretation. Rather, Paul valued glossolalia (when interpreted) on a par with prophecy, as the self-revealing manifestation of the redeeming God confronting, challenging, comforting and instructing the people he redeems and loves. Interpreted tongues may thus be said to be a sign of the presence of salvation, in that it witnesses to God's immediate self-communicating presence in and to the community — the reversal of the alienation of the 'fall'. But Paul also understood it as a gift for use in private prayer, both as inspired charismatic praise, and, perhaps, as the means of communication of inner groanings and longings which the person could not put into words of his or her own. There is no indication that he thought that any of these functions of tongues would be eclipsed by (e.g.) the establishment of something like a canon of Scripture, and so nothing to suggest he thought tongues should rapidly pass away, or that God would remove them before the Parousia. But that takes us to issues we shall need to discuss more fully in Chapters 16 and 17.

---

[70]See Turner, *Power*, chs. 12–13.

Chapter Fourteen

Gifts of Healings in the New Testament

When we come to the 'gifts of healings' (*charismata iamatōn*) of 1 Corinthians 12:9,30, there is perhaps less doubt about the essential nature of the phenomena in question — examples of the healing miracles of Jesus, of the apostles and of others (e.g. Philip) are strewn through the pages of the Gospels and Acts.[1] It is the significance of these, rather than their nature, that is most keenly debated. Before we launch into the debates, however, we should make seven initial observations about the subject matter of our inquiry: (i) we are concerned here not just with divine healing in general, but especially with occasions where individuals are seen as the locus of God's healing of others: cf. 'to another, gifts of healings (are given)'; (ii) in this phrase, the plural 'gifts (of healings)' probably emphasizes that each event is the work of God, rather than that the ability to heal on any and every occasion is granted the charismatic in question;[2] (iii) we are concerned primarily with stereotypical healings, rather than (e.g.) healings by apostolic shadow (Acts 5:15) or by pieces of apostolic clothing (19:12), which Luke specifies as 'out-of-the-ordinary healings' (*ou . . . tychousas* 19:11); (iv) we should probably not simply *assume* all such claimed healings were immediate (this is not the case even in the gospel tradition: cf. Mk. 8:22–26; Lk. 17:14; Jn. 9:6,7[3]); (v) it is probably not possible to distinguish sharply between healings granted as response to prayer (e.g. the situa-

---

[1] Wilkinson (mis-)uses Bittlinger's understanding of *charisma* to imply the gift of healing in 1 Cor. 12:9 is 'a natural gift of sympathy or empathy combined with a capacity of knowing the right thing to do in the individual situation and with any individual patient', with the Spirit merely sharpening this ability (*Health*, 109). Such would be far more likely had Paul first mentioned it in the list of gifts at 1 Cor. 12:28-30. Its place in 1 Cor. 12:9 amongst the spectacular *pneumatika* the Corinthians prize, indicates more overtly 'divine' healing, and healings seen as specific answers to the prayer of faith.

[2] See Dunn, *Jesus*, 210–11.

[3] The next item in the list in 1 Cor. 12:10 is 'the working of acts of power' (= 'miracles'). Were all healings instantaneous one might expect them to be collapsed into this category.

tion envisaged by Jas. 5:15,16) and those performed by someone with 'gifts of healings'; especially where the latter prays for the one healed, or lays on hands;[4] (vi) while exorcisms and raisings from the dead are special types of 'healings', they are related, and we shall need to consider them alongside more prototypical healings, and (vii) we probably should distinguish Jesus, as one gifted to heal, from the disciples, at least at one point: for the author of Luke-Acts, the post-Easter miracles of the disciples (which parallel those of Jesus) are in some way worked *by* the exalted Jesus, as a continuation and extension of the work of the ministry: cf. the paradigmatic 'Aeneas, Jesus Christ heals you.' (Acts 9:34, cf. 3:12; 14:3; 11:21, etc.)[5]

I. THE SIGNIFICANCE OF GIFTS OF HEALINGS

Were they, for example, a temporary phenomenon (along with other 'sign-miracles', like prophecy and tongues) intended merely to legitimate Jesus and the apostles and to attest their revelation (as cessationists have argued)? Or, to go to the other extreme of interpretation, does healing belong so intrinsically to the gospel itself that those with authentic Christian faith should *expect* healing in *all* circumstances (as proponents of the Health and Wealth Gospel claim)? And if there is a middle way, how do we define the New Testament expectation?

1. Healing Miracles as Evidence of Divinity?

Traditionally, Jesus' healings were understood as miraculous signs attesting his divinity and validating the gospel.[6] From Aquinas onwards, the conclusion of Jesus' divinity could to some extent be made to depend on the very meaning of 'miracle'. Whereas Augustine had focused 'miracle' as unusual events that transcend the expectation and powers of the marvelling observer (thus placing the emphasis on the observer's subjective appraisal), Aquinas defined miracle as an unusual event that 'transcends the powers of nature' as well as the expectations of the marvelling observer. That is, for Aquinas, 'the emphasis has clearly shifted from the witnessing person to the nature of the effect produced

---

[4]Elders called regularly to pray for the sick might soon come to be thought of as those with 'gifts of healings'.
[5]For elucidation, see Turner, 'Luke and the Spirit', 139–46.
[6]Cf. C. Brown, *Miracles and the Critical Mind* (Exeter: Paternoster, 1984), chs. 1–8. For our definition of miracle, see Ch. 15 (n.31) and Ch. 19.

and to its adequate cause'.[7] We need to understand that when he speaks of transcending 'the power of nature' he means something that surpasses the possibilities of *all* created powers not merely of material or human ones. From this it follows that a 'miracle' is the sort of event that *only God can perform*, and it becomes clear how miracles attest Jesus' divinity, especially when it is maintained he performed such events in his own name.[8] We shall see, in Chapter 16, how a similar understanding becomes central to Warfield's position.

2. Jesus' Healing Miracles in a General First-Century Context of Belief in Miracles

It fell principally to Alan Richardson[9] and those after him to clarify that this evidentialist understanding was a misunderstanding of Jesus' healings and other works of power. Jesus' exorcisms, healings and occasional raisings from the dead, would certainly not themselves easily have been understood by his contemporaries to evince *deity* as such (for similar phenomena were claimed of the prophets, and of Jesus' contemporaries[10]). Other explanations were readier to hand, as is shown by the typical responses to his acts of power. Some, who were unconvinced that he was a man of God at all, explained his capacities in terms of magic and sorcery (*b.Sanh.* 43a[11]), or demonic empowerment (Mk. 3:22

---

[7]R. Latourelle, *The Miracles of Jesus and the Theology of Miracles* (New York: Paulist Press, 1988), 270 (and see his whole section on Aquinas, 268–71).

[8]Latourelle makes the important point that Aquinas' definition was by no means all he had to say on the subject: he saw the miracles as *signs* displaying God's redemptive grace too.

[9]A. Richardson, *Miracle-Stories of the Gospels* (London: SCM, 1941). For a good critical summary, see C. Brown, *Miracles*, 253–62.

[10]For brief but careful consideration of the parallel claims on behalf of Galilean charismatics, the 'sign prophets', Apollonius of Tyana, Vespasian and others, see J.P. Meier, *A Marginal Jew: Rethinking the historical Jesus* (Vol 2: New York: Doubleday, 1994), 576–601: cf. also, C.A. Evans, 'Jesus and Jewish Miracle Stories', in *Jesus and His Contemporaries* (Leiden: Brill, 1995) 213–43, and the excursus on 'Jesus and Apollonius of Tyana', 245–50.

[11]M. Smith, *Jesus the Magician* (San Francisco: Harper and Row, 1978), and D. Crossan, *The Historical Jesus* (Edinburgh: Clark, 1991), 137–67, 303–32, have both claimed Jesus may be described as a magician, and that at the phenomenological level there would be no distinguishable difference between Jesus' works and those of magicians. Working with a more neutral sociological definition of magic (performing of acts of power outside the sanctioned religious system), even David Aune has claimed Jesus *used* magic (but is better characterized as a

and parallels, etc.). A rather larger group would have thought of him as a man of the Spirit, a powerful prophet, like the wonder-workers Elijah and Elisha (Lk. 7:16; Mk. 6:15; 8:28 and parallels; cf. Lk. 13:32,33; Jn. 6:14; 9:17). In this respect it is notable that Josephus can characterize Jesus as a teacher and 'worker of miraculous deeds' (*Antiquities* 18:63–64), while polemicizing against the so-called 'sign prophets' that they merely *promised* the people signs of deliverance.[12] A very small group of disciples came to the further conclusion he was the 'Son of God' (Mk. 8:29 and parallels) — not a title of divinity, before Pentecost, but a messianic title taking up the ancient theme of Israel's king as God's 'son', cf. Ps. 2:7, etc.). In these latter cases we meet different types of the typical Jewish assumption that Jesus might be an agent of God's power, like others before him, and to follow, and, indeed, similar miracles were attributed to the disciples both before (Lk. 10:9–11,17) and after Pentecost.[13]

What was the purpose of these acts of power? It is immediately apparent that Jesus did not work miracles to compel faith from the

---

(footnote 11 continued)
messianic prophet of a millenarian movement, than as a magician): 'Magic in Early Christianity', *ANRW* II/23.2, 1507–57, esp. 1523–39. By contrast, Meier argues the category 'magic' is almost entirely inappropriate. On a cline between pure 'miracle' (an act of liberating or provisionary power performed for someone in need by simple intelligible command, and directed to elicit faith/repentance towards God) and pure magic (the technical manipulation or coercion of supernatural personal or impersonal forces, by incantations, spells, etc. to obtain desired concrete 'benefits' (including harmful and punitive ones directed at enemies)), Jesus' works are quite clearly better characterized as 'miracles', even if there may be occasional traits of magic (use of spittle, etc.): see *Marginal Jew*, 2:537–52.

[12] See Meier, *Marginal Jew*, 2:592.

[13] One might argue that the so-called 'nature miracles' were unparalleled, but do they point in the direction of *deity*? This would not be probable for such cases as, (a) the cursing of the fig-tree (Mk. 11:12–14, 20,21//Mt. 21:18–20); (b) the miraculous catches of fish (Lk. 5:1–11 and Jn. 21:1–14); (c) the miracle of water into wine (Jn. 2:1–11), and (d) the feedings of the multitudes (Mk 6:32–44 and//s — for which there was in any case an Elishianic parallel in 2 Kgs. 4:42–44). Could not a mere angel be thought capable of such acts? More promising, perhaps, are (e) the stilling of the storm (Mk. 4:35–41 and//s) and (f) the walking on the water (Mk. 6:45–52 and//s), which is actually told in such a way as to evoke OT theophanic passages (Jb. 9:8b; 38:1; Hab. 3:15; Ps. 77:19; Isa. 43:16, etc.). But these latter two reflect a faith that has seen more significance in the event than the bare occurrence itself requires (which is to say no Jew would find it difficult to believe that a powerful heavenly being might walk on water, and a 'phantom' (Mk. 6:49) was just one of the many possibilities).

reluctant; *per contra*, in Mark 8:11,12 (and parallels) he refuses with an oath to provide miracles that would 'demonstrate' his God-given authority when requested to, and elsewhere he commands silence in respect of his miracles. Indeed, faith was often more obviously a *condition* of healings than their *goal*. Matthew's rendering of Mark 6:5,6 explains, 'He did not do many mighty works there *because of their lack of faith*' (13:58). With this we may compare those places where the faith of those who come to Jesus seeking a miracle is commended: e.g. Luke 7:1–10 (Q)); Mark 2:1–12 and//s.; Mark 5:25–34 and//s., especially verse 34, 'Your faith has healed you. Go in peace' (cf. also Mk. 10:52 and//s, and Lk. 17:19). We shall need to return to this question of the relation of miracles to faith later, but the healings were not intentionally worked as 'messianic proofs'.

3. Jesus' Healings and Exorcisms in the Context of Jewish Eschatological Hopes

What Richardson (followed by Kallas and Van der Loos) was able to show was that the healing miracles were part and parcel of Jesus' eschatological message.[14] They were concrete expressions of God's inbreaking reign. This is to be seen against the background of Jewish belief that saw all illness, deformity, insanity, demonism and death as expressions of the work of Satan and his powers. Whether direct expressions, or very indirect ones,[15] they were aspects of Satan's dominion in the world (along with alienation from God, and alienation from each other). The longing for the kingdom of God — God's reign — was precisely that the rule of Satan in all its manifestations be broken and evil destroyed. It was the hope for a transformed creation, free from death, disease and demonic interference. The (mainly pre-Christian) *Testaments of the Twelve Patriarchs* expresses this in typical fashion:

> And thereafter the Lord himself will arise upon you, the light of righteousness with healing and compassion in his wings. He will

---

[14]J. Kallas, *The Significance of the Synoptic Miracles* (London: SCM, 1961); H. van der Loos, *The Miracles of Jesus*, (Leiden: Brill, 1965).

[15]Jews did not regard all illness as demonic: cf. E. Yamauchi, 'Magic or Miracles? Diseases, Demons and Exorcisms', in D. Wenham and C. Blomberg (eds.), *Gospel Perspectives 6: The Miracles of Jesus* (Sheffield: JSOT, 1986), 89–185. For the beginnings of a Jewish/Christian typology of medicine, see P. Borgen, *Paul Preaches Circumcision and Pleases Men, and Other Essays on Christian Origins* (Trondheim: Tapir, 1983), 115–30; H.C. Kee, *Medicine, Miracle and Magic in New Testament Times*, (Cambridge: CUP, 1986).

liberate every captive of the sons of men from Beliar, and every spirit of error will be trampled down (*Test. Zebulon* 9.8).[16]

We would misunderstand this if we thought of it purely or even primarily in individualist terms. It was part of a broader hope that God would forgive Israel her sins and restore her as a united people, living in God's peace, and under his blessing, as the light of the world. Another important expression of this soteriology was what has come to be called an 'Isaianic New Exodus' hope, namely that a Spirit-anointed Davidic/Mosaic Servant would release Israel from her state of 'exile'/'captivity' and lead her along 'the way' through a transformed wilderness (with miracles of provision) to a restored Zion/Jerusalem, where God would reign. Of this, 4Q521 claims:

> The Heavens and the earth will obey His Messiah [2] and all that is within them . . . [6] Over the meek will his Spirit hover, and the faithful will he restore by his power. [7] He shall glorify the pious ones on the throne of the eternal kingdom. [8] He shall release the captives, make the blind see, raise up the downtrodden . . . [12] then He will heal the sick, resurrect the dead, and to the Meek announce glad tidings.[17]

Given this climate of expectations, Jesus' hearers could hardly have failed to make the connection between Jesus' preaching and his healings, exorcisms and raisings from the dead. If he was preaching that God had begun his long-hoped-for reign (Mk. 1:14,15, etc.), he could naturally be anticipated to understand his various works of power not

---

[16]Similar expressions are found elsewhere in the Testaments: cf. *Test. Jud.* 18.12, 'And Beliar shall be bound by him. And he shall grant to his children the authority to trample on wicked spirits'; *Test. Sim.* 6.6, 'Then all the spirits of error will be given over to being trampled underfoot. And men will have mastery over the evil spirits'; *Test. Dan* 5.9–11, '[9] Therefore when you turn back to the Lord, you will receive mercy, and he will lead you into his holy place, proclaiming peace to you. [10] And there shall arise for you from the tribe of Judah and (the tribe of) Levi the Lord's salvation. He [God? or the Messiah?] will make war against Beliar . . . [11] And he shall take from Beliar the captives, the souls of the saints; and he shall turn the hearts of the disobedient ones to the Lord. . . .' For similar views at Qumran see, e.g., 4Q525 and 11QMelchizedek. All passages concern the final restoration of Israel.

[17]It is not clear whether the miracles of line 12 are worked by the Messiah, or by the Lord who is spoken of in line 6: we have argued elsewhere that probably both together are meant (the Messiah acting as God's agent in the liberating transformation): see *Power*, ch. 4 §3.

merely as *symbols* of the dawning of the promised kingdom, *but also as its very first fruits*. From Jesus' perspective, his exorcisms were the despoiling of Satan's house, and the liberation of his captives: these works were thus *concrete expressions* of the Good News that God has begun his reign (cf. Lk. 11:20 (Q)). Similarly with the other healing miracles. It has been noted, for example, by A.E. Harvey that the miracles attributed to Jesus were largely unparalleled in type in contemporary Judaism, being mainly the bringing of sight to the blind, speech to the dumb, hearing to the deaf, and mobility to the lame and paralysed.[18] But these are exactly the miracles (along with some raisings of the dead according to 4Q521) that Isaiah 35:5,6 and 61:1,2 anticipate of the 'New Exodus' or 'new age' of liberation and restoration. It is hardly surprising that the evangelists can present Jesus as expecting people to understand the significance of the mighty works. The villages, towns and cities visited by the disciples in the ministry of Jesus are to witness people being healed (Lk. 10:9 — Jesus' command to his disciples) and thereby to understand that the kingdom of God has dawned (Lk. 10:9–11), and their guilt is the more dramatic if they do not (10:11–15 (Q)). In its broad lines this view of the relation between Jesus' works of power and his proclamation has now received such general acceptance that it is critical orthodoxy.[19] It is also deeply embedded in the theological framework of the evangelists.

---

[18]A.E. Harvey, *Jesus and the Constraints of History* (London: Duckworth, 1982), ch. 5.

[19]For a more general review of Jesus' miracles in the Gospels, see C. Brown, *Miracles*, ch. 11; idem, *That You May Believe: Miracles and Faith Then and Now* (Exeter: Paternoster, 1985); W.J. Bittner, *Heilung — Zeichen der Herrschaft Gottes* (Neukirchen-Vluyn: Aussaat Vlg., 1984); B. Blackburn, 'Miracles and Miracle Stories', *DJG*, 549–60; idem, 'The Miracles of Jesus', in Bruce Chilton and Craig A. Evans (eds.), *Studying the Historical Jesus* (Leiden: Brill, 1994), 353–94; Blomberg, 'Healing', in *DJG*, 299–307; M. Brown, *Israel's Divine Healer* (Carlisle: Paternoster, 1995), ch. 5; Dunn, *Jesus*, §§8–9, 12; L.P. Hogan, *Healing in the Second Tempel* (sic) *Period* (Göttingen: Vandenhoeck & Ruprecht, 1992), 232–55; Latourelle, *Miracles*; Meier, *Marginal Jew*, 2: chs. 14–16, 20–23 (and see 522–24 (note 4) for bibliography); H.K. Nielsen, *Heilung und Verkündigung* (Leiden: Brill, 1987); G. Theissen, *The Miracle Stories of the Early Christian Tradition* (Edinburgh: T. and T. Clark, 1983); Van der Loos, *Miracles*; J. Wilkinson, *Health and Healing: Studies in New Testament Principles and Practice* (Edinburgh: Hansel, 1980.

4. The Miracles as Legitimation of Jesus' Revelation?

It was commonplace in the ancient world to expect prophetic figures to be legitimated (at least in part) by 'miracles'.[20] But we need to distinguish between two rather different ways in which an act of power might 'legitimate' a prophet or revealer: extrinsic and intrinsic types of legitimation.[21] In the case of extrinsic legitimation, there is no necessary connection of content between the allegedly legitimating act and the message/ revelation it purports to sanction. As an example, we may consider Josephus' account of the confrontation between Micaiah and Zedekiah before Ahab (*Antiquities* 8:408, cf. 1 Kgs. 22:24; 2 Chr. 18:23). Departing from the biblical narrative, he has the false prophet request Ahab to allow a test of Micaiah's credentials: 'But you [Ahab] shall know whether he [Micaiah] is really a true prophet and has the power of the divine Spirit; let him right now, when I strike him, disable my hand as Jadon caused the right hand of king Jeroboam to wither [*scil.* 1 Kgs. 12:32–13:10]'. Here the power to frizzle Zedekiah's arm would be taken to legitimate Micaiah as a prophet, even though there is no material connection between the content of the prophecy of Ahab's doom and the punitive miracle on Zedekiah. The only connection is the middle term — the Spirit — and the logic is that if Micaiah has the Spirit of power he has the Spirit of prophecy. In this case the relation between the message and the legitimating act is what I mean by *extrinsic*. Let us imagine, however, for a moment, that Micaiah's message had instead been for Zedekiah himself, warning him that God would bring a judgement upon him for his false prophecies to Ahab. Were now Zedekiah to pose the same test, and his arm became withered, this would legitimate Micaiah's message in an *intrinsic* way: the act would be the direct expression of the message.

A cessationist position tends to construe the relation between Jesus' miracles and his revelation wholly or largely in extrinsic manner.[22] The

---

[20] For a survey, see Anitra B. Kolenkow, 'Relationships between Miracle and Prophecy in the Greco-Roman World and Early Christianity', in W. Haase (ed.), *ANRW* 23.2 (Berlin: de Gruyter, 1980), 1471–1506.
[21] For this distinction see, e.g. R.E. Brown, 'The Gospel Miracles', in R.E. Brown *et al* (eds.), *The Jerome Biblical Commentary* (London: Chapman, 1968), 784–8, esp. 787; Ruthven, *Cessation*, 116; M. Brown, *Healer*, 225–7.
[22] Gaffin's more nuanced cessationism recognizes the healing miracles have a more intrinsic relation to the salvation announced, but only in the sense that they are signs of that total healing that will be accomplished through the eschatological resurrection: cf. *Perspectives*, 45. But this appears to miss the thrust of Jesus' teaching on the presence of the kingdom of God: cf. Deere, *Surprised*, 285–6.

miracles demonstrate once for all that Jesus and his apostles were in-dwelt in fulness by the God of power, and this extrinsically attests the parallel fulness of their soteriological revelation. Thereafter the soteriological revelation can be received without further miracles.

The position of Jesus and of the evangelists, however, is quite differ-ent. Luke-Acts, for example, envisages an *intrinsic* relationship between Jesus' message and the acts that legitimate it. For Luke 'salvation' is not merely forgiveness of sins, contentment of soul, and a bright future hope; it is a holistic liberation and social renewal of God's people. It is the sort of transformation of Israel envisaged in Zechariah's prophecy (Lk. 1:68–79), and being fulfilled in the new community.[23] Jesus' pro-gramme is summed up in the quotation and application of the New Exodus text, Isaiah 61:1,2, in Luke 4:18–21. To this programme, deliver-ance from evil powers and healing of the sick are not merely extrinsic factors, they are themselves very much part of the salvation announced. Thus Jesus heals blind Bartimaeus with the command, 'Receive your sight' (18:42 (diff. Mk.)) which matches the programmatic 'to proclaim . . . sight to the blind', of 4:18. Similarly, his healings are typically the setting at liberty of Satan's captives (cf. Lk. 13:10–17[24]), and the freeing of 'the oppressed' (Lk. 4:18,19; Acts 10:38), as much as his exorcisms are (11:14–22;10:18–20). For the Lucan Jesus, to withhold healing (on the Sabbath) may be to 'kill' (even though the man concerned is in no mortal danger); but to heal is both 'to do good' and to 'save' (6:9). And when John the Baptist sends his disciples to Jesus, to ask whether he is the expected Coming One, Jesus answers (according to Luke 7:20–22//Mt.) with a demonstration of miracles, and an interpretive word concerning them, which together directly evoke the Isaianic New Ex-odus hopes referred to above: 'the blind receive their sight, the lame

---

[23]Cf. ch. 3, IV, §3. For Luke's view of 'salvation' (in addition to what is said in Chapter 3 above) and its relation to healing, see Turner, *Power*, chs. 5–14 (esp. ch. 9); Green, *Theology*, ch. 4 and ch. 6, esp. 134–5; Hogan, *Healing*, 238–56; J.T. Carroll, 'Jesus as Healer in Luke-Acts', in E.H. Lovering (ed.), *Society of Biblical Literature 1994 Seminar Papers* (Atlanta: Scholars, 1994) 33, 269–85 (and for the broader picture see his 'Sickness and Healing in the New Testament Gospels', *Int* 49 (1995), 130–42; L.T. Johnson, 'The Social Dimensions of *Sōtēria* in Luke-Acts and Paul', in E.H. Lovering (ed.), *Society of Biblical Literature 1993 Seminar Papers* (Atlanta: Scholars, 1993), 32, 520–36.

[24]'In Luke there is no sharply drawn boundary between healing and the driving out of demons', Hogan, *Healing*, 247 (and 247–50); Böcher, *Dämonenfurcht und Dämonenabwehr. Ein Betrag zur Vorgeschichte der christliche Taufe* (Stuttgart: Kohlhammer, 1972), 117. See also J.B. Green, 'Jesus and a Daughter of Abraham (Luke 13:10–17): Test Case for a Lucan Perspective on Jesus' Miracles', *CBQ* 51 (1989), 643–54; D. Hamm, 'The Freeing of the Bent Woman and the Restoration of Israel: Luke 13.10–17 as Narrative Theology', *JSNT* 31 (1987), 23–44.

walk, . . . the deaf hear, the dead are raised, [these] "the poor" have good news brought to them' (cf. Isa. 61:1,2). These miracles legitimate the message, *of which they are a part*, that the prophesied time of liberation from evil has dawned, as well as the messenger who is revealed as the Isaianic prophetic Servant-liberator. They do this, not merely in parallel to the preaching, far less as external attestation of the speaker, but because they are concrete expressions of the message: first fruits of the dawning kingdom and Isaianic New Exodus itself.

Are we able to go beyond this? Alongside the motif of miracles requiring faith (see above) we have seen other places where the miracles are expected to invite towards faith because they embody the kingdom of God that is preached (e.g. in the missions of the disciples, and in the implication of the condemning words on the cities that do not respond to the signs performed, etc.). Similarly, miracles may even strengthen questioning faith (e.g. John the Baptist's). The Fourth Gospel builds on this theological stance: the signs, the author tells us, are written so that the readers may believe that the Christ, the Son of God, is none other than Jesus, and that in such faith they may find 'life' (20:30,31). How do they lead to such belief? Undoubtedly part of the answer is that the signs testify Jesus is the messianic bearer of salvation, sent from the Father (cf. 5:36). But this is certainly not merely to be construed as extrinsic legitimation (crude proofs that God is with him, so one should believe him): Jesus does not trust himself to those who believe in him simply because they have seen the signs he performs (2:23,24; 3:2; 6:14,15). As we have seen, in John, 'salvation' means revelatory encounter with the God who is light and life. This raises perhaps most acutely the question of what it *means* to claim that Jesus' miraculous provision of bread (Jn. 6), his healing the blind (Jn. 9), or his raising of Lazarus (Jn. 11), constitute such an encounter (and for whom and when they do so). Under what conditions do such miracles reveal that the Father is in full and reciprocal revelatory unity with the Son (14:7–11; cf. 10:37,38)? Or to, put it another way, under what conditions does Jesus' miraculous provision of ordinary bread (Jn. 6:11–14) lead to the conclusion he is the bread of life (6:35,51); how does the resuscitation of Lazarus suggest Jesus *is* the resurrection and the life (11:25)? It is surely not simply because the gift in the material realm may be taken as a symbol which assures Jesus' ability to provide the spiritual counterpart (Elijah raised the dead, but no one consequently confesses him to be 'the resurrection and the life'). Clearly, one condition is Jesus' glorification in the cross and resurrection; before that the disciples do not 'penetrate' the signs. But afterwards (illuminated by the Spirit) Jesus' signs may *'lead to (authentic) faith when one discerns in them the manifestation of the character of God as life-giving and responds to Jesus as mediating that life'.*[25] As God had given Israel the bread necessary for life in the wilderness, now he gives material bread again miraculously, through Jesus, as the creator and sustainer of all life. And the gift of God through the compassionate initiative of Jesus is a self-revealing and self-giving of the Father with the Son which later come to a climax in the cross. The case is essentially the same (*mutatis mutandis*) in the gifts of healing and resuscitation. In this subtle and penetrating sense the miracles of Jesus (interpreted by the word of Jesus and illuminated by the Spirit-Paraclete) give a deeper 'legitimation' of Jesus, and lead to a higher christology, than is indicated in the Synoptic accounts of the miracles. But it must be recognized we have moved far from an eviden-tialism that can leave miracles as having done their job. Precisely this Johannine understanding makes continuing healings, performed through those who believe and pray in Jesus' name, theologically relevant. The move from 14:7–11 to vv. 12–14 is not accidental. Such works done by his disciples in Jesus' name will provide echoing (if lesser) 'signs' of the unity of the Father with the Son in creation and redemption.

5. Gifts of Healing in the Post-Resurrection Church of Acts

The holistic understanding of 'salvation' in Jesus' ministry had obvious implications for Jesus' disciples and for the church that would result from their witness. As Jews, they were hardly liable to abandon a soteriology which embraced the bodily dimension of existence for a more platonic view of the importance of the soul. Nor were they likely to ignore the possibility of redemption from the demonic in exorcisms. The attempt by some cessationists to argue that the commissions to heal, which characterized the period of the mission in Israel (cf. Mk. 6:7–13 and//s; cf. esp. Lk. 9:6; 10:9,17 (Q)), were not specifically repeated to the disciples in the post-Easter commissions (Mt. 28:19; Lk. 24:47–49) is largely irrelevant. (1) While Jesus did, according to Luke, imply a significant change to one of the conditions of the forthcoming mission (22:35,36), he rescinded no other (and certainly not the holistic substance of the fundamentally Jewish soteriology). (2) The charge in Matthew 28:19 assumes the making of 'disciples' will follow roughly the pattern of the discipleship shared by the earlier disciples except where this evidently requires change. (3) The accounts of the commissioning of the disciples in Mark and Q are usually considered to have

---

[25]Marianne Thompson, 'Signs and faith in the Fourth Gospel', *BBR*, 1 (1991), 89–108, 96 (and sim. at 107).

been preserved by the earliest church because they were considered paradigms for the Christian mission. (4) Luke deliberately portrays the mission of the church in *continuity* with the pattern of Jesus' ministry in respect of healings (including exorcisms and raisings from the dead); he accomplishes this especially through a careful set of crafted parallels between the miracles of Jesus and those of Peter and Paul.[26] The miracles of the church, for Luke, attest that Jesus continues his soteriological role, healing those under the power of the devil (Acts 10:38; cf. 1:1,2 and cf. 3:16 and 9:34, 'Aeneas, Jesus Christ heals you'). There is no reason to believe Luke thinks the miracles in the church legitimate the message other than *intrinsically*, i.e. as in the Gospel account, by dynamically exemplifying important aspects of how God's 'salvation' breaks through into joyful reality. Evidently this was more prone to be understood by Jews than by those with little knowledge of Israel's hopes. The healing of the paralytic at the Temple in Acts 3 is thus thematically and lexically connected with the proclamation of salvation in Acts 3–4,[27] and Acts 8 puts Philip's miracles in Samaria firmly within the context of the proclamation of the word (8:6), i.e. (as 8:12 clarifies) 'the good news about the kingdom of God and the name of Jesus'. That miracles of healing were exemplars of the message would be less prone to be understood on Gentile soil and in a pagan setting, such as Lystra (Acts 14:8–18). Here indeed they are understood to legitimate Paul and Barnabas, albeit not in the way Warfield would have hoped! Now the ambiguous miracle must be clarified by the kerygma — but we may note that Paul's preaching sets it precisely against the background of God's witness to his own gracious 'doing good' (14:17) for humankind in creation and redemption.[28] As in the case of Jesus, the miracles of the disciples confirm the message in part by bringing it to expression and *simultaneously* by indicating God is

---

[26]See, e.g. A.J. Mattill, 'The Purpose of Acts: Schneckenburger Reconsidered', in W.W. Gasque and R.P. Martin (eds.), *Apostolic History and the Gospel: Biblical and Historical Essays Presented to F.F. Bruce on his 60th Birthday* (Exeter: Paternoster, 1970), 108–22; C.H. Talbert, *Literary Patterns, Theological Themes and the Genre of Luke-Acts*, (Missoula: Scholars, 1974); R.F. O'Toole, 'Parallels between Jesus and His Disciples in Luke-Acts: A Further Study', *BZ* 27 (1983), 195–212; F. Neirynck, 'The Miracle Stories in the Acts of the Apostles. An Introduction', in J. Kremer (ed.), *Les Actes des Apôtres* (Gembloux: Duculot, 1979) 169–213 (esp. 172–88); Susan M. Praeder, 'Jesus-Paul, Peter-Paul, and Jesus-Peter Parallelisms in Luke-Acts: A History of Reader Response', in H.K. Richards (ed.), *Society of Biblical Literature 1984 Seminar Papers* (Chico: Scholars, 1984), 23–49; Carroll, 'Jesus as Healer', 282–3.
[27]See Wilkinson, *Health*, 90–1.
[28]The verb *agathourgeō* here chimes with the *agathopoiēsai* ('to do good') of Lk. 6:9, and the *euergeteō* of Acts 10:38.

'with' the messenger (cf. Acts 10:38). As such, Luke thinks they encourage belief (without compelling it) and draw away from magic: cf. 2:43;3:1–4:22,30; 5:12,13;8:6–13;9:35,42;13:12; 14:3;16:30,33; 19:17.[29] Naturally they could also challenge, comfort and strengthen the faith of disciples (e.g. 2:43; 20:12).

6. Healing in the Epistles

(1) In Paul

Paul uses the terminology of physical healing surprisingly rarely, though we may infer from his holistic soteriology that he would have counted healings as expressions of God's saving intervention. The fact that he attributes certain illnesses and deaths amongst the Corinthians to God's judgement upon their sin (1 Cor. 11:30) also carries the natural corollaries that the Corinthians might otherwise have expected health and vigour, and that repentance might lead to healing (though we shall note below the limits Paul places on these corollaries).[30] When he speaks of his own ministry, he talks of having 'fully preached the gospel of Christ', with word and deed, and with 'signs and wonders', in the power of the Spirit (Rom. 15:18,19: cf. 1 Thess. 1:5). Similarly, in 1 Corinthians 2:2–5 he reminds the Corinthians his gospel came not merely in word, but in demonstration of the Spirit's power (cf. also Gal 3:1,5). Healings of various kinds would almost certainly be the *main* (though by no means exclusive) content intended by the language of 'signs and wonders' (especially if we may be informed by the usage in Acts, where this phrase — or similar collocations — is found most often),[31] and these would be the most obvious candidates for 'demon-strations of the Spirit's power' too

---

[29]See J. Achtemeier, 'The Lucan Perspective on the Miracles of Jesus: A Preliminary Sketch', *JBL* 94 (1975), 547–62, esp. part II; also Dunn, *Jesus*, 163–70 and 189–93, and Hogan, *Healing*, 254. Masters argues that healings, signs and wonders, were not performed as an aid to evangelism; they were not performed in public, but for believers, to help Christians identify which people were the 'true apostles' and so bearers of infallible revelation, and pen-men of Holy Scripture (so *The Healing Epidemic* (London: Wakeman Trust, 1988), 71–4, 74–81, 133, etc.). This, however, is incredible: it is quite clear that Luke considered (*inter alios*) Stephen (Acts 6:8) and Philip (Acts 8:6,13) to perform signs and wonders of healing before the public (explicitly at 6:8; 8:6), and it is equally clear he considered these to elicit faith amongst unbelievers (explicitly at 8:6). Of the view that such miracles were wrought to identify trustworthy apostles as bearers of infallible revelation there is not the slightest hint.
[30]See G.H. Twelftree, 'Healing, Illness', in *DPL*, 378–81.
[31]In the OT and Judaism the language is most typically used to describe the miracles performed in the context of the Exodus redemption (cf. Acts 7:36). But

— after all, there are so few other such 'demonstrations' ever referred to
in the context of proclamation of the 'good news', and redemptive healings were especially apposite as demonstrations of the gospel's content.
In 2 Corinthians 12:12, while reticent to draw attention to them at all, Paul
again reminds the Corinthians that he too worked 'signs and wonders
and mighty works'. That he refers to the same phenomena as 'signs of a
true apostle' earlier in the verse should not be taken to mean these actions
were purely extrinsic 'legitimation' of his calling, or some distinctive kind
of miracles that only an apostle might be capable of. If the apostles are
especially marked by healings (etc.), that is because the apostles are *par
excellence* manifestations of the dying-and-rising of Jesus (2 Cor. 4:10–12;
1 Cor. 4:9–13, etc.); but all Christians are incorporated in this, and so Paul
evinces no surprise, but rather the expectation, that others besides
apostles will work miracles and healings (1 Cor. 12:28–30).

(2) In James.

James 5:14–18 anticipates that the 'prayer of faith will save the sick, and
the Lord will raise them up' (5:15) — once again an interesting (but
now anticipated) pregnant association of healing and salvation terminology, and expressed with little overt qualification on the expectation of healing. A first reading suggests that once the issue of sin is
dealt with, healing in response to prayer may be *expected*; as part, perhaps, of what it *means* to belong to the community of the saved.[32] But
the first reading may mislead us. There is reason to think 'the prayer of
faith' is not simply the fervent prayer of the faithful, but a prayer
informed by a charismatic insight into God's specific will and timing,
such as Elijah's prayer, given as an example (5:17,18[33]). It is thus

---

(footnote 31 continued)
through the New Exodus theme the expression 'sign' (often collocated with
'wonder' or some equivalent) comes *especially* to mean dramatic redemptive
healings (including exorcisms), both in Luke-Acts (cf. Acts 2:22,43; 4:16,22,30;
5:12 (cf. v.15); 6:8; 8:6,7,13; 14:3 (cf. vv.8–11); 15:12) and in John (4:48,54; 6:2;
9:16, etc.): see e.g. Gary S. Grieg, 'The Purpose of Signs and Wonders in the
New Testament: What Terms for Miraculous Power Denote and their Relationship to the Gospel' in G.S. Grieg and K.S. Springer (eds.), *The Kingdom and the
Power* (Ventura (CA): Regal, 1993), 133–74.
[32]J.C. Thomas, 'The Devil, Disease and Deliverance: James 5.14–16', *JPT* 2
(1993), 25–50 (I am grateful to the author for a copy of his paper).
[33]See Keith Warrington, 'The Significance of Elijah in James 5:13–18', *EvQ* 66
(1994), 217–27, and cf. the perceptive suggestions in Tim Geddert's essay, 'We
Prayed for Healing . . . But She Died', in J.R. Coggins and P.G. Hiebert (eds.),
*Wonders and the Word: An Examination of Issues Raised by John Wimber and the
Vineyard Movement* (Winnipeg: Kindred Press, 1989), 85–91, esp. 87–8.

possible James allows there may be times when the elders are not given this faith. With that possibility we turn to the question of qualifications on the expectation of healing in the New Testament.

II. THE EXPECTATION OF HEALING IN THE NEW TESTAMENT

Our argument so far has been that various types of healings were regarded as integral to the holistic (somatic, social and spiritual) pattern of salvation envisaged by the New Testament writers.[34] They were not merely extrinsic legitimating miracles performed on the body as a symbol of a salvation available at present only in the soul. The problem posed by the New Testament is not 'Why do others, besides Jesus and the apostles, work healings?. It is rather, 'Why, if it is part of God's eschatological restoration, is not healing universal among Christians?' The answer to that question — which is beyond the scope of this chapter — is to be found in the eschatological tension between the 'already' and the 'not yet' of the kingdom of God. But we may briefly consider the different types of expectation that tension imposes on our different classes of healings.

1. Resuscitations of the Dead

It is transparent how Jesus' raisings from the dead (Mk. 5:21–43//s; Lk. 7:11–17; Jn. 11:1–46, and cf. the summaries in Mt. 11:5//Lk. 7:22[35]) would be considered eschatological signs of the presence of the reign of God which he proclaimed. In this age, humankind characterized by sin was doomed to death; the fulness of the kingdom of God, salvation and life were the antithesis of this condition. Hence to raise the dead is included within the mission programme for the disciples according to Matthew 10:8, as attestation of the kingdom of God. From this it would be easy to draw the false conclusion that wherever the kingdom of God makes itself present, the dead should universally be brought to life. Such a conclusion, however, fails sufficiently to distinguish the remarkable sign and first fruits (resuscitation to mortal life) from its corresponding eschatological reality (resurrection life in the new creation). Because they are related, then where the kingdom of God is powerfully present one might hope for occasional instances of such resuscitation. But there were not many in Jesus' own ministry, and Acts mentions

---

[34]For the holistic pattern of Jewish soteriology, contrasted with the dualistic Platonic one, see e.g. G.E. Ladd, *The Pattern of New Testament Truth* (Grand Rapids: Eerdmans, 1968), ch. 1.

[35]See Meier, *Marginal Jew*, 2:773–873, for a critical discussion of these.

only two (9:36–42 and 20:7–12). These last were evidently regarded as exceptional. No one, as far as we know, suggested (e.g.) that Stephen should be resuscitated after his martyrdom, rather than buried and lamented (8:2). Nor is it likely anyone proposed that James, the brother of John, might be brought back to life, after being put to the sword (12:2), so that he might continue his valuable service as one of the twelve. For Paul, as we saw in Chapter 8 (part V), bodily death, the fruit of humanity's solidarity with sin in Adam, remains the Christian's normative and divinely appointed experience too, even though God may occasionally rescue from the very teeth of death as a further sign that he is the God of resurrection, life and hope (2 Cor. 1:8–10).

2. Exorcisms.

We have seen that Jesus explained his own exorcisms as the release of Satan's captives and the very presence of God's future eschatological reign (Lk. 11:17–23 and//s). As G.H. Twelftree observes, 'For Jesus his ministry of exorcism was not preparatory to the kingdom, nor a sign of the kingdom, nor an indication that the kingdom had arrived, *but actually the kingdom itself in operation.*'[36] Once again the relationship is transparent for the first-century believer: the invasion of the body by evil spirits and the resulting captivity (which the church traditionally termed 'possession', as opposed to 'oppression', the infliction of harm from without) betokened a fulness of Satan's rule in the life of the individual. The kingdom of God (or the New Exodus liberation) was not merely its warring antithesis, but its rout (at least — as with *1 Enoch* 10:4–6 — in the phase before the eschatological judgement): the parable of the strong man (Mk. 3:27//Mt. 12:29; Lk. 11:21,22), based in Isaiah 49:24,25, proclaims fulfilment of the Jewish New Exodus hopes for liberation from this sort of captivity to Beliar's hosts (and cf. Lk. 10:18). It is fairly clear that, for the Gospel writers, successful exorcism of those turning to Christ would be the expected *norm*, wherever such states of possession were detected. Similarly, for Paul any form of 'fellowship with' demons and allied spiritual powers was to be shunned absolutely as belonging to the pre-Christian past (1 Cor. 10:14–22); even their more all- pervasive obsessions and 'influences' were to be recognized as alien and to be resisted (cf. Rom. 8:38,39; Eph. 2:1–3; 6:10–18)[37]. It is inconceivable that any New

---

[36]G.H. Twelftree, 'Demons, Devil, Satan', in *DJG*, 167–72 (here 168 (italics added)); but for the detailed argument, see his *Jesus the Exorcist*, (Tübingen: Mohr, 1993).
[37]See, e.g. D.G. Reid, 'Principalities and Powers', *DPL*, 746–52; *idem*, 'Satan, Devil', *DPL*, 862–7, etc.

Testament writer would regard the persistence of a state of 'possession' as God's will for the Christian in the same way as bodily death was (and we may trace the abhorrence at such a thought right through to the early church routine incorporation of exorcism into the catechumenate, and the later practice of exorcistic *exsufflatio* in infant baptism).

3. Physical Healing of Ailments.

If merciful resuscitations from the dead were rarely to be expected, and deliverances from possession virtually always to be, where on the cline of expectations should we place anticipation of gifts of healing? Several observations suggest the expectation was high:

(a) As Pentecostal writers have regularly argued, the summaries in the Gospel narratives typically affirm that Jesus healed everyone who came to him (e.g. Mt. 9:35, 'Jesus went about all the cities . . . preaching the gospel of the kingdom of God, and healing *every* disease and *every* infirmity' (cf. 4:23,24; 14:35,36)); there are no stories of his failing to heal (except where there was lack of faith: Mk. 6:5,6 and//s), nor any of his refusing a petitioner. The inference is drawn that Matthew holds out a universal expectation of healing for the faithful. But this type of argument is not entirely convincing. We would hardly expect gospel stories about Jesus *failing* to heal people (even were there such cases), or of his turning them away, for such stories would have little or no survival value in the oral tradition of the church. As for the summaries, they naturally aim to highlight Jesus' success, but the adjective *pas* ('all'), translated above as 'every', should not necessarily be made to absolutize. While the adjective *can* mean 'every single case without exception', it was also regularly used as a weaker generalizing adjective meaning 'the majority' or even just 'a representative proportion', similar to our 'all of Watford turned out to see the Queen' (cf. Mt. 3:5; 8:34, etc.). The locution in the summaries undoubtedly indicates reverent awe at the scale and diversity of Jesus' healings, but may fall short of affirming that *each* and *every* case was dealt with (for which the adjectival *heis hekastos* 'each one' would have served better). Other passages may suggest Jesus was selective in whom he healed: John 5:3 thus speaks of *many* invalids seeking God's healing in the pool called Bethzatha, and Jesus chooses compassionately to offer healing to but one, whose condition had been especially chronic (5:5–9). Similarly, Mark 1:37 implies the gathering again of crowds from Capernaum, drawn by the healings performed the previous evening (1:32–34). But Mark appears to understand their desire for Jesus' further (healing) ministry as a temptation to abandon the primary thrust of his mission, and accordingly Jesus, on this occasion, refuses to continue his work amongst them.[38] While the healings were thus a major expression of the compassionate reconciling and redemptive thrust of Jesus' ministry, the narratives hardly imply that the physical healing of all, and of every sickness, was at the top of Jesus' agenda. In addition, we need to ask whether the Gospel writers and their first readers would not have had a higher expectation of Jesus' own earthly ministry than they would of the risen Lord acting through people with the gifts of healing in their own communities (just as they evidently had a higher expectation of the Lord working such acts through apostles, and through men like Stephen and Philip (cf. Acts 6:8; 8:6-13), than through other members of the congregation[39]).

(b) Another consideration regularly advanced on the basis of Matthew's Gospel has focused on the use of Isaiah 53:4,5 ('he took our infirmities and healed our diseases') in Matthew 8:17, where it is specifically applied to healings. It was claimed, by T.L. Osborn, R.A. Torrey, K.E. Hagin, and others,[40] that this meant healing was 'in the atonement', and so as much assured to all in the present age as the 'forgiveness of sins'. But this has long been recognized as a misunderstanding. From the perspective of the New Testament writers, *all* the benefits of Christ (including resurrection life) may be said theologically to be 'in (or through) the atonement', but that does not mean they thought all were fully available in the present age to all.[41]

(c) A more significant consideration is the argument above that

---

[38]See W.L. Lane, *The Gospel According to Mark* (London: MMS, 1974), 78–83.

[39]At a popular level, Pentecostal preachers have appealed to Hebrews 13:8 to plug this gap, but the appeal must be discounted. This verse is no more intended to demonstrate that Jesus today heals all petitioners who come to him than it is to prove he now wears sandals or sleeps, or that he is eternally crucified (etc.). The point is rather that the resurrected and exalted High Priest that the readers came to know through the proclamation they originally heard ('yesterday') remains true to his character and priesthood ('today' and beyond), even if the leaders who introduced them to the faith have passed away.

[40]See J. Wimber and K. Springer, *Power Healing*, 165–8, and notes on 291–2.

[41]See D. Moo, 'Divine Healing in the Health and Wealth Gospel', *TrinJ* 9 (1988), 191–209, and J. Wilkinson, 'Physical Healing and the Atonement', *EvQ* 63 (1991), 149–67. See also, e.g., Wimber and Springer, *Power Healing*, 164–71, for rejection of this view, and for secondary literature. I am aware that in the early part of the debate a distinction was made between 'in' the atonement (meaning 'available now') and 'through' the atonement, but do not find this use of the prepositions helpful.

healings are aspects of the holistic salvation announced as dawning with Jesus. Healing and health had been associated with the favour of God through most of the Old Testament, and sickness and disease largely (with notable exceptions, such as Job) seen as a form of God's wrath on alienation and sin.[42] The time of promise, precisely because it was to be the great day of reconciliation, was essentially anticipated as one of full well-being (physical, social and religious) in a renewed creation. To the extent that New Testament writers maintain this perspective, they will expect continuation of healings (unless other factors require consideration). Luke-Acts is probably the most positive in this regard. Healings, such as that of the lame man in the Temple (Acts 3:6–8), are celebrated instances of the 'times of refreshment' or 'of respite (from hardships)' that the Lord may be expected to send (3:20). They are also expressions of the kingdom of God at work (cf. 8:4–12). But it is doubtful that Luke considered such miracles to be theologically *indispensable* expressions of God's reign through Christ (the transformed community of faith, joy, unity, worship, and witness in the power of the Spirit, is more significant for him in this regard), and, by contrast, the present can also be categorized as a period of *sufferings* until the kingdom of God comes (14:22). While 'sufferings' may not necessarily mean 'illnesses' (though surely include them), they nevertheless imply there is an eschatological limitation on the degree to which salvation is completely 'holistic' in the present age. There is an evident theological tension here, but it is not unlike that which we have already observed in the Pauline soteriology. In short, Luke appears to encourage a positive *expectation* of healings. They are vivid demonstrations of God's redemptive reign, which embraces all aspects of the believers' life (physical, mental, social and religious), but his theology does not guarantee them universally to the righteous.

If the Gospels and Acts maximize expectation, the note is perhaps a little less triumphant in Paul.[43]

(a) Mention may be made of three co-workers of Paul who do not appear to benefit from 'gifts of healing', despite their obvious standing in the Christian community and strategic usefulness to it. According to Philippians 2:27, Epaphroditus 'was ill and almost died'. 'But', we are told, 'God had mercy on him . . . to

---

[42]See M. Brown, *Healer*, chs. 2–4.
[43]Cf. Hogan, *Healing*, 286–90.

spare me sorrow upon sorrow', which suggests that in God's grace he 'survived' the illness rather than that he experienced a miracle of healing. In 1 Timothy 5:23 Paul needs to advise Timothy, 'take a little wine for the sake of your stomach and your *frequent ailments*', and in 2 Timothy 4:20 Paul admits, 'Trophimus I left sick in Miletus'.

(b) More significant is Paul's own experience: in Galatians 4:13,14 he reminds his readers, 'As you know it was because of an illness that I first preached the gospel to you. Even though my illness was a trial to you, you did not treat me with contempt or scorn'. With this too we probably need to take 2 Corinthians 12:7–9, with its mention of the 'thorn in the flesh' that Paul three times besought the Lord to remove. Despite a measure of doubt on the matter, the most likely referent of the 'thorn' remains a physical disease (rather than opponents or sexual temptation, or whatever[44]). Even if one presses for a different solution to this difficult exegetical puzzle, one is left with a Paul whose Lord permits him (for the sake of his humility) a Satanically-orchestrated device which causes the apostle considerable anguish, and reduces him to such a level of weakness that Christ's own power is seen the better through him. Such a description (especially when taken with Paul's preceding boasting in his many sufferings: 2 Cor. 11:23–33) indicates that Paul does not see his own present 'wholeness', 'peace' and 'well-being' as central to the salvation in which he rejoices, but even believes his own sufferings and 'many deaths' (2 Cor. 11:23) bring 'life' to others (2 Cor. 4:8–12; Col. 1:24). As we have indicated earlier, for Paul, the believers' present Christian experience is as much one of the *dying* of Jesus as it is of his resurrection 'life' (2 Cor. 4:10–12).[45] This in turn inevitably somewhat marginalizes the importance and expectation of the charismata of physical healings.

---

[44]See e.g. Wilkinson, *Health*, ch. 11, or V. Furnish, *II Corinthians* (New York: Doubleday, 1984), 548-551; Martin, 412-16. Peter Masters says there is no doubt on the issue: according to him, those who suggest the thorn is opposition are indulging in far-fetched exegetical gymnastics, driven by the anxiety to prove no Christian should suffer sickness (*Epidemic*, 160). As in so many of the exegetical decisions in which he is certain, he appears sadly unaware of the sweat and tears of hard New Testament scholarship (compare Martin's cautious conclusion on this issue: 'We will probably never know the truth' (416)). With respect to many other controversial exegetical issues on which he is equally confident, he seems unaware that New Testament scholarship as a whole (Evangelical and otherwise) entirely opposes the judgements he represents.

[45]See Dunn, *Jesus*, 326–38; Hafemann, *Suffering*.

In sum, the witness of the New Testament writers is that God will indeed grant miraculous gifts of healing, and that these are joyful experiences of, and pointers to, the holistic nature of God's eschatological salvation, the first fruits of the consummation to come. From a New Testament perspective, healings are thus perhaps *especially* appropriate to the Christian community and to its witness to outsiders (though only in the context of a transformed and vibrant community life and worship). But for both Luke and Paul the present is shaped by the whole Christ-event; not merely by the resurrection, but by the cross too. And both these poles of the Christ-event are experienced as much in the physical as in the social and in the spiritual life of the community.

Chapter Fifteen

The Charismata of God and the Spirit in the Life of the Pauline Churches

I. TOWARDS A STEREOTYPE OF 'SPIRITUAL GIFTS' IN PAUL?

We have examined three prototypical gifts from Paul's list in 1 Corinthians 12:8–10.[1] Are we now able to provide a list of typical characteristics that unite the three and enable us (at least potentially) to identify all further members of the class denoted by the expression 'spiritual gifts'?

Our three gifts are very diverse. What unites healing, prophecy and tongues? What features have they in common? Paul draws attention to six significant traits in 1 Corinthians 12:1–7. In each case the phenomena in question are simultaneously:

(1) *energēmata* ('workings') of God (v.6),

(2) *diakoniai* ('acts of service') given by the Lord (v.5),

(3) *phanerōsis* ('manifestation') of the Spirit (v.7) and so, as a consequence,

(4) *pneumatika* ('things of the Spirit'[2]), things the Spirit endows/enables (v.1, cf. 14:1),

(5) for the common good: i.e. of the church (v.7) and, finally

(6) *charismata* ('gracious gifts') granted by the Spirit (vv.4, 8)[3].

The scarlet thread running through the whole discussion in 12:1–10 is that the phenomena Paul lists are regarded as events in which the Spirit

---

[1] For NT surveys of the sense and significance of the other gifts, see, e.g. A. Bittlinger, *Gifts and Graces: A Commentary on I Corinthians 12–14*, (Grand Rapids: Eerdmans, 1967); Dunn, *Jesus*, 209–58; Carson, *Showing the Spirit*, 31–42 and 77–100; Fee, *Presence*, 164–75; R.P. Martin, *The Spirit and the Congregation: Studies in I Corinthians 12–15*, (Grand Rapids: Eerdmans, 1984).

[2] The plural genitive *pneumatikōn* may derive from a masculine (*pneumatikos*, 'spiritual (person)' (cf. 2:15; 3:1 and 14:37) or a neuter (*pneumatikon*), as taken here, but understood in a broader sense than the common 'spiritual gifts'.

is made manifest (*phanerōseis*): that is, the Spirit's activity coming to relatively clear, even dramatic, expression. They are workings of God in which the presence and activity of divine power is judged — rightly or wrongly — to be a matter of immediate perception; expressions of the Spirit's activity in which man's natural talents and abilities, honed in this world, are least visible.

Are we then to assume that for Paul *pneumatika* and *charismata* are semi-technical terms for what Pentecostalism and the Charismatic movement has called 'supernatural spiritual gifts' (however problematic it might be to define the borders of the extension of such an expression)? May we simply give as a stereotype of 'spiritual gifts' that they be immediately- perceived workings of God, events in which the Spirit is made manifest, and given by Christ to enable the service of his body for the common good? Such a view has been most ably presented by Professor Dunn, but we shall argue (part III) that this misrepresents what Paul is attempting to communicate to the Corinthians. Such a stereotype would be closer to the Corinthians' own view than to Paul's, and merely provides the starting point which he modifies. But the real force of Professor Dunn's argument derives mainly from a more consensus view of what Paul means by the word χάρισμα, and it is to this that we turn first.

II. THE MEANING OF Χάρισμα IN PAUL

There are no known textually secure pre-Pauline uses of the word *charisma*, and of the 17 New Testament occurrences all but one (1 Pet. 4:10) are in the Paulines (though it is unlikely he coined it, as he uses it without explaining it to his readers). In determining its meaning we must thus rely on analysing (a) what can be learned from the word-formation; (b) how the findings suggest it relates to other words meaning 'gift', and (c) Paul's own usage.

Siegried Schatzmann states a widely-held assumption when he maintains, 'χάρισμα is derived from the root χάρις' (*charis*, 'grace').[4] Understandably, like Dunn before him,[5] he then provides a summary of χάρις in Paul, and concludes, 'this understanding of χάρις, then, leads to its correlate, χάρισμα'.[6] Similarly Dunn claims, '*Charisma can*

---

[4]S. Schatzmann, *A Pauline Theology of Charismata* (Peabody: Hendrickson, 1987), 1.
[5]Dunn, *Jesus*, 199–256.
[6]Schatzmann, *Theology*, 2.

only be understood as a particular expression of charis',[7] or, more specifically, *'charisma* is an *event'* of grace,[8] and *'charisma* means, by definition,
manifestation, embodiment of grace (*charis*[9])'. This alleged 'event' character of *charisma* has far-reaching significance for Dunn's whole theology of 'spiritual gifts' and their relation to ministry. With respect to the
former, the very use of the term *charisma* might suggest that a spiritual
gift is a short-term burst of Spirit-given activity. And 'ministry' —
which he thinks for Paul is always simply the exercise of *charismata* —
must be the actual deed or word in which God's Spirit becomes
manifest (short-term *functions*, never persons or human abilities or
talents[10]). For this reason Dunn finds it difficult to accept that Paul
would have condoned any concept of church 'offices': *charisma*, for him,
cannot be institutionalized; the Pastorals (with their interest in appoint-
ments of elders and deacons) represent an 'early catholic' fading of the
Pauline vision.[11] A lot of theological freight is being carried on the back
of apparently innocent linguistic assertions and assumptions here!

---

[7]*Jesus*, 253 (Dunn's italics). Dunn's position is over-simplified here: for more
nuanced treatment see Max Turner's 'Modern Linguistics and the New
Testament', in Joel B. Green (ed)., *Hearing the New Testament: Strategies for Interpretation* (Carlisle: Paternoster, 1995), 156–8.
[8]*Jesus*, 254.
[9]J.D.G. Dunn, 'Ministry and the Ministry: The Charismatic Renewal's Challenge
to Traditional Ecclesiology', in C.M. Robeck (ed.), *Charismatic Experiences in
History* (Peabody: Hendrickson, 1985), 81–101, 82. As far as I am aware the view
that *charisma* was used as a technical expression for a short-term event of God's
grace derives from F. Grau, 'Der Neutestamentliche Begriff "Χάρισμα" ', unpublished PhD dissertation, Tübingen, 1946. For criticism, see U. Brockhaus,
*Charisma und Amt: Die paulinische Charismenlehre auf dem Hintergrund
frühchristlichen Gemeindefunktionen* (Wuppertal: Brockhaus, 1975[3]), 128–39. Many
who hold to the view that Paul's use of *charisma* is based in his understanding
of *charis* ('grace') nevertheless reject the view that this necessarily denotes a
short-term charismatic 'event': see *inter alios* Fee (who states that the noun
charisma was formed from *charis* and means 'a concrete expression of grace' [in
DPL, 340], while clearly rejecting any view that it is necessarily of short duration) and Hemphill ('Concept', *passim*), not to mention Turner (whose view of
the relation of *charisma* to *charis* ['Spiritual Gifts: Then and Now', *VoxEv* is
(1985), 30–32] I am now modifying).
[10]Dunn, *Jesus*, 253.
[11]*Jesus*, §57. For criticism of Käsemann's very similar views, see R.Y.K. Fung,
'Charismatic versus Organized Ministry. An Examination of an Alleged
Antithesis', *EvQ* 52 (1980), 195–214; *idem.*, 'Function or Office? A Survey of the
New Testament Evidence', *ERT* 8 (1984), 16–39.

I have argued elsewhere that, in terms of the discipline of lexical semantics, the crucial assertions in this case are entirely implausible.[12]

(1) The word *charisma* derives from the verb *charizomai* ('to give graciously'), not from *charis*. (Even were it otherwise we should still need to resist the temptation to read the whole Pauline theology of grace into the lexeme *charisma*!)

(2) The *-(s)ma* suffix added to the verbal root signifies 'result of' not 'event of'. The word-formation of *charisma* as a resultative noun from *charizomai* would thus suggest the meaning is 'gift' in the sense 'thing (graciously) given', or 'favour bestowed' rather than 'event of grace'.

(3) What distinguishes *charisma* as a word for 'gift' from other related words in the same semantic field (such as the relatively neutral *doma*, or *dōron* and *dōrea* which perhaps highlight the trait 'free (gift)', or the more formal *dōrēma*) is that a speaker's choice of *charisma* tends more to highlight the thing(s) described as 'gracious and generous gifts, and signs of the giver's good will and favour'. Of course in Paul's uses the giver in question happens always to be God, but that does not mean he thinks the word *charisma* itself *means* 'divine gift'. We must not confuse sense and reference. I see no *linguistic* reason why Paul should not have spoken of human benefactors granting *charismata* to other people, or civic institutions, whether of finance, prestigious offices, or other benefits.

(4) The sense outlined clearly accounts for Romans 5:15,16 where Paul wishes to highlight God's great graciousness in the justification of sinful humankind. Here he uses the word *charisma* interchangeably with other words for 'gift' in the same context (including *dōrea*, *dōrēma* and *charis*). The same sense is to be discerned at 6:23 where Paul uses charisma to denote God's gracious gift of eternal life (*not* a short term 'event' we hope!). In Romans 11:29, Paul chooses the term *charismata* to refer to Israel's irrevocable covenant benefits (cf. 9:4); probably in order to highlight God's graciousness in giving these, and Israel's consequent accountability. Similarly Paul calls the ability of the celibate believer to remain chaste a *charisma* 'from God' (1 Cor. 7:7: again, a long-term ability, and the additional 'of God' would be uncalled for if the word itself always *meant* 'divine gift' as such). In the opening section of his letter to the Romans, Paul expresses his hope he will be able to impart some *charisma*

---

[12]Max Turner, 'Modern Linguistics' 146–74 (155–65).

pneumatikon to them (1:11): the gift in question is not glossolalia or the like, but most probably upbuilding spiritual teaching which he hopes *they* will perceive as God's gracious gift through him, for he hopes for their support for the mission to Spain. And it should be noted the term *charisma* hardly itself means 'spiritual gift'; Paul *adds* the adjective *pneumatikon* to bring that sense. Similarly, at 2 Corinthians 1:11 the *charisma* in question is 'the gracious activity of God on Paul's behalf in rescuing him from a deadly peril, from which at one point he did not expect to recover'.[13]

(5) On each of the occasions above it would be unacceptable to argue that *charisma* has a *sense* like 'supernatural manifestation of the Spirit' (and we have accounted for half of the uses of *charisma*). Those who still wish to claim Paul uses *charisma* in such a way need to argue that Paul distinguished two quite different senses of the word: a general one covering the examples above and a 'technical' one for 'spiritual manifestations' in 1 Corinthians 12–14 and Romans 12 (Schatzmann indeed posits *four* different senses in the Paulines[14]). Of course, polysemy is widespread to language, and there is no intrinsic problem with the supposition that Paul may have developed a special sense — but appeal to such a development should only be made where one discovers a set of linguistic uses of a word that cannot reasonably be explained in terms of the known or expected 'normal' meanings. As we shall see, all the remaining occasions (1 Cor. 1:7; 12:4,9,28,30,31; Rom. 12:6; 1 Tim. 1:14 and 2 Tim. 1:6) are readily enough explained in terms of the sense indicated above.[15]

So for what reason has so much significant scholarship deduced a 'technical sense' (= 'spiritual gifts') in 1 Corinthians 12–14 and Romans 12? I

---

[13]Fee, *Presence*, 286.

[14]Schatzmann, *Theology*, 4–5, cf. 15–22. But see the critique of this in Turner, 'Modern Linguistics', 160–65.

[15]The first of these (1 Cor. 1:7) will not be treated below. NRSV translates: 'so you are not lacking in any spiritual gift as you wait for the revealing of our Lord Jesus Christ'. With Fee (*Presence*, 86), I agree the addition of the word 'spiritual' here is somewhat gratuitous (there is no specific Greek word in the text), though evidently from the co-text of vv.5,6 the gifts he is referring to are (a) from God and (b) principally what *we* might call 'spiritual gifts'. That does not mean, however, that the word *charisma* here itself carries the *sense* 'spiritual gifts' as though Paul could not have used *doma*, *dōron*, or some other word for 'gift' here instead.

suspect it derives from a more widespread tendency in New Testament scholarship to confuse the 'sense' of a word with what the word is used to 'refer' to.[16] Undoubtedly in 1 Corinthians 12:4, Paul uses the word *charismata* to *refer* to phenomena which we recognise as 'spiritual gifts', but that does not mean he thinks the word itself means this. After all, in the same fashion he also uses the words *energēmata* ('workings'), *diakoniai* ('acts of service') and *phanerōsis* ('manifestation') to refer to the same phenomena, but none would suggest these too have become 'semi-technical terms' for spiritual gifts. In this context the simplest explanation is probably the best one: Paul refers to the phenomena in question as *charismata in the ordinary sense of the word*. I suggest he does so because the Corinthians were prone to understand prophecy, tongues, and the like as signs of their own *pneumatikos* nature, and this could easily lead to a boasting elitism amongst those who experienced these gifts. Paul chooses to refer to these phenomena as *charismata* and *diakoniai* by way of corrective. The lexical choice of the former term is made in order to *interpret* prophecy, tongues, charismatic wisdom (etc.) as examples of the many 'gracious gifts' (some of which are more 'spiritual', some more 'natural') which God gives to his people. They are thus things to be humbly grateful for and used appropriately, not grounds for boasting. The subsequent choice of *diakoniai* is made in order to indicate what sort of 'use' is 'appropriate' for these manifestations: it is use in Christ's service to build up the church. Both these points are then developed explicitly in chapters 12–14.

In sum, the word *charisma* in Paul probably means no more than simply '(gracious) gift'. It is not primarily related to Paul's concept of grace, but to other words in the semantic domain of 'gift'.[17] Nor has it

---

[16]See Cotterell and Turner, *Linguistics and Biblical Interpretation* (London: SPCK, 1989), chs. 3 and 5.

[17]To avoid potential misunderstanding I must clarify that I mean simply that linguistically *charisma* is derived from *charizomai*, and so only secondarily (and before Paul) related to the lexeme *charis*, which is not to be confused in a simplistic way with Paul's concept of 'grace' (see Cotterell and Turner, *Linguistics*, ch. 4). I am aware, of course, that Paul relates *charisma* to God's grace quite directly at 1 Cor. 1:4,7; and at Rom. 12:6. That should not surprise us: what else is any 'generous gift' from God other than an expression of his grace? But that is no reason to think he believes the lexeme *charisma* itself semantically *means* 'expression of grace', and that Paul might not equally appropriately have substituted *dōrea*, *dōrēma* or *doma* in its place as he does in Rom. 5:15,16; 2 Cor. 9:15, and most striking is the close parallel to Rom. 12:6 (with 1 Cor. 12:7) in Ephesians 4:7,8. In short, *charisma* is not significantly more closely associated with *charis* than are the other words in the semantic domain of 'gift', except in the obvious assonance, and in their mutual (but differing) lexical relations to *charizomai*.

any privileged (linguistic) relation to 'Spirit': it does not have the specific sense 'spiritual gifts', even when it refers to such.[18] Finally, nothing about the word's formation or use suggests it applies only to 'events', and it is demonstrable that Paul does not restrict it to mean 'short-term' events. We shall need to see whether this general understanding is confirmed by examination of the relevant passages.

III. GOD'S GIFTS IN 1 CORINTHIANS 12–14 AND ROMANS 12 AND THEIR RELATIONSHIP TO THE SPIRIT

Under this broad heading we can only point briefly and in summary fashion to some important areas of debate.[19] We shall first examine Paul's uses of *charisma/ta* in 1 Corinthians 12–14 and Romans 12 in relation to the respective discourse strategies.

1. Paul's Teaching in 1 Corinthians 12–14[20]

The list of gifts Paul specifies in 12:8–10 is not a neutral one but reflects (1) the interest of the Corinthians in the spectacular and (2) Paul's preparation for his specific pastoral advice on the manner and practice of gifts in 1 Corinthians 13–14: issues which have been raised by the Corinthian letter to him. Furthermore, we need to remember that the pressing issue that Paul has in mind is especially the over-exaltation of (uninterpreted) 'tongues', perhaps as a sign of spiritual status (it is

---

[18]'As a rule of thumb, some contextual reason must usually be present in order for us to understand this word as referring to the activity of the Spirit', Fee, *Presence*, 286.

[19]The literature on the subject is enormous, and the reader is simply directed to the summaries of issues and secondary sources by Bittlinger, *Gifts*; H. Schürmann, 'Die geistlichen Gnadengaben in den paulinischen Gemeinden', *Ursprung und Gestalt* (Düsseldorf: Patmos, 1970), 236–67; Dunn, *Jesus*, part III; S. Schulz, 'Die Charismenlehre des Paulus', in J. Friedrich, W. Pöhlmann and P. Stuhlmacher (eds.), *Rechtfertigung: Festschrift für Ernst Käsemann zum 70. Geburtstag* (Tübingen: Mohr, 1976), 443–60; R.Y.K. Fung, 'Ministry, Community and Spiritual Gifts', *EvQ* 56 (1984), 3–20; Martin, *Spirit*; Carson, *Showing the Spirit*; Schatzmann, *Theology, passim*; Fee, *Presence, passim*, but esp. ch. 15; *idem*, 'Gifts of the Spirit', *DPL*, 339–47 (which probably provides the best single brief introduction).

[20]For an outline of the problems relating to these chapters, see the introductory essay by J. Dupont, 'Dimensions du problème des charismes dans 1 Co. 12–14', in De Lorenzi (ed.), *Charisma*.

possibly in this sense that the Corinthians thought tongues were 'a sign to believers', a view which Paul subverts in 14:22).[21] While he will only deal with this issue directly in chapter 14, he prepares the way by his careful positioning of his mentions of tongues at the end of the lists at 12:10 (with interpretation) and 12:28.

Paul starts in 12:1–3 by broadening what was probably a narrow Corinthian view of who the 'spirituals' in the congregation were (was it just those who had gifts of inspired speech, especially tongues?). He lays an important foundation for his anti-elitist response by asserting that all who profess 'Jesus is Lord' do so by the Spirit (and so are in the most important sense *pneumatikos*[22]). He then re-interprets the Corinthian *pneumatikos* terminology, and redirects their interest in the overtly manifest activities of the Spirit (such as in 12:8–10), by setting the whole debate within the broader framework of God's 'gracious gifts' and 'ministrations' (*diakoniai*) intended for the benefit of Christ's body (12:4–7, and see part II, above). Taken within such a framework, the more manifest workings of the Spirit were less liable to become the objects of prideful boasting or divisive elitist practice.

After the brief characterization of gifts of the Spirit in verses 4–7, and Paul's initial list thereof in verses 8–10, he returns to the point that the Spirit distributes the *diversity* of gifts to each as he wills. The *hekastō(i)* ('to each') of verses 7,11 remains ambiguous (is the point merely that the Spirit distributes his diverse gifts to an elite of charismatics, or is Paul saying that *each believer* receives some gift?[23]). So far the Corinthians could read the letter on the assumption that *charismata/pneumatika* denote only the sort of gifts listed in verses 8–10, and that Paul is talking about the Spirit's work only amongst an inner circle of *pneumatikoi*. But that he is not becomes clearer in 12:12–31. While the main argument of this section is the need for *diversity* of gifting in the one body, subsidiary motifs insist once again (cf. 12:1–3) that the whole body is pneumatic and broaden out the class of God's 'gifts' well beyond the kind grouped together in 12:8–10. Thus Paul starts with the insistence that the Spirit has made all members one body: *all* were given the one Spirit to drink (12:13). The body imagery, which he next develops, not only allows him to insist on the need for diversity making

---

[21]Cf. Forbes, *Prophecy*, 175–81 and 260–5 for a discussion of whether prophetic elitism was a key issue.

[22]So, e.g. Grudem, *Gift*, 156–73, esp. 170–3; K.S. Hemphill, *Spiritual Gifts Empowering the New Testament Church* (Nashville: Broadman, 1988), 55–8; idem, 'Concept', 68ff.; Fee, *Presence*, 151–8.

[23]For the view that Paul does *not* believe all have gifts, see the list of writers in Brockhaus, *Charisma*, 204 n.3.

up the one unity, but permits him also to raise the possibility that the parts of the body that seem weaker, less honourable, or less presentable, may prove indispensable and more honoured (vv. 22–24), God giving greater honour to the 'inferior' part. In this Paul is preparing to say that some divine workings which the Corinthians have played down are in fact of greater significance than the list of highly prized items in verses 8–10.

The trap is then sprung in verses 28–31. In verse 18 Paul had spoken of God 'setting' (*etheto*) the diverse members in the body, 'according to his will'. This deliberately echoes the conclusion of the previous paragraph, viz. that the Spirit distributes the diverse gifts 'according to his will' (12:11). Only the precise range of 'members', or 'gifts', is so far left unclear (though 12:13 has already hinted in a universalizing direction). Now in verses 28–31 it is spelt out. We are told God has 'set' (*etheto*) in the pneumatic body of the church (v.28; cf. v.18) first apostles, then prophets, then teachers, etc. — a listing which immediately gives some priority to leadership which some of the Corinthians were wont to downplay (cf. 1 Cor. 1–4; 16:15,16). Paul appears to be pointing out that these functions, too, are God's gifts to the interdependent spiritual body, and by the same token the abilities enabling teachers (etc.) to function are no less 'spiritual' than those vaunted by any self-styled *pneumatikoi*. Under the same rubric come 'helps' (*antilēmpseis*) and 'administrations' (*kybernēseis*), which the Corinthian enthusiasts probably did not reckon amongst 'God's workings' or 'gifts' at all (though the reference to 'acts of service' (12:5) might have given them pause). It is possibly with these in mind (and the Corinthian attitude to them!) that Paul introduced the 'unseemly' and the 'weak' members into his analogy earlier (vv.22–24[24]). The rhetoric of Paul's whole discourse to this point appears thus deliberately to broaden out the notion of the locus of the Spirit's work, and simultaneously (at least potentially) to extend the class of 'gifts' granted to (or 'set in') the church. It is within this broader, more diverse and corporate setting that he can finish with the exhortation to 'seek the greater gifts (*charismata* 12:31)' — greater, that is, in the sense he is to elucidate in chs. 13-14.

Chapter 13, which follows, does not attempt in any sense to commend love *instead of* such manifestations of the Spirit as outlined in 12:8–10, but rather to state the manner in which the genuine *pneumatikos* exercises those gifts[25] — in love, for the benefit of the rest

---

[24]Cf. Hemphill, 'Concept', ch. 3; *idem, Spiritual Gifts*, ch. 2, 67–69.

[25]A point well elucidated by Carson, *Showing the Spirit*, 56–57: cf. Hemphill, 'Concept', 100; S. Lyonnet, 'Agapè et Charismes selon 1 Co 12,31' in De Lorenzi (ed.), *Charisma*, 509–27.

of the church (and it is precisely the intelligible *charismata* that build up most which constitute the 'greater' gifts to be sought[26]) — and this is spelled out in practical terms in chapter 14,[27] which resumes 12:31 with an opening exhortation to seek the things the Spirit gives, especially prophecy (14:1).

In sum, this discourse may begin by suggesting the term *charismata* denotes a narrow range of phenomena — namely the dramatic demonstrations of the Spirit — but by the end of the discourse Paul has suggested a quite different perspective; one that recognizes even apparently 'mundane' services as God's work in and gifts to the pneumatic body of Christ.[28] It is not (as Dunn would have it) that Paul is saying only the most striking acts of 'administration' or 'help' can be called *charismata*, ones that powerfully demonstrate the Spirit's work; rather even relatively ordinary 'weak' services that are 'not honoured' may be perceived as such by the spiritual person.

We are finally in a position to comment more specifically on the uses of the term *charisma/ta* in this section. We have dealt with 12:4. The word then appears three times in the plural form *charismata iamatōn* ('gifts of healings': 12:9,28,30). That abilities to heal on particular occasions are what some might call 'supernatural spiritual gifts' is not in dispute. But in so far as such occurrences are merely part of a much larger class of benevolent gifts (and Paul could as easily have substituted other lexemes such as *domata iamatōn* without substantially affecting the sense), there is no cause to appeal to a new technical sense for this use of *charisma*. Similar considerations apply to the remaining case in the exhortation in 12:31 to seek the greater gifts (*zeloute de ta charismata ta meizona*). As emerges in chapter 14, the gift he has first and foremost in mind is prophecy (so 14:1), and perhaps with it also interpretation of tongues (14:5!) and the other intelligible charismata mentioned in 12:8–10. Co-textual (discourse) factors may thus indicate the only gracious gifts he is talking about happen to be a subgroup of what a twentieth-century Pentecostal might call 'supernatural spiritual gifts'. But that does not mean we have sufficient evidence to claim he has now formulated a technical term to add to the Greek Lexicon —

---

[26]Hemphill, 'Concept', 97–122.

[27]For the argument of ch. 14, see L. Hartman, 'I Co. 14, 1–25: Argument and Some Problems', in De Lorenzi (ed.), *Charisma*, 149–69; Carson, *Showing the Spirit*, chs. 3–4; Fee, *Presence*, 214–71 (who is less convinced the issues in the chapter concern elitism related to tongues; but see e.g. Gillespie, *Theologians*, 156–60; Forbes, *Prophecy*, 170–81 and 260–5).

[28]Hemphill, 'Concept', 82–92; cf. Brockhaus's summary, 'Die Korinther engten den Kreis der Pneumatiker ein; Paulus weitet ihn aus' (*Charisma*, 204).

χάρισμα2 (= 'divine grace in supernatural manifestations of the Spirit') as a hyponym of χάρισμα1 (= '(gracious) gifts'). In this case the general sense is quite adequate to account for the specific usage, and the Corinthians have every reason to know Paul uses the word *charisma* in the more general sense, for he has done so at 7:7, and implied it in his textual strategy leading up to 12:28.

2. Romans 12:6–8

This need not delay us long. The teaching made pointedly and contingently in 1 Corinthians 12 is offered more neutrally here. Once again (12:3,6) Paul associates *charismata* with God's *charis*; once again the issue of the conduct of God's various 'gifts' is raised within an ethical structure (here Paul's treatment of the theme is the filling in an ethical/paraenetic sandwich, 12:1–3,9–21); once again the unity and diversity in the one body is the main illustration (12:4,5), and, as in Corinthians, Paul intimates the need truly to understand the role of each as contributing to the whole (12:3–5). In verse 6 this is spelt out, 'we have gifts that differ according to the grace given to us'. The phrase translated 'according to the grace given to us' signals that God's *charis* (here with the active sense 'his bestowal of kindness') takes different (and varying) 'shape' or character to each (cf. v.3), issuing in different giftings (*charismata*). In what follows, the believers are urged to express or to live out their giftings in step with and within the limits of God's initiative towards them. The list of *charismata* which follows is instructive for the meaning of the lexeme *charisma* here. The list includes (in order) prophecy, service of some kind (*diakonia*), teaching, encouraging, charitable giving, leading (*proistamenos*, or is it 'caring for others'?), and performing acts of mercy. The exact denotation of some members of the list is disputed; but its mixed quality is not.[29] One thing is clear: the lexeme *charismata* here must mean '(gracious) gifts' in the general sense we have already outlined. As Fee observes:

> There seems no way for the Romans to have understood vv. 6–8 as a listing of "Spiritual gifts." Both the immediate context of v. 6 and all other uses of the word χάρισμα in this letter in fact point in the opposite direction: that they would not think of this . . . word as having special associations with the Spirit at all, but with the gifts of

---

[29]Contrast Dunn, *Jesus*, §42; Hemphill, 'Concept', 189ff; J.S. Bosch, 'Le Corps du Christ et les charismes dans l'épître aux Romains', in L. De Lorenzi (ed.), *Dimensions de la vie chrétienne* (Rome: PBI, 1979), 51–72.

God. In 1:11 it took the adjective πνευματικόν to turn this word into a "*Spirit* gifting", and all the other uses have to do with a gift from God (5:15,16; 6:23; 11:29). . . . Thus, we probably have overstepped legitimate exegetical boundaries by a fair margin when we use this "list," alongside 1 Corinthians 12–14, to develop a theology of "Spiritual gifts."[30]

We may go further: if 1 Corinthians 12:4 and 31 are the only places in Paul where the term *charisma* could (even theoretically) bear the specialized meaning 'divine grace in miraculous[31] manifestations of the Spirit', and if even there it is by no means a *required* sense (in that one can explain the usage perfectly naturally in terms of the broader sense), then *the claim that Paul coined a hyponym of* χάρισμα *for a distinct class of miraculous spiritual gifts should be dropped once for all.*

The evidence of Ephesians 4:7–16 follows suit. This section is in continuity with both 1 Corinthians 12 and with Romans 12, though some themes are developed in a specialized way in accordance with the perspective of the letter as a whole. Here again we find the ethical framework (4:1–3,5,16); similarly, we meet the same insistence that each believer is part of the one body of Christ constituted by the one Spirit, and that each receives an appropriate expression of God's grace apportioned by Christ (4:5-8; cf. 1 Cor. 12:5). This *charis*, however, is not said to be revealed in *charismata* but in *domata* — a word forced on the writer by its appearances in Psalm 68:18,

---

[30](*Presence*, 606). Dunn attempts to safeguard his position by insisting that human activities listed in e.g. Rom. 12:6–8 are not charismata merely by virtue of being performed in and for the community: 'charisma can properly be exercised only when it is recognized as the action of the Spirit, for *charisma is characterized not by the exercise of man's ability and talent but by unconditional dependence on and openness to God*' (*Jesus*, 256). But this (and the whole and perceptive discussion in §43) really pushes well beyond Paul in an idealizing way (perhaps to sharpen his thesis): Paul does *not* say the activities of caring, supporting, encouraging, teaching, etc. only *become charismata* when performed in the consciousness of being empowered by the Spirit, or that they are only 'properly' *charismata* when they come as a 'manifestation of the Spirit' to others.

[31]I use the term 'miracle' here, and elsewhere, in the semi-technical sense of an event which combines the following traits: (1) it is an extraordinary or startling observable event, (2) it cannot reasonably be explained in terms of human abilities or other known forces in the world, (3) it is perceived as a direct act of God, and (4) it is usually understood to have symbolic or sign value (e.g. pointing to God as redeemer and judge). For similar definitions in more detail see Latourelle, *Miracles*, 276–80; Meier, *Marginal Jew*, 2:512–15. Of these traits, (1) and (2) should be taken sufficiently loosely to allow for imparting of knowledge that could not otherwise be known by the human agent (as in prophecy).

which is quoted, and the gifts of Christ in question are the apostles, prophets, evangelists, pastors and teachers, whose function it is to equip the saints, and with them to serve in building towards the eschatological unity.[32] In brief, unless one wishes to argue that the writer of Ephesians has made *domata* into a 'technical term' too, the parallel with the use of *charismata* in 1 Corinthians 12 and Romans 12 suggests we need not invoke the theory of the creation of a technical expression in the earlier two letters either.

IV. CHARISMATA AND THE SPIRIT IN PAUL

Having hopefully cleared away some linguistic confusions, we may return to the theological issues.

1. General Considerations

(1) We have indicated that the term *charisma* in Paul is itself neutral with respect to the Spirit. But the Spirit's relation to at least some of God's '(gracious) gifts' is marked: either by co-textual indicators (such as the addition of *pneumatikon* at Rom. 1:11) or by specific assertions of the Spirit's activity in them (e.g. 1 Cor. 12:4,7,8–10 and frequently in statements about prophecy and tongues in ch. 14). Beyond this we can infer that other divine 'gifts' were enabled by the Spirit on more general theological grounds. The 'teaching' and 'encouraging' of Romans 12:7 may be expected to depend at least in part on the Spirit of prophecy furnishing wisdom and insight, and enhancing skills in communication, while the more humanitarian functions of Romans 12:8 are evidently deeply rooted in the Spirit's renewing work and in what might be called the fruits of the Spirit (cf. Gal. 5:22). Thus, while we have emphasized that *charisma* does not itself *mean* 'miraculous spiritual gift', and that some are neither miraculous nor directly related to the Spirit, clearly some divine gifts were regarded by Paul as 'miraculous spiritual gifts' (including most of the list in 1 Cor. 12:8–10, and more besides) and others were gifts *enabled* by the Spirit even if not 'miraculously'.

(2) As many have pointed out, though none more clearly than Dunn, there are many 'gifts' of God enabled by the Spirit that are not included in 1 Corinthians 12:8–10 and Romans 12:6–8.

---

[32]See Turner, 'Mission', 149–51.

The former is a contextually defined list chosen to match the Corinthian expectations, the latter an *ad hoc* illustrative group. For example, amongst the more 'miraculous' gifts of the Spirit (at least according to Paul's account of them) not mentioned are the deeply charismatic intercessory groan of Romans 8:26,27,[33] and the visions and revelations of the Lord of 2 Corinthians 12:1, etc. More to the point, for Paul the whole Christian life is strongly pneumatic, if in less 'miraculous' fashion, and its many and varied experiences of the Spirit might all have a claim to be called God's 'gifts', especially when these were in the service of the church: hence the problem of providing anything more than a vague stereotype for the category 'spiritual gift'.

(3) We cannot artificially reduce this last problem to simplicity by insisting (with Grau and Dunn) that 'spiritual gifts' should be defined strictly in terms of *energēma* (1 Cor. 12:6) or *praxis* (Rom. 12:4).[34] For Dunn, this means that in Paul *charismata* are 'concrete actions, actual events, not . . . latent possibilities and hidden talents'.[35] Consequently, only particular occasions of teaching, leadership, pastoralia etc., or specific events of prophecy, tongues etc., can be *charismata*, and then only when they are *manifestly* of the Spirit. Other than the major lexical problem we have raised above concerning the use of the Greek word *charisma*, there are two related obstacles in the path of any attempt to restrict 'spiritual gifts' to the supernaturally 'manifest' expressions.

(i) There are no clear demarcations on the cline between the Spirit irrupting in miraculous transcendent fashion and the Spirit's more 'silent' presence and activity (which might,

---

[33]Unless, of course, this is 'private' tongues, as Fee argues (*Presence*, 579–86) against E. Käsemann, who took it as public expression of tongues ('The Cry for Liberty in the Worship of the Church', *Perspectives on Paul* (London: SCM, 1971), 122–37), and E.A. Obeng, who takes it as *unspoken* intercession ('The Origins of the Spirit Intercession Motif in Romans', *NTS* 32 (1986), 621–32). The main difficulty for Fee and Käsemann is the adjective 'inarticulate' (*alalētos*), though Fee makes a plausible case that it should be understood to mean 'uncomprehended', and that the other features of the passage align the intercession in question with the praying 'with the Spirit'/'not with the mind' of tongues in 1 Cor. 14:14,15. Cf. also A.J.M. Wedderburn, 'Romans 8:26 — Towards a Theology of Glossolalia', *SJT* 28 (1975), 369–77.

[34]*Contra* Grau, see Hemphill, 'Concept', 187 n.77.

[35]Dunn, *Jesus*, 209.

for example, only be discerned *retrospectively* from the fruit produced in the church). The majority of expressions of the Spirit may well have fallen in the middle ground. One has only to ask of every sermon one hears whether or not the Spirit was 'manifest' in it to appreciate the problem of demarcating 'charismata' on such a basis. One would have similar if not greater problems with discerning when exactly it was appropriate to say a particular believer had received the gift of spiritual wisdom and insight of the kind for which the writer of Ephesians prays in 1:17; 3:16–19.

(ii) Hemphill rightly criticizes Dunn's formulation of the antithesis as between either activities of the Spirit in the moment or latent possibilities and hidden talents. Here too there is room for middle ground — especially concerning activities which demand a wide range of competence such as leadership or pastoralia. Could not Paul speak of an ability possessed, which was recognized and dedicated to God, and used for the upbuilding of the church (even recognized ultimately as being the work of a God who fashions man from the womb) as a 'gift' from God, used and enhanced by the Spirit? And would such then not qualify to be described both as a χάρισμα (cf. 1 Cor. 7:7) and as a 'spiritual gift'? As Hemphill points out, if Paul thought of spiritual gifts merely as momentary activities of the Spirit he could effectively have quenched all Corinthian boasting by saying no one possesses any gifts. But in fact he speaks freely of people 'having' gifts, and gives practical instructions for utilizing the gift one 'has' (ch. 14) — indeed *charismata* can only threaten the community at all if they are 'possessed in stewardship' (cf. 1 Pet. 4:10) and hence subject to immature misuse by the one who 'has' the gift.[36]

2. Only One 'Gift' Per Believer?

1 Corinthians 12:7–11 could give the impression that Paul taught each member of the body receives just one type of spiritual gift: each has his own *charisma* from God, as 1 Corinthians 7:7 puts it (to quote out of context!). But such a view would misunderstand Paul. Three points need to be clarified here:

---

[36]Hemphill, 'Concept', 78 n.92.

(1) What is said in 1 Corinthians 12:7–11 (cf. 29–31) concerns only those gifts which are *manifestations* of the Spirit *in the assembly*: i.e. the kinds of gift exemplified in 12:8–10, especially tongues, interpretation and prophecy which he will deal with in detail (ch. 14), and for which he prepares in ch. 12.

(2) Certainly he expects the church to be characterized by a variety of such gifts, and for these to be distributed in such a way that individual members of Christ are dependent on each other — but this must be made to suggest neither that each is a specialist with just one operation of the Spirit, nor, worse, that the Spirit's distribution of gifts is like some endless heavenly game of musical chairs with a different allocation of types of manifestation of the Spirit each time the assembly meets. The point, I think, is that the broad sense Paul attributes to *charisma* allows him to use it at different levels. While he actually speaks of individual instances of healing as *charismata iamatōn* ('gifts of healings' 1 Cor. 12:9), he might equally have said 'to another (is given) the gift of healing(s)', with the singular thereby summing up all the specific instances generally as God's gracious enabling. Similarly he could easily have spoken of one receiving *charismata* of prophecy or interpretation of tongues (viewing each instance as God's gift) but as readily speaks of God giving the *charisma* of interpretation of tongues (12:10 — an expression denoting a regular ministry of this, rather than a specific instance: cf. 1 Cor. 14:28 *diermeneutēs* = 'an interpreter'); even of God giving 'prophets' (e.g. Eph. 4:11; cf. 1 Cor. 12:28,29). *Charisma* can denote the instance, or sum up a series of instances of the same enabling.

(3) But similarly, even concerning 'manifestation of the Spirit' in the assembly, Paul expects that a person might have the gift of more than one gift — if one may put it that way. He expects the one with tongues to pray for the gift to interpret his tongues (1 Cor. 14:13), and presses all (individually? corporately?) to seek prophecy (14:1).

When we move to a more general perspective than is afforded by his discussion of 'manifestations' in the congregation, we need to remember that Paul recognizes as God's gifts to the church, pastors, evangelists, teachers, and administrators (1 Cor. 12; Rom. 12; Eph. 4). Whether we view these as functionaries or as functions, the point remains that each 'gift' itself comprises a whole nexus of gifts. For example, the teacher needs understanding of Scripture and tradition, personal insight into his congregation, power of *paraklēsis* (cf. Rom. 12:8), etc. And

Paul can speak of his own apostolate as God's 'working' (Gal. 2:8) and God's gift (*charis*: Rom. 1:5; 15:15[37]) — he could as easily have said it was God's *charisma* (cf. Eph. 4:11 where it is *doma*) — yet this apostleship seems to include the gifts of wonders, healing, tongues, prophecy and teaching, *etc.* Whatever God enables a person to do for the church is at the same time his gifts (severally) and his gift (viewing the separate instances of gracious enabling collectively, as one): cf. (1) above.

3. Are the Believers' Gifts 'Fixed'?

1 Corinthians 12 emphasizes that it is the Spirit or God who has apportioned diverse gifts according to his will (12:6–11,18,28,29) and that there is consequently no room for boasting, jealously or inferiority (vv. 12–30). This has led not a few commentators to portray Paul as a fatalist in respect of the distribution of gifts, and the analogy of the body has been taken to mean that the nature of any particular believer's gifting will be as constant as the functions of the bodily organs.[38] Grudem,[39] probably rightly, sees Paul as countering such an attitude in verse 31 — 'Eagerly desire the greater gifts.' (cf. 14:1, 39[40]). God's wise distribution is his choice — and not all will receive the same manifestation of the Spirit — but his choice is not independent of the believer's humble prayerful seeking.[41] The sovereignty of the giver does not negate human responsibility. Some, over-impressed by Paul's statements of divine sovereignty in the passage, have claimed for *zēloun* its classical meaning 'to practise zealously' rather than 'to seek'.[42] This does not really circumvent what they perceive to be the difficulty; for Paul, as we have seen, definitely advises in 14:13 that the one who speaks in tongues should pray to be enabled to interpret too. Further, it seems most natural to interpret *zēloun* semantically (in 14:1) as something like 'seek', for it is qualified 'especially that you might prophesy' (and Paul is evidently commending this).

---

[37]For the senses of *charis*, two of which are simply 'gift' (whether as 'event of giving' or as 'thing given'), see Turner, 'Modern Linguistics', 165.
[38]The latter argument is pressed by Schürmann, 'Gnadengaben', 248; but see the response of Schatzmann, *Theology*, 78–9.
[39]*Gift*, 54–7, 259–61.
[40]The hortatory character of the passage and the parallel with 14:1 demand *zēloute* be imperative, not indicative: so Grudem, *Gift*, 56. R.P. Martin argues for an indicative, *Spirit*, 18, 57; but for the difficulties with this see, e.g., Fee, *Presence*, 196–7.
[41]Hemphill, 'Concept', 124.
[42]Edgar, *Gifts*, 319ff.

4. Spiritual Gifts and Natural Abilities

For Paul, as for the Old Testament, God is sovereign in the world, and that means that all that he grants or enables are his 'gifts' amongst humankind (cf. Rom. 11:29; 1 Cor. 7:7); though the apostle would not characterize them all as 'of the Spirit' as such. In the case of the three prototypical gifts that we examined (prophecy, healing and tongues) it is quite clear that Paul does not consider them to be in any way linked to natural abilities. The same may be said for the rest of the gifts listed in 1 Corinthians 12:8–10. But when Paul includes apostleship, teaching, pastoralia, administration and service in various ways in his listing of God *charismata/domata*, it is obvious that the question of the relationship of natural abilities to spiritual gifts becomes more relevant. For all Paul has to say in 1 Corinthians 2:11–13, it is clear that not a few of the fundamental structures of his teaching only awaited christocentric focusing, reorganization and crystallization in the Damascus Road epiphany to become his apostolic teaching. And for which of his rhetorical and communication skills did he not serve at least some measure of apprenticeship in Judaism? Similar questions might be asked concerning the 'teachers', 'administrations' and 'leaders' of 1 Corinthians 12:28,29, and those with the caring functions of Romans 12:8.[43] Ultimately Paul's language of 'gift/gifting' is neutral with respect to the question of the part played by 'natural ability' — which is only proper for one who can say, 'God . . . set me apart from the womb' (Gal. 1:15[44]).

5. Spiritual 'Gifts' and the 'Fruit of the Spirit'

Galatians 5:22,23 uses the metaphor of 'fruit of the Spirit'[45] to refer to an *ad hoc* list of virtues which are the result of the Spirit's work in the believer (and in contrast with the 'works of the flesh': 5:19–21). The contrast between *gifts* of God worked through the Spirit and *fruit* brought about by the Spirit is inevitably not as sharp as one might at first think, especially if we do not artificially restrict *charismata* to special short-term startling 'manifestations' of the Spirit (or even simply to enablings for service as such: *contrast* e.g. Rom. 5:15,16; 6:23; 11:29, etc.). We have noted the overlap between the caring 'gifts' of Romans 12:8

---

[43]Cf. Bittlinger, *Gifts*, 70–2.
[44]See Schatzmann, *Theology*, 73–6, for a review of differing opinions on the relation between divine enabling and natural ability.
[45]See D.S. Dockery's article by this name in *DPL*, 316–19.

and the socially-orientated 'fruit' of the Spirit in Galatians. There is little obvious *a priori* (semantic) reason why Paul could not have referred to individual prophecies as the 'fruits' of the Spirit, nor why he should not have referred to the various ministries of Ephesians 4:10,11 together as the 'fruit' of the Spirit. And similarly it is possibly merely fortuitous that he did not refer to the ethical qualities in Galatians 5:22,23 together as the 'gift' of the Spirit (or of God).[46] One distinction may perhaps have influenced his choice. One would not expect sharply different types of fruits from a single source (e.g. a tree) and this perhaps made the metaphor of 'fruit' less appropriate for contexts where Paul wishes to place the emphasis on the *variety* of different and complementary workings of the Spirit enabled in different Christians (the point of 1 Cor. 12:7–30; Rom. 12:3–8). Of course, Galatians 5:20–22 lists differing virtues, but there is a much greater conceptual cohesion between them: one could not easily envisage a believer having all 'self-control' but lacking 'patience' in the same way as one could conceive of believers with tongues but without interpretation! Moreover, Paul anticipated that *all* believers should share in and strive for all such fruit (for the absence of them meant action 'according to the flesh' instead).

6. Spiritual Gifts and Church Office

Considerations of space do not permit us to trace the vigorous debate from R. Sohm (1892[47]) onwards on the question of the relationship between charismatic ministry and church office.[48] What I propose, instead, is to address some comments to Dunn's position, which stands at this end of the broad (albeit wiggly) line from Sohm through Käsemann, von Campenhausen, and Schweizer to today.[49]

For Dunn the issues are relatively clear: Paul's concept of *charismata*

---

[46]His choice of 'fruit' is not intended to suggest that these qualities are produced 'automatically' by the Spirit without human participation and effort: see Ch. 8 above.

[47]R. Sohm, *Kirchenrecht*, Leipzig 1892.

[48]For a full account see Brockhaus, *Charisma*; more briefly H.A. Lombard, 'Charisma and Church Office', *Neotestamentica* 10 (1976), 31–52 (esp. 31–7), and cf. the discussion in Schatzmann, *Theology*, ch. 4.

[49]H. von Campenhausen, *Ecclesiastical Authority and Spiritual Power in the Church of the First Three Centuries*, (London: Black, 1969) (ET of 1965 work in German); Käsemann, 'Ministry and Community in the New Testament', *Essays*, 63–94; E. Schweizer, *Church Order in the New Testament*, (London: SCM, 1961); Dunn, *Jesus*, §§44–57; *Unity*, §§29–30.

as events manifesting the Spirit — 'gifts given for a particular instance';
never a talent 'on tap' — means that for Paul there is no place for
formally appointed church office, merely for charismatic leadership
functions which could be regularized in an individual (e.g. prophet or
teacher) and in less well-defined ministries. Starting with the latter, let
Dunn speak for himself:

> They included preaching, a wide range of services, administration
> and/or some kinds of leadership, and acting as a church delegate or
> serving in the Gentile mission as a co-worker with Paul (see par-
> ticularly Rom. 12:7–8; 16:1,3,9,21; 1 Cor. 12:28; 16:15–18; 2 Cor. 8:23;
> Phil. 1:1; 2:25; 4:3; Col. 1:7; 4:7; 1 Thess. 5:12f.). These diverse forms
> of ministry were by no means clearly distinguishable from one
> another — for example, the ministry of exhortation overlaps with
> that of prophecy (Rom. 12:6–8) and the ministry of "helping" (1 Cor.
> 12:28) with the "sharing, caring and giving" of Romans 12:8. The
> explanation of this diversity is obvious: any form of service etc.
> which any individual member of the charismatic community found
> himself regularly prompted to by the Spirit and which benefited the
> church was (or at least should have been) recognised as a regular
> ministry by the church (1 Thess. 5:12f.; 1 Cor. 16:16, 18). Consequent-
> ly these ministries should not be thought of as established or official
> ministries, and they were certainly not ecclesiastical appointments or
> church offices. Indeed we are told specifically in the case of
> Stephanas and his household that "they *took upon themselves* their
> ministry to the saints" (1 Cor. 16:15). The only ones which took a
> form which may have provided the beginnings of a pattern for the
> future were the 'overseers (bishops) and deacons' of Philippi (Phil.
> 1:1). There it would appear that some of the less well defined areas
> of administration and service mentioned above had begun to be
> grouped together or to cohere into more clearly outlined forms of
> ministry, so that those who regularly engaged in them could be
> known by the same name (overseer or deacon).
>
> The 'evangelists' and 'pastors' of Eph. 4:11 may also denote more
> clearly defined ministries, though in Ephesians the (universal)
> Church is possibly viewed from a later (post-Pauline?) perspective . . .
> Yet even here the words seem to denote functions rather than offices
> and are not yet established titles.[50]

Dunn goes on to emphasize the congregational responsibility for ministry in Paul's letters. In contrast to all this, he finds the Pastorals much
closer to Ignatius than to Paul. Elders, overseers and deacons are now

---

[50]Dunn, *Unity*, 112–13.

church offices (1 Tim. 5:17–19; Tit. 1:5; 1 Tim. 3:1–13; Tit. 1:7–9), and Paul's concept of *charisma* has become narrowed and regulated: it is a single gift, given once for all in the course of ordination: it has become the power and authority of office (1 Tim. 4:14; 2 Tim. 1:6). This is seen as the result of the fusing of Pauline and Jewish-Christian patterns, and as the decay of Paul's charismatic vision.[51]

Apropos of this structure we make the following observations:

(1) The whole structure rests on the unsubstantiated claim that *charisma* can only denote an event, or a gift given for a particular instance, the latter being regarded (quite arbitrarily) as of short duration — which certainly does not match Paul's view e.g. of his own apostolate.[52]

(2) Dunn argues that Paul's preference for participles such as *ho didaskōn* ('the [one] teaching'); *ho parakalōn* ('the [one] exhorting'), and *ho proistamenos* (Rom. 12:7,8: cf. *ho katechoumenos* 'the [one] instructing' (Gal. 6:6)) indicates that he conceives the *charismata* as functions not offices. This is true in what it asserts and false in what it denies. The participles indeed focus functions but this is because the discourse context and themes of Romans 12 concern ethics and praxis, and so with what God enables and how those *charismata* are to be exercised. Paul is not discussing, far less defining, church polity as such.[53] Dunn's statement is wrong in what it denies for two reasons: (a) to say, for example, that in Romans 12 Paul is concerned to emphasize how the one who teaches should teach, and that he does so by God's *charis*, in no way suggests or implies that Paul had reservations about using the titular form *didaskaloi* ('teachers'; cf. 1 Cor. 12:29; Eph. 4:11); nor can we infer that he probably did not know of an 'office' of 'teacher' (as Dunn virtually admits). But by the same reasoning, the use of participles to denote other leadership functions (when it is the functions as such which are in focus) in no way suggests that Paul was unaware of corresponding 'offices'. (b) Dunn's statement implies that there is some necessary antithesis between charismatic functions and church offices. The writers of the Pastorals (even on

---

[51]Dunn presses the implications of this for a reformation of ministerial patterns, especially that of what he regards as the questionable category of the 'ordained ministry', in his 'Ministry and the Ministry', 81–101.

[52]See above, and F. Fraikin, ' "Charismes et ministères" à la lumière de 1 Co 12–14', *Église et Théologie* 9 (1978), 455–63.

[53]A point well made by H.A. Lombard, 'Charisma', 47.

Dunn's hypothesis) and of Luke-Acts certainly did not think this to be the case.[54] Nor is the 'necessity' a logical one.[55]

(3) Indeed, for Paul we are forced to accept that some of the charismatic functions were simultaneously church 'offices' (at least of a rudimentary type) — if by 'office' we mean a function (a) with an element of permanency, (b) recognized by the church (e.g. with a title), (c) authorized and hallowed in some way, (d) with formal commissioning (e.g. through laying on of hands), and possibly (e) legitimated (e.g. through letter of commendation), and (f) remunerated.[56] Thus Brockhaus and Holmberg can point, for example, to Paul's legitimation of the leaders in 1 Thessalonians 5:13, and of Stephanas and household in 1 Corinthians 16:15,16 (to whom Paul requests congregational *hypotassesthai* ('subjection'), to paid teachers (Gal. 6:6) and to the titles such as *diakonoi; episkopoi*, etc. (Phil. 1:1 etc.) as indications of office, even if we would be hard-pressed to define their precise nature.[57] How Dunn knows these last were not offices, but functions, eludes scrutiny. His conclusion probably rests on the fact of unsubdued chaos in Corinth (1 Cor. chs. 5, 6, 10, 12–14). This, of course, hardly shows that Corinth had charismatic leadership as opposed to institutional leadership — it merely shows that Corinth had ineffectual leadership. But that could be due to a variety of causes, including: (i) personal failures, (ii) lack of precedents and norms at this early stage by which *episkopoi* might guide, and especially (iii) unclear specification of role-responsibilities between leaders and, in particular, the other strongly pneumatic elements in the congregation. Are there no modern church leaders, even with definite ecclesiastical polity, who find it difficult to know how to relate their office to strong charismatic elements in their churches? In the earliest days of Paul's churches, when recognition was of *episkopoi* — a very unspecific title and one that carried none of the theological and

---

[54]See M. Dumais, 'Ministères, charismes et Esprit dans l'oeuvre de Luc', *Église et Théologie* 9 (1978), 413–53. V.C. Pfitzner, 'Office and Charism in Paul and Luke', *Colloquium* 13 (1981), 28–38, argues that Luke and Paul take similar positions on the relation of office to *charisma*.

[55]Against a similar antithesis in Käsemann's writings, see R.Y.K. Fung, Charismatic versus Organized Ministry', 195–214.

[56]The criteria of 'office' are essentially those of Brockhaus, *Charisma*, 24–25; cf. B. Holmberg, *Paul and Power* (Lund: Gleerup, 1978), 110–11.

[57]See Holmberg, *Paul*, 110–23.

organizational baggage perhaps associated with *presbyteroi* (at least not until the period of the close of Paul's ministry)[58] — lack of clear definition of role may at times have been quite paralysing.

(4) The antithesis between the earlier Paulines and the Pastorals on ministry is overdrawn. Interestingly, J.S. Bosch confesses he started his essay on pastoral charisma in the Paulines with the firm conviction that the Pastorals were non-Pauline, but changed his mind in the writing. The similarity (at deep-structure level) of what Paul had to say on the issue in the earlier letters and what is said in the Pastorals forced him to regard the question of authorship as open after all.[59] Dunn's handling of the question of *charisma* in the Pastorals (1 Tim. 4:14; 2 Tim. 1:6) seems quite inadequate. Why must *charisma* now be nothing other than the power and authority of office? No office is actually mentioned (in connection with Timothy). Is Dunn merely reading these letters through the spectacles of second-century ministerial patterns? It does not seem any less plausible, for example, to envisage a scene modelled on Acts 13:2,3 where Paul during worship prophesies God's setting apart and empowering of Timothy (cf. 1 Tim. 4:14) and accordingly consecrates him for the specified purpose with laying on of hands. Did Paul himself not receive a divine commission (in an initiating event) with empowering to carry it out? The parallel in 2 Timothy 1:6,7 clearly indicates that the gracious 'gift' in question is an empowering and enabling of the Spirit, but of any subordination of this to 'office', ritual or tradition, or of any simple equation of it with ecclesial authority, there is not the slightest hint.[60]

(5) We conclude by quoting some words from Holmberg and from Lombard. Holmberg writes: 'In Paul's mind there exists no opposition between χάρισμα and office, or χάρισμα and institution, as the term signifies any gift, task, or benefit to the whole church that a Christian has been enabled by God to practise'.[61] Lombard sums up a section of his findings:

---

[58]This does not necessarily mean Luke was mistaken to report Paul setting up *presbyteroi*, e.g. Acts 14:23. In Luke's day the terms *presybyteros* ('elder') and *episkopos* were virtually synonyms.

[59]J.S. Bosch, 'Le Charisme des Pasteurs dans le Corpus Paulinien' in De Lorenzi (ed.), *Paul*, 363–97.

[60]See e.g. Fee, *Presence* 772–6; 785–9.

[61]Holmberg, *Paul*, 123.

In no passage of Scripture whatsoever does one encounter the alleged antithesis between charisma and church office, between Spirit and church polity, between Gentile pauline charismatic church and Jewish Palestinian institutionalized church in Jerusalem: Charismata were and are by no means church offices! As gifts of the Spirit they enable and make one competent to serve Christ and his church. It must be clearly understood that the institutional church (with its offices, laws and polity) could and still can in no way exercise and fulfil its duty otherwise than by endowment of the Spirit, viz, by the received and operating charismata.[62]

This more closely represents Paul's teaching on the relationship of gifts and spiritual gifts to church office than the antithetical formulations of Käsemann and Dunn.[63]

V. CONCLUSION

Paul refers to a wide variety of entities as *charismata*, of which some were charismatic irruptions that rendered the Spirit's presence and activity a matter of immediate perception, in others the Spirit was more 'immanent', and to some the Spirit is not directly related at all. The second group could be swelled in ranks by all those occasions where Paul indicates the Spirit is responsible for enhanced abilities of any kind given for the service of Christ (including, e.g. understanding of the gospel, and wisdom in how to apply it and communicate it), *even though he does not specifically use the word χάρισμα to describe them*. Paul does not appear to have a 'concept' of 'spiritual gifts' (at least, not in the sense of a distinct class one could readily isolate, and this term only appears once, and then in the singular: Rom. 1:11). We may appropriately use the English phrase 'spiritual gifts', however, of all the manifestations and abilities Paul relates in one way or another to the Spirit. It is then clear that the whole body of believers is expected in this broader (English) sense to be 'charismatic', even if Paul did not neces-

---

[62]H.A. Lombard, 'Charisma', 48; cf. also Brockhaus, *Charisma*, 210–18.
[63]See Fung, 'Charismatic versus Organized Ministry', 195–214; *idem*, 'Function or Office?', 16–39; *idem*, 'Ministry', 3–20.

sarily think that all believers personally experienced the kind of manifestations exemplified in 1 Corinthians 12:8–10.[64] To the New Testament expectation concerning these we may now turn.

---

[64]As Fee notes, we cannot tell just what percentage of the congregation experienced the *charismata* of 1 Cor. 12:8–10. When Paul says 'to each is given the manifestation of the Spirit for the common good' the point is not necessarily that *all* receive such gifts, nor even that a high proportion does, but that each who does receive a gift receives something complementary to what is received by other believers and for the good of all.

Chapter Sixteen

Cessationism and New Testament Expectation

In this chapter we shall come face to face with cessationist issues. We shall first provide a brief critical account of the modern Protestant cessationist position, beginning with B.B. Warfield. The cessationist position relies on three kinds of argument: (i) the New Testament itself anticipated the cessation of miraculous gifts; (ii) they in fact disappeared in church history, and (iii) there are no modern counterparts to the miraculous gifts of the New Testament. Parts II and III of this chapter address the first two of these; subsequent chapters the third.

I. MODERN PROTESTANT CESSATIONISM

Warfield's cessationist arguments did not fall as a bolt from the blue.[1] Already some of the Church Fathers (Victorian of Petau; Chrysostom; Augustine and Gregory the Great) had explained the comparative lack of miraculous gifts in their own day as due to the more special need of them at the beginnings of the church — i.e. to accredit the Christian message. Aquinas, by defining 'miracle' as an event which transcends *all* the powers of nature, had virtually turned them into 'proofs' of their divine source and of the truth of the Christian doctrines taught by Christ and his disciples. As this was (in his view) the purpose of the miracles, he naturally inclined to the belief that they had done their job and that no more were necessary. Calvin took up this view and used it in his polemic against Catholicism: miracles claimed on behalf of the saints or relics in order to justify Catholic teaching were to be suspect as counterfeit miracles. The effect of the Enlightenment was to sharpen the distinction between events in nature, governed by scientific laws, and 'miracles' of supernature. The essentials of Warfield's position are here, but he was to reshape them into a 'hard' cessationism that

---

[1] For antecedents to Warfield's position, see J. Ruthven, *Cessation*, ch. 1.

brooked no further true miracles beyond the apostolic age (unlike Aquinas and Calvin).

B.B. Warfield (1855–1921), a staunch Calvinist, became professor of didactic and polemical theology at Princeton Theological Seminary in 1887, at a time when the tide of liberalism was fast rising. He sought to provide a robust apologetic for Christianity, and it was in this context that he penned what to many Evangelicals is his best-known work, *The Inspiration and Authority of the Bible.*[2] Nine years earlier, however, he published another work, which remains profoundly influential in conservative Evangelical circles to this day. His *Counterfeit Miracles*[3] was a trumpet blast against all claims for miracles that might be used to substantiate religious teachings beyond or different from that of the apostles (whether Catholic, Christian Science, or whatever). While Warfield largely ignored emerging Pentecostalism,[4] his *Counterfeit Miracles* has since been used extensively by traditional Evangelicalism to combat Pentecostal and Charismatic affirmations that (*inter alia*) healings, tongues and prophecy should be expected by the church today.

One other important stream, however, coursed powerfully into Warfield's apologetic: it was Scottish Common Sense Philosophy.[5] The Enlightenment had shifted the focus of knowledge away from revealed truth to the knowing subject, the inquiring critical mind. But the earlier confidence of the movement was fragmenting into Humean scepticism and even phenomenalist idealism ('The only realities I can be sure of are the (subjective) sensations of data I have'). Such subjectivist philosophies left little base on which a solid Calvinist could build a secure theological apologetic (even if they left scope for Schleiermacher's quite different project). To the rescue of the redoubtable Presbyterians came Scottish Common Sense Philosophy, a brand of Realism developed in the Scottish Divinity faculties in the mid-to-late eighteenth century. Essentially it cut the epistemological Gordian knot, by maintaining God had set in the intellectual constitution of humankind a set of self-evident principles and logical abilities that enabled objective knowledge and true understanding of the real world. The cat I 'observe' is not merely a product of visual data subjectively organized (by my mind), which might or might not correspond with external reality: I am so built that I truly see the cat and can

---

[2]Posthumously edited by S.G. Craig, and published in 1927 (New York: OUP).

[3]New York: Scribners, 1918.

[4]He deals, however, with its more gentrified sociological sister, the Irvingite movement (*Counterfeit Miracles*, 131–53).

[5]For the influence of this on Warfield, see Ruthven, *Cessation*, ch. 2, especially, 44–52.

veritably 'know' I have done so. This faculty to organize evidence objectively, in accordance with reality, and to perceive its logical relations to other areas of reality is humankind's 'common sense'. It was a short step from this to asserting that if one put together a suitable collection of empirically reliable evidence for Christianity, 'common sense' should inevitably infer the truth of its claims.

It is within the framework of this latter expectation that we may best understand Warfield's approach to miracles. Following Aquinas, he understands miracles as observable entirely supernatural events (not merely God's spectacular and providential use of natural forces, or the product of other natural forces which we do not understand). The divine origin and nature of the miracles of Christ and the apostles are transparent to 'common sense' by their great quantity and utter perfection (in contrast, e.g. to the partial healings alleged whether at Lourdes or in Christian Science). The essentials of his position may be summed up in six points:

(1)   In the Bible there is an 'inseparable connection of miracles with revelation, as its mark and credential': the miracles thus gather around the periods of revelation — (i) the Exodus and possession of the land; (ii) the struggle between true and false religion in Elijah-Elisha's time; (iii) the Exile, when God showed his superiority over the pagan gods through Daniel, and (iv) the introduction of Christianity.[6]

(2)   The miracles of Christ and the apostles were performed as signs of God's revealing power, to fully accredit the message which was to become Scripture.

(3)   'When the revelation of God in Christ had taken place, and become in Scripture and church a constituent part of the cosmos, then another era began':[7] i.e. with the last revelations of the apostles, miracles duly ceased.

(4)   The theological rationale for this cessation is (with Bavinck) that with the completion of Scripture, 'God the Holy Spirit had made it His subsequent work, not to introduce new and unneeded revelations into the world, but to diffuse this one complete revelation through the world and to bring mankind into saving knowledge of it'.[8] There was no further revelation to

---

[6]See Warfield, 'A Question of Miracles', in SSWW II, 167–204; *idem*, 'Miracles', in J.D. Davis (ed.), *Dictionary of the Bible* (Grand Rapids: Baker, 1954), 505; cf. *Counterfeit Miracles*, ch.1.
[7]*Counterfeit Miracles*, 27 (quoting Bavinck).
[8]As quoted by Ruthven, *Cessation*, 76.

attest, and further miracles would only distract from the uniqueness of those worked by Christ and the apostles.

(5) All subsequent claims to miracles are as transparently false (to critical reason) as those of the Bible are true, being either connected with heterodoxy (in which case by definition not divine miracles), or trivial, or providential and natural, or representing credulous claims.

(6) Once the New Testament Scripture was given, the transparently divine miracles it recounts were for ever after to be, for 'common sense', the objective evidence and morally compelling accreditation of the gospel. There was no need for God to continue to accredit his revelation 'atomistically . . . to each individual'.

We may highlight a number of important ways in which Warfield's teaching differs from earlier forms of cessationism:

First, while Gregory the Great and most after him considered that God had graciously 'watered' the church with regular miracles until it took firm root in the world (third to fourth century AD), Warfield saw there was no clear logic to such a cessation (on such a supposition one might expect miracles at least where the gospel came to new frontiers — as indeed Calvin allowed — and where the church was weak).[9] He argued instead, with Conyers Middleton,[10] there is no good evidence for miracles in the post-apostolic age. Or, more precisely (with Bishop Kaye[11]), they did not run beyond those upon whom the apostles had laid hands to confer gifts of miracles (as signs of the apostles), with the outer limits set by (e.g.) Poycarp, Ignatius, Papias, Clement, and Hermas.[12]

Second, the miracles are tied more tightly than ever before to 'special revelation'. As we have seen, this was developed by later cessationist writers like Farnell and Gaffin. For them, the gift of prophecy was granted *principally to assure the infallibility of the inscripturated revelation* (though also to guide the church until the canon was complete): tongues, healings and other wonders were granted purely as (evidentialist) apostolic signs accompanying the special revelation (cf. 2 Cor. 12:12; Heb. 2:3b–4).

Third, Warfield's is a 'hard' cessationism, in that he does not appear (if Ruthven's account is fair to him) to allow for charismatic moments of inspired speech, or of penetrating illumination, inner testimony of

[9] See Warfield, *Counterfeit Miracles*, 35–6.
[10] *A Free Enquiry*, London 1749.
[11] *The Ecclesiastical History of the Second and Third Centuries*, (London 1825).
[12] *Counterfeit Miracles*, 22–31.

the Spirit or distinct events of guidance. He dismisses these as but versions of the mystic dream. In doing so he departs from (e.g.) a Puritan or Pietistic spirituality which gave considerable scope for such experiences. Nor is Warfield's position on this point upheld by many cessationists, who adopt a milder form of the position. J.I. Packer, for example, can even commend Pentecostal glossolalia as an aid to spirituality, and appears mainly concerned to deny that the contemporary phenomena are a restoration of healing, prophecy, tongues and interpretation with anything approaching the revelatory power and 'sign' quality of the New Testament counterparts.[13]

How should we assess these arguments? Warfield's argument is vulnerable to a number of criticisms:

(1) The Scottish Common Sense Philosophy that undergirds Warfield's approach is no longer tenable. The fatal weakness proved to be that the 'common sense' in question is not so common: different observers regularly draw opposing conclusions from the same evidence. If the divine nature of miracles were plainly transparent, and if God-given 'common sense' naturally deduced from them what Warfield imagined, then there should be no unbelievers in the world.[14] In fact, as we have seen (Ch. 14), what Warfield took to be the 'common sense' understanding of the miracles would not have been held at all by the first-century groups amongst whom they were worked!

(2) The case that miracles were tied to periods of special revelation, and above all to the process of inscripturation, is also demonstrably false. This position overlooks the phenomenon of prophecy itself, which was not restricted to these periods. It also

---

[13]Packer, *Keep in Step*, ch. 5. And see now the important collection of essays in W. Grugem (ed.), *Are the Miraculous Gifts for Today: Four Views* (Leicester: IVP, 1988).

[14]In order to protect his thesis at this point Warfield is forced to the assertion that the dead soul cannot respond to the evidence. In order to explain Darwin's *loss* of faith, he argues that Darwin's over- indulgence in his one scientific endeavour permitted other aspects of his mind to atrophy. And to explain competing theological models and movements among Christians he invokes the suppression of 'common sense' by opposed dangers of enthusiasm and rationalism (cf. Ruthven, *Cessation*, 49–52: one suspects Warfield found 'common sense' only amongst like-minded Calvinists). These devices effectively concede that 'common sense' does not provide a sure foundation for apologetics.

[15]See J. Deere, *Surprised by the Power of the Spirit* (Eastbourne: Kingsway, 1994), 253–66, which responds in detail to the similar case made by J. MacArthur, *Charismatic Chaos*, (Grand Rapids: Zondervan, 1992).

turns a blind eye, on the one hand, to the many other sorts of miracles scattered throughout Genesis, Judges, 1 and 2 Samuel, etc.[15] and, on the other hand, to the *lack* of such 'substantiating miracles' in connection with the writings of the pre- exilic prophets. Furthermore, as Ruthven points out, such a limitation is specifically denied by Jeremiah 32:20, which rather affirms a *continuum* of signs and wonders from the Exodus to the prophet's own day.[16]

(3) That miracles were thought to attest God's messengers need not be doubted; but that that was their *prime*, if not *exclusive*, purpose was in no way demonstrated by Warfield (nor by his cessationist successors). As we have seen, within Jesus' proclamation, healings and exorcisms were regarded as expressions of the salvation announced. Similarly, the prophecy and tongues of the apostolic church were not related to the preparation of Scripture, nor understood as 'sign gifts' in an evidentialist sense. They performed a wide range of beneficial functions within the church, and in individual discipleship, and were not in any way rendered significantly less 'needed' (nor less desirable) by the completion of the canon (as cessationists claim).[17] One can only stand in amazement at the mixture of rationalism, hard-headed evidentialism and sheer biblicism that sometimes declares that once the record of the miracles were in Scripture for all to read, further signs and wonders, prophecies, tongues and healings were effectively rendered obsolete and theoretically irrelevant to the church's continuing life and mission.

(4) An important plank in the cessationist argument has been that signs and wonders and healings were in fact performed only by the apostles and by a few on whom they laid hands to convey such powers (so Bishop Kaye, Warfield, and most modern cessationists)[18] — thus even the latter cases might (allegedly) properly be subsumed under the title 'signs of the apostles'.[19]

---

[16]Ruthven, *Cessation*, 73.

[17]See Chs. 12 and 13 above.

[18]Warfield, *Counterfeit Miracles*, 23 (depending on Kaye). Most recently Masters, *Epidemic*, 69–70 (who would almost reduce those involved to Philip, Stephen, and Barnabas), and Gross, *Miracles, Demons and Spiritual Warfare: An Urgent Call for Discernment* (Grand Rapids: Baker, 1990), 46–9.

[19]But as Deere observes, there is a logical problem here: if the miracles are given precisely to authenticate apostles, the dissemination of miracles to others could only weaken their value distinctively to authenticate apostles (*Surprised*,

But there is no scrap of evidence that apostles *ever* laid hands on *anyone* in order to confer the power to work miracles. To say (as Bishop Kaye did) that the Samaritans in Acts 8:14–17 'all received power of working signs by the laying on of Apostolic hands', and that this was paradigmatic,[20] totally misunderstands Luke's point. Laying on of hands indeed there was, and signs there were too — both at the time and possibly later — but Luke is concerned to depict the Samaritan reception of the Spirit promised in Acts 2 (vv. 17-21,33,38,39) *to all*; not a special charism for working apostolocentric authenticating signs![21] Nor is it the case that what cessationists mean by 'miracles' were wrought by the apostles and their 'deputies' alone. Warfield was forced to admit the obvious exceptions of Ananias (Acts 9:17,18) and Cornelius (10:44–46).[22] But there were evidently many more who experienced prophecy, tongues, interpretation of tongues, healing, or other 'miraculous' gifts, concerning whom only a global argument from silence allows us to assume they received these things through the laying on of apostolic hands.[23] In particular we may note that Warfield's treatment of New Testament miracles has little to say concerning the gift of prophecy itself, which Paul evidently considered might be widespread in any single congregation, such as at Corinth (cf. Ch. 12, above).[24]

(5) Cessationists often appeal to Hebrews 2:3,4 for their case that miracles were worked only through the apostolic circle, and for the sole function of once-for-all confirmation of the gospel. But as Grudem observes, Hebrews 2:3 does not limit 'those who heard him' to the apostles, and, more important, while 2:4 affirms their message was attended by signs and wonders, it does

---

[20]Warfield, *Counterfeit Miracles*, 22.
[21]See ch. 3 above.
[22]*Counterfeit Miracles*, 21–2.
[23]See Deere, *Surprised*, 230–3.
[24]And for a broader perspective, see Chapter 15. Later cessationist writers, as we have noted, have attempted to fill the gap in the argument here by insisting 'prophecy' was given both to provide Scripture and to accredit the Scripture writers. The completion of the canon then allegedly left no further occasion for the phenomenon, and hence it passed away. The objections to this, however, have been stated in Chapter 12: the hypothesis is baseless, because neither the OT writers, nor their NT equivalents, equate prophecy with inscripturation, and the NT phenomenon is not primarily concerned with this.

not suggest that similar confirmation would be lacking when others preached.[25]

Two other important criticisms require more detailed treatment. First, the New Testament writers themselves evidently expected the continuation of healing, prophecy, tongues, and other related gifts, until the Parousia. Second, Warfield's claim that all such miracles ceased with the close of the sub-apostolic period is based in a polemical re-writing of history, and one that reveals a fundamental incoherence in his very notion of 'miracle'. It is to these criticisms that we now turn.

II. THE NEW TESTAMENT EXPECTATION OF CONTINUATION OF CHARISMATIC GIFTS

1. Healings

As we have seen (Ch. 14), nothing in the New Testament suggests that healings would cease, and Warfield's attempt to restrict their function to apostolic accreditation is baseless and reductionist. For the New Testament writers, the healings were not externally attesting signs, but part of the scope of the salvation announced, which reached beyond the merely spiritual to the psychological and physical. The dawning of salvation, viewed holistically, was the beginning of the reversal of Satan's oppression (Lk. 4:18–21; 7:20–22; Acts 10:38, etc.). As such, the healings were still regarded as having legitimating function with respect to Jesus and to the apostles (around whom they clustered with especial intensity), but essentially the exorcisms and healings belonged as part of the first-fruits of the kingdom of God, and so as part of the message of salvation which the church announced.[26] So, if there are sick in the church, James can expect (as a rule of thumb?) that the elders' prayer of faith will bring healing (Jas. 5:15). The relationship

---

(footnote 25 continued)
[25]See W. Grudem, 'Should Christians Expect Miracles Today? Objections and Answers from the Bible', in Grieg and Springer (eds.), *Kingdom*, 55–110 (esp. 67–8). When K.L. Sarles ('An Appraisal of the Signs and Wonders Movement' BSac 56 (1988), 57–82) deduces from the use of the aorist *ebebaiōthē* ('it was confirmed') that such confirmation of the gospel no longer continues (75–6), he simply shows lack of understanding of current research on the nature of the aorist (on which see e.g., S.E. Porter, *Verbal Aspect in the Greek New Testament: With Reference to Tense and Mood*, (New York: Lang, 1989).
[26]See Ruthven, who argues the biblical view of the kingdom of God, and its inauguration through Jesus, is inimical to cessationism (*Cessation*, 115–23).

which healing sustains to the kerygma of the dawning kingdom of God suggests that the New Testament writers did not envisage the two ever being separated.

2. Tongues and Prophecy: 1 Corinthians 13 and the Pauline Evidence

(1) 1 Corinthians 13.

Paul explicitly states the expectation that prophecy, tongues and knowledge will cease or be done away with (1 Cor. 13:8–12).[27] The reason they will cease, Paul states, is that they are 'partial' (*ek merous*) and when 'the perfect' (*to teleion*) comes they will be done away with as unnecessary (vv. 9,10). Three interpretations of this have become widely current:

(1) The first is that by *to teleion* Paul denotes the completed canon of *Scripture*: when this comes, the gifts which correspond to merely partial knowledge will be done away with. This position is exegetically indefensible, and is not held in serious New Testament scholarship.[28] The objections to it are strong: (a) There is no evidence that Paul expected the formation of a canon after the death of the apostles; indeed he half expected he might himself survive to the Parousia (1 Thess. 4:15,16; 1 Cor. 15:51), though he was not sure. (b) He cannot have expected the Corinthians to perceive from the phrase *to teleion* that he was referring to a canon of Scripture (and he was not aware of writing to anyone else). (c) In any case, the completed canon of Scripture would hardly signify for the Corinthians the *passing away of merely 'partial' knowledge* (and prophecy and tongues with it), and the arrival of 'full knowledge', for the Corinthians already had the Old Testament, the gospel tradition (presumably), and (almost certainly) more Pauline teaching than finally got into the canon. (d) More important still is that in verse 12b Paul states that (with the coming of 'the perfect') our 'partial knowledge' will give way to a measure of knowledge that is only matched by the way *we are now known* (i.e. by God[29]). This

---

[27]On the exegetical fallacy involved in the claim that the verb *pausontai* implies tongues will cease of their own accord (and so before the Parousia 'puts an end to' prophecy and 'knowledge'), see D.A. Carson, *Exegetical Fallacies* (Grand Rapids: Baker, 1984), 77–9, and Ruthven, *Cessation*, 136–7.
[28]Conceding this, the more informed cessationists (including Farnell and Gaffin) have moved to variants of the second explanation below: but R.L. Thomas, 'Tongues . . . Will Cease', *JETS* 17 (1974), 81–9, still attempts to defend the possibility (alongside the explanation below).
[29]Cf. G. Bornkamm, *Early Christian Experience* (London: SCM, 1969), 185.

contrast between the Corinthians' knowledge before and after the arrival of *to teleion* is so sharp that Paul can express it, 'Now we see but a poor reflection; then we shall see face to face' (v.12a, NIV). This last statement is in fact the language of theophany,[30] and makes it all but certain that Paul is talking of the Parousia — so sure that Calvin was able to say: 'It is stupid of people to make the whole of this discussion apply to the intervening time.' However much we respect the New Testament canon, Paul can only be accused of the wildest exaggeration in verse 12 if that is what he was talking about. (e) Finally, we note that this view rests partly on the assumption that prophecy was an interim revelation of doctrine to be transcended by the canon. But, as we have seen, prophecy was *not* primarily authoritative revelation of theology, but had much wider content and function, much of which would not be affected in the least by completion of the canon.

(2) A second widely-held interpretation is that *to teleion* means 'maturity', and that tongues, prophecy (etc.) would end when the church reached maturity in love and knowledge of God. Lexically this is possible, and the illustration in verse 11 is sometimes taken to confirm it.[31] But to suggest that this may apply to some pre-Parousia maturity of the church is, once again, simply to trivialize the language of verses 10 and 12.[32] Besides which we must note (a) that Paul so highly ranks prophets and prophecy that it is unlikely he would envisage them excluded from even the most mature church (cf. 1 Cor.

---

[30]Grudem, *Gift*, 213 n.57.

[31]Furthermore, it is held that the 'faith' and 'hope' that (together with 'love') 'remain' (according to v.13) beyond tongues, prophecy and 'knowledge', cannot be virtues that belong to the *post*-Parousia situation, when they are displaced by 'sight' (so R.L. Thomas, 'Tongues . . .', 83–4; E. Miguens, '1 Cor 13:8–13 Reconsidered', *CBQ* 37 (1975), 76–97). This argument, however, is insecure on a number of grounds: (1) C.K. Barrett (*A Commentary on the First Epistle to the Corinthians* (London: Black, 1971), 308–11) and Carson (*Showing the Spirit*, 74–6) argue that for finite human beings, 'faith' and 'hope' will always have a place (with love) in a person's relationship to God, even beyond the Parousia; (2) it is less than certain that the 'now' is temporal, rather than logical; and so (3) whether 'remain' means 'endure beyond the arrival of *to teleion*', or simply 'are left as evidently more important than the charismata'.

[32]Furthermore, as Forbes observes, the closest parallel to the idea of the church maturing to the point of becoming the *anēr teleios* ('mature man') is Eph. 4:13, where the reference is eschatological, not to some pre-Parousia temporal maturity (*Prophecy*, 88–91: against the view that Eph. 4:13 represents temporal maturity, see, e.g., Turner, 'Mission', 150–1).

14:1,39), and (b) Paul in 1 Corinthians 1:7 clearly regards revelatory and other charismata as strengthening the church as it awaits the Lord's return. The point in 13:11 is not that the apostolic church will give rise to a more mature one on earth, in which knowledge will no longer be *ek merous*; but that the whole existence of the church on earth is characterized by partial knowledge (prophecy etc.) when seen from the perspective of the coming Parousia. Paul's polemical point is that 'the spiritual manifestations of this age, no matter how magnificent they may seem (to the Corinthians) are childish in comparison with the fulness to be possessed when the kingdom is fully realized'.[33] Love will *then* prove eternal, but all phenomena characterized by partial revelation will be transcended: so the former must now be the matrix for the latter, and the gifts must be exercised for loving upbuilding of the church which awaits Christ.

(3) Only the third — the eschatological — interpretation of verses 8–12 satisfactorily accounts for Paul's language.[34] With it, however, goes the corollary that Paul expects prophecy, 'knowledge' and (possibly) tongues to continue (note the adversitive *de* of v. 10); it is only the advent of the Parousia, and the conditions it introduces, that makes prophecy otiose (cf. *katargēthēsetai* vv. 8,10); not some unspecified event or condition before it.

(2) Other Pauline passages.

Ruthven appeals to a large number of other Pauline texts as evidence of expectation of charismata until the Parousia,[35] but it must be admitted

---

[33]Hemphill, 'Concept', 116.

[34]See Grudem, *Gift*, 210–21; Hemphill, 'Concept', 113–20; Carson, *Showing the Spirit*, 66–76; Fee, *Presence*, 204–14; Ruthven, *Cessation*, 138–51; Forbes, *Prophecy*, 85–91.

[35]See his treatment of Eph. 4:11–13; 1:13–23; 3:14–21; 4:30; 5:15–19; 6:10–20; Phil. 1:5–10; Col. 1:9–12; 1 Thess. 1:5–8; 5:11–23; 2 Thess. 1.11,12, in *Cessation*, 151–79. From the non-Paulines he treats 1 Pet. 1:5; 4:7–12; 1 Jn. 2:26–28, and Jude 18–21 (*Cessation*, 179–86). But of the latter, the references in 1 Peter and Jude are far too general (while both imply the presence of revelatory or prophetic gifts, and both speak of the imminent end, they do not address the question of whether similar gifts might be anticipated were there a long church history). Similarly, 1 Jn. 2:26–28 speaks of the Spirit teaching disciples, but this could be a matter of the kind of spiritual 'illumination' of the gospel that most cessationists (though perhaps not Warfield) readily admit continues.

that his handling does not always show the critical acumen of the earlier chapters of his work.

> Thus, for example, on 1 Thess. 1:5–8 he presses Paul's assertion 'you became imitators of us' to mean the Thessalonians became charismatics with the power of the Holy Spirit (as Paul in 1.5), and *so* a model to other believers in Macedonia and Achaia.[36] On 1 Thess. 5.11–24, Ruthven assumes prophecy will endure to the end on the grounds that the horizon of Paul's guidance on prophecy contains an eschatological note (cf. v.23 'and be kept blameless at the coming of Jesus'[37]), but the words on prophecy belong to the paraenesis of vv.12–22, while the eschatological note only appears in a separate section commencing in v.23, that is, in the letter's concluding prayer, exhortation and benediction of vv.23–28. Again, 2 Thess. 1:11,12 refers to God fulfilling 'by his power' in believers every 'good resolve and work of faith'. Ruthven somewhat surprisingly takes this to refer to miraculous *charismata*, but the reference should almost certainly be taken in a far more general sense (the same pertains to his treatment of Col. 1:9–12 and Eph. 1:17–21). Eph. 1:3,14 certainly speaks of the Spirit as the believers' guarantee of the eschatological inheritance, but Ruthven's conclusion that the writer means the Spirit will be experienced in miraculous charismata until the end rests on unsupported assumption (and similarly he gratuitously assumes the reference to the 'word of God'/'sword of the Spirit' in 6:17 is to prophecy[38]). Eph. 4:7–13 expects Christ's gifts of various ministries to guide the church's growth towards eschatological unity, but (*contra* Ruthven) that does not necessarily underwrite a continuing line of apostles and prophets to the end (any more than 2:20 and 3:5 necessarily precludes it): it was at least potentially possible that their contribution would persist merely through others (evangelists, pastors and teachers) later building on the foundation they provided. Ruthven offers no justification for his claim that 'exegetically, the gifts continue or cease as a single group'.[39]

Some of his texts (particularly the prayers of Col. 1:9–12; Eph. 1:17–21 and 3:14–21) are effective against Warfield's hard cessationism, in that they show appropriation of the gospel was not through 'common sense' recognition of the miracles of the apostles and consequent rational belief in the veracity of their teaching. It was rather a matter of Spirit-enabled understanding. But while this may constitute an argument against Warfield, it would not contribute much to the debate with other milder cessationists, who could willingly pray Paul's prayers and expect corresponding spiritual illuminations. None of Ruthven's texts (other than those in 1 Corinthians) address their question, which is

---

[36]*Cessation*, 173–4.

[37]*Ibid.*, 174–8.

[38]*Ibid.*, 200, but cf. 169.

[39]*Ibid.'* 156.

whether the distinctively miraculous gifts of prophecy, tongues, interpretation, healings and the like were expected to continue. In Chapters
12–13 above we have argued that prophecy and tongues had no special
relationship to apostolicity, inscripturation or authentication of the gospel in Paul. They were enjoyed for the other benefits they brought the
church, corporately and individually, including the revealing of God's
specific insight, judgement or guidance on questions Scripture could
not address (e.g. the diagnostic prophecies of Rev. 2–3, each specific to
the circumstances of a single congregation), enhancing private prayer,
etc. So there would have been no reason for Paul to assume such gifts
would pass away until the Parousia made them otiose (at least in the
'partial' and flawed form in which Paul then knew them).

3. Tongues and Prophecy: The Evidence of Acts 2:16–39

The nature of the gift of the Spirit which Peter promises to *all* who call
on the name of the Lord (Acts 2:38,39) — even to the hearers' children's
children — is a Christianized version of Joel's promise of the 'Spirit of
prophecy'. Prototypical to this are gifts of revelation, wisdom,
prophecy and charismatic praise (see chs. 1 and 3). It would quite
literally be nonsense to suggest the writer of Luke-Acts *anticipated* the
cessation of these: if indeed they ceased, such a state of affairs could
only have come as a considerable surprise to him. It would inevitably
have seemed like a failure at the very heart of what Joel's promise of
the Spirit was all about.

III. DID PROPHECY, TONGUES OR HEALINGS CEASE IN THE
SUB-APOSTOLIC PERIOD?

Unfortunately we have no critical history of any of the three gifts we
chose to discuss; though this is not to say we lack for semi-popular or
highly partisan surveys. Where detailed work has been performed, it
has all too often been vitiated by strong confessional or theoretical bias.
Some of these confessional or theoretical biases have been well exposed
by Colin Brown's *Miracles and the Modern Mind*. And nowhere are they
more obvious than in the work of Warfield, whose book swings violent-
ly from a confessionalist, and somewhat naive evidentialist, treatment
of miracle in the apostolic age, to an extreme scepticism towards any
claims of miracles in the church in the post-apostolic period, quite
clearly dependent on Conyers Middleton.[40] Had Warfield shown the

---

[40]See C. Brown, *Miracles*, 64–8, 198–204. Cf. also Ruthven, *Cessation*, 82–92.

same openness — some would say credulity — towards post-apostolic claims that he evinced when discussing New Testament miracles, which of the miracles of the saints would not have received his defence, if not indeed his approbation? And, had he turned the degree of scepticism manifest in his treatment of post-apostolic writers onto the New Testament accounts, what scant few miracles of the apostles (or of the Lord himself) would have escaped his sharp wit and criticism! (For Warfield the Scriptures authenticated the miracles every bit as much as the miracles authenticated the Scriptures.[41]) Certainly the church never universally claimed the gift of healing to have ceased: as Warfield himself admits, the number of claims appears to grow in the third and fourth centuries.

Ruthven observes that a comparison of Warfield's treatment of the biblical miracles with his negative response to later claims for miracles reveals an epistemological incoherence at the heart of his view of 'miracle'.[42] On the one hand, he expects the biblical miracles to be transparent to 'common sense' (i.e. it is 'evident' they are God's own work, not that of some created power), while on the other, even so well-attested an event as the complete and spontaneous healing of Pierre de Rudder's badly broken legs at Lourdes is not permitted the title 'miracle' on the grounds that the healing might turn out to be explicable in terms of as yet unknown and mysterious natural forces.[43] How then is 'common sense' supposed to detect that the power unleashed to heal the man at the Beautiful Gate, who had been lame from birth (Acts 3:2–8), was God alone, and directly, rather than a providential use of the same mysterious as-yet- unknown-to-us natural forces? The answer, of course, is that we have *no* independent means for making such a distinction.[44] Any assertion that a 'miracle' has taken place in the sense Warfield intends is ultimately a confessional and theological assertion, with a fideistic *a priori*, not simply the result of observation processed through 'common sense'.[45] That said, Warfield's whole dismissal of post-biblical 'miracles' would require a complete review, and we would need to scrutinize each claim using the kind of criteria advanced by Meier in his analysis of the historicity of Jesus'

---

[41]See Ruthven, *Cessation*, 67–71.

[42]*Ibid.*, 63–71.

[43]*Counterfeit Miracles*, 119–20.

[44]This is why Meier argues the historian cannot (*qua* historian) assert any miracle to have taken place: see *Marginal Jew* 2: ch. 17.

[45]See the careful discussion of the issue in respect of Jesus' miracles in Meier, *Marginal Jew*, 2: ch. 17.

[46]See *Ibid.*, chs. 18 and 19.

miracles.[46] Undoubtedly many of the claims rest in rumour or were generated by a mixture of superstition and hagiographical concerns; but the evidence for others (especially healings and exorcisms) is much better, and occasionally based in reliable first-hand witness of the Fathers or of others.[47]

Is the matter different with respect to tongues and prophecy? For the former, Middleton once bravely ventured:

> And I might risk the merit of my argument on this single point; that, after the Apostolic times, there is not in all history one instance, either well attested, or even so much as mentioned, of any particular person, who had ever exercised this gift, or pretended to exercise it, in any age or country whatsoever.[48]

But John Wesley was able to respond fairly quickly with a reminder that the phenomenon was known as close to home, and as recently, as amongst the Camisards[49] — and historians have shown that Wesley's counter-claim could be widely illustrated in other centuries too.[50] Of course we have no guarantee that these claims were authentic, but we simply cannot in true Middletonian fashion try to read church history as though they were not there. They were. And the evidence for the critical early church period is that tongues were a claimed phenomenon

---

[47]For the early period, see R.N. Kydd, *Charismatic Gifts in the Early Church: An Exploration into the Gifts of the Spirit in the First Three Centuries of the Christian Era*, (Peabody: Hendrickson, 1984). Warfield laments that many of the claims for miracles come from such leading theological thinkers as Jerome, Gregory of Nyssa, Athanasius, Chrysostom and Augustine (*Counterfeit Miracles*, 38). He then disposes of the claims by turning upon them the heavy guns of his radical scepticism; but it is largely because he 'knows' on *a priori* grounds that miracles 'could not' happen after the apostolic age that he does not find sufficient hard evidence for them. For a more balanced account of the witness of the fourth- and fifth-century Fathers, see M.T. Kelsey, *Healing and Christianity* (London: SCM, 1973), ch. 8.

[48]*Free Enquiry*, 120 (as cited in M.P. Hamilton (ed.), *Charismatic Movement*, 78).

[49]In a letter to Middleton (4 January 1749): for details see in Hamilton (ed.), *Charismatic Movement*, 78–9. On the Camisard phenomenon see G.H. Williams and E. Waldvogel, 'A History of Speaking in Tongues and Related Gifts', in Hamilton (ed.), *Charismatic Movement*, 75–80; D. Christie-Murray, *Voices from the Gods: Speaking in Tongues* (London: RKP, 1978), 47–50.

[50]To the list of historical studies in R. Laurentin, *Catholic Pentecostalism* (London: DLT, 1977), 94–6; 213–22, add Williams and Waldvogel, 'History', 61–113; Christie-Murray, *Voices*, chs. 4–5; H. Hunter, 'Tongues-Speech: A Patristic Analysis', *JETS* 23 (1980), 125–37.

at least to the time of Tertullian, Novation (writing AD 240), and possibly to Pachomius (290–346) and Ambrose (339–97).[51] Chrysostom, Augustine and Pope Leo the Great were the first to suggest that tongues had ceased and to attempt a theological rationale (namely that apostolic and later tongues were symbolic of that extension of the church through the nations which was now fulfilled).[52] As for 'prophecy', the word itself has suffered such redefinition (principally in terms of 'preaching') that it will be especially difficult to write a history of the phenomenon.[53] But we shall find some evidence of its continuation (see Ch. 18 and 20).

We have implied that it is not possible to answer the question whether any of the prototypical gifts ceased. All that we can say is that claims to them were made, even if relatively sparsely. From this it may probably be inferred that these gifts were at least less prominent in the later church than at the beginning. What theological significance would such an observation carry? Certainly, if the outright assertion that 'all spectacular gifts ceased with the immediate apostolic circle' could be justified, this might support a cessationist understanding of the gifts. But such a position would require a sharp end to all credible Christian claims to prophecy, tongues and healings by Justin's day. Not a few dispensationalists have attempted to read the patristic evidence that way, but only at some cost to their claim to objectivity.[54] The sharp line is not there; nor anywhere else. And, anyway, the New Testament itself does not encourage the view that these gifts were merely 'signs', or provisional substitutes for the canon.

The only claim that can be made with confidence is that our prototypical gifts gradually became marginalized. But it would be very unwise to give a single and theological reason for this, such as, for example, the alleged sinfulness or dryness of the post-apostolic church.[55] The factors concerned were probably very complex. Prophecy may well have become increasingly peripheral, as Aune suggests, (i) because Christian doctrine, tradition and norms were gradually established and fell within the province of teachers and pastors to administer, and (ii) as, sociologically, the church became more integrated

---

[51]Though Chrysostom was not aware of the phenomenon at Antioch in the same period. See the brief but careful examination by Forbes, *Prophecy*, 75–84.

[52]See G.H. Williams and Waldvogel, 'History', 77–8; Hunter, 'Tongues-Speech', *passim*.

[53]See, e.g. Packer, *Keep In Step*, 229.

[54]See the criticisms of such attempts by Hunter, 'Tongues-Speech', *passim*.

[55]Cf. the reasons offered by the Pentecostal churches for the withdrawal of miraculous gifts, C.F. Williams, *Tongues*, 73–4.

with its environment, and less prone to the dynamics of a millenarian sect. As for incomprehensible 'tongues', they had little built-in survival value, and it is hardly surprising that they became peripheral until they were made the hallmark of Spirit-baptism in early Pentecostalism, and until later culturally and existentially orientated factors could under-gird them in Charismatic circles. Healing of the body soon came to be detached from the gospel proper, by platonizing of the latter, and so became eclipsed, only to re-emerge in the church with an entirely different theological significance (accreditation).

In general, we may echo, at least as a suggestive possibility, the commonplace hypothesis that searching before God for personalized spiritual experiences, including the more spectacular gifts, is characteristically a phenomenon of the church in periods of insecurity, introspection and historical instability, rather than in those of consolidation and self- confidence. In addition, the phenomena sought of God (e.g. in revivalist periods) seem to have been determined to some extent by cultural-theological expectations within the church. So a wide range of cultural, sociological and theological factors may have been at play in the shaping of the expectation, and consequent distribution, of gifts in the church. And the theological significance — or insignificance — of the (temporary) cessation of any one manifestation is almost impossible to assess.

Chapter Seventeen

Tongues Speech Today

The Pentecostal and Charismatic renewal movements have put the issue of contemporary 'tongues' very much on the agenda for study, even if they may rightly feel that what is a *distinctive* mark of their spirituality is not an especially important one.[1] What relationship exists between the glossolalia of the Acts and 1 Corinthians and various types of 'tongues speech' today? As Laurentin laments, the subject is 'a tangled skein', and it takes some effort to unravel it. We will begin with an overview of the contemporary scene (part I), then turn to the relationship between modern tongues speech and New Testament glossolalia (part II).

I. TONGUES SPEECH IN THE CHURCH TODAY

In social sciences the term *glossolalia* is used for a variety of phenomena, found both outside Christianity and within it. The earliest work was in fact done on spiritist glossolalia in the first decade of this century, but research was soon broadened to include not only Pentecostal tongues, but also other related types of utterance.[2] Early attempts to classify the different types of glossolalia include the important distinctions made by Lombard between ascending levels of linguistic 'competence', starting with so-called *phonations frustres* (rough sounds, inarticulate cries, murmurs or stutterings), then moving to 'pseudo-language' (sounds simulating a discourse, but with no evident correspondence of sounds to groups of ideas), and finally, at the highest level, various forms of xenoglossia (speaking of foreign languages).[3] L.C. May was later (1956)

---

[1] See, e.g., Laurentin, *Pentecostalism*, 60.

[2] The magisterial work on the whole topic is that by H.N. Malony and A.A. Lovekin, *Glossolalia: Behavioural Science Perspectives on Speaking in Tongues*, (Oxford: OUP, 1985). On early studies of spiritist tongues, see 13–16 (and see on May, below).

[3] E. Lombard, *Glossolalie*. For an overview of his position see Malony and Lovekin, *Glossolalia*, 16–19.

to develop a six-fold taxonomy to account for parallel shamanistic utterances. He distinguished (i) the language of spirits, (ii) sacerdotal languages, (iii) language of animals, (iv) *phonations frustres*, (v) xenoglossia, and (vi) interpretations of tongues.[4] We are not sure how useful these typologies are for the discussion at hand, though they are helpful in reminding us that when we speak of glossolalia we may be referring to a number of quite distinct phenomena. We propose instead to begin with two definitions which we adopt (with modification) from Vern Poythress.[5] The first, 'free vocalization', is the more generic; the second, 'tongues speech', is more specific to religious contexts:

(a) 'free vocalization' is a term used to denote the production of connected sequences of speech sounds, not identified by speakers as a language known to them, lexically opaque to them, not capable of being repeated by them (except in very small snatches), and which sounds to an average hearer like an unknown language. We may now more narrowly circumscribe the area of our interest (to exclude baby-talk, pseudo-languages used on the stage, etc.) by defining Tongues Speech.

(b) 'tongues speech' is 'free vocalization' for religious purposes by one competent in his native tongue.[6] It will be clear that this definition excludes some Christian glossolalic phenomena, especially of the type that Lombard and May would have categorized as *phonations frustres*, 'rough' sounds or the repetitive use of just a few syllables, etc.

What is today's 'tongues speech', and how does the practice of it in the church relate to the phenomenon of *glōssais lalein* in the New Testament? Modern glossolalia of various types, and Christian 'tongues speech' in particular, have been subject to widespread research.[7] With

---

[4]L.C. May, 'A Survey of Glossolalia and Related Phenomena in Non-Christian Religions', *American Anthropologist* 58 (1956), 75–96, reprinted in W.E. Mills (ed.), *Speaking in Tongues: A Guide to Research on Glossolalia* (Grand Rapids: Eerdmans, 1986), 53–82. For review, see Malony and Lovekin, *Glossolalia*, 19–21.
[5]V.S. Poythress, 'Linguistic and Sociological Analyses of Modern Tongues-Speaking: Their Contributions and Limitations', *WTJ* 42 (1980), 367–88 (esp. 369–70).
[6]Poythress includes in his definition the criterion that the speaker be a Christian — but this makes a useful term inapplicable to the closely related phenomena in other religious circles. In practice we shall only be discussing 'tongues speech' amongst Christians, but we desire to leave the definition more open.
[7]The best brief summary account is in C.G. Williams, *Tongues*; but the standard work is Malony and Lovekin, *Glossolalia*.

respect to Christian 'tongues speech' we may offer the following brief summary of contemporary conclusions:

(1) Contrary to earlier claims, there is no evidence that 'tongues speech' is correlated with low intellect, education, social position or pathological psychology. The distribution figures are normal with respect to psychological types.[8] Early studies to the contrary by Cutten, Thomas, etc.[9] — widely quoted as authoritative in anti-charismatic circles — were based on studies made of psychotic patients in mental institutions, and even (in Thomas' case) of counsellees in a suicide prevention clinic.[10] Who is now surprised that glossolalia examined at such centres was heavily correlated with disturbed psychology? Similarly, attempts to correlate glossolalia in its various forms with hypnotic suggestibility, mass contagion, and low ego controls, seem largely to be 'the function of prejudgements and bias on the part of researchers or of attempts to discount deviant religious expressions'.[11]

(2) Psychologically, 'tongues speech' is not the product of what is usually meant by 'ecstasy' (though it may attend it[12]). Leading charismatics with the facility of 'tongues speech' claim they can start and stop at will; usually, again, without any acknowledged loss of awareness of surroundings, or even, necessarily, loss of concentration on some other activity (reading a book;

---

[8]Compare E.M. Pattison, 'Behavioural Science Research on the Nature of Glossolalia', *JASA* 20 (1968), 76, and J.P. Kildahl, 'Psychological Observations', in M.P. Hamilton (ed.), *Charismatic Movement*, 124–42, with the more positive appraisals of C.G. Williams, *Tongues*, 126–35: Malony and Lovekin, *Glossolalia*, chs. 3–5; *idem*, 'Debunking Some of the Myths About Glossolalia', in C.M. Robeck (ed.), *Experiences*, 102–10, and S.E. Gritzmacher, B. Bolton, and R.H. Dana, 'Psychological Characteristics of Pentecostals: A Literature Review and Psychodynamic Synthesis', *Journal of Psychology and Theology* 16 (1988), 233–45.
[9]G.B. Cutten, *Speaking with Tongues: Historically and Psychologically Considered*, (New Haven: Yale UP, 1927); K. Thomas, 'Speaking in Tongues', unpublished paper, Berlin Suicide Prevention Centre, 1965.
[10]Cf. C.G. Williams, *Tongues*, 126–7.
[11]Malony and Lovekin, *Glossolalia*, 93.
[12]See Ch. 12, II, §1 and Ch.13, III, §2 above. Cf. Hollenweger's distinction between 'hot' tongues (ecstatic, if not 'outside oneself') and 'cool' tongues (with no more hint of ecstasy than one would associate with a foreign language heard on the radio: *Pentecostals*, 344).

driving a car, etc.).[13] This claim appears now clearly to be borne out by detailed studies.[14]

> Felicitas Goodman provided the strongest case for the view that glossolalia is associated with some level of trance. To be more precise, she argued there is a common linguistic pattern of glossolalic utterance, across seven quite different cultural contexts, and even amongst people with four different native languages. Every pulse (smallest sound unit) begins with a consonant, there are no initial consonant *clusters*, the pulse is nearly always open (does not end in a consonant), bars (groups of pulses separated by pauses) are usually of equal duration, primary stress falls on the first pulse of each bar, and decays at the end, etc.[15] This cross-cultural and cross-linguistic constancy, she argued, which was not a natural feature of e.g. the English or Spanish normally spoken, was best explained if glossolalia was itself a bodily reflex to a particular kind of mental state. Her field work thus (in her opinion) confirmed her hypothesis that, '*the glossolalist speaks the way he does because his speech behaviour is modified by the way the body acts in the particular mental state, often termed trance, into which he places himself.* In other words . . . the glossolalia utterance [is] an artifact of a hyperaroused mental state . . . the surface structure of a non-linguistic deep structure, that of the altered state of consciousness'.[16] She sees this latter state as induced by e.g. rhythmic singing, hand-clapping, ejaculative acclamations and invocations, etc.[17] But extensive physiological tests designed by G. Palmer to investigate previous claims that glossolalia was ecstatic have produced an overwhelmingly negative verdict: skin-conductivity, EEG patterns, blood-pressure and heart rate tests taken during glossolalic utterance were virtually the same as those of control groups, or of the same groups praying in English.[18] Similarly, Spanos and Hewitt tested the level of consciousness of surroundings and ability to perform mental tasks during glossolalia, and concluded that the glossolalist was as receptive to external information, and as able to

---

[13]Kilian McDonnell states, 'There would be almost universal rejection on the part of all Pentecostals and charismatics of the position that tongues is usually spoken in an ecstatic state or that it represents a product of trance' (as quoted by Malony and Lovekin, *Glossolalia*, 105: the quote is from K. McDonnell, *Charismatic Renewal and the Churches* (New York: Seabury, 1976), 82).

[14]Cf. C.G. Williams, *Tongues*, 135–46.

[15]For the linguistic/phonetic traits of glossolalic utterances she analysed see F. Goodman, *Speaking in Tongues: A Cross-Cultural Study of Glossolalia* (London: University of Chicago Press, 1972), 121–2.

[16]*Ibid.*, 8.

[17]*Ibid.*, 60, 74–9, 90–2.

[18]G. Palmer, 'Trance and dissociation: A cross-cultural study in psychophysiology', unpublished Master's thesis, University of Minesota 1966.

process it and react to it during bouts of glossolalia, as (e.g.) when he or she was reading aloud a short story in English.[19] All this means that while 'tongues speech' *can* accompany trance, it certainly does *not require* any significant altered state of consciousness or dissociation (beyond that involved, e.g., in driving a car while thinking about what to have for tea). W.J. Samarin was able to account for the alleged linguistic similarities in the phonetic and intonational patterns on the grounds that some of the features were widespread to speech, others were indigenous to the Pentecostal sub-culture, yet others were to be accounted for as common to the anomalous form of speech involved in the production of linguistic utterances that do not make sense to the individual (e.g. amongst secular graduate students attempting to 'free vocalize' within Samarin's experiments[20]).

(3) In form, most 'tongues speech' is not xenolalia (real 'foreign' languages[21]). When 'tongues speech' broke out at the beginning of the Pentecostal movement, virtually all involved thought it was the gift of foreign languages granted for evangelistic purposes, and Charles Parham continued to believe this view till his death in 1929, despite mounting counter-evidence:[22]

(i)   Some claims to recognized xenolalia have been made this century, but most of them are ill- documented, often at second-or third-hand, and the languages prove to have been 'recognized' by people who were not competent speakers of the tongue in question, and who merely thought they recognized some words.

      For example, Harold Bredesen claimed his tongues speech had been identified by hearers as Polish and (on a different occasion) as Coptic Egyptian, but when samples of it were submitted to linguists this was not confirmed.[23] Samarin

---

[19]N.P. Spanos and E.C. Hewitt, 'Glossolalia: Test of the trance and psychopathology hypotheses', *Journal of Abnormal Psychology* 88 (1979), 427–34.
[20]See Malony and Lovekin, *Glossolalia*, 105–9, for a review of the ongoing debate between Goodman and Samarin.
[21]See C.G. Williams (*Tongues*, ch. 8) and Malony and Lovekin (*Glossolalia*, ch. 2) for the best short summaries W.J. Samarin, *Tongues of Men and Angels: The Religious Language of Pentecostalism* (London: Collier-Macmillan, 1972), chs. 4–6, for a more detailed discussion (which, nevertheless, is updated by Malony and Lovekin).
[22]See J.R. Goff, 'Initial Tongues in the Theology of Charles Fox Parham', in G.B. McGee (ed.), *Evidence*, 57–71; and, in the same volume, C.M. Robeck, 'William J. Seymour and "the Bible Evidence" ', 72–95.

playfully draws an analogy with Poe's story, 'The Murders in Rue Morgue'. The witnesses have each heard the 'murderer's' cry, but it 'sounds like' Spanish to the Frenchman, French to the Irishman, German to an English-man, English to a Spaniard, etc. but the real culprit is dis-covered to be an orang-utan.[24]

In none of the numerous examples of taped 'tongues speech' of known pedigree submitted to competent linguis-tic analysis has there yet been any occasion of recognized xenolalia.[25] This is not to say there have not been a number of what sound like reliable testimonies of recognized xenolalia where the documentation of the incident, and reliability of those testifying, is such that it makes the claims believable.[26] But even these do not meet the very rigorous criteria required before a case of xenolalia would be said to be scientifically proven (viz. a good tape-record-ing of considerable length; living authorities recognizing the language; full documentation of the speaker's history to exclude earlier subconscious contact with the language, etc.)[27]. And such cases of possible xenolalia are very rare.

(ii) Of the many tapes of 'tongues speech' submitted for analysis, few if any have been recognized as demonstrating the linguistic structure, or grammar, of human languages. What is more, the frequency of repetition of consonants

---

[23]See Malony and Lovekin, *Glossolalia*, 28 (and cf. Christie-Murray, *Voices*, 248–52); and for another example of two Englishmen who claimed to speak in Temne (a language spoken in Sierra Leone), but whose claim was subsequently rejected by native speakers, see *Glossolalia*, 29.

[24]Samarin, *Tongues*, 114–15, and reused by Laurentin, *Pentecostalism*, 67.

[25]The best attested examples of xenolalia are thus perhaps those from outside the Christian movement (for examples in spiritist circles: see Christie-Murray, *Voices*, ch. 19; Malony and Lovekin, *Glossolalia*, 28–9).

[26]With Poloma, *Charismatic Movement*, 65. For documentation see, e.g., Laurentin, *Pentecostalism*, 67–70; C.G. Williams, *Tongues*, 180–3; Poythress, 'Analyses', 374 n.17; Malony and Lovekin, *Glossolalia*, 26–9.

[27]One of my BA students, J. Modha, then a recent convert from Hinduism, reports an incident that was important to him, which took place at Millmead Baptist church, Guildford. An English person behind him, speaking in tongues, repeatedly uttered the words, 'Peace be with you, peace be upon you' in Modha's native tongue. But as only one or two lexemes were concerned (*Gujurati*), such an incident could no doubt be explained away as 'coincidence'. A longer discourse in tongues, recognized as a foreign language, would be necessary to convince a more sceptical inquiry that *xenolalia* had taken place.

seems usually (not always) to be that of the speaker's native language, and the vowels to be the open vowels of his or her vernacular. In other words, according to W.J. Samarin, the pioneer of serious linguistic research of 'tongues speech', the samples prove to be 'strings of syllables, made up of sounds taken from among all those that the speaker knows, put together more or less haphazardly'.[28] This verdict perhaps oversimplifies. There is some contrary evidence: thus, (a) Goodman's own evidence (that the glossolalic sounds were not like the speaker's own delivery of their native languages) could be taken to support the view that the 'tongues speech' was some other type of language, and (b) some glossolalists appear to be able to produce different types of tongue, one or other (or both) of them more closely related to other known languages in their phonetic structure than to their native language.[29] But, once again, linguists are fairly confident that given an adequate portion of 'tongues speech' they could reach a verdict on *whether* it was a language (even if they could not identify it). Dr Peter Cotterell (a fellow of the Institute of Linguists) indicated in a personal interview that it should take a competent linguist little more than perhaps twenty minutes to decide whether there was sufficient evidence of linguistic structure. And yet the taped examples have not provided clear cases of such.

Not surprisingly, many Charismatic leaders have acknowledged that the evidence at present is against the view that tongues are usually miracles of xenolalia (whether human languages, past or present, or those of heaven); especially as it is clear that 'free vocalization' can be a learned phenomenon inside and outside of Christian — even of religious — settings. They tend instead to elucidate it as a natural phenomenon which simply becomes a spiritual gift when orientated towards the Lord, in a way similar to that in which speech in the vernacular can become a spiritual gift.[30]

(4) Functionally, 'tongues speech' can convey meaning: even the

---

[28]Samarin, *Tongues*, 81.

[29]For the more positive evidence, see Malony and Lovekin, *Glossolalia*, 34–8.

[30]E.g. H. Mühlen, *A Charismatic Theology* (London: Burns and Oates, 1978), 152–6; F.A. Sullivan, *Charisms*, 143–4; Laurentin, *Pentecostalism*, 93–4.

more hostile analyses admit that 'tongues speech' conveys meaning in its prosodic contour (metre, stress, intonation, etc.) and one can distinguish pleading, grieving, thanking, praising 'tongues speech', etc. Just how much more information is being precognitively coded in the 'tongues speech', however, is beyond direct scrutiny. But that 'tongues speech' is not usually human language does not require that it cannot *function* as language.[31] So it would be possible to suggest that in 'tongues speech' the Spirit interacts with people at the subconscious level (cf. Paul's 'my spirit prays') and communication is 'encoded' non-lexically through the otherwise natural mechanism of 'free vocalization'.[32] C.S. Lewis approached this sort of account of tongues when he analysed it in terms of what he called 'transposition', in which a richer system may come fully to expression within a poorer one, just as a whole orchestral piece might be represented (for one who knew the fuller reality) on a piano, or a three- dimensional reality in a two-dimensional drawing.[33] This perception clarified the possibility that even a 'learned behaviour' or a form of utterance initially psychologically induced might (in God's grace, and when directed to him in a doxology of love) *become* a 'supernatural' divine gift (even if not a 'miraculous' one), in the same fashion as a person's natural teaching gifts may become on occasion the spiritual gift of powerful preaching that 'brings all heaven down' to listeners.[34]

(5) Beyond conveying meaning (in the sense of message), the Christian may well claim his 'tongues speech' has functioned to deepen his relationship with, and worship of, the Lord; has made him more aware of the indwelling christocentric Spirit, and so has led, in turn, to fuller dedication. Such claims could easily be true even were the tongues itself simultaneously (if reductionistically) 'explicable' to others on a naturalistic basis. For any one individual, renewing experiences of God may become closely linked

---

[31]Poythress, 'Analyses', 374–5; Carson, *Showing the Spirit*, 85–7.

[32]Some writers from within the Charismatic movement no longer appear to assume that semantic content is encoded, only mood: cf. Sullivan, *Charisms*, ch. 8, esp. 133–4.

[33]C.S. Lewis, *Transposition and Other Addresses* (London: Bles, 1949), 9–20.

[34]Various anti-Charismatic writers too readily assume that a psychological explanation itself disproves the claim tongues is a spiritual gift: cf. A.A. Hoekema, *What About Speaking in Tongues?* (Grand Rapids: Eerdmans, 1966), 132; MacArthur, *Charismatic Chaos*, 176; Budgen, *Charismatics*, ch.4.

with 'tongues speech': occasions of the latter may become 'moments' of a renewed faith that God is at work in her life and hears even the Spirit's unutterable groans through her (cf. Rom. 8:26,27).[35] These 'sighs too deep for words' may become what Käsemann called 'the cry for liberty',[36] and then the cry of joy.[37]

(6) Putting the last two approaches together, Malony and Lovekin have developed Lewis' portrayal of glossolalia in terms of transposition by drawing on Troeltsch's analysis of glossolalia, and the practice of other 'spiritual gifts'.[38] He saw these as evidence of a third type of religious grouping alongside the Weberian categories of 'church' and 'sect', which he called 'mysticism'. Its essence is the pursuit of meaning and vitality through *contact* with the divine; the search for renewal, even within the available religious structures, through the *experience* of the transcendent. It is in this context that most Pentecostals and charismatics would probably wish to place their 'tongues speech'. For earlier Pentecostal writers, such as Donald Gee and Carl Brumback, tongues was significant especially as an immediate experience of God's presence.[39] For them this was not merely a formal deduction from what seemed to them necessarily to be a miraculous gift. They evaluated tongues this way because both initial and subsequent moments of tongues speech were so often combined with a direct sense of numinous encounter. Tongues thus verged on the theophanic and mystical.[40]

(7) While most research on tongues has focused on the individual speakers' experiences of this, we need perhaps to remember that early Pentecostalism valued the gift as much, if not more,

---

[35]Poythress, 'Analyses', 377–80.

[36]Käsemann, *Perspectives*, 122–37; cf. the subtle treatment in Theissen, *Aspects*, 315–20, 332–41.

[37]Cf. the subtle and suggestive analysis of F.D. Macchia, 'Sighs', 47–73. For a recent theological (but not critical) appraisal of the place of tongues in spirituality, see J.R. Williams, *Renewal Theology: Salvation, the Holy Spirit, and Christian Living* (Grand Rapids: Zondervan, 1990), ch. 9, esp. part V.

[38]See Malony and Lovekin, *Glossolalia*, ch. 14.

[39]See D. Gee's address to the World Pentecostal conference 1952 (as reported by Macchia, 'Sighs', 49) and C. Brumback, *What Meaneth This? A Pentecostal Answer to a Pentecostal Question* (Springfield: Gospel Publishing, 1947), 131.

[40]Cf. the description of tongues as a 'mysticism of sound' (C.G. Williams, *Tongues*). W. Mills too sees the essence of glossolalia in the New Testament as a visible sign of the Spirit's dynamic presence, even if it was only one such sign, and not a form liable to be helpful to many believers today, who, he thinks, will need to find other forms as symbols of God's presence (so *Approach*, ch. 5, esp. 118–26).

for its congregational contribution. Here we may note two different uses. (a) One relatively widespread practice during worship, usually on occasions when the congregation senses some
special 'presence' of God in grace, is a corporate response of
harmonic singing in tongues. On these occasions the tongues
(which usually last from less than thirty seconds to a maximum
of two or three minutes) are not interpreted; but are understood
as free inspired doxology. There is no direct precedent for this
in the New Testament, though we could find such in the invasive charismatic praise of the Old Testament and in Judaism
(see Ch. 1, part II, §1 above). Some criticize the phenomenon as
a breach of Paul's instructions in 1 Corinthians 14:27,28 (cf.
v.23), but those instructions pertain more specifically for the
second kind of use.[41] (b) Individuals may feel a strong impulse
to address a period of tongues to God or to the congregation
(e.g. at times of congregational waiting on God, within the worship), with the understanding that this is a divine prompting,
and that the resulting utterance will be interpreted (in line with
Paul's advice in 1 Cor. 14:13,27,28). Tongues, followed by interpretation, function like prophecy within the congregation (see
Ch. 18, below). From the point of view of the spiritual benefit
conveyed, however, the emphasis perhaps falls more on the
interpretive moment (cf. 1 Cor 14:4,5,13). But this does not
render the tongues otiose. In the dynamic of the congregation's
meeting, they function as a herald of the divine presence and of
the Lord's intention to address the congregation, and so raise
expectation and increase dependence on God for the interpretive phase of this charismatic partnership.[42] In both kinds of use
of congregational tongues, the glossolalia functions as a relatively powerful symbol of God's immediate presence, marking
both humanity's remaining 'distance' from God (that God
speaks in words that cannot themselves be understood is a
mark of humankind's fundamental alienation) and, simul-

---

[41]Paul's limitations in 14:23, 27,28 protect against the domination of the assembly by pneumatics flaunting their tongues; they do not pertain to brief moments
of corporate doxology.
[42]Compare Samarin's suggestion (made in a slightly different context) that tongues says, 'God is here', in the way a Gothic cathedral says, 'God is majestic':
Tongues, 154, 232 (taken up by Macchia, 'Sighs', 53). M.B. McGuire's sociological study has put this on a firmer basis: see 'The Social Context of Prophecy:
"Word-Gifts" of the Spirit among Catholic Pentecostals', *Review of Religious
Research* 18 (1977), 134–47.

taneously, God's redemptive grace (because he makes himself present to speak to his people, he gives understanding of the tongue, and because tongues are themselves understood as a sign of eschatological renewal[43]).

II. TONGUES SPEECH AND NEW TESTAMENT GLOSSOLALIA

How then does all this tie in with the New Testament? It is certainly a far cry from the evangelistically orientated sign on the day of Pentecost, and on that basis Edgar and Packer (*inter alios*) have said modern tongues are not the same phenomenon as we discern in the New Testament. But, as we have argued, the whole interpretation of New Testament tongues is at fault. Pentecost was rather the exception than the rule in the New Testament — and, as such, it could be paralleled by some of the exceptional cases of recognized xenolalia reported this century. But, we noted, neither Luke nor Paul elsewhere presents tongues as an evangelistic sign-gift; that interpretation of 1 Corinthians 14:22,23 completely misreads Paul's irony. On the whole (*contra* Edgar, we argued) Paul considers 'tongues speech' a gift mainly (but not exclusively) for private worship — and what Luke has to say elsewhere in Acts is also tolerant of this view. Here the New Testament understanding matches the present-day phenomenon. Where tongues and interpretation are in evidence as features of contemporary *congregational* worship, the relationship to what is envisaged in 1 Corinthians 14 appears at first sight even more transparent (though we have yet to establish appropriate criteria for testing the validity of 'interpretations' in the modern context[44]).

But there are still problems involved in identifying the New Testament phenomenon with today's 'tongues speech'. Paul's language more naturally suggests he was thinking of xenolalia. And one may feel this is enough to justify the view that what Paul denotes, and 'tongues speech' today, are in the final analysis different phenomena. However, caution is required. It would have been virtually impossible for Paul to

---

[43]See Macchia, 'Sighs', 55–60.

[44]In one investigation of which I am aware, tape-recorded glossolalic utterances were submitted for 'interpretation' by a variety of practitioners, and mixed among them were control samples of Arabic and the Australian national anthem spoken backwards (!). The interpretations given were mutually contradictory, and bore no correlation to the known content of the control samples. But a test undertaken within the dynamic of a church, and with warning that non-glossolalic controls had been introduced, might have been more appropriate and searching.

distinguish xenolalic 'tongues speech' from non-xenolalic 'tongues speech' performing a similar function — so he could well simply have lumped together, phenomenologically, what we would regard as two distinct types of 'tongues speech'. Alternatively, his rather enigmatic *genē glōssōn* ('(different) kinds of tongues') could include not only xenolalia and angelic speech, but also 'tongues speech' of the type highlighted by modern research. There is certainly no room for the dogmatism that today's glossolalia are not the same phenomena as Paul knew.

Even if Paul were speaking about a different manifestation, that would not necessarily mean that 'tongues speech' today is less of a 'spiritual gift'. As we have suggested above, following Lewis, Poythress and Malony and Lovekin, the question is ultimately one of whether modern 'tongues speech' functions in a doxological, christocentric, faith-supporting (e.g. personality-integrating, cohesive, anxiety-minimizing) and up-building way — perhaps along merely parallel lines with Paul's *glōssais lalein*. Here the testimony of those who claim the gift — and of a number of the more recent specialist psychiatric investigations — is that it does (and, indeed, like the Corinthian phenomenon, that it can be subject to misuse too[45]). But there remains much room for further empirical research in this area.

---

[45]See C.G. Williams, *Tongues*, ch. 7 (esp. 163); Malony, 'Debunking', 107–8, and Malony and Lovekin, *Glossolalia*, 10–12. For a positive appraisal of the religious function of tongues speech, see Laurentin, *Pentecosalism*, 79–82, and note Samarin, *Tongues*, chs. 7–10.

Chapter Eighteen

Prophecy Today

I. INTRODUCTION

Pentecostalism and the Charismatic renewal movements have thrust the question of 'prophecy' onto the agenda for lively church debate.[1] Surprisingly, there are no comprehensive critical discussions of prophecy in the modern church. The phenomenon of Christian 'oracular speech' — the rendering of a message considered by a believer to have been imparted to him or to her directly by the Spirit in (e.g.) a 'word' or vision — has not generated anything like the serious academic interest and field research invested in 'tongues'. A significant start has, however, been made by Mark J. Cartledge in a recent MPhil dissertation, and in subsequent articles.[2] We shall use his findings, along with other observations, as the basis for comparing the New Testament understanding of prophecy with that in the various Pentecostal and Charismatic Renewal movements today.

1. Sources

The descriptions of contemporary phenomena which follow are based on three different kinds of sources: (i) we have available a large number of popular and semi-popular works with anecdotal accounts of prophetic experiences (both first-hand and second-hand, and from sources of varying reliability). (ii) From time to time journals such as

---

[1] For a rapid overview of 'prophecy' in church history, written at the popular/semi-popular level, see D. Pytches, *Prophecy in the Local Church* (London: Hodder, 1993), chs. 14–20 (with bibliographies).

[2] M.J. Cartledge, 'Prophecy in the Contemporary Church: A Theological Examination', unpublished MPhil dissertation, Oak Hill, 1989; *idem*, 'Charismatic Prophecy and New Testament Prophecy', *Themelios* 17 (1991), 17–20; *idem*, 'Charismatic Prophecy: A Definition and Description', *JPT* 5 (1994), 79–120; *idem*, 'Charismatic Prophecy', *JET* 8 (1995), 71–88. I am grateful to the author for supplying me with several of these articles.

Prophecy Today publish approved prophetic 'words'. Here, at least, there can be no doubt about the *content* (wording) of the messages concerned. (iii) Finally, we have Cartledge's own field research amongst Anglicans in the diocese of London. This was based on a sample of 34 people who claimed prophetic experiences, all drawn from some nine Anglican churches. The study was conducted by questionnaire and interview.[3] Such direct field research is, of course, of great value for assessing the kinds of claims made in the (more dogmatically interested) literature.

II. SIMILARITIES BETWEEN NEW TESTAMENT PROPHECY AND CONTEMPORARY PROPHECY

There are obvious complicating factors in making such an analysis. There are differences between the type of utterances one regularly hears during 'ordinary' congregational worship, and the (usually much more specific) prophecies of those more widely regarded by Charismatic and Pentecostal communities as 'prophets'. Then again, there are differences of style, focus and content within the latter group between, say, the rather more nationally (and internationally) orientated prophecy of Clifford Hill, and the more personal and ecclesial prophecies of the Kansas City Prophets.[4] Despite these diversities, modern prophecy roughly coheres with New Testament patterns at the following points:

(1) *The understanding of prophecy is that it is oracular speech based on a perceptible revelatory event or impulse.* The oracular nature of the speech-event is usually marked by some standard formula such as 'The Lord says . . .' or the like, followed either by direct or (more rarely) indirect speech understood as expressing the content of the oracle, or by description of a visionary phenomenon.

    The revelatory event or impulse in question may take the form (*inter alia*) of (a) a picture' (a mental impression, whether static or cinematic); (b) a dream or vision (the latter term being used for a more pronounced 'sighting' than a mere 'picture'); (c) a 'word' (whether a single word, or clause, or short message); (d) a reception of a 'package' of knowledge concerning some person or event (e.g. through a mixture of the above); (e) Scripture verses coming

---

[3]For details, see *JET* 8 (1995), 77–8; 'Prophecy' (1989), 84–92 (the questionnaires and analysis are included in the Appendices, 208–222).

[4]This generalization is a crude one, and should not be permitted to give the impression there is not considerable overlap.

to mind (e.g. with some compelling intensity); (f) physical sensations (e.g. a pain, or grief, that the person believes is not her own, but pertains to another); (g) a simple and growing compulsion or impulse to speak (or write) without any known 'content', etc.[5] These various revelatory events or 'impulses' come with a parallel conviction that they originate with the Lord, and that they are to be passed on. They may be experienced either immediately prior to the utterance of the prophecy, shortly before it, or (with the exception of (g)) even days, weeks or months before it. In comparing with intertestamental Judaism and the New Testament, one immediately recognizes types (b) and (c) as standard forms of non-invasive prophecy,[6] and (g) as invasive prophecy.[7] The other types ((a), (d), (e) and even, possibly, (f)) appear to be forms related in different ways to (b) or (c).

In answering questions concerning the 'clarity' with which the revelation comes, the range of answers is from relatively indistinct 'pictures' or silent 'words' to what seem to the recipients to have been like quite audible voices (sufficient to make the person concerned turn about seeking the speaker), or strikingly 'objective' and tangible visions. But two other aspects concerning the 'clarity' of the revelatory event require mention: (i) a number report the phenomenon that while what is 'received' may itself be 'clear' in the sense of 'sharply perceived', the picture or word is so fragmentary that its *significance* is at that stage minimal. Some would claim the initial revelatory event occasionally provides such incomplete information that they per-

---

[5]For this typology I roughly follow Cartledge, *JET* (1995), 80–2, whose analysis is based on his field research. These may be compared with what others describe in the literature on the subject (for which see Cartledge, *JPT* (1994), 82–6). The variety of ways in which the initial revelatory impulse comes to the recipient indicates the close relationship between 'prophecy' and such other gifts as 'words of wisdom', 'words of knowledge', interpretation of tongues; discernment of spirits, etc. (a point well made by Cartledge, *JPT* (1994) 88–98).

[6]The use of Joel 2:28 in Acts 2:17b almost marks reception of revelation in dreams and visions as paradigmatic, while Luke 3:2 echoes other Old Testament formulae in saying that the '(a) word of God' came to John in the wilderness (not, it would appear, a message or specific oracle he immediately gave). As we have seen, the prophecies of 1 Cor. 14:26, 29–32 appear to be of the non-invasive type (as too Agabus' oracles: Acts 11:27,28 and 21:11 — the implication being that he travelled in order to deliver them, though that is not certain).

[7]For examples of invasive prophecy (that are not merely invasive charismatic praise), cf. Lk. 1:41, 67.

ceive the need (and call) to pray for further clarificatory detail or interpretive understanding before they can take the matter further. (ii) The recipient has then usually further to determine when and how the matter should be related.

> For example, Dr. Clifford Hill reports an occasion when, in Jerusalem, he was awoken early in the morning of Friday with the words 'Danger! Beware Monday 16th April'. Thinking it concerned his family, he prayed and received the further clarification, 'There will be an attack launched against Israel by Syria on Monday 16th April, and you must warn the nation'. He then had the problem of ascertaining the appropriate person to communicate it to, etc.[8]

In the sampling taken by Cartledge (both from field research and from literary sources), most of those prophesying presented their final 'message' with an introductory, 'Thus says the Lord' or 'My children' (or the like) and in direct speech.[9] This may, however, represent the speaker's choice of rhetorical form and his or her understanding of 'prophetic convention' rather than having been part of the revelatory 'event' — especially if the latter were visual rather than in words. Earlier in the history of the twentieth-century prophetic movements prophecies were regularly given in the archaic language of the King James Version, but this was recognized as the speaker's linguistic choice, rather than integral to the prophecy itself, and teachers began to discourage it.[10] Similarly, others such as Bickle and Grudem (for different reasons) discourage the use of 'Thus says the Lord', and first person address in contemporary prophecy,[11] and there

---

[8]He goes on to record how the circumstances unfolded allowing him to pass on the warning, and that the danger was subsequently verified by Israeli intelligence discovery of mass Syrian army deployment pending a probable surprise strike over Passover (the Monday). For the details of the account and the outcome, see C. Hill, . . . *And They Shall Prophesy: A New Prophetic Movement in the Church Today* (London: Marshall Pickering, 1990), 29–34. For similar occasions, see 38–39, 61–71; also M. Bickle (with M. Sullivant), *Growing in the Prophetic* (Eastbourne: Kingsway, 1995), 194–98 and 200–203.

[9]See the claims by D. Atkinson, *Prophecy* (Bramcote: Grove Books, 1977), 3; Cartledge, *JPT* 5 (1994) 89 and 108–114.

[10]Cf. B. Yocum, *Prophecy: Exercising the Prophetic Gifts of the Spirit in the Church Today* (Ann Arbor: Servant Books, 1976), 81–3; Grudem, *Prophecy*, 164–5; Bickle, *Growing*, 115–17.

[11]See Grudem, *Prophecy*, 167–8 (who thinks such style is appropriate to canonical prophets and NT apostles alone); Bickle, *Growing*, 116 (who thinks it should be used by the experienced or when the 'prophecy' has been received with exceptional clarity or power).

is a corresponding growth in the use of indirect or other 'distancing' forms of speech (e.g. description of how the 'message' came, with corresponding 'application' for the target audience).

(2) Usually *the psychological condition of the one uttering prophecy varies from the 'normal' state to that of mild dissociation*: i.e. the one concerned may experience a rising 'prompting' to speak (often attributed to the oncoming of an 'anointing of the Spirit'), and this may be attended by the physiological effects of mild excitement or nervousness (e.g. slightly faster and stronger pulse, tremor). Occasionally this approaches 'controlled trance' state; but such is unusual within the western and middle-class culture of the Charismatic renewal movements. The psychological condition at the (earlier) moment(s) of revelation is regularly that normal to the recipient's usual state in (e.g.) prayer or meditation, or Christian counselling, or that of whatever varied circumstance happens to be the occasion into which the revelation intrudes. There is, in other words, no special psychological state conducive to such reception, which sometimes occurs at quite unexpected moments and in entirely secular situations.

> For example, John Wimber reports an occasion when, relaxing and looking casually round the plane cabin, he was arrested by 'seeing' the word 'adultery' written across a passenger's face. He then received the name of the other party involved, and the warning the man would not live if he did not repent. (This disclosure of his sin came as a bombshell to the man concerned, and led to his conversion).[12]

(3) *The content of prophetic pronouncements is rarely if ever primarily doctrinal: rather, they are particularistic and contingent.* Prophecies in the Pentecostal and Charismatic movements thus tend to provide contemporary parallels to biblical (and more general near-Eastern and hellenistic) prophetic utterances. That is, they are functional equivalents of (*inter alia*):

  (i)   oracles of assurance (the majority of the 'I am with my people . . .' type).

  (ii) prescriptive oracles (advising particular individuals, teams, congregations, denominations, etc., on such issues as how to relate to specific circumstances of encroaching sin, whether to make overtures to another church group in matters of oversight or some other joint venture, directing mis-

---

[12]See J. Wimber, *Power Evangelism* (London: Hodder, 1985), 44–6.

sion, even (e.g.) whether to go ahead with a church building,[13] etc.).

(iii) oracles of judgement and/or of salvation (e.g. warning of
the danger of specific judgement in relation to either personal or corporate sin, often accompanied with a promise
of the alternative of blessing on repentance.[14] These types
of oracles are expected only from people with regular and
tested 'ministries' of prophecy).

(iv) legitimation oracles and personalized predictive oracles
(i.e. 'words' addressed to particular leaders or other individuals announcing God's calling of them to some
specific role/ministry, and/or warning them of particular
difficulties to be faced ahead, etc. These were relatively
rare, but became a feature amongst the Kansas City
Prophets[15]).

In other words, the modern charisma of prophecy seems to
operate chiefly within the area which is not directly the focus of
Scripture, and where specific knowledge or guidance may be
required.[16]

(4) *Modern congregational prophecy (as opposed to that of the more
specialized 'prophets') is especially seen to fulfil the role expressed
in 1 Corinthians 14:3* of encouragement, strengthening and ex-

---

[13]See the example of this type offered by D. McBain, *Eyes That See* (Basingstoke: Marshall, 1981), 98 (and cited by Cartledge, *JPT* (1994), 112).

[14]Cf. the prophecy concerning the Anglican communion delivered by Tony Higton in Canterbury Cathedral (1978), and that of Patricia Higton (warning against inter-faith developments) in the same place, ten years later: both published in C. Hill *et al.*, *Blessing the Church?* (Guildford: Eagle, 1995), 16–18.

[15]For a popular commendatory introduction to the Kansas City Prophets, see e.g., D. Pytches, *Some Say It Thundered*, (London: Hodder, 1990). For a view from within the circle (albeit at points critical), see Bickle, *Growing*. For critical reaction to the circle, see Hill, *They Shall Prophesy*; Hill *et al.*, *Blessing*.

[16]Clifford Hill has accused Paul Cain (at least by implication) of prophetic support for some entirely dubious Latter Rain teachings (such as the rise of a generation of dread warriors for the Lord, endowed with all manner of miraculous powers): see Hill, *They Shall Prophesy*, ch. 6; Hill *et al.*, *Blessing*, 127–32. The passages he quotes, however, appear to be from Cain's *teaching*, rather than prophetic oracles (though see *Blessing* 162 which refers to these sections as prophetic oracles). From within the circle of the Kansas City Prophets, Bickle insists strong prophetic gifts do not guarantee the prophet's *doctrines*, which are rather their human understanding of Scripture and tradition (see *Growing*, 71–4).

hortation of the church.[17] Thus, for example, Meredith McGuire's sociological study of American Catholic charismatics shows that prophecy (particularly in the form of tongues and interpretation) significantly effects the cohesion, assurance and unity of groups that practise these, as well as raising their expectation of God.[18]

(5) *Contemporary prophetic oracles share the same mixed and enigmatic quality of authority evinced in 1 Corinthians 14 and 1 Thessalonians 5.* Three observations should be made here:

(i) Charismatic leaders and teachers distinguish prophecy operating at different levels. Joyce Huggett applies the distinction to each specific occasion of prophetic speech, and differentiates 'low-level prophecies' of general encouragement from 'higher-level' prophecies giving more particularistic guidance, and 'highest-level prophecy', 'which causes people to bow down and worship God . . . because they know "The Lord has spoken" '.[19] Bickle, assuming prophecy to be a mixed phenomenon of perceived divine revelation and merely human interpretation, prefers to distinguish points on a spectrum between weak prophetic words (where the human element predominates) and strong prophetic words (where the human element is minimal). He tends to correlate this with a fourfold typology running from level I, 'simple prophetic' words of general encouragement, to level IV, 'prophetic office' (parallel with OT prophets, and attended by signs and wonders, though not necessarily infallible). Between the two, Bickle places 'prophetic gifting' (regular gifting and with more specific content, but without much understanding of how the prophecies should be applied) at level II, and 'prophetic ministry' (which receives prophetic revelations and the un-

---

[17]David Hill believes Pentecostal prophecy is dominated by exhortation (*Prophecy*, 210, following Hollenweger). Poloma, however, finds this unusual of Pentecostal circles, but more characteristic of neo- Pentecostal and Charismatic gatherings (*Charismatic Movement*, 57). Both, of course, wrote before the Kansas City Prophets entered the scene.

[18]McGuire, 'Social Context', 134–47.

[19]J. Huggett, *Listening to God* (London: Hodder, 1986), 133 (as quoted by Cartledge, *JPT* (1994), 90). Huggett's typology depends on Alex Buchanan. For other similar typologies, see Cartledge, *ibid.* n.55.

derstanding to implement them in the church) at level III.[20]
While there is nothing sacrosanct about any of the
proposed typologies, they do at least recognize that current
'prophecy' is not a simple black-or-white matter, but falls
within the scales of grey. This recognition aligns the
modern phenomenon with the New Testament call for discernment of prophecies, and the retaining of what is good
even from 'weak' prophecies that were in danger of being
despised (see Ch. 12 above). Cessationists appear unable to
come to terms with the possibility that God can 'reveal'
himself, and his will, in less than infallible ways: this is
curious, as the obvious analogy of teaching and preaching
in the church (let alone that of being 'led' by God) very
strongly suggests that God can make himself known
through spiritual gifts of enormously mixed quality.

(ii)   Prophecies are not to my knowledge treated at the same
level of authority as Scripture. They are sometimes even
passed over quite rapidly and without comment if the congregation evaluates them as lacking in charismatic
authority. More striking oracular speech usually provokes
actual response by way of discussion or leadership comment, which in turn is guided, where relevant, by Scripture
and tradition. If, then, the prophecy is prescriptive (or if
diagnostic, but implying required action) the church may
decide that the oracle is binding on it — but only in the
way more traditional churches might feel 'led' to some
specific decision by God, and so adopt it. Some churches
may (accidentally) have marginalized biblical exposition in
their zeal for the prophetic word for today, but I have no
reliable account of any congregation actually formally accepting a proposition to the effect that charismatic
authority stands on a par with Scripture, far less above it.
Almost invariably, Scripture is given an absolute authority
— at least in theory — while prophetic words are accorded
only relative, albeit sometimes substantial, authority.[21]

---

[20]Bickle, *Growing*, 133–42. Bickle considers these categories simply as a guide
(not as sharply distinguishable classes). Level IV prophecy he considers rare,
but he thinks Paul Cain is an example (cf. *Growing*, 141).

[21]Clifford Hill has rather surprisingly accused the Charismatic movements of
treating prophetic revelations as 'the direct word of God, on a par with
Scripture' (*Blessing*, 112), but he does not substantiate the remark, and against
his view stands not merely the explicit denials (which he admits), but the

Even in those movements which claim 'apostles', the title is not used to imply that their prophetic speech is to be regarded as carrying canonical status.[22]

(c) The secondary nature of the authority of prophecy for the churches in the Pentecostal and Charismatic movements is surely indicated both by the widespread practice of discernment of prophecies (which goes beyond the simple decision of whether they are true or false) and by the growing amount of teaching on the mixed character of prophecies. With respect to the former, we may note that concord with the Scriptures themselves is usually regarded as the supreme 'test' of prophetic utterances.[23] With respect to the latter, attention has been focused especially on the important interpretive stage in the process which leads from the revelatory event(s) to the (possibly considerably later) presentation of the prophecy. We have already noted that these 'revelatory events' could be very fragmentary and require clarification. It is thus theoretically more than possible for the 'prophet' to infer some wrong conclusions.

Bickle gives the example of a prophecy made over an individual which included the affirmation, 'You have a music ministry. You're called to be a singer. . .'. But the man concerned did not play or sing at all. Checking up, Bickle discovered the 'prophet' had merely had a 'vision' of the man surrounded by musical notes, and had jumped to the conclusion represented in his utterance with no further attempt to discern the issue. In fact the man in question was the owner of a music shop. Bickle and Hill would

---

(footnote 21 continued)
whole *rhēma/logos* distinction developed in the Apostolic Renewal Movement. According to this distinction, God's word of Scripture, as *Logos*, is unchangeable and of final authority, while God's prophetic word (*rhēma*) is particularistic, contingent, and of secondary authority. That this account of the two Greek lexemes for 'word' is semantically dubious is neither here nor there: the point is that it articulates two different levels of divine authority and purpose. Others, in the mainline Charismatic movements make similar distinctions between the primary authority of Scripture and the secondary authority of prophetic utterances: see Cartledge, *JPT* 5 (1994), 90–1.

[22]See M.M.B. Turner, 'Ecclesiology in the Major "Apostolic" Restorationist Churches in the United Kingdom', *VoxEv* 19 (1989), 83–108.

[23]See Cartledge, *JPT* 5 (1994) 114–20 for an overview of approaches to discernment of prophecies in Charismatic circles.

presumably respond that the 'prophet' in question had either only done half the job or that he should have given a more neutral account of this element of his prophecy (e.g. 'Music surrounds you . . .').[24]

Another very significant factor affecting this interpretive stage will naturally be the prophet's own theological pre-understanding (too often lacking in nuance, or even positively ill-informed).

Deere reports a prophecy of Paul Cain to a couple, Kevin and Regina Forest.[25] The prophecy contained a detailed disclosure of events in the couple's life, including that their daughter had recently died [Kevin had in fact lost his former faith precisely because he blamed God for the death of their daughter]; that Regina's brother had also recently died; that Kevin had committed adultery and was considering running away and creating a new identity. The prophecy went on to assert that all this was a great Satanic attack on them, and that Satan was out to destroy twenty-eight year old Kevin before he was thirty [Kevin was indeed already seriously considering suicide as the alternative to running away]. God, however, would turn all this to blessing if Kevin repented and if Regina gave up her bitterness and forgave him. Cain's assertion that it was not God, but Satan who had killed their daughter, coupled with Cain's detailed insight into their situation, provoked a deep repentance (not just in the Forests), reconciliation and renewal of marriage vows. One may readily discern 'revelatory elements' of some kind in this, while wondering about the rather crudely dualistic view of Satan inherent in such affirmations as 'He has a contract on your [Kevin's] life', and the explanation, 'Satan wants to kill you because he knows what God has for you and Regina'. Might a discerning group of reverent theologians not perhaps be forgiven for suspecting that these latter views simply reflect Cain's own theological pre-understanding, which he has used as the 'stage' for the prophetic play?

Further factors may affect this and other stages in the process leading up to prophetic utterance. The very fact that some of the 'revelatory events' described were experienced as *faint* or *tentative* impressions in the prophet's

---

[24]Bickle, *Growing*, 194–203, for this and other similar mistakes.

[25]Deere, *Surprised*, 209–12. My resumé necessarily simplifies Deere's quite lengthy account.

psyche, rather than sharp communications, opens up a number of possibilities (beyond the simple one of Satanic counterfeit!). Some such impressions may simply be the result of too much rich food late at night; others may come from deep within the human psyche; others still by an inner and natural resonance or empathy akin to telepathy (e.g. in a congregational setting),[26] and not a few out of sheer inner theological conviction. One suspects that many of the prophecies to the effect that David Watson would not die of the cancer that afflicted him were most probably mothered by the firm *belief* that the Lord was bound to heal such a man of God. While we cannot preclude the Spirit from using some of these 'natural' mechanisms (see Ch. 13 above), they also increase the probability of error. This may especially be the case in times of turmoil or strife within the Christian community (one is aware how often contending parties both feel sure they are 'led of the Lord!', and different parties prophesy both for and against, e.g., the 'Toronto blessing'), or where the prophet's reputation is somehow at stake.[27] It will be evident that spiritual discernment of contemporary prophecies is inevitably a delicate affair.[28]

---

[26]Cf. the suggestive treatment by N. Wright in Smail, Walker and N. Wright, *Renewal*, 82–3, and by D.C. Lewis in Wimber, *Power Healing*, 260–3 (on the parallel phenomenon of what Pentecostals mean by 'words of knowledge'). It should be noted, however, that Lewis' position has changed, and he no longer thinks the comparison with 'natural' telepathic abilities is fruitful. He argues that the information imparted in 'words of knowledge' and prophecies (at the Harrogate Wimber conference) was often much more specific and detailed than can be compared with natural ESP/telepathy statistical results: see D.C. Lewis, *Healing: Fiction, Fantasy or Fact?* (London: Hodder, 1989), ch. 3, and compare his shorter account in Grieg and Springer (eds.), *Kingdom*, 327–8.

[27]Cf. the example of the competing prophets criticized by Bickle, *Growing*, 160–5.

[28]Not so delicate, it would appear, for C. Hill, who thinks he can at least dispense with all of the triumphalistic prophecies of great supernatural blessing to come on the grounds that, 'God never sent prophets to Israel to pronounce blessing. He never sent his prophets toherald times of peace and prosperity. It was the false prophets that came with these messages' (in Hill *et al.*, *Blessing*, 105 (and ch. 4, *passim*)). But this is an over-simplification both of the Old Testament (cf. Isa. 40–66) and of those he attacks (who do not prophesy blessing *alone*). In earlier works, Hill puts a question mark over the prophecy of Paul Cain and other Kansas City Prophets on the grounds (a) those involved hold Latter Rain beliefs, and (b) real *prophets* address the nation(s), and the church as a whole, not merely individuals (cf. *They Shall Prophesy*, chs. 4–6; cf. C. Hill, *Prophecy Past and Present*, (Crowborough: Highland Books, 1989). We may agree

III. POINTS OF DISSIMILARITY BETWEEN NEW TESTAMENT PROPHECY AND CONTEMPORARY PROPHECY

Moving to points of difference, we might note:

(1) Except for somewhat stereotyped openings and (more rarely) endings, modern oracular speech is relatively lacking in distinctive prophetic forms (though archaizing language was formerly commonplace).[29] This difference may, however, be more apparent than real, for: (a) it is precisely the well-formed oracles embedded in the early literature that tend to be 'rediscovered'; (b) in the New Testament there is already a tendency to mixture of Old Testament forms, and to the formless (so Aune);[30] (c) there is evidence that some oracular speech in the New Testament period consisted not merely of declaration of revelation, but that this was mixed with response by the prophet (e.g. Acts 21:4, where Paul is urged 'through the Spirit not to go on to Jerusalem': this is often — rightly I think — interpreted as revelation of Paul's fate and a prophetic response urging that he should avoid it (see Ch. 12, II, §6)). Similarly, as we have noted, 1 Corinthians 14:30 envisages a situation where one actually prophesying is expected to draw his speech to a close if another signals he has received revelation. This makes most sense if what the first stops is not the declaration of his revelation as such but his exposition or elucidation thereof. If revelation were declared in indirect speech and integrated with response, typical oracular speech-forms would be lost.

(2) Another difference might be found to lie in the fact that some modern 'prophecy' does not rest on previous reception of the word of the Lord by the individual; but is regarded as a simultaneous reception and transmission of the oracle or vision. Where the Old Testament prophet said, 'I saw . . .', the modern

---

(footnote 28 continued)

with many of Hill's criticisms of the style of the Kansas City Prophets' ministry, but these criteria are too simplisitic to reduce the task of discernment: occasional theological beliefs may corrupt prophecies, without vitiating them entirely, and biblical prophets gave personal and individual prophecies (see Ch. 12) as well as oracles for Israel and the nations (and, indeed, whatever we make of them, Cain's prophecies address broader ecclesial and national matters too).

[29] The examples cited by Poloma, *Charismatic Movement*, 58, however, have clear form.

[30] Aune, *Prophecy*, ch. 10.

[31] Not exclusively: see Poloma, *Charismatic Movement*, 59.

prophet more often says, 'I see. . .'[31] But this contrast is perhaps not particularly significant either. Philo provides an example of the latter type; that is, of simultaneous charism and delivery (*Life of Moses* 2, 280–1 and compare, e.g., 250–2); and so does Stephen (Acts 7:55,56[32]). Furthermore, we have noted that the category of invasive charismatic speech (whether prophecy or doxology), while rarer than non-invasive prophecy, was nevertheless prototypical to Jewish understanding of the 'Spirit of prophecy'. The quite widespread practice in congregational prophecy today of speaking on 'impulse' from the Spirit, without any conception of the content in advance, may thus have some credible antecedents in biblical prophetism. It should be pointed out, however, that this kind of prophesying, which eliminates the possibility of prior evaluation of a 'word' before it is given out, entails even higher risks of merely human contribution and error,[33] and generally yields what have been regarded as the weaker forms of prophecy.

The differences, then, do not appear to be material, and we may cautiously conclude that at least *several* forms of modern 'prophecy' correlate well in mechanism, content, function and purpose, with *some types of New Testament* prophetic speech. The same factors that gradually marginalized prophecy in the early church (see Ch. 16, part III), along with the vast increase in theological resources and guides available to church leaders, ensure it at most a secondary place within the tasks of teaching, building up, and challenging Christians today. We would certainly be surprised if anyone tried to add to or tamper with the fundamental structures of theology in the name of some revelatory experience (albeit that, as theologians, we sometimes tamper with them in the name of less godly authorities!). In practice, such prophetic adjustment is not seriously attempted outside sectarian movements. But within the broad framework of 'established' theology, there is still need for the illumination, the interpretation (in the sense of application of original sense to twentieth-century situations), and the fresh and timely 'representation' of gospel truth and apostolic praxis. There is need, too, for deep spiritual diagnosis of individuals and congregations, and of specific leading on a host of practical issues. And these are the areas in which the revelatory gifts of 1 Corinthians 12:8–10, including prophecy, still have contemporary relevance.

Of course the wise pastor, leader or interpreter today has infinitely

---

[32]On this phenomenon, see Aune, *Prophecy*, 148–51.
[33]See the warning by Grudem, *Gift*, 261.

more by way of aid in the precedents and norms laid down in centuries of church history and reflection. But ultimately it is still only by the Spirit's work that God gives shape to his church and directs its growth, and we cannot identify the Spirit's work with the natural workings of the pastor's mind simpliciter. The Spirit works sovereignly in the mind of the man of God without his necessarily being conscious of it (cf. 1 Cor. 2:16) — this we need not deny. He brings fruit through our disciplined study. But the New Testament lesson is that the Spirit also works at the level at which he is immediately perceived as giving direction. The pastor or leader today is as much in need as ever of such immediate charismata of wisdom, direction and heavenly knowledge — occasions where he is aware of these things breaking in on his existence as events of the Lord's grace and guidance, given specifically in answer to prayerful seeking, or sovereignly in response to a prayerful life. Where more traditional ('non-Charismatic') Christians seek the Lord this way, the difference between them and Pentecostals/Charismatics on the issue of the relation of theology and revelatory events is minimalized.

Chapter Nineteen

Healing Today

'An opinion survey published by George Gallop in 1989 found that about 82 per cent of Americans polled believed that "even today, miracles are performed by the power of God" '.[1] It is within the context of such widespread belief that Christians, and many of other faiths, believe in different sorts of spiritual healings. But while most Christians believe that God (in his sovereign freedom) at least occasionally heals (and not necessarily rapidly) in response to prayer,[2] there is considerable controversy on other related questions.[3] From the side of the Pentecostals and Charismatics, we regularly hear the claim that the healing ministries of Jesus and the apostles are normative for the church. Correspondingly, miracles of exorcism and healing (and even occasional raisings from the dead) are widely reported in the popular and semi-popular literature, and in the preaching of evangelists and others with healing ministries. From the opposing side, cessationists insist point

---

[1]So Meier, *Marginal Jew* 2: 520. Only 6% disagreed with the proposition, and could be listed as potential supporters for Bultmann's famous affirmation that 'it is impossible to use electric light and wireless . . . and at the same time to believe in the New Testament world of . . . miracles'.

[2]The confessions of most Church bodies is that *God Does Heal Today* (to take the title of Robert Dickinson's study (see below), which is perhaps the most comprehensive available).

[3]For various aspects of the modern debate, see: N. Baumert, 'Evangelism and Charismatic Signs' in Harold D. Hunter and Peter D. Hocken (eds.), *All Together In One Place: Theological Papers from the Brighton Conference on World Evangelization* (Sheffield: SAP, 1993), 219–26; W.J. Bittner, *Heilung* (Neukirchen-Vluyn: Aussaat Vlg., 1984); D. Bridge, *Power Evangelism and the Word of God* (Eastbourne: Kingsway, 1987); *idem, Signs and Wonders Today* (Leicester: IVP, 1985); Brown, *That You May Believe*; H.R. Casdorph, *The Miracles* (Plainfield: Logos, 1976); J.R. Coggins and P.G. Hiebert (eds.), *Wonders*, 109–52; Robert Dickinson, *God Does Heal Today* (Carlisle: Paternoster, 1995); V. Edmunds and C.G. Scorer, *Some Thoughts on Faith Healing* (London: IVP, 1956); Ann England (ed.), *We Believe in Healing* (London: MMS, 1982); G.D. Fee, *The Disease of the Health and Wealth Gospels* (Costa Mesa: Word for Today, 1979); R. Gardner,

blank that such New Testament *ministries* of healing were granted simply to accredit the bearers of new revelation, and passed away with the completion of the canon of Scripture.[4] They dismiss the contemporary claims to miracles as credulity or even as occult counterfeit. Coming to the issue with a different perspective are the medical experts. We might at least expect their professional objectivity to settle the matter, once for all, of whether there are many (or any) miraculous healings to talk about, or whether we can all go home and have a quiet night. But, alas, the doctors are found supporting both sides.[5] Beyond that debate, we have further questions being asked about the right context for healing (is it in evangelism, the church's worship, or the bedroom, with the assembled elders?); about the extent to which we

---

(footnote 3 continued)
Healing Miracles (London: DLT, 1986); J. Goldingay (ed.), *Signs, Wonders and Healing* (Leicester: IVP, 1989); W. Grudem, *Power and Truth: A Response to Power Religion* Vineyard Position Papers 4 (Anaheim: Vineyard Churches, 1993); M. Israel, *The Quest for Wholeness* (London: DLT, 1989); P. Jensen and A. Payne (eds.), *John Wimber: Friend or Foe?* (London: St. Matthias, 1990); D. Kammer, 'The Perplexing Power of John Wimber's Power Encounters', *Churchman* 106 (1992), 45–64; M.T. Kelsey, *Healing*; Latourelle, *Miracles*; D.C. Lewis, *Healing*; M.D. Lloyd-Jones, *Healing and Medicine* (Eastbourne: Kingsway, 1987); F. Mac-Nutt, *Healing* (Notre Dame: Ave Maria Press, 1974); *idem, The Power to Heal* (Notre Dame: Ave Maria Press, 1977); M. Maddocks, *The Christian Healing Ministry* (London: SPCK, 1987); D. McConnell, *The Promise of Health and Wealth: A Historical and Biblical Analysis of the Modern Faith Movement* (London: Hodder, 1990); Masters, *Epidemic*; L. Monden, *Signs and Wonders: A Study of the Miraculous Element in Religion* (New York: Desclée, 1966); Moo, 'Divine Healing'; W.A. Nolan, *Healing: A Doctor in Search of a Miracle* (New York: Random House, 1974); J. Richards, *The Question of Healing Services* (London: DLT, 1989); L. Sabourin, *The Divine Miracles Discussed and Defended* (Rome: Catholic Book Agency, 1977); K.L. Sarles, 'Appraisal'; D.J. West, *Eleven Lourdes Miracles* (London: Duckworth, 1957); Wilkinson, *Health*; Wimber, *Power Evangelism; idem, Power Healing* (London: Hodder, 1986); F. Wright, *The Pastoral Nature of Healing* (London: SCM, 1985).
[4]Masters can thus affirm, 'Miracles and healings still occur today, by the power of God, and in answer to prayer. But sign-miracles wrought through the hands of gifted individuals, for the purpose of authentication, belong to the age of the apostles' (*Epidemic*, 133).
[5]Those returning a predominantly negative verdict on reports of miraculous healings include, most recently, Professor Verna Wright (in Masters, *Epidemic*, ch. 11; but note that D.C. Lewis criticizes Wright's material as largely opinions based on second-hand reports: *Healing*, 163–5) and Peter May (in Goldingay (ed.), *Signs*, 75–81). Those giving a positive verdict on miracles include Rex Gardner (*Miracles*) and Tony Dale (in Goldingay (ed.), *Signs*, 53–74).

can *expect* healing (and on what basis), and about the relationship of sickness and healing to demonology.

There is more than enough here for a book, let alone a chapter. Our primary interest is to assess the extent to which we find contemporary parallels in the church today to the spiritual gifts of healings in the New Testament discussed in Chapter 14. We shall begin by asking whether there are reliable reports of miraculous physical healings by God within the Pentecostal/Charismatic churches today (part I). Considerations of space unfortunately preclude a parallel study of 'exorcism and deliverance'[6] and 'inner healing'. We shall then briefly compare the alleged healing miracles today with those described in the New Testament (part II). Finally, we shall venture brief remarks on the significance of occasions where there is no apparent healing (part III). We shall not be able to enter further into the other main area of dispute,

---

[6]Demons and evil spirits were fast disappearing from academic and serious pastoral theological discourse until the publication of John Richards', *But Deliver Us From Evil*, (London: DLT, 1974) (Richards was a member of the Bishop of Exeter's committee on exorcism, the findings of which were published two years earlier (Dom Robert Petitpierre (ed.), *Exorcism: The Findings of a Committee Convened by the Bishop of Exeter*, (London: SPCK, 1972)). But in Pentecostal and Charismatic circles there has been an increased interest from the publication of Jesse Penn-Lewis' *War on the Saints* (New York: Thomas Lowe, 1973) and Frank and Ida Mae Hammond's, *Pigs in the Parlour* (Missouri: Impact Books, 1973) onwards. What has made the issue of especial interest is the claim that *Christians* can be at least demonized or 'oppressed' by demonic powers, and may require the 'minor' exorcism of 'deliverance ministry'. This claim in itself would not constitute a break with more traditional Christianity (which allowed for the occasional case). But the element of demonization of Christians became a major focus through Ern Baxter, Don Basham, and Derek Prince (members of the so-called Fort Lauderdale Five), and in the ministries and writings of Bill Subritzky and Peter Horrobin (of Ellel Grange). It has reached the point where Andrew Walker speaks of a Paranoid Universe: i.e. the conception of the Universe as infested with demons which cluster like flies on people's heads (or penetrate them), and empower every manner of temptation and minor personality weakness. We have a Paranoid Universe when we regard most Christians as requiring deliverance ministry (see Walker, 'The Devil You Think You Know' in Smail, Walker and N. Wright, *Renewal*, ch. 6). For a brief account of the rise of such views, in addition to Walker's survey, see S. Hunt, 'Deliverance: The Evolution of a Doctrine', *Themelios* 21 (1995), 10–13. For a theologically considered account, cf. N. Wright, *The Fair Face of Evil*, (London: Marshall Pickering, 1989). Between Richards and Subritzky/Horrobin, a middle ground is occupied by Wimber (see *Power Healing*, ch. 6) and D.C. Lewis (see *Healing*, ch. 2).

namely that of the relationship of healings as 'signs and wonders' to evangelism.[7]

I. RELIABILITY OF CONTEMPORARY CLAIMS TO PHYSICAL HEALINGS

According to John Wimber, miracles of healing are numerous. Speaking merely of what is happening within his own fellowships he made the following oft-quoted claim:

> Today we see hundreds of people healed every month in Vineyard Christian Fellowship services. Many more are healed as we pray for them in hospitals, on the streets and in homes. The blind see; the lame walk; the deaf hear. Cancer is disappearing!

And other groups make parallel affirmations. But while the claims are many, the substantiating evidence is somewhat thinner on the ground. As Andrew Walker (himself sympathetic to the Charismatic movement) warns:

> It is precisely at the level of rigorous investigation into the miraculous that the Pentecostal movements, since their earliest days,

---

[7]See Chapter 14 above, for our view of the New Testament position(s): in short, the more manifest healings effectively illustrate the gospel, and partially legitimate the messenger of the gospel. As such they often led to, or promoted acceptance of, the message (a point made most strongly and regularly in Acts), but they did not compel it, nor were they *necessary* to effective evangelism (cf. Acts 8:26–39; 16:14; 17:1–4, 11,12; 18:5–8; 19:8,9). Traditional evangelicalism has attacked Pentecostal and Charismatic 'over-emphasis' on signs and wonders in evangelism, and especially Wimber's more focused association of the two (see *Power Evangelism, passim*). As Packer affirms, 'The line of thought . . . that says evangelism is not evangelism until it has a particular kind of miracle attached to it . . . is an overstatement, a real error' (in Grieg and Springer (eds.), *Kingdom*, 213). But as Packer also affirms, 'Nevertheless, it is not wrong to want to evangelize in a way that impresses and blesses people because it convinces them that all this talk about a new life in Christ through God's power is for real' (*ibid.*), and while he thinks the witness of transformed lives offers the best 'power encounter', he also criticizes the Reformers' reaction against the supernatural in the lives of God's people, and affirms the rightness of bringing it into prominence and of raising Christians' expectation with regard to healings, empowering for preaching, etc. (210–12). Worthwhile essays (clarifying potential misunderstandings) in the same volume include W. Grudem's, 'Should Christians Expect Miracles Today?' (*Kingdom*, 56–110), and Gary S. Grieg's, 'Purpose', in *Kingdom*, 133–74. That is not to say there is no further need for nuance and corrective!

have let themselves down. In the euphoria and excitement of revival, miracles have been testified to in abundance, but rarely verified. Testimonies are direct, successful and personal means of communication, but they are by definition prone to exaggeration or capable of incorrect assessment. Congregations awash with the emotion of enthusiasm feed off rumour, conjecture and hearsay. When you know that God heals, what you look for is not empirical evidence but tacit confirmation of your beliefs, in the form of positive reports, reconstructions of events, or books replete with amazing stories.[8]

The point here, of course, is not that those who make such claims are charlatans. It is rather a question of what evidence is taken to substantiate the claim that a miracle of healing has taken place. For those at an inspiring healing service, some change of feeling in the part of the body affected, combined with a conviction that God is healing, may be enough. For the investigating doctor with a professional reputation to maintain, however, there needs to be a competent and documented medical history of the condition before the healing, and clear evidence of change that cannot simply be accounted for in terms of temporary or spontaneous remission. Though we could wish otherwise, it needs to be said, in all honesty, that there are relatively few occasions that stand up to such rigorous medical analysis. A further complicating factor is introduced by the various different senses of the word 'miracle' in current use.[9] While in popular usage the word 'miracle' may be applied to almost any act attributed to God, such as the disappearance of a headache after prayer, those attempting a more critical examination set the requirements higher. In this book we have assumed (with Latourelle and Meier) that to qualify as 'miracle' we must be satisfied the phenomenon in question meets the following criteria:

(a) it is an extraordinary or startling observable event,
(b) it cannot reasonably be explained in terms of human abilities or other known forces in the world,
(c) it is perceived as a direct act of God, and
(d) it is usually understood to have symbolic or sign value (e.g. pointing to God as redeemer and judge).[10]

---

[8] T. Smail, A. Walker and N. Wright, *Charismatic Renewal: The Search for a Theology* (London, SPCK, 1995), 125.

[9] See Meier, *Marginal Jew*, 2: 524–5, for a survey.

[10] Of these traits, the first two should be taken sufficiently loosely to allow for imparting of knowledge that could not otherwise be known by the human agent (as in prophecy). For similar definitions in more detail, see Latourelle, *Miracles*, 276–280; Meier, *Marginal Jew* 2, 512–515.

From the perspective of this definition, of course, many alleged miracles of healing will fall at the second step: those healings which might potentially be 'explained' as 'psycho-somatic' would all be excluded, for while we do not know the precise mechanism of all of these, it is still widely assumed they are largely *natural* mechanisms. As most claimed healings belong to the category of functional diseases rather than organic ones, it is not surprising that doctors (Christian and otherwise[11]) find little evidence of real 'miracles',[12] and some gradually become suspicious of finding any hard cases at all.[13] Could not all claimed healings be explained away as ordinary physiological processes resulting in return to health, as the completion of the natural history of the disease cycle, as the normal kind of spontaneous remissions,[14] as cases of incorrect initial diagnosis (whether by the medically uninformed sufferer, or even by the competent specialist), as hypnotic removal of pain, or as psychosomatic effects?[15] We may be relatively sure many 'testimonies' could be accounted for in such ways.

But while fairly radical methodological scepsis and hard medical evidence may be needed in order to secure the verdict 'proven miracle' in the Academy, it is not surprising that a few have felt this critical approach concedes a little too much to the doubters. Rex Gardner's analysis leads him to the conclusion that there are indeed incidents well-enough attested to count as secure 'miracles of healing', e.g. Dr Anne Townsend's case of the total healing of an 'incurably' deaf girl (audiograms taken the day before the healing confirmed the condition; those two days later showed complete healing).[16] But he would also argue that in many instances where physicians might appeal to (e.g.) unusual spontaneous remission, or to faulty earlier diagnosis, these are not so much 'explanations' as admissions that a more plausible medical account is not forthcoming.[17] Under certain conditions the Christian may legitimately

---

[11]Atheists or radical agnostics will naturally exclude virtually all claims at step three.

[12]Casdorph (*The Miracles*) endorses miracles in Kathryn Kuhlman's ministry, but is only able to find ten sufficiently strong cases.

[13]See, e.g., West's scepticism concerning some of the best of the Lourdes cases (*Miracles, passim*), but note, e.g., the response of Sabourin, *Miracles*, 156–9.

[14]Edmunds and Scorer, *Thoughts*, observed that statistically Christians did not evince a higher percentage of 'remissions' of, e.g. cancer than non-Christians.

[15]Such are the explanations offered by Professor Wright in Masters, *Epidemic* 204–14; but see Gardner, *Miracles*, ch. 2, for important reconsiderations.

[16]Gardner, *Miracles*, 202–5.

[17]Cf. D.C. Lewis' comments in Grieg and Springer (eds.), *Kingdom*, 326. Lewis cites a particular case of healing of infantile fibrosarcoma, which the consultant labelled 'spontaneous remission', even though the medical literature on this type of tumour knows of no such cases.

count these as 'healing miracles', Gardner suggests. This is especially the case when the 'spontaneous remission' in question takes place, e.g. in a healing meeting, accompanied perhaps by strong physical sensations of God's healing 'touch', or when the healing follows a 'word of knowledge', or some other indication from God that he is going to answer prayer for healing in the instance in question.

> As one of several similar examples, Gardner instances the case of a young trainee General Practitioner in 1975, admitted to hospital near death, suffering from meningococcal septicaemia (from which no one had recovered in that hospital). Prayer meetings in Rhyl, Llandudno, Caernarfon and Bangor interceded that evening, and independently and simultaneously came to believe she would be completely healed. At 8.30 the same evening she dramatically improved, and recovered consciousness four days later. A haemorrhage, however, had left one eye blind, with no (medical) prospect of healing. But the eye too was completely restored. In this case there is no doubt about the diagnoses, and the full recovery was 'unique'. One might call this an inexplicable remission, but Gardner rightly points to the significance of the earlier God-given conviction (in different prayer meetings) that she would be healed. The coincidence makes a purely 'natural' explanation less convincing.[18]

Gardner, himself a senior medical officer, has documented some twenty-one contemporary and international 'cases' (including two raisings from the dead)[19] where a verdict of 'healing miracle' might reasonably be recorded. Beyond instances like these we can probably anticipate a much larger class of healings in response to prayer where the borderline between 'miracle' and God's providential use of natural means (e.g. psychosomatic healings) is much fuzzier.

But where does all this get us? It suggests we may need to recognize the quotation from John Wimber, with which we started, as an impassioned and programmatic confession of Jesus' ability to heal today, rather than as a precise report on the typical nature and number of healings in Vineyard fellowships. Elsewhere, Wimber has freely admitted that in praying for children with Down's Syndrome he had seen improvement in only one in about two hundred cases, and then the improvement was only slight.[20] In the same context he claims between 3 per cent and 8 per cent success in prayer for different types of blind-

---

[18]Gardner, *Miracles*, 20–1.

[19]*Ibid.*, 137–41. These are amongst the weaker documented cases, depending more on first-hand testimony than clear medical histories: compare also Deere, *Surprised*, 203–6.

[20]Admitted in an interview with three leading evangelicals shortly before the Spiritual Warfare Conference, Sydney 1990. The substance of the interview is

ness. If we were to take a mean figure of approximately 5 per cent, this would certainly suggest healing is an occasional and minority phenomenon, rather than that it is a norm. Some of his critics suggest his healings are largely of trivial complaints subject to psychosomatic treatment (unmeasurable 'backaches' and 'headaches'), and feel that these figures may be accounted for in terms of a mere placebo effect.[21] This charge does not appear, however, to be borne out by analysis. David Lewis, a social anthropologist, conducted a wide-ranging and thorough survey of those prayed for at Wimber's Harrogate conference in 1986. Of the 867 who received prayer for healing, some 32 per cent reported a significant high measure of healing; 42 per cent indicated little or none, and 26 per cent an intermediate 'fair amount' of healing. This means some 58 per cent noticed some perceptible improvement. More significantly, of a random sample of 100 followed up nearly a year later, 57 per cent claimed the level of their healing had persisted or even improved since the occasion of prayer.

A group of 27 are discussed in more detail. In two cases, Lewis put the claim to improvement down to 'fantasy'; i.e. the person concerned reported healing (and may have felt better), but medical tests showed none (or even aggravation in the state of the disease condition). Four further cases appear to have involved the loss of chronic pain or other disturbing symptoms, even though medical examination showed no alteration in the disease (e.g. cervical spondylitis [crumbling of the spine with age]). Some other cases were unremarkable, or, while more striking, rested purely in the testimony of the one healed, without any medical corroboration of the diagnosis.[22] Three cases might perhaps squeeze into the category of (minor) miracle: one, a case of painfully sensitive teeth healed, another, the lengthening of a leg by 1½ inches (overcoming a bad rolling limp caused by failure in bone repair following an accident), and, third, the marked improvement in the hearing of a retired missionary.[23]

(footnote 20 continued)
written up by Philip Jensen as 'John Wimber Changes His Mind', in P. Jensen and A. Payne (eds.) *Wimber*, 6–11 (7–8 for the discussion of the extent of healings in his ministry).

[21] Dummy pills (placebos), administered to patients who believe them to be genuine pharmaceutical drugs, may stimulate a measurable improvement along the lines of the patients' expectations. Jensen argues 'Wimber heals in the "sugar pill area" ' (Jensen and Payne (eds.), *Wimber*, 8).

[22] E.g. the the case of a nurse who had signs of a tumour on the side of the head (with distressing swelling, attendant left-side headaches, pain in left eye, and buzzing sensation in the ear), but out of fear had not told anyone of it (D.C. Lewis, *Healing*, 40–44). The same nurse also claimed healing of retroverted uterus.

[23] D.C. Lewis, *Healing*, 37–43.

x

These various healings clearly do not quite match the rhetoric of Wimber's affirmation with which we opened this section, and there can be little doubt that the percentages would be less impressive had the survey been conducted amongst hospital patients, or even in an average church, instead of amongst those attending a conference on Signs and Wonders. There does appear, however, to be sufficient evidence to suggest that an otherwise unexpected number and variety of healings took place, and that a few at least verged on the 'miraculous', in the sense that we have defined.

II. COMPARING NEW TESTAMENT AND CONTEMPORARY HEALING

Two main kinds of contrasts are suggested. (1) As we have indicated, even adamant cessationists are prepared to admit God's sovereign freedom and power to heal, especially where the injunctions of James 5:13–16 are followed. It is the *mandate* to heal, and the possibility of people with *ministries* of healing that are most in question. And then, (2), there is the question of quantity and quality. In the apostolic church, it is held, the model for healing was inevitably that of the apostles, and of Christ himself. Their healings were instantaneous and visibly striking, without failure, irreversible, great in number and covering all manner of diseases, dependent on the charisma of the healer not the faith of the seeker, and so a sign to the unevangelized. Pentecostal and Charismatic healers show no such track record.[24] Both contrasts, I would suggest, need re-examination, and we shall tackle them in reverse order.

(1) The sharp contrast between healing ministries in the New Testament and those today rests partly on unproven assumptions about the former. Thus, for example, (a) we simply do not know that all Jesus' miracles were instantaneous (naturally the most remarkable are the ones recorded, but we do not know about the greater number covered merely by the summaries — and Mk. 8:22–25, Lk. 17:11–19, and Jn. 9:2–7 relate to healings which, however remarkable, were not necessarily instantaneous[25]). Nor do

---

[24]E.g., Packer, *Keep in Step*, 213–14; cf. MacArthur, *Charismatic Chaos*, 215, for the view that those who had miraculous gifts could use them at will, independent of faith in others. Against this quasi-magical view, see e.g. Deere, *Surprised*, 58–64.

[25]Packer argues the miracle in Mk. 8:22–25 was in two stages, but that at each stage the healing was instantaneous (*Keep in Step*, 213). This appears to be special pleading to which modern Charismatics might make similar appeal in respect of their own multi-stage healings.

we know they were 'irreversible' (the Gospels are not concerned to provide any 'follow up' on the people healed, and Jesus' own warnings in Matthew 12:44,45 and John 5:14 suggest the opposing possibility). As for the inference that Jesus' miracles were not dependent on the faith of the seeker, but merely on Jesus' own power,[26] this both seriously misunderstands the nature and purpose of Jesus' healings and clearly contradicts a number of the Gospel stories (cf. Mk. 6:5,6; Mk. 5:34 and//s; Mk. 10:52 and//s, and Lk. 17:19, etc.). (b) What we have just said concerning Jesus' miracles applies more especially to healings worked through the apostles. Undoubtedly some were instantaneous and remarkable 'signs and wonders', but it is quite unwarranted to claim they all were: the summaries do not provide the kind of information that would be required. Mark 9:18, 28,29 (and parallels) suggest rather that some types of exorcism were anticipated to take time. And there were indeed occasions when even the apostles were apparently unable to heal (Gal. 4:13,14; Phil. 2:27; 1 Tim. 5:23; 2 Tim. 4:20, etc.: cf. Ch. 14, part II). (c) The assumption that Jesus' own most striking miracles were the pattern for *all* the 'gifts of healings' referred to in 1 Corinthians 12:9,29,30 is gratuitous. We perhaps do not have sufficient evidence to draw any really safe conclusions about these gifts in the Pauline congregations. But, if anything, the implied contrast with those given to work 'miracles' (1 Cor. 12:10,29) points to these healings as being less remarkable. And if Stephen worked 'great' signs and wonders (Acts 6:8), and Paul 'extraordinary' miracles at Ephesus (Acts 19:11), the implication is of a gradation in the phenomena, with God working in greater power through some people, at particular times and places, than in others (as is evidently the case with other spiritual gifts, such as empowering for preaching, teaching gifts, etc.). In short, the New Testament evidence is consistent with the possibility that healings performed by Jesus were more remarkable than many of those performed by his disciples, and that theirs in turn differed in quality and number from the broader circle of those with 'gifts of healings'.[27] It is worth noting that Deere (and now Wimber too) specifically distinguishes the more general gifts

---

[26]It would be more accurate to say he performs them through the power of the Spirit: so Mt. 12:28 and Lk. 4:18–21.

[27]The 'greater works' anticipated by John 14:12 of Jesus' followers cannot be reduced to conversions (see Grieg and Springer (eds.), *Kingdom*, 393–7): as the syntax and co-text require, they are indeed to include the sort of works envisaged in 14:11. But they will be 'greater' not in the sense that they will be more spectacular or prodigious. We need to remember that the purpose of the works

of healings in 1 Corinthians 12:9,10,30 from those of Jesus and the apostles, and compares contemporary healing in Charismatic circles directly with the former, not with the latter.[28]

(2) The view that the pre-Easter mission mandate to heal was not renewed in the final commissions of the gospels has been dealt with above.[29] As for the assertion that beyond the apostolic period the only pattern for healing is James 5:13–15, and that none were to have 'gifts of healings' any more, such an affirmation is simply arbitrary and rests on the misunderstanding that 'gifts of healings' means the quasi-magical ability to perform evidentialist healings at *will* in order to authenticate the gospel.[30] Such a view has no place in serious New Testament scholarship.

Given these considerations, the relationship between New Testament healings and healings today may not be so sharply polarized as some have considered it. There do appear to be some events that Christians may reasonably call 'miracles' (in the sense defined above) because sufficiently well documented and analysed by competent professional parties. If they are comparatively rare, similar cases may have been rare in parts of the early church too. There are many more 'lesser' healings. While these do not compare directly with those of Jesus or the apostles in quality or quantity, they may be comparable to some of the apostolic healings, and (even more probably) to those with 'gifts of healing' scattered through the Pauline congregations. Even if we cannot be sure of this last, it may still reasonably be claimed that these modern healings are spiritual gifts that are in *theological continuity* with healings of Jesus and of the apostles. That is, they are experienced by the beneficiaries as

---

(footnote 27 continued)
is to reveal the glory of the Father in the Son. Within the ministry, the significance of Jesus' mighty acts is not fully disclosed because Jesus is not yet glorified and the Paraclete is not yet available to 'interpret' them to people (see Ch. 4–5 above). Beyond his ascension, even less spectacular acts, if they are performed in answer to prayer to the Father in the name of Jesus (14:13), will have greater power to reveal the unity between the Father and the Son (cf. 14:11–14). It is primarily in this latter sense that the works of the disciples will be 'greater works'.

[28] Deere, *Surprised*, 64–71. For Wimber's 'change of mind' on this (his earlier works used Jesus and the apostles as the direct models for healing today), see Jensen and Payne (eds.), *Wimber*, 8.

[29] See above, Ch. 14, part I, §5: cf. also Appendices 2 and 3 (on Jn. 14:12 and Mt. 28:18–20 respectively) in Grieg and Springer (eds.), *Kingdom*, 393–7 and 399–403.

[30] *Per contra* see Deere, *Surprised*, 58–64, and Appendix 4 to Grieg and Springer (eds.), *Kingdom*, 405–11.

lesser or greater acts of liberation and as fresh inbreakings of God's
reign into their lives. Such healings can make them joyfully aware anew
of Christ's presence in their lives through the Spirit, and point afresh to
his compassion and glory, as well as to the fuller salvation to come
through resurrection into the new creation. In some instances the healings in question have freed the believer to fresh service that would have
been impossible (or very difficult) without it. When experienced by
outsiders prayed for by Christians, even relatively minor healings have
been discovered to confront the person with the reality of God in such
a way as to prepare for the gospel. More spectacular healings have
functioned, like some of the 'wonders' of Acts, as a 'sign' to whole
families, neighbourhoods, or other sections of a community. Often healings (even some of the most spectacular cases) have come as answers to
the prayers of individuals or of small groups, acting within the
guidance of James 5:13-15. But the majority centre on the ministry of
specific persons (K. Kuhlman, Oral Roberts, A.A. Allan, Smith Wiggles-
worth, the Jeffreys brothers, Morris Cerullo, Colin Urquhart, J. Wimber,
Reinhard Bonnke, etc.). As such people tend to deny emphatically that
they are healers, but to insist instead that God regularly brings healings
through them, one is inclined to think a good way to describe them
might be 'those with gifts of healings'. In these ways the contemporary
phenomena may reasonably be claimed as parallels to at least some
New Testament healings.

III. INTERPRETING OCCASIONS OF THE LACK OF HEALING?

Pentecostalism and its spiritual children have forcefully reminded us
that the kerygma addressed whole men and women (as part of a physical creation that was to be restored) not platonic or aristotelian disem-
bodied 'souls'.[31] They put healing back into the spiritual agenda, and
located it firmly in the atonement (cf. Mt. 8:17; Isa. 53:4), where it rightly belongs — indeed what benefit of salvation does not derive from the
atonement? However, we do not enjoy all the benefits yet; and Pentecostalism has set for itself an ideal that it has not been able to live up
to, where it has maintained that God certainly wills to heal all (with

[31]For Pentecostal attitudes to healing, see Hollenweger, *Pentecostals*, ch. 25; for
those of neo-Pentecostalism and the Charismatic Renewal movements, see
Poloma, *Charismatic Movement*, ch. 5. There were, of course, non-Pentecostal
antecedents: Hollenweger, *Pentecostals*, 353–4; C.E. Hummel, *Fire in the Fireplace*
(London: Mowbray, 1979), 197–9; Kelsey, *Healing*, 232–42, and see Taylor, 'Historical Perspective', below (n.36).

faith) *now*.[32] Amongst those who have 'gone forward' (to be healed)
there have been many failures — indeed the majority.[33] The question
becomes how these occasions are best interpreted.[34]

One answer that must be totally rejected is that of the so-called
'Health and Wealth Gospel', propagated by Kenneth Hagin, Kenneth
and Gloria Copeland, and Fred Price.[35] In brief, their answer is that in
Christ all believers *are* already healed. Sickness is effectively merely an
illusion. It is not merely the right, but the duty, of Christians to acquire
their healing. Faith is the divinely appointed means, and active confession ('I am already healed in Christ') is the power, which by immutable
law draws the spiritual healing into the earthly body. In the meantime,
Satan sows doubts (e.g.) in the form of 'physical symptoms', and inspires negative confessions ('I am ill'), which just as inexorably draw
that 'reality'. Exercise faith properly, and a person should not die
before the allotted one hundred and twenty years (cf. Gen. 6:3). This
view, which stems from E. Kenyon and his associations with the New
Thought Metaphysics of Emerson College (a precursor of Christian
Science[36]), is heretical in its major assertions. Its fundamental dualism
of matter and spirit is essentially gnostic; it leads to a denial of the

---

[32]By no means all Pentecostal or Charismatic practitioners of healing believe
that God necessarily heals all today, conditional only on faith: see, for example,
the warnings voiced by Hummel, *Fire*, 203–7; MacNutt, *Healing*, ch. 18; Wimber,
Power Healing, ch. 8; Deere, *Surprised*, ch. 11.

[33]It will be remembered that, in Lewis' sample, the percentage claiming a significant measure of healing was 58 per cent, but this was a somewhat un-
representative sample (and only 32 per cent claimed more than a moderate
degree of healing).

[34]On Charismatic minimizing of dissonance, see Poloma, *Charismatic Movement*,
98–100.

[35]For a brief introduction to the movement, see Thomas Smail, Andrew Walker,
and Nigel Wright, ' "Revelation Knowledge" and Knowledge of Revelation:
The Faith Movement and the Question of Heresy', *JPT* 5 (1994), 57–77 (also in
Smail, Walker and N. Wright, *Renewal*, 134–51, 171–5). But the fullest treatment
is that of McConnell, *Promise*. See also Fee, *Disease*; Moo, 'Divine Healing'.

[36]As McConnell has shown, Hagin is dependent on Kenyon to the point of
considerable plagiarism (*Promise*, 6–14). An important article by Malcolm
Taylor, however, shows that many elements of the 'positive confession' teaching were already being related to healing both inside early Pentecostalism, and
in other pre-Pentecostal Christian faith-healing enterprises, before Kenyon published his first work. And significant aspects of the thinking of Christian
Science were mediated to later Pentecostal and Positive Confession teaching by
A.A. Boddy's journal, *Confidence*: see M. Taylor, 'A Historical Perspective on the
Doctrine of Divine Healing', *Journal of the European Pentecostal Theological Association* 14 (1995), 54–84.

efficacy of the cross (Jesus' physical death is irrelevant; he needed to die spiritually, whether in Gethsemane, earlier, or in hell, later, to deal with spiritual matters of sin, poverty and sickness), and implicitly to the incoherent view that the trinity became, at least for a period, a binity. Its view of 'faith' makes the latter an absolute power independent of relation to God (unbelievers can apply the same spiritual laws), rather than a way of expressing a filial relationship of dependence. According to this view, then, if people are not healed it is entirely their own fault. They have made negative confessions; they have not applied 'faith'. And of course this theological diagnosis can lead to disastrous pastoral consequences. Larry Parker took Hagin's teaching to its logical conclusion when he carried on confessing his baby son's healing, and refused to believe the 'Satanic symptoms', until little Wesley died in an insulin coma. He believed this too was a Satanic counterfeit, and that God would raise him, so he and his wife would not permit the child's burial, and held a resurrection service instead. But Wesley was not raised. Tragically, they persisted in their 'faith' that the death was just a counterfeit, and that God would raise up their son, for over a year![37]

A second 'answer' assumes that healing for all is made available in the atonement, and that faith should always receive it, unless, for example, there is unrepented sin. This relatively widespread view does not contain the same dualism of matter and spirit, it is based in a much more orthodox Christology and interpretation of atonement, in which 'faith' means trust in God, and his promises to heal, rather than the power of positive thinking. This view can fairly naturally claim both that disobedience is a denial of faith, and so a barrier to healing, and also that texts such as 1 Corinthians 11:30 even suggest some sickness is itself divine judgement. There are, however, considerable problems with such an explanation (some common to the next interpretation), of which two may be singled out. First is the assumption that the benefits of the atonement are all universally 'available' *now*.[38] A second is that it leads to the conclusion that fundamentally what was wrong with Paul, Epaphroditus, Timothy and Trophimus, when they continued to be ill, was either that they did not have enough faith or that they had not repented sufficiently radically. But were they really less authentic in their faith and commitment than all those healed by Jesus in the ministry? And if Paul and his co-workers could not achieve the necessary conditions, what realistic probability, we might ask, has anyone else?

A third position may be distinguished, which still regards sickness

---

[37] When they came to terms with what had happened, Larry wrote up their story as the book, *We Let Our Son Die*, (Irvine, California: Harvest House, 1980).
[38] Against this, see Ch. 13, II.

as theologically 'abnormal', but anticipates more 'complicating factors'. This is essentially the position of Wimber's *Power Healing*. He regards continuing sickness essentially as an anomaly on the grounds that heal- ing is a core aspect of the presence of the kingdom of God. Jesus' ministry reveals sickness as intrinsically demonic, and that God's will is to liberate from it. Failure to receive healing is thus largely at- tributable to human causes. Accordingly he asserts: 'There are many reasons why people are not healed when prayed for. Most of the reasons involve some form of sin and unbelief'.[39] But he includes amongst these such factors as, e.g. disunity, failure to prevail in prayer in cases of chronic illness, incomplete or incorrect diagnoses resulting in wrong prayer, terminal disease at a natural time to die, etc. Rather surprisingly, almost as an explanation for a *minority* of cases, he cites the eschatological tension between the 'already' and the 'not yet', and comments:

> The examples of Epaphroditus, Timothy, Trophimus and Paul — and my own situation — are humbling reminders that the fullness of our salvation is yet to be revealed . . . that though the atonement provides for divine healing we have no right to presume that unless God heals in every instance there is something wrong with our faith or his faithfulness.[40]

But he immediately follows this with an analysis that suggests that 'the most fundamental reason' for failure is lack of persistence in prayer, and he concludes, 'There will be more . . . divine healing if only we persist in seeking him' (171). The whole treatment thus tends to play down the significance of the eschatological tension, to which Ladd him- self (whose position Wimber seeks to apply) gives far more emphasis.[41]

---

[39]Wimber, *Power Healing*, 164.
[40]*Power Healing*, 169.
[41]On Wimber's debt to Ladd's view of the kingdom of God, see, e.g. Sarles, 'Appraisal', 57–82 (71–76). There are evident problems in Wimber's position that still require more careful thinking through, including his somewhat over- exaggerated dualism between Satan and God, which risks compromising God's sovereignty, and such tensions as that between his assertions that God wishes to heal all, and that he is specifically *selective* about whom he heals (for the latter, see *Power Healing*, 164, appealing to, e.g., Jn. 5:1–9). Another tension is that between Wimber's assertions that the *main* reasons for failure are lack of faith and his assertion that he never blames the sick person for lack of faith if healing does not occur (so 186). For a discussion of the tensions in Wimber's position, see N. Wright, 'The Theology and Methodology of "Signs and Wonders" ', in Smail, Walker and N. Wright, *Renewal*, 71–85.

Here his associate, Deere, is more nuanced, recognizing that God may allow suffering and physical illness (the Satanic messenger/thorn in the flesh of 2 Cor. 12:8–10) for beneficial redemptive purposes, that there are ebbs and flows of God's outpourings of grace (and not merely in healing) in different places and periods of history, and that in many particular cases his sovereign will is simply beyond scrutiny.[42] In addition, Nigel Wright has pointed to the further 'complicating factor' of disease caused by societal and environmental factors, where healing may not be possible without fundamental restructuring of its human causes. Healing a case of asthma may thus simply bring temporary relief if the real problem is stress caused by work pressures and financial burdens, combined with living in an area with industry-related poor air quality. A return to the asthma, or some other illness, awaits in the wings if the causative structures are not dealt with.[43]

Our own position may be distinguished from Wimber's in regarding both healing and the lack of it as in different ways 'normal' in this age. Both the destruction of death and the resurrection of life fundamentally mark the believer.[44] With the former belong all sufferings, including not merely those encountered as a result of embracing the gospel and bearing witness, but those inherent in the particular forms of fallen society in which believers live, natural disaster, and the progressive impairments of people's energies and abilities which come with age, as well as particular diseases, whether epidemic, or genetic, or whatever.[45] With resurrection and life belong rescues from dangers and all forms of healing and deliverances from diseases, but also all individual and corporate experiences of Christ's self-revealing presence and transforming blessing, including gifts of grace to endure with thankfulness in adversity, and to recognize sufferings as fellowship in the sufferings of Christ.

---

[42]Deere, *Surprised*, 155–9. Compare also Henry H. Knight III, 'God's Faithfulness and God's Freedom: A Comparison of Contemporary Theologies of Healing', *JPT* 2 (1993), 65–89. God's sovereign freedom in healing was also emphasized by Kathryn Kuhlman (see Knight, 'God's Faithfulness', 74–8).

[43]N. Wright, 'Theology and Methodology', 80–82.

[44]See Chs. 8, V, and 14, II.

[45]We agree thus with P.G. Hiebert's assertion (criticizing Wimber's position), 'We need a theology of sickness, injury, suffering and death. These consequences of sin cannot be divorced from each other. The processes of aging and death are at work in humans from the moment of their conception. The side effects of this are sickness and bodily suffering. While God often does heal us by natural and by extraordinary means, our full delivery is only after death, when we receive our new body': cf. 'Healing and the Kingdom', in Coggins and Hiebert (eds.), *Wonders* , 109–52, esp. 138–9.

We agree with (e.g.) John Wimber and Nigel Wright that Jesus' ministry of healing clearly and uniquely expresses the ultimately *redemptive* divine will and desire of God. We may entirely agree with them, too, that both Jesus' ministry and that of the apostolic church strongly suggest that the holistic pattern of eschatological salvation *is a pattern that God wishes to display in history*. This would appear to imply that we should have a positive *expectation* of God's healing interventions as continuing demonstrations of the new level of his redemptive rule inaugurated in Christ. But this expectation should not be permitted to eclipse the equally biblical perception (understood most clearly by Paul) that God's will is also one of wrath and judgement on the present form of our sinful humanity. This judgement requires the destruction of our present bodily and historical existence, even if God's ultimate intention is for 'life'. Paul expresses the paradox neatly in Romans 8:10. Within the over-arching context of this paradox, believers should be able to combine a truly christocentric and lively expectation of God's saving interventions with an equally cruciform acceptance of weakness, sufferings, and death, knowing that the latter will ultimately lead to resurrection in Christ. The community of believers all experience both sides of the 'paradox', in different measures, in different individuals, and at different times. Their eschatological hope should always vitally inform their present expectation, and stretch their faith towards 'saving' interventions in the community, but (at least theoretically) they should not be confounded by various forms of sufferings (including illness), which is part of their sharing in the suffering of Christ. They should not view their differing 'lots' as evidence of a capricious deity, but see them both in a personal, and in a broader community, relational and historical context. The God who seeks to create a new humanity of reconciliation may permit an illness in one, e.g. for the greater goal of drawing the community together in supplication, support and love, almost as readily as he might heal to bring joy and glory to his name. Any worthwhile theology of 'healing' must fully allow for the diversity and complexity, in this age, of God's ultimately beneficial workings. Such a death-and-resurrection theology can best account for Frost's perception that God sometimes heals and at other times withholds healing from the same person, without there being any perceptible change in their spiritual condition.[46] It can also best account for Deere's 'ebbs and flows' of healing grace in history, while nevertheless anticipating not merely Lewis' distribution of healing and non-healing, but also his observation that in the Bible and in the world, God's healings appear to

---

[46]Henry Frost's, *Miraculous Healing* (London: MMS, 1951), remains one of the most balanced accounts on most issues.

have a bias towards the poor and the young.[47] In short, the gospel may be expected to raise the believer's expectation of healing, and bring him or her to confident prayer for such intervention, but it cannot guarantee healing on any specific occasion. It is the duty of faith — not merely the individual faith of the sufferer, but the corporate faith of his or her church — to discern and rest in God's will.

---

[47]See D.C. Lewis, *Healing*, 63–8.

Chapter Twenty

Concluding Reflections: The Spirit and 'Spiritual Gifts' in the Life of the Church Today

In September 1909, some fifty-six leaders of the Gnadau Alliance (the Pietist-Holiness current in German evangelical protestantism) published the infamous 'Berlin Declaration' (*Die Berliner Erklärung*), which essentially maintained that the Pentecostal Movement was 'not from on high, but from below', and that demons were at work in it. Amongst the reasons for branding it so were the curious manifestations (notably tongues), and the (alleged) propensity for prophecy to replace obedience to the word of God. By 1990, the Pentecostal churches, together with their spiritual children in the Charismatic Renewal movements, and New Church movements, together formed 23.4 per cent of the totality of the world's church-member Christians (and much the largest group in Protestant Christianity).[1] The Pentecostal denominations are now respected members of broader evangelical alliances,[2] and the Charismatic streams within the traditional denominations are similarly regarded. The earlier demonizing interpretation of the movement would receive little, if any, assent, except in the more bigoted extremes.[3] Those who doubt the validity of the 'spiritual gifts' being manifest in the various parts of the Renewal movement would tend rather to contrast what they regard as weak contemporary phenomena with the (allegedly) demonstrably miraculous nature of the corresponding New Testament gifts. Armed with this sharp contrast, they are then in a position to criticize the former as largely self-deception, hysteria,

---

[1]See D.B. Barrett, 'Statistics, Global', in S.M. Burgess and G.B. McGee (eds.), *Dictionary of Pentecostal and Charismatic Movements* (Grand Rapids: Zondervan, 1988), 811–30.

[2]A sign of its growing respectability, no doubt, is that Sheffield Academic Press publishes the *Journal of Pentecostal Theology*, and an allied monograph series.

[3]In Germany, however, the Berlin Declaration has left a legacy of division and sharp suspicion of the Pentecostal/Charismatic movements: see the history of its influence in L. Eisenlöffel, . . . *bis alle eins werden: Siebzig Jahre Berliner Erklärung und ihre Folgen*, (Erzhausen: Leuchten, 1979).

telepathy, altered states of consciousness, or some mixture of these, along with other 'natural' powers.

In the previous three chapters, we have noted that there is reason to suspect this hard contrast. It rests on a somewhat credulous idealizing understanding of the New Testament phenomena (especially in relation to prophecy and tongues), combined with a hermeneutic of suspicion in relationship to contemporary claims. In any case, cessationist critics have not sufficiently allowed for the possibility of a middle ground in relation to the phenomena today. That is, in claiming that modern prophecy and healing cannot be compared with the infallible, perfect gifts of these in the New Testament period, they have not explored the possibility that the present-day phenomena, while weaker than some of the New Testament manifestations, are nevertheless in real (theological and functional) continuity with them. It is this that we have claimed to be the case.

In what follows we face two questions. First, we must ask whether the spiritual gifts we have given attention to are unique to the Pentecostal and Charismatic streams of Christianity. Second, we ask whether there is any biblical, theological or practical reason to assume that reception of these and other related 'charismata' depends upon a post-conversion crisis experience.

I. ARE THE PROTOTYPICAL SPIRITUAL GIFTS UNIQUE TO PENTECOSTAL OR CHARISMATIC FORMS OF CHRISTIANITY?

We are compelled to answer 'No',[4] at least with respect to two of the three prototypical gifts we chose to study. Tongues is the only phenomenon that appears to be without parallel in the church today outside Pentecostal/Charismatic streams of Christianity. But even in this case, we need to qualify the apparent 'uniqueness' of tongues to the Pentecostal movements. As we have noted,[5] other groups in the past experienced glossolalia.[6] Furthermore, tongues is in any case a type of invasive speech, and so related to other forms of the latter, including, e.g. invasively empowered preaching or witness, which is found quite commonly outside the Pentecostal/Charismatic sector.

---

[4]Cf. Packer's telling criticism of Pentecostal/Charismatic claims to the effect that 'spiritual gifts' have been 'restored' to the church in these movements alone: *Keep in Step*, 197ff.

[5]See Ch. 16, §III.

[6]Charismatics unwarrantedly tend to take the phenomena as evidence that the practitioners were 'baptized-in-the-Spirit' arch- Pentecostalists.

Claims to healings and to some kinds of prophecy are relatively commonplace in the church outside the Pentecostal/Charismatic sector. Healings can be found outside the Charismatic tradition and independent of it, for example, typically in 'the Guild of Health' and 'the Guild of St. Raphael' in Anglicanism; the Iona Community; at Lourdes, etc.,[7] and in many of the more traditional churches which (encouraged by Charismatic practices) have begun to arrange occasional healing services. While it is true that such claims in regard to healing are less widespread and less emphasized than in the Pentecostal and Charismatic traditions, they cannot be ignored.

Prophecy too, when rightly understood, is located in many if not all streams of evangelicalism, and the pietist traditions of other churches. By this we do not mean to condone the generalizing of the term to the point where it connotes God-enabled preaching, teaching, or 'any verbal enforcement of biblical teaching as it applies to one's present hearers'.[8] These are spiritual gifts indeed (so Paul would teach us), and related in different ways to prophetism, but they are not oracular speech (cf. Chs. 12 and 18 above). But the phenomenon of oracular speech itself, in some form, is exercised by many believers outside the Pentecostal movements and their offspring. Spiritually-minded Christians often seek God's guidance on decisions which they know the Bible cannot settle for them; and many expect that God will sometimes give them a definite and direct indication — a 'word from the Lord' on the matter.[9] Where such is experienced, and related to others to whom it is also directed, we have the dynamics of what the New Testament means by 'prophecy', and of what is experienced in Charismatic circles and labelled 'prophecy' there. Many traditional evangelicals, for example,

---

[7]See Kelsey, *Healing*, ch. 9; Gardner, *Miracles*, chs. 3–4; Taylor, 'Historical Perspective', 54–6.

[8]So Packer, *Keep in Step*, 215.

[9]Gentry lists a number of 'orthodox' reformed teachers who discount the possibility of the Spirit giving any direct guidance or impressions other than through the plain meaning of Scripture (on the grounds that all such claims are tantamount to the claim to new revelation, beyond Scripture, and so threaten the unique authority of the latter; *Gift*, 91–4), but this is not a usual view, nor a credible one. Modern 'prophecy' (and related phenomena) is not given the same authority as Scripture, for the reasons explained in Ch. 18. Furthermore the whole argument forces Gentry to the special pleading that Paul's words in (e.g.) Phil. 3:15, and the whole prayer in Eph. 1:17–19 (sim 3:15–19), were intended only for the apostolic period, after which such a 'Spirit of wisdom and revelation in the knowledge of [God]' was withdrawn from the church, which had the Bible instead (cf. Gentry, *Gift*, 60–1, though see 62 for a different explanation).

would not be unduly surprised if a pastor approached a member of his congregation, and said something like, 'While I was praying for you, I think the Lord told me I should speak to you about going into the ministry. I have the sense he has a great work for you ahead.' I suggest that such instances (and they are regular) *are* forms of prophecy (in the sense we have defined). Similarly, preachers and teachers in the same tradition not infrequently claim that God has especially 'given' them some particular message (or some specific point) for a congregation. Here again, we have the essential *dynamic* of New Testament prophecy. The persons concerned first become aware that God wishes to address a particular issue. They then attempt to elucidate what they understand God wishes to say to the congregation, whether through expounding a Scripture passage to which they feel especially led, or by some other means. Depending on the degree of elaboration by the preacher/teacher, one might call the result 'prophecy' (if he keeps as close as possible to what he thought he 'heard' from God) or 'prophetic preaching/teaching' (if he expounds and applies the received 'message' as a full sermon). The real difference between the Charismatics and (e.g.) more traditional evangelicals, on the spiritual realities of what we have called 'prophecy', are perhaps not so much ones of substance, but rather matters of *semantics* (different understandings of what the word 'prophecy' means), of *expectation* (Charismatics/Pentecostals seek and expect such phenomena much more frequently), and of *presentation* (the Charismatic may say, 'The Lord showed me in a picture', where her evangelical counterpart is more likely to say, e.g. 'The Lord laid it on my heart that . . .'). There may also be differentia in the range of content and in power of delivery — but the more traditional evangelical experiences cannot be sharply divided off from the Charismatic: they too lie within the boundaries of the ancient patterns of oracular speech. As to the clarity of perception of the initial revelatory experience, there are no necessary differences between the two groups: some evangelicals claim (occasionally) remarkably strong and clear 'words' or other types of leadings (rarely, however, visionary leading) on an issue; many Charismatics would confess very indistinct 'reception' of some prophecies. The strongest dividing line within these phenomena may lie not across the evangelical/Charismatic border, but within Pentecostal/Charismatic circles — that is, the line between those who open their mouths and speak out a 'prophecy' without any idea of what is coming (for which there is perhaps less firm New Testament basis) and those who have at least some notion of the message before they speak at all.[10] If traditional evangelicals and others hesitate to use the term 'prophecy'

---

[10]See Yocum, *Prophecy*, 75–9.

to denote the sort of phenomenon we have described, it is perhaps due to a mistaken understanding of New Testament prophecy, namely as a primarily doctrinal revelation parallel in authority to canonical prophecy. Here Grudem's thesis that congregational prophecy was a mixed phenomenon, in which elements of revelation were combined with human and fallible interpretation, may serve to tumble the barriers between Pentecostals/Charismatics and the more traditional forms of Christianity with which they otherwise belong.

When we say the Pentecostal or Charismatic experience of the prototypical spiritual gifts is not unique, but found in other churches, to some degree, we do not of course imply that it is necessarily found in those churches in biblical or ideal measure. If Pentecostal and Charismatic churches are in danger of overemphasizing some gifts in relation to others, it may well be that the more traditional churches have marginalized and underemphasized them.

II. DOES RECEPTION OF THE PROTOTYPICAL CHARISMATIC GIFTS DEPEND ON A POST-CONVERSION CRISIS EXPERIENCE?

Is there any biblical, theological or practical reason to assume that reception of such charismatic gifts as tongues, interpretation, prophecy and gifts of healings, depends on a post-conversion crisis experience of empowering?

1. Biblical/Theological Reasons?

As we have seen, there is no basis for such a view in Paul.[11] He does not restrict charismata to a special, 'Spirit-baptized', group. The lesson of Paul in 1 Corinthians 12–14 (and Romans 12) is that the whole body of Christ is differently enabled for mutually supportive acts of service. And Paul's very point is that the charismata dealt with in 1 Corinthians 12:8–10 cannot be segregated from the rest; they are not allocated to a special group of pneumatics — that is precisely the Corinthians' misunderstanding. Rather he expects the different gifts to be granted to the prayerful seeker and in accordance with God's will (cf. 1 Cor. 14:1,13). More important, for Paul (as for John[12]) the Spirit of Christ that is necessary for the new covenant life of eschatological sonship is above all the Spirit of prophecy who makes the Father and the Son manifest

---

[11]See Chs. 7-8, 10 and 15 above.
[12]See Chs. 4–6.

to the disciple, and affords the wisdom which enables the believer to grasp the meaning of the gospel and to be led deeper into it.[13] This means the gift of the Spirit of prophecy cannot be a *second* distinct gift, or *donum superadditum* (even if there may be subsequent renewing *appropriations* of this gift, e.g. for new spheres of ministry).

Pentecostals and neo-Pentecostals wish to read Luke-Acts as in a special sense *their* story. They identify the disciples' progress towards authentic Easter-faith in Jesus, and their deepening relationship with him, with conversional belief and reception of salvation. And they understand reception of the Spirit at Pentecost as paradigmatic of their own subsequent Spirit-baptism (empowering for mission). The Samaritan experience in Acts 8 is seen as confirmation of the pattern. But, as we have seen, this reading is profoundly problematic.[14] Undoubtedly, Pentecostals are right to recognize that 'salvation' is much more than coming to believe the gospel's offer of forgiveness of sins. It has more to do with the reversal of the alienations of the 'fall', and so Pentecostals are right to stress that salvation is fundamentally about coming into existential relationship with the Father in and through the Son. But this takes us to the heart of the problem with the Pentecostal reading. Before the ascension it was perhaps possible for the disciples to enter a deepening relationship with their Lord, without receiving the Spirit, for Jesus was there alongside them, to see, to touch, and to hear (even so, as John clarifies for us, the disciples' entry into this saving self-revelation of the Father in the Son was very limited before Easter). On our side of the ascension, however, there is simply *no way of coming into existential or 'experienced' relationship with the risen Lord, except through the Spirit of prophecy who makes him manifest*, e.g. in gifts of revelation, illumination, wisdom, and inspired speech. The gift of the Spirit, promised in Acts 2, is thus no *donum superadditum* of power. It is rather the gift of the Spirit of prophecy promised by Joel; the organ of communication between the risen Lord and the Father, in the heavenlies, and the disciples on earth. Without this gift the disciples could not have continued meaningful Christian existence as we know it; nor could any others come under Christ's lordship and rule. That is why from Acts 2 onwards the gift of the Spirit is normally attached to conversion-initiation, and why the suspension of the Spirit from baptism (as at Acts 8) is regarded as an anomaly to be corrected as soon as possible. The advent of the Spirit of prophecy does not create a special class of spiritually-gifted Christians over against others. Rather, reception of this gift initiates and enables that relationship to the heavenly

---

[13]See Chs. 7–8.
[14]See Chs. 3 and 10, above, or Turner, *Power, passim*, esp. ch. 14.

Lord which marks true Christian existence. It brings to each the means of receiving not only 'communion with the Lord' viewed generally, but also the same concretely specified in charismata of heavenly wisdom and knowledge. These may then inform the teacher, guide the missionary, lead in individual decisions, give diagnosis to the pastor, 'irresistible wisdom' and power to the preacher, or be related as prophecy to the congregation or other individuals. The 'power' received by the apostles (cf. Acts 1:8) was not something in addition to Joel's promised gift, but precisely an intense experience of some of the charismata which are part and parcel of the operation of the Spirit as Joel's promised Spirit of prophecy.[15]

The separation of reception of the Spirit by the Samaritans from their faith in Christ certainly is not blamed by Luke on inadequate faith, as Dunn suggests, but nor can the separation be regarded as paradigmatic — had Philip, or the apostles, left the situation unrectified, the Samaritans' faith, aroused by Philip's preaching, could never have been consummated in ongoing Christian life under the active day-to-day lordship of Jesus.[16] At this point we need again to question the Pentecostal interpretation of the Samaritan experience. Many Pentecostals draw a direct comparison between the Samaritans of 8:4–16 and most believers outside the Pentecostal/Charismatic sector of the church, including even e.g. pious and fervent evangelicals. This is surely quite contrary to Luke's intention. If the Samaritan believers were praying with the spiritual depth and inspiring reverence of a William Still, or preaching and teaching with the spiritual wisdom, power and influence of a John Stott or Dick Lucas, or even if they were simply marked with a lively joy in the gospel and love for Christ, neither the apostles nor Luke would have concluded that the Spirit of prophecy had not yet come upon them. Such a conclusion could only be reached where there was no sign of the Spirit as God's self-revealing presence, i.e. no apparent sense of existential encounter with the risen Lord, no vital spiritual wisdom and understanding, no immediate sense of God's love or of his dynamic grace at work in them, and no flowering of doxological response. One does come across such cases within largely nominal Christianity, and it may be correct to challenge such people with the words Luke attributes to Paul, in Acts 19:2, 'Did you receive the Spirit when you "believed"?' But such a challenge is *not* appropriate when addressed to healthy, vigorous and witnessing forms of Christianity. And it is particularly incongruous to suggest that effective evangelists, or pastors of spiritually lively and growing churches, may not have

---

[15]See ch. 3 above, and *Power*, chs. 10–14.

[16]Against Dunn, *Baptism*, ch. 5, see Turner, *Power*, chs. 12 (esp. §2.2) and 13.

received what Luke means by the gift of the Spirit, when Luke himself so strongly emphasizes the Spirit's work precisely as empowering mission to the outsider and to the church (cf. Chs. 2–3, above).[17]

It is not surprising that scholars in the Charismatic movement have tended to concede that post-ascension reception of the Spirit in John, Paul and Luke-Acts marks the beginning of Christian life, not a second level. Nor can the language of 'filled by' or 'full of' the Spirit be successfully correlated with a second-blessing theology.[18] There has consequently been a tendency, especially in Catholic Charismatic circles, to differentiate between theological and objective Spirit baptism/reception, tied to initiation, and subjective experience of the same, introducing people to the world of charismata.[19] The immediate response must be that there is no separate theoretical or biblical basis advanced for this, and so the position is really a theologizing of the practical argument to be looked at next.

---

[17]David Pawson effectively falls into these traps when he insists that receiving the Spirit is itself a discernible experience (normally attended by definite audible or visible phenomena), and concludes that many evangelicals have simply believed in Jesus without receiving the Spirit if they have not had a conscious 'moment' of Spirit-reception; see *Fourth Wave* (London: Hodder, 1993), ch. 9; *idem, Birth*, esp. ch. 35. In the latter, he speaks of a type of person 'who having repented and believed was baptized and has continued in the Christian life for many years, growing in grace and holiness, maturing in trust and obedience, being faithful and fruitful in service, and being devoted and dependable in character — yet never having had an experience which could be called "baptism in the Spirit" ' (291). He concludes that such people have yet to receive the Spirit. But certainly in Pauline terms this is simply incoherent. It is the gift of the Spirit which enables precisely these graces. The mistake comes in the assumption that the moment of the Spirit's coming upon a person must itself be consciously perceived. The real test, however, is not whether there was some *initial* consciously experienced Spirit-reception at conversion-initiation, but whether the Spirit's activity has subsequently become apparent in the person's life. And as Pawson includes amongst the activities of the Spirit received the heart-felt 'abba', the awesome sense of God's holy presence, the flood of love prompting to new relationships, spontaneous prayer, etc. he should surely be willing to recognize that believers who have experienced such things have 'received the Spirit', even if they did not have a conscious initial experience of Spirit-reception.

[18]See above, Ch. 10.

[19]See Hummel, *Fire*, 171; T. Smail, *Reflected Glory* (London: Hodder, 1975), chs. 6 and 10; L.J. Suenens, *A New Pentecost* (London: DLT, 1975), 80–1, and Lederle, *Treasures*, chs. 3–4.

2. Empirical Reasons?

It is often alleged today that in practice Christians only receive empowering and charismatic gifts after some initiating, and consciously realized, spiritual experience. This is usually, though not always, expected to be associated with speaking in tongues. Pentecostals and neo-Pentecostals identify this package with their understanding of Acts, and interpret their experience as an empowering 'baptism in Spirit', while sacramentalists are more likely to explain the experience as the initial 'flowering of baptismal (or Confirmational) grace'. Reality, one suspects, is much more complex than the theory. Of those who claim to fit the pattern there seem to me to be at least three types:[20]

(i) A few who have had an intense crisis-experience of the Spirit with vigorous manifestations. Testimonies to this are not lacking. Such people call themselves 'Spirit-baptized'.

(ii) A much larger group who, for example, were prayed for at a Pentecostal or Charismatic meeting and who have had a subjectively strong, but not especially vigorously manifested experience, probably spontaneously spoke in tongues, and may even have been 'slain in the Spirit', or the like.

(iii) Again a large group, who, when prayed for, had no spontaneous experience (other than mild euphoria), but were persuaded to initiate tongues speech, and, on achieving this, accepted (by faith) that they had received the same package as types (i) and (ii) — though they may even register disappointment concerning their experience if pressed.

All three types usually discover changes in their pattern of spirituality after the 'crisis experience', perhaps most marked in type (i), but not necessarily so. There are usually claims to greater awareness of the Lord, deepened and more expectant faith, greater joy, and development of a new range of charismata. At first sight this provides an impressive argument for the view that a second blessing type of crisis experience is the key to reception of the kind of charismata described in 1 Corinthians 12:8–10. However, there are serious counter-considerations.

(1) One cannot but feel that testimonies from those with type (i) experiences tend to become the stereotype for those with types (ii) and (iii), and that this leads to the preaching and teaching of

---

[20]I base this merely in informal discussions and questioning amongst students and church members. There is an evident need for a formal and rigorous empirical investigation.

an exaggerated experiential dualism (much, or all, was sin, doubt and weakness before; much, or all, is faith, power and victory now). Where such teaching is accepted, it is of course liable to become self-fulfilling, creating a negative expectation in people with respect to the possibility of 'gifts' before their own 'crisis-experience', and a positive one afterwards. Worse, the exaggerated personal experiential dualism tends to be projected onto (e.g.) the Charismatic/traditional Christian divide so as to create a claimed experiential dualism between relatively powerless traditional Christianity, lacking charismata, and Charismatics living in victory, power and the plenitude of charismata. It is this last dualism which popularly undergirds the 'practical argument' for pursuing a post-conversion crisis 'appropriation' of the Spirit, as 'Spirit-baptism', 'filling with the Spirit', 'release of the Spirit', or whatever.

(2) A major problem facing the practical argument is that the dualism breaks down when examined. Healing is not a gift confined to the Pentecostal/Charismatic streams of the church, even if it is practised more often by them. Similarly, we have seen, 'words of the Lord' or 'revelations' (in the general New Testament sense, not in the technical systematic theological one) are not imparted just to Pentecostals and Charismatics. They are widely reported (albeit in different language) in the evangelical, pietist, puritan, Quaker, and traditional mystical literature too. In other words, on closer examination, there is no sharp dividing line between Pentecostal/Charismatic experience and that of many other forms of vibrant Christianity. There is no question of 'leaving the realm of natural Christianity' and entering, by the gateway of Spirit-baptism, into 'supernatural Christianity', as it is popularly put; nor of leaving a charisma-less Christianity for a charismatic one. The basic difference is one of degree and not of kind; one of emphasis, and not absolute. Pentecostalism and its spiritual children happen to enjoy and emphasize charismata, many of which are exercised under a different name, and paid less attention, in other Christian circles. Being forced to accept that one stands on the wrong side of an experiential dualism, and so to seek 'Spirit-baptism' as the gateway to greener pastures, may be one way of passing from more traditional forms of Christianity to the Charismatic pole. But it is neither a necessary way, nor a particularly appropriate way, for the very reason that it suggests passage from one kind of Christian experience to another of a different kind.

(3) There is evidence that people receive charismata of prophecy,

etc., without any immediately related crisis experience. In this context we may note that the large group we earlier labelled 'type (iii)' crisis experiences do not in reality involve an *experience* as such at all, but merely an apparent transition from one sort of spirituality to a different set of expectations and experiences. Equally, there are plentiful testimonies of people who have initiated tongues speech, or felt it quietly to be 'liberated' through them, in their own times of spiritual devotion, without any particular accompanying 'experience'.

(4)   As we have seen, the charismata of tongues, interpretation, prophecy, words of knowledge (etc.) are not so different in nature and spiritual dynamic from inspired preaching, teaching, and other ministerial gifts of discernment and wisdom which are widely accepted as current outside the Pentecostal/Charismatic sector, that one would wish to suggest that some crisis experience should be necessary in order to pass from a spirituality involving the latter set to one that embraces the former too. If the evangelical Christian wishes in his or her heart to become a 'Charismatic' (we only mention that direction of 'conversion' as it is the more common), what he or she should need is not laying on of hands and a crisis-experience, but merely the sort of teaching given in 'Charismatic' circles to the 'freshly Spirit-baptized' as to how to 'develop their gifts'. The Pentecostal teacher considers his fledglings to have the potential of any of the 'gifts', and to need only to learn how to discern and use them. In such circles, Christians are regarded as having this potential by virtue of having been Spirit-baptized. Our counter-thesis is simply that it is not by virtue of some second 'Spirit-baptism', but by initially receiving the Spirit as Luke's promised Spirit of prophecy, that any Christian has such potential. Indeed, believers in the more traditional forms of Christianity are already experiencing many of the charismata of this same Spirit and, were they to wish to become 'Charismatics', they should only need, before God, to redirect their emphases and expectations.

In sum, the practical argument for the actual *need* for a second crisis experience of appropriation of the Spirit (under whatever name) rests on a misunderstanding. The essence of this lies in the creation of a set of false experiential dualisms and the absolutizing of one of them, thereby suggesting that 'Pentecostal' experience is fundamentally different in kind — i.e. in a different realm from (e.g.) traditional evangelical experience. Such a view, but only such a view, should *require* a second and gateway 'reception' or 'appropriation' of the Spirit. This is not to deny that God will occasionally equip a believer for some whole new area of ministry through a 'crisis' experience of spiritual empowering (as with Jesus at Jordan). It is, however, to say that such an experience is by no means the *only* way to spiritual empowering (for many this comes instead as a gradual series of growth experiences), nor is it a paradigmatic and normative way for believers.

III. BRIEF CONCLUDING COMMENTS

The whole thrust of our study has suggested a *via media* in spirituality between Pentecostalism and more traditional forms of Christianity. The Spirit's gifts are manifold, and involve varying degrees of divine inspiration and human interpretation or skill. Some of the positive emphases of both sides of the debate are right. With Pentecostals we may affirm the essentially holistic nature of salvation, its presence in (e.g.) exorcism and healing, and the availability of God's direct leading in prophecy and related gifts. With other sectors of Christianity (including cessationists) we may affirm the great importance of spiritual preaching and teaching, and the fundamental import of the Spirit's work in illuminating the Christ-event to faith, and in showing how the apostolic teaching should be appropriated in our day. It may be admitted these groups have some justification for their fear that the Pentecostal/Charismatic contribution has been unhelpful in the way it has downgraded thoughtful understanding of the gospel (and of its application to our world) in favour of the immediacy of 'experiences'. Without a rigorously disciplined and profound analysis of the Christian gospel, and of its relationship to discipleship and to the world, the church can only expect more pastoral disasters, more ecclesial divisions over avoidable misunderstandings, and the further loss of credibility in the world. At the same time, the Pentecostal/Charismatic emphases have correctly pointed the church to the fact that Christianity is not merely a set of rational propositions about God, to be apprehended by the intellect. It involves every level of the church's individual and corporate being. And Pentecostalism has rightly pointed to the fact that contemporary 'experiences' of God may resonate with the biblical revelation in such a way as to open the believer's eyes to aspects of that revelation to which more traditional and 'rational' forms of Christianity have often simply been blind. The positive way forward for the church lies in the combining of the wisdom of both sides, not in the often arrogant and alienating polemics between them. In this context we may perhaps be permitted to conclude with words drawn from the exhortation of Ephesians 4:3–6, and which reflect the centre of the theology of Jesus, Paul and John:[21]

> With all lowliness and meekness, with patience, forbearing one another in love, *strive eagerly to maintain the unity of the Spirit in the bond of peace.* For the body is one, and the Spirit is one, just as you were called to the one hope . . . one Lord, one faith, one baptism, one God and Father of us all, who is above all, and through all and in all.

---

[21]For justification of this claim, see Turner, 'Mission', *passim.*

Select Bibliography

Atkinson, W., 'Pentecostal Responses to Dunn's *Baptism in the Holy Spirit: Pauline Responses', JPT* 7 (1995), 49–72

Aune, D.E., *Prophecy in Early Christianity and the Ancient Mediterranean World* (Exeter: Paternoster, 1983)

von Baer, H., *Der Heilige Geist in den Lukasschriften* (Stuttgart: Kohlhammer, 1926)

Barclay, J.M.G., *Obeying the Truth: A Study of Paul's Ethics in Galatians* (Edinburgh: T. & T. Clark, 1988)

Barrett, C.K., *The Holy Spirit and the Gospel Tradition* (London: SPCK, 1966)

Beasley-Murray, G.R., *Gospel of Life: Theology in the Fourth Gospel* (Peabody: Hendrickson, 1991)

Belleville, L.J., *Reflections of Glory. Paul's Polemical Use of the Moses-Doxa Tradition in 2 Corinthians 3.1–18* (Sheffield: JSOT Press, 1991)

Best, E., 'The Interpretation of Tongues', *SJT* 28 (1975), 45–62

——, 'Prophets and preachers', *SJT* 12 91959), 129–50

——, 'Spirit-Baptism', *NovT* 4 (1960), 236–43

Betz, O., *Der Paraklet* (Leiden: Brill, 1963)

Bickle, M. and Sullivant, M., *Growing in the Prophetic* (Eastbourne: Kingsway, 1995)

Billington, A., Lane, T. and Turner, M. (eds.), *Mission and Meaning: Essays presented to Peter Cotterell* (Carlisle: Paternoster, 1995)

Billington, A., 'The Paraclete and Mission in the Fourth Gospel', in Billington, Lane and Turner (eds.), *Mission and Meaning*, 90–115

Bittlinger, A., *Gifts and Graces: A Commentary on I Corinthians 12–14* (Grand Rapids: Eerdmans, 1967)

Bittner, W.J., *Heilung – Zeichen der Herrschaft Gottes* (Neukirchen-Vluyn: Aussaat, 1984)

Boring, M.E., *The Continuing voice: Christian Prophecy and the Gospel Tradition* (Louisville: Westminster/John Knox, 1991)

Bovon, F., *Luke the Theologian: Thirty-three Years of Research (1950–1983)* (Allison Park: Pickwick, 1987)

Breck, J., *The Origins of Johannine Pneumatology* (Crestwood: St. Vladimir's Seminary Press, 1991)

Brockhaus, U., *Charisma und Amt: Die paulinische Charismenlehre auf dem Hintergrund frühchristlichen Gemeindefunktionen* (Wuppertal: Brickhaus, 1975³)

Brown, C., *Miracles and the Critical Mind* (Exeter: Paternoster, 1984)

——, *That You May Believe: Miracles and Faith Then and Now* (Exeter: Paternoster, 1985)

Brown, M., *Israel's Divine Healer* (Carlisle: Paternoster, 1995)

Brown, R.E., 'Appendix V: the Paraclete', in *The Gospel According to Saint John* (2 vols.; London: Chapman, 1971), 1135–44

——, 'The Paraclete in the Fourth Gospel', *NTS* 13 (1966–67), 113–32

Budgen, V., *The Charismatics and the Word of God* (Welwyn: Evangelical Press, 1985)

Burge, G.M., *The Anointed Community: The Holy Spirit in the Johannine Community* (Grand Rapids: Eerdmans, 1987)

Burgess, S.M. and McGee, G.B. (eds.), *Dictionary of Pentecostal and Charismatic Movements* (Grand Rapids: Zondervan, 1988)

Carroll, J.T., 'Jesus as Healer in Luke-Acts', in Lovering (ed.), *Society of Biblical Literature 1994 Seminar Papers* 33 (Atlanta: Scholars, 1993) 269–85

Carson, D.A., *Showing the Spirit* (Grand Rapids: Baker, 1987 and Carlisle: Paternoster, 1995)

Cartledge, M.J., 'Charismatic Prophecy', *JET* 8 (1995), 71–88

——, 'Charismatic Prophecy: A Definition and Description', *JPT* 5 (1994), 79–120

——, 'Prophecy in the Contemporary Church: A Theological Examination', unpublished MPhil dissertation, Oak Hill, 1989

Casdorph, H.R., *The Miracles* (Plainfield: Logos, 1976)

Chevallier, M.A., 'Luc et l'Esprit, à la Mémoire du P. Augustin George (1915–77)', Recherches de Science Religieuse 56 (1982), 1–16

——, '«Pentecôtes» lucaniennes et «Pentecôtes» johanniques', in J. Delorme and J. Duplacy (eds.), *La Parole de Grâce: Études lucaniennes à la Mémoire d'-Augustin George* (Paris: Recherches de Science Religieuse, 1981), 301–14

Childs, B.S., *Biblical Theology of the Old and New Testaments* (London: SCM, 1992)

Christie-Murray, D., *Voices from the Gods: Speaking in Tongues* (London: RKP, 1978

Coggins, J.R. and Hiebert, P.G. (eds.), *Wonders and the Word: An Examination of Issues Raised by John Wimber and the Vineyard Movement* (Winnipeg: Kindred Press, 1989)

Congar, Y., *I Believe in the Holy Spirit* (vols. 1–3; London: Chapman, 1983)

Cotterell, P. and Turner, M., *Linguistics and Biblical Interpretation* (London: SPCK, 1989)

Crone, T.M., *Early Christian Prophecy* (Baltimore: St Mary's UP, 1973)

Dautzenberg, G., *Urchristliche Prophetie* (Stuttgart: Kohlhammer, 1975)

Davies, J.G., 'Pentecost and Glossolalia', *JTS* 3 (1952), 228–31

Deere, J., *Surprised by the Power of the Spirit* (Eastbourne: Kingsway, 1994)

Dunn, J.D.G., *Baptism in the Holy Spirit: A Re-Examination of the New Testament Teaching on the Gift of the Spirit in Relation to Pentecostalism Today* (London: SCM, 1970)

——, *Christology in the Making* (London: SCM, 1980)

——, *Jesus and the Spirit* (London: SCM, 1975)

——, *The Partings of the Ways* (London: SCM, 1991)

——, *The Theology of Paul's Letter to the Galatians* (Cambridge: CUP, 1993)

——, *Unity and Diversity in the New Testament: An Enquiry into the Character of Earliest Christianity* (London: SCM, 1977)

——, 'Baptism in the Spirit: A Response to Pentecostal Scholarship on Luke-Acts', *JPT* 3 (1993), 3–27

——, 'I Corinthians 15:45 – Last Adam, Life-giving Spirit', in Lindars and Smalley (eds.), *Christ and Spirit*, 127–42

——, 'Jesus – Flesh and Spirit: An Exposition of Romans I.3–4', *JTS* 24 (1973), 40–68

——, 'Ministry and the Ministry: The Charismatic Renewal's Challenge to Traditional Ecclesiology', in Robeck (ed.), *Experiences*, 81–101

——, 'Spirit and Fire Baptism', *NovT* 14 (1972), 81–92

Edgar, T.R., *Miraculous Gifts* (New Jersey: Loiseaux, 1983)

Ellis, E.E., *Prophecy and Hermeneutic in Early Christianity: New Testament Essays* (Tübingen: Mohr, 1978)

Engelsen, N.I.J., 'Glossolalia and other Forms of Inspired Speech according to 1 Corinthians 12–14', unpublished PhD dissertation, Yale University, 1970

Ervin, H.M., *Conversion-Initiation and the Baptism in the Holy Spirit: A Critique of James D.G. Dunn Baptism in the Holy Spirit* (Peabody: Hendrickson, 1984)

Evans, C.A., *Jesus and His Contemporaries* (Leiden: Brill, 1995)

Farnell, F.D., 'Does the New Testament Teach Two Prophetic Gifts?', *BSac*150 (1993), 62–88

——, 'The Gift of Prophecy in the Old and New Testament', *BSac* 149 (1992), 387–410

——, 'When Will the Gift of Prophecy Cease?', *BSac* 150 (1993), 171–202

Fee, G.D., *The Disease of the Health and Wealth Gospels* (Costa Mesa: Word for Today, 1979)

——, *God's Empowering Presence: The Holy Spirit in the Letters of Paul* (Peabody: Hendrickson/Carlisle: Paternoster, 1994)

——, 'Christology and Pneumatology in Romans 8:9–11 – and Elsewhere: Some Reflections on Paul as a Trinitarian', in Green and Turner (eds.), *Jesus of Nazareth*, 312–31

Forbes, C., *Prophecy and Inspired Speech in Early Christianity and its Hellenistic Environment* (Tübingen: Mohr, 1995)

Franck, E., *Revelation Taught: The Paraclete in the Gospel of John* (Lund: Gleerup, 1985)

Franklin, E., *Luke: Interpreter of Paul, Critic of Matthew* (Sheffield: SAP, 1994)

Fung, R.Y.K., 'Charismatic versus Organized Ministry. An Examination of an Alleged Antithesis', *EvQ* 52 (1980), 195–214

——, 'Function of Office? A Survey of the New Testament Evidence', *ERT* 8 (1984), 16–39

——, 'Ministry, Community and Spiritual Gifts', *EvQ* 56 (1984), 3–20

Gaffin, R.B. *Perspectives on Pentecost: Studies in New Testament Teaching on the Gifts of the Holy Spirit* (Phillipsburg: Presbyterian and Reformed, 1979)

Gardner, R., *Healing Miracles* (London: DLT, 1986)

Gentry, K.L., *The Charismatic Gift of Prophecy* (Memphis: Footstool Publications, 1986 and 19892)

George, A., 'L'Esprit Saint dans l'Oeuvre de Luc', *RB* 85 (1978), 500–42

Gillespie, T.W., *The First Theologians: A Study in Early Christian Prophecy* (Grand Rapids: Eerdmans, 1994)

Green, J.B., *Hearing the New Testament: Strategies for Interpretation* (Carlisle: Paternoster, 1995)

——, *The Theology of the Gospel of Luke* (Cambridge: CUP, 1995)

——, and McKnight, S. (eds.), *Dictionary of Jesus and the Gospels* (Leicester: IVP, 1992)

——, and Turner, M. (eds.), *Jesus of Nazareth* (Grand Rapids: Eerdmans/Carlisle: Paternoster, 1994)

Grieg, G.S. and Springer, K.S. (eds.), *The Kingdom and the Power* (Ventura, CA: Regal, 1993)

Grieg, G.S., 'The Purpose of Signs and Wonders in the New Testament: What Terms for Miraculous Power Denote and their Relationship to the Gospel', in Grieg and Springer (eds.), *Kingdom*, 133–74

Grudem, W., *Are the Miraculous Gifts for Today: Four Views* (Leicester: IVP, 1996)
———, *The Gift of Prophecy in 1 Corinthians* (Washington: UPA, 1982; short title *Gift*)
———, *The Gift of Prophecy* (Eastbourne: Kingsway, 1988; short title *Prophecy*)
———, '1 Corinthians 14:20–25: Prophecy and Tongues as Signs of God's Attitude', *WJT* 41 (1979), 381–96
———, 'Should Christians Expect Miracles Today? Objections and Answers from the Bible', in Grieg and Springer (eds.), *Kingdom*, 55–110
Gundry, R.H., ' "Ecstatic Utterance" (NEB)', *JTS* 17 (1966), 299–307
Gunkel, J., *The Influence of the Holy Spirit: The Popular view of the Apostolic Age and the Theology of the Apostle Paul* (Philadelphia: Fortress, 1979)
Hafemann, S.J., *Suffering and the Spirit: An Exegetical Study of II Cor 2.14–3.3 Within the Context of the Corinthian Correspondence* (Tübingen: Mohr, 1986)
Hamilton, M.P. (ed.), *The Charismatic Movement* (Grand Rapids: Eerdmans, 1975)
Hamilton, N.G., *The Holy Spirit and Eschatology in Paul* (Edinburgh: Oliver and Boyd, 1957)
Harrisville, R.A., 'Speaking in Tongues: A Lexicographical Study', *CBQ* 38 (1976), 35–48
Hatina, T.R., 'John 20,22 in its Eschatological Context: Promise of Fulfilment?', *Bib* 74 (1993), 196–219
Haya-Prats, G., *L'Esprit Force de l'Église* (Paris: Cerf, 1975)
Hemer, C.H., *The Book of Acts in the Setting of Hellenistic History* (Tübingen: Mohr, 1989)
Hemphill, K.S., *Spiritual Gifts Empowering the New Testament Church* (Nashville: Broadman, 1988)
———, 'The Pauline Concept of Charisma: A Situational and Developmental Approach', PhD dissertation, Cambridge, 1977
Hermann, I., *Kyrios und Pneuma: Studien zur Christologie der paulinischen Hauptbriefe* (Munich: Kösel, 1961)
Hill, C., *Blessing the Church?* (Guildford: Eagle, 1995)
———, *. . . And They Shall Prophesy: A New Prophetic Movement in the Church Today* (London: Marshall Pickering, 1990)
———, *Prophecy Past and Present* (Crowborough: Highland Books, 1989)
Hill, D., *Greek Words with Hebrew Meanings* (Cambridge: CUP, 1967)
———, *New Testament Prophecy* (London: MMS, 1979)
———, 'On the Evidence for the Creative Role of Christian Prophets', *NTS* 20 (1974), 262–74
Hogan, L.P., *Healing in the Second Tempel* (sic) *Period* (Göttingen: Vandenhoeck & Ruprecht, 1992)
Hollenweger, W.J., *The Pentecostals* (London: SCM, 1972)
Holmberg, B., *Paul and Power* (Lund: Gleerup, 1978)
Holwerda, D.E., *The Holy Spirit and Eschatology in the Gospel of John* (Kampen: Kok, 1959)
Horn, F.W., *Das Angeld des Geistes: Studien zur paulinischen Pneumatologie* (Göttingen: Vandenhoeck & Ruprecht, 1992)
———, 'Holy Spirit', in D.N. Freedman (ed.), *The Anchor Bible Dictionary* (vol. 3; New York: Doubleday, 1992), 265–78
Hunter, H.D., *Spirit-Baptism: A Pentecostal Alternative* (Lanham: UPA, 1983)
———, 'Tongues-Speech: A Patristic Analysis', *JETS* 23 (1980), 125–37
Hurtado, L.W., *One God, One Lord* (London: SCM, 1988)
———, 'Normal, but Not a Norm: Initial Evidence and the New Testament', in McGee (ed.), *Evidence*, 189–201

Isaacs, M.E., *The Concept of Spirit* (London: Heythrop Monographs, 1976)

Johnston, G., *The Spirit-Paraclete in the Gospel of John* (Cambridge: CUP, 1970)

Käsemann, E. *Essays on New Testament Themes* (London: SCM, 1964)

——, *New Testament Questions of Today* (London: SCM, 1969)

——, *Perspectives on Paul* (London: SCM, 1971)

Kelsey, M.T., *Healing and Christianity* (London: SCM, 1973)

Kim, H.S., *Die Geisttaufe des lukanischen Doppelwerks* (Berlin: Lang, 1993)

Kydd, R.N, *Charismatic Gifts in the Early Church: An Exploration into the Gifts of the Spirit in the First Three Centuries of the Christian Era* (Peabody: Hendrickson, 1984)

Lampe, G.W.H., *God as Spirit: The Bampton Lectures* (Oxford: Claredon, 1977)

——, 'The Holy Spirit in the Writings of Saint Luke', in D.E. Nineham (ed.), *Studies in the Gospels: Essays in Memory of R.H. Lightfoot* (Oxford: Blackwell, 1955), 159–200

Latourelle, R., *The Miracles of Jesus and the Theology of Miracles* (New York: Paulist Press, 1988)

Laurentin, R., *Catholic Pentecostalism* (London: DLT, 1977)

Lederle, H.I., *Treasures Old and New: Interpretations of 'Spirit-Baptism' in the Charismatic Renewal Movement* (Peabody: Hendrickson, 1988)

Levison, J.R., 'Did the Spirit withdraw from Israel? An Evaluation of the earliest Jewish Data', *NTS* 43 (1997), 35–57

Lewis, D.C., *Healing: Fiction, Fantasy or Fact?* (London: Hodder, 1989)

Lindars, B. and Smalley, S.S. (eds.), *Christ and Spirit in the New Testament* (Cambridge: CUP, 1973)

Lombard, E., *De la glossolalie chez les premiers chrétiens et des phénomènes similaires* (Lausanne: Bridel, 1910)

Lombard, H.A., 'Charisma and Church Office', *Neotestamentica* 10 (1976), 31–52

de Lorenzi, L. (ed.), *Charisma und Agape (1 Ko 10–14)* (Rome: PBI, 1983)

——, *Paul de Tarse: Apôtre du Nôtre Temps* (Rome: PBI, 1979)

van der Loos, H., *The Miracles of Jesus* (Leiden: Brill, 1965)

Ma, W. and Menzies, R.P., *Pentecostalism in Context: Essays in Honor of William W. Menzies* (Sheffield: SAP, 1997)

MacArthur, J., *Charismatic Chaos* (Grand Rapids: Zondervan, 1992)

MacNutt, F., *Healing* (Notre Dame: Ave Maria Press, 1974)

McConnell, D., *The Promise of Health and Wealth: A Historical and Biblical Analysis of the Modern Faith Movement* (London: Hodder, 1990)

McGee, G.B. (ed.), *Initial Evidence: Historical and Biblical Perspectives on the Pentecostal Doctrine of Spirit Baptism* (Peabody: Hendrickson, 1991)

McGuire, M.B., 'The Social Context of Prophecy: "Word-gifts" of the Spirit among Catholic Pentecostals', *Review of Religious Research* 18 (1977), 134–47

Macchia, F.D., 'Sighs too Deep for Words: Towards a Theology of Glossolalia', *JPT* 1 (1992), 47–73

——, 'The Spirit and Life: A Further response to Jürgen Moltmann', *JPT* 5 (1994), 121–7

Mainville, O., *L'Esprit dans l'Oeuvre de Luc* (Montreal: Fides, 1991)

Malony, H.N. and Lovekin, A.A., *Glossolalia: Behavioural Science Perspectives on Speaking in Tongues* (Oxford: OUP, 1985)

Malony, H.N. 'Debunking Some of the Myths About Glossolalia', in Robeck (ed.), *Experiences*, 102–10

Martin, R.P., *The Spirit and the Congregation: Studies in I Corinthians 12–15* (Grand Rapids: Eerdmans, 1984)

Masters, P., *The Healing Epidemic* (London: Wakeman Trust, 1988)

Meier, J.P., *A Marginal Jew: Rethinking the historical Jesus* (vol. 2; New York: Doubleday, 1994)

Menzies, R.P., *The Development of Early Christian Pneumatology with Special Reference to Luke-Acts* (Sheffield: SAP, 1991, short title *Development*)

——, *Empowered for Witness: The Spirit in Luke-Acts* (JPTS 56; Sheffield: SAP, 1994, short title *Empowered*)

——, 'Luke and the Spirit: a Reply to James Dunn', *JPT* 4 (1994), 115–38

——, 'Spirit and Power in Luke-Acts: A Response to Max Turner', *JSNT* 49 (1991), 11–20

——, 'Spirit-Baptism and Spiritual Gifts', in Ma and Menzies (eds.), *Pentecostalism*, 48–59

Mills, W.E. (ed.), *Speaking in Tongues: A Guide to Research on Glossolalia* (Grand Rapids: Eerdmans, 1986)

——, *A Theological/Exegetical Approach to Glossolalia* (London: University Press of America, 1985)

Moltmann, J., *The Church in the Power of the Spirit* (London: SCM, 1975)

——, *The Spirit of Life: A Universal Affirmation* (London: SCM, 1992)

Montague, G.T., *The Holy Spirit: Growth of a Biblical Tradition* (New York: Paulist Press, 1976)

Moo, D.J., 'Divine Healing in the Health and Wealth Gospel', *TrinJ* 9 (1988), 191–209

Morgan, R., *The Nature of New Testament Theology* (London: SCM, 1973)

Müller, U.B., *Prophetic und Predigt im Neuen Testament* (Gütersloh: Mohn, 1975)

Packer, J.I., *Keep in Step with the Spirit* (Leicester: IVP, 1984)

Panagopoulos, J. (ed.), *Prophetic Vocation in the New Testament and Today* (Leiden: Brill, 1977)

——, 'Die urchristliche Prophetie: Ihr Character und ihre Funktion', in Panagopoulos (ed.), *Vocation* 1–32

Pawson, D., *The Normal Christian Birth* (London: Hodder, 1989)

Poloma, M., *The Charismatic Movement: Is There a New Pentecost?* (Boston: Twayne, 1982)

Porsch, F., *Pneuma und Wort. Ein exegetischer Beitrag zur Pneumatologie des Johannesevangeliums* (Frankfurt: Knecht, 1974)

Poythress, V.S., 'Linguistic and Sociological Analyses of Modern Tongues-Speaking: Their Contributions and Limitations', *WJT* 42 (1980), 367–88

Price, R.M., 'Contribution and Charisma', *SLJT* 33 (1990), 173–82

Räisänen, H., *Beyond New Testament Theology* (London: SCM, 1990)

Reiling, J., 'Prophecy, the Spirit and the Church', in Panagopoulos (ed.), *Vocation*, 58–76

Robeck, C.M. (ed.), *Charismatic Experiences in History* (Peabody: Hendrickson, 1985)

Rowdon, H.H. (ed.), *Christ the Lord* (Leicester: IVP, 1982)

Ruthven, J., *On the Cessation of the Charismata: The Protestant Polemic on Postbiblical Miracles* (Sheffield: SAP, 1993)

Samarin, W.J., *Tongues of Men and Angels: The Religious Language of Pentecostalism* (London: Collier-Macmillan, 1972)

Sandnes, K.O., *Paul – One of the Prophets?* (Tübingen: Mohr, 1991)

Sarles, K.L., 'An Appraisal of the Signs and Wonders Movement', *BSac* 56 (1988), 57–82

Satterthwaite, P.E. and Wright, D.F. (eds.), *A Pathway into Holy Scripture* (Grand Rapids: Eerdmans, 1994)

Schatzmann, S., *A Pauline Theology of Charismata* (Peabody: Hendrickson, 1987)

Schlatter, A., 'The Theology of the New Testament and Dogmatics', in Morgan, *Nature*, 117–66

Schürmann, H., *Ursprung und Gestalt* (Düsseldorf: Patmos, 1970)

——, 'Die geistlichen Gnadengaben in den paulinischen Gemeinden', in Schürmann, *Ursprung*, 236–67

Schweizer, E., *The Holy Spirit* (London: SCM, 1981)

——, 'πνευμα', *TDNT* VI: 389–455

Shelton, J.B., *Mighty in Word and Deed: The Role of the Holy Spirit in Luke-Acts* (Peabody: Hendrickson, 1991)

Shepherd, W., *The Narrative Function of the Holy Spirit as Character in Luke-Acts* (Atlanta: Scholars, 1994)

Smail, T., *The Giving Gift: The Holy Spirit in Person* (London: Hodder, 1988)

——, *Reflected Glory* (London: Hodder, 1975)

——, Walker, A. and Wright, N., *Charismatic Renewal: The Search for a Theology* (London: SPCK, 1995)

Stronstad, R., *The Charismatic Theology of Saint Luke* (Peabody: Hendrickson, 1984)

Sullivan, F.A., *Charisms and Charismatic Renewal: A Biblical and Theological Study* (Dublin: Gill and Macmillan, 1982)

Talbert, C.H., *Literary Patterns, Theological Themes and the Genre of Luke-Acts* (Missoula: Scholars, 1974)

Taylor, M., 'A Historical Perspective on the Doctrine of Divine Healing', *Journal of the European Pentecostal Theological Association* 14 (1995), 54–84

Theissen, G., *Psychological Aspects of Pauline Theology* (Edinburgh: T. & T. Clark, 1987)

Thiselton, A.C., 'The "Interpretation" of Tongues: A New Suggestion in the Light of Greek Usage in Philo and Josephus', *JTS* 30 (979), 15–36

Thomas, R.L., 'Tongues . . . Will Cease', *JETS* 17 (1974), 81–9

Turner, M., *Power From On High: The Spirit in Israel's Restoration and Witness in Luke-Acts* (Sheffield: SAP, 1996)

——, 'Jesus and the Spirit in Lucan Perspective', *TynB* 32 (1981), 3–42

——, 'Luke and the Spirit: Studies in the Significance of Receiving the Spirit in Luke-Acts', unpublished PhD dissertation, Cambridge, 1980

——, 'Mission and Meaning in Terms of "Unity" in Ephesians' in Billington, Lane and Turner (eds.), *Mission and Meaning*, 138–66

——, 'Modern Linguistics and the New Testament', in J.B. Green (ed.), *Hearing the New Testament*, 156–8

——, 'The Significance of Receiving the Spirit in John's Gospel', *VoxEv* 10 (1977), 24–42

——, 'The Spirit of Christ and "Divine" Christology', in Green and Turner (eds.), *Jesus of Nazareth*, 413–36

——, 'Spirit Endowment in Luke-Acts: Some Linguistic Considerations', *VoxEv* 12 (1981), 45–63

——, 'The Spirit of Christ and Christology' in Rowdon (ed.), *Christ the Lord*, 168–90

——, 'The Spirit and the Power of Jesus' Miracles in the Lucan Conception', *NovT* 33 (1991), 124–52

——, 'The Spirit of Prophecy and the Power of Authoritative Preaching in Luke-Acts: A Question of Origins', *NTS* 38 (1992), 66–88

——, 'Spiritual Gifts: Then and Now', *VoxEv* 15 (1985), 7–64

——, and Burge, G.M., '*The Anointed Community*: A Review and Response', *EvQ*

62 (1990), 253–62

Twelftree, G.J., *Jesus the Exorcist* (Tübingen: Mohr, 1993)

Warfield, B.B., *Counterfeit Miracles* (New York: Scribners, 1981)

West, D.J., *Eleven Lourdes Miracles* (London: Duckworth, 1957)

Wijngaards, J., *The Spirit in John* (Wilmington: Glazier, 1988)

Wilkinson, J., *Health and Healing: Studies in New Testament Principles and Practice* (Edinburgh: Hansel, 1980)

——, 'Physical Healing and the Atonement', *EvQ* 63 (1991), 149–67

Williams, C.G., *Tongues of the Spirit: A Study of Pentecostal Glossolalia and Related Phenomena* (Cardiff: UWP, 1981)

Williams, G.H. and Waldvogel, E., 'A History of Speaking in Tongues and Related Gifts', in M.P. Hamilton (ed.) *Charismatic Movement*, 75–80

Wilson, R., 'Prophecy and Ecstacy: A re-examination', *JBL* 98 (1979), 321–37

Wimber, J. and Springer, K., *Power Healing* (London: Hodder, 1986)

Wimber, J., *Power Evangelism* (London: Hodder, 1985)

Wrede, W., 'The Task and Methods of "New Testament Theology" ', in Morgan, *Nature*, 68–116

Wright, N., 'The Theology and Methodology of "Signs and Wonders" ', in Smail, Walker and Wright, *Charismatic Renewal*, 71–85

Wright, N.T., *The New Testament and the People of God* (London: SPCK, 1992)

——, 'Reflected Glory: 2 Corinthians 3:18', in Hurst, L.D. and Wright, N.T. (eds.), *The Glory of God in the New Testament: Studies in Christology in Memory of George Bradford Caird* (Oxford: Clarendon, 1987), 139–50

Yates, J.E., *The Spirit and the Kingdom* (London: SPCK, 1963)

Yocum, B., *Prophecy: Exercising the Prophetic Gifts of the Spirit in the Church Today* (Ann Arbor: Servant Books, 1976)

York, J.O., *The Last Shall Be First: The Rhetoric of Reversal in Luke*, (Sheffield: SAP, 1991)

Note: Three notable works of a more systematic-theological orientation came to my attention too late to be included in this work –

John McIntyre, *The Shape of Pneumatology* (Edinburgh: T. & T. Clark, 1997)

Clark H. Pinnock, *Flame of Love: A Theology of the Holy Spirit* (Downer's Grove: InterVarsity Press, 1996)

Michael Welker, *God the Spirit* (Minneapolis: Augsburg/Fortress, 1994)

References to them would no doubt have appeared with regularity in this volume had I been able to access them earlier.

Scripture Index

Genesis

1:2	2
2:7	2,91,**96–100**,124
8:11	28
22:18	54

Exodus

8:19	31
14,15	11
16:4	64
19:3	53
28:3	4
31:3	4,9
34:34	116,118
35:31	4
40:35	24

Numbers

11:17,19	4
11:24–30	4,10,**192,198**
22:38	10
23,24	10
24:2	4
27:18	4

Deuteronomy

8:3	64
18:15,16	4,18
18:19–22	192
32:35	207

Judges

3:10	3,14
6:34	3,14

11:29	3,14
13:25	14
14:6,19	14,192
15:14	14

1 Samuel

9:3–10	193
10:1–13	4,192,198
16:13	4
19	11
19:20–24	4,192,198

2 Samuel

12:25	191

1 Kings

12:32–13:10	247
13:20,21	193
18:12	14
20:35	193
22:24	247

2 Kings

1:2	193
2	193
2:9–16	14,133
8:7–15	193

1 Chronicles

25:1–7	192,193

2 Chronicles

18:23	247

Author Index

Page numbers in italic give bibliographic details.

Chuck
715-479-4327